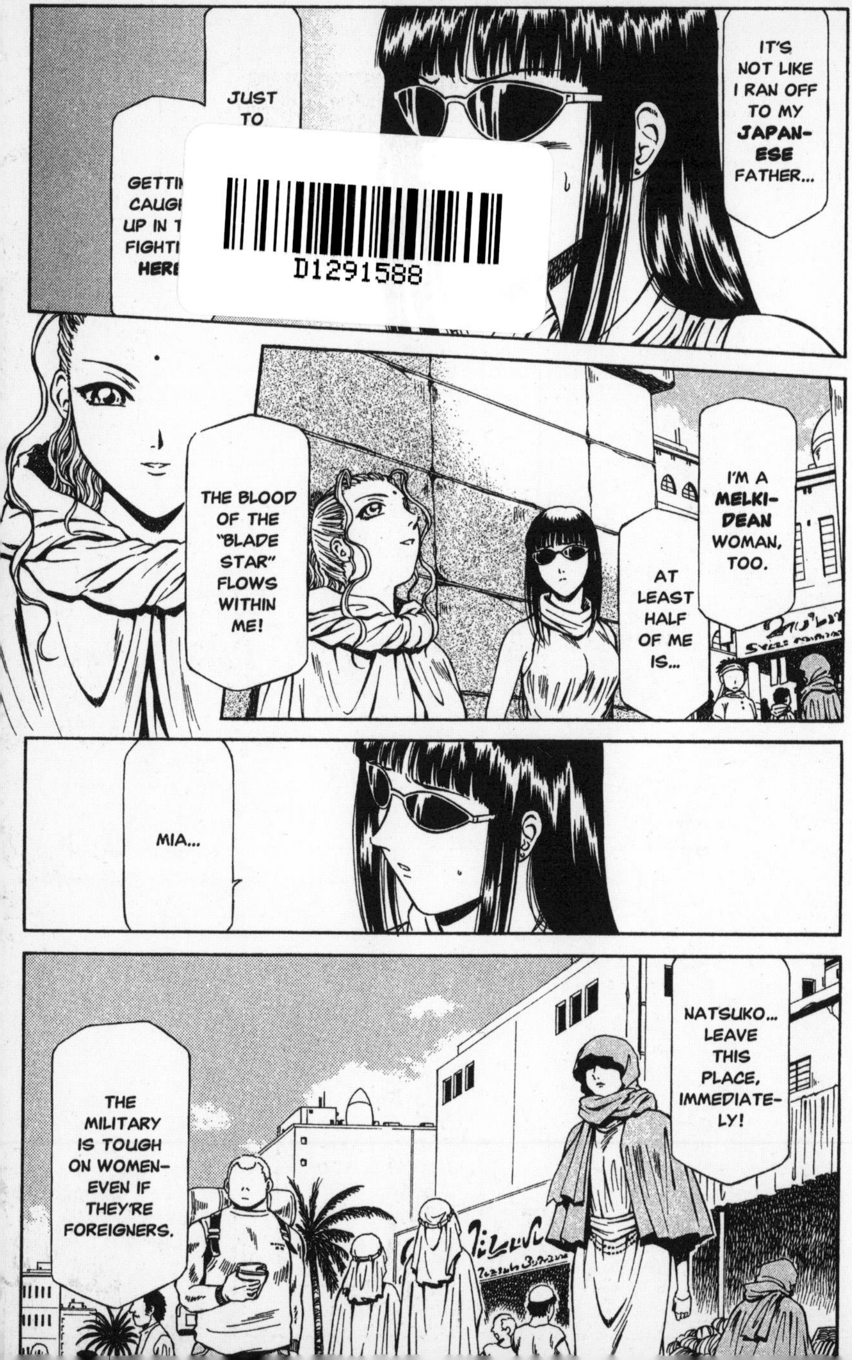
IT'S NOT LIKE I RAN OFF TO MY JAPANESE FATHER...
JUST TO
I'M A MELKIDEAN WOMAN, TOO.
AT LEAST HALF OF ME IS...
THE BLOOD OF THE "BLADE STAR" FLOWS WITHIN ME!
MIA...
NATSUKO... LEAVE THIS PLACE, IMMEDIATELY!
THE MILITARY IS TOUGH ON WOMEN-EVEN IF THEY'RE FOREIGNERS.

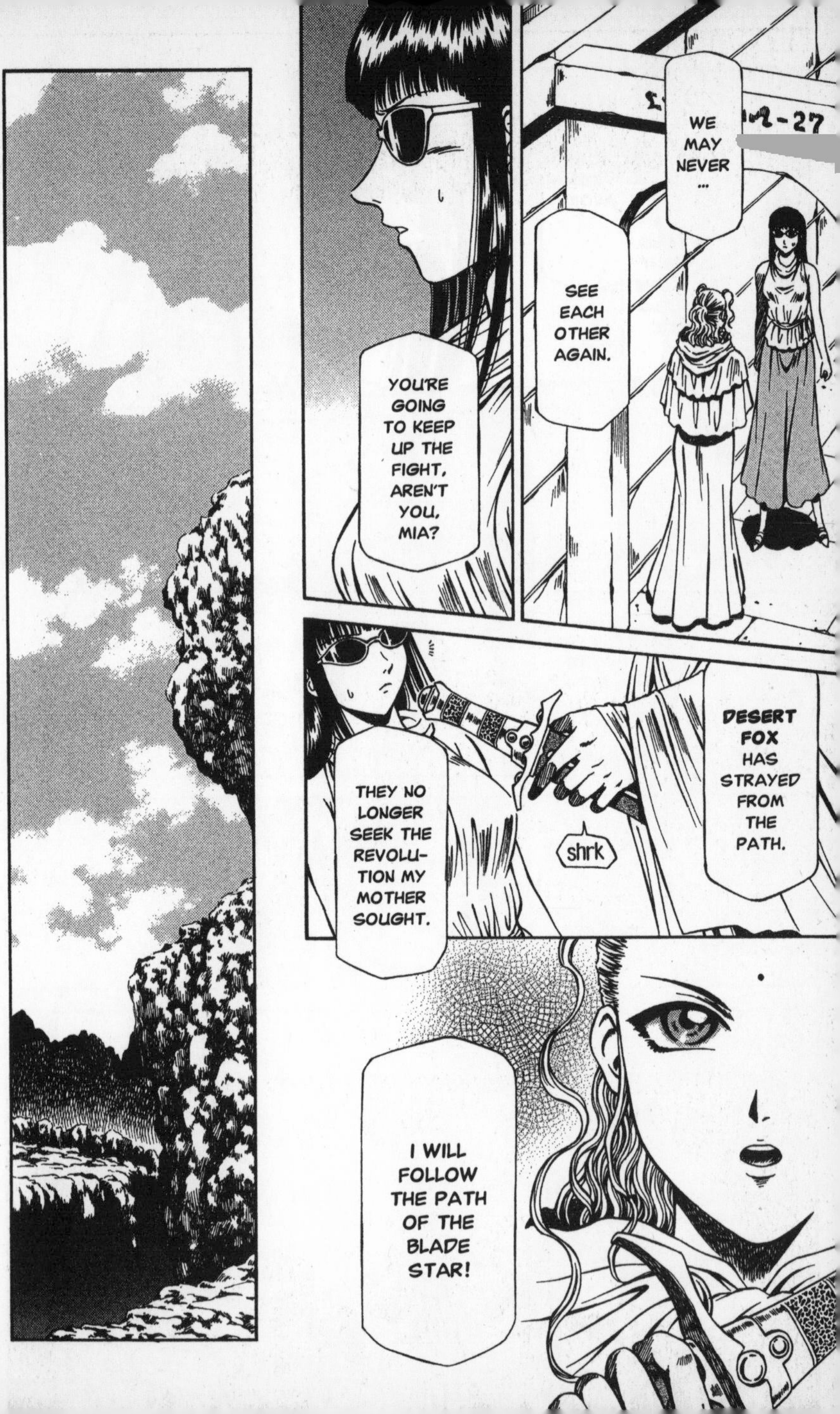

WE MAY NEVER ...
SEE EACH OTHER AGAIN.
YOU'RE GOING TO KEEP UP THE FIGHT, AREN'T YOU, MIA?
DESERT FOX HAS STRAYED FROM THE PATH.
shrk
THEY NO LONGER SEEK THE REVOLU-TION MY MOTHER SOUGHT.
I WILL FOLLOW THE PATH OF THE BLADE STAR!

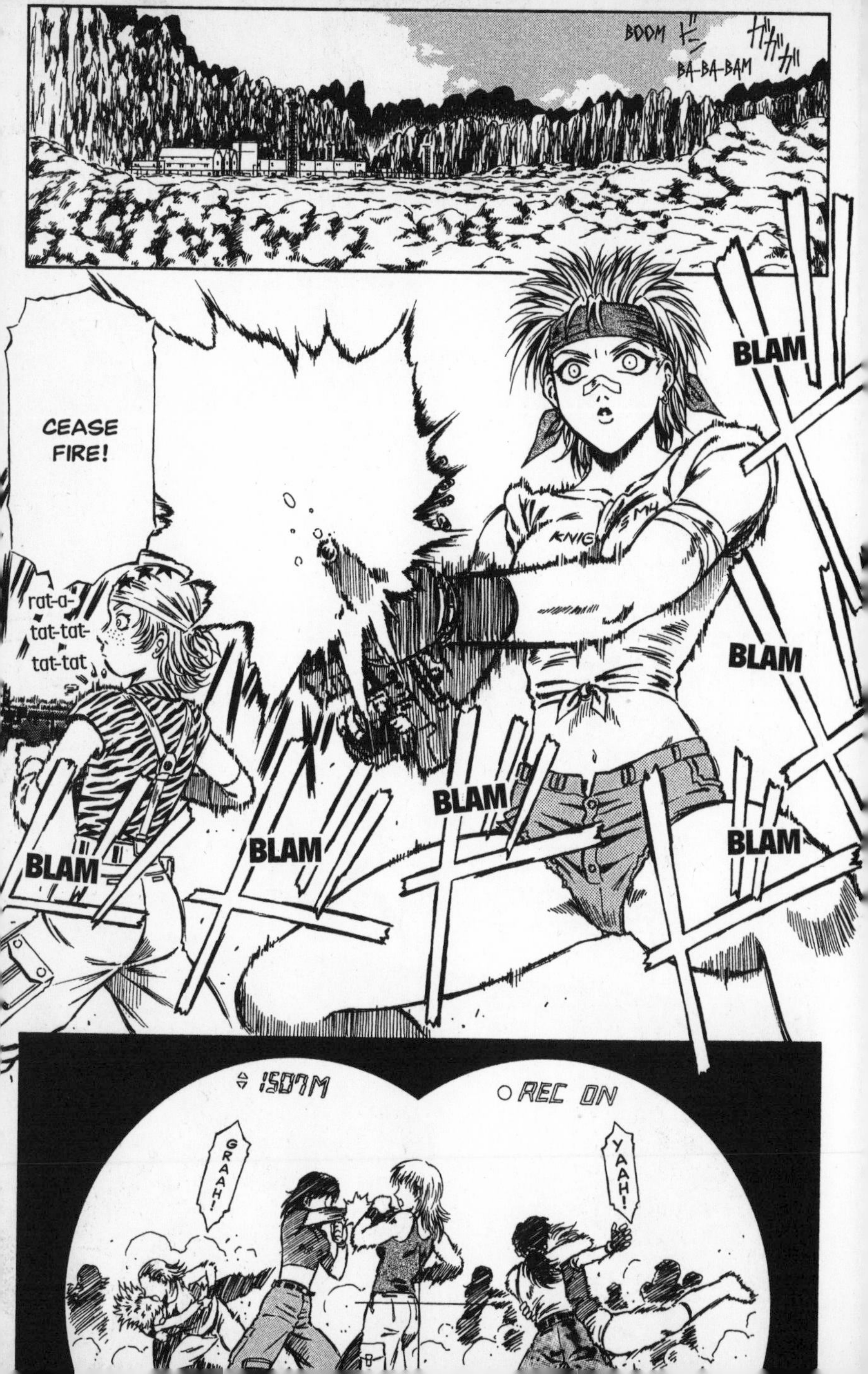
BOOM
BA-BA-BAM
CEASE FIRE!
BLAM
BLAM
BLAM
BLAM
BLAM
BLAM
rat-a-tat-tat-tat-tat
1507M
REC ON
YAAH!
GRAAH!

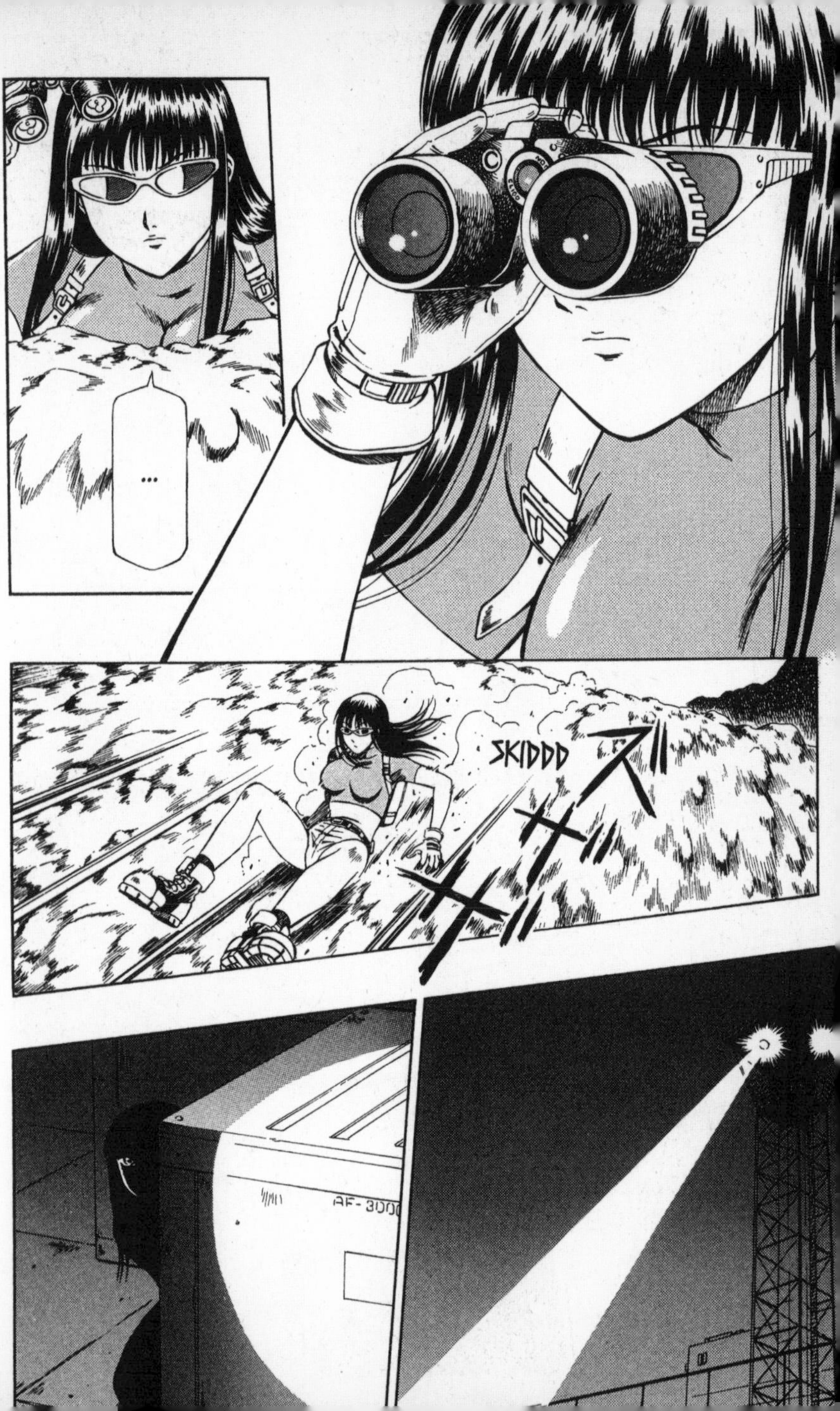
...
SKIDDD
AF-3000

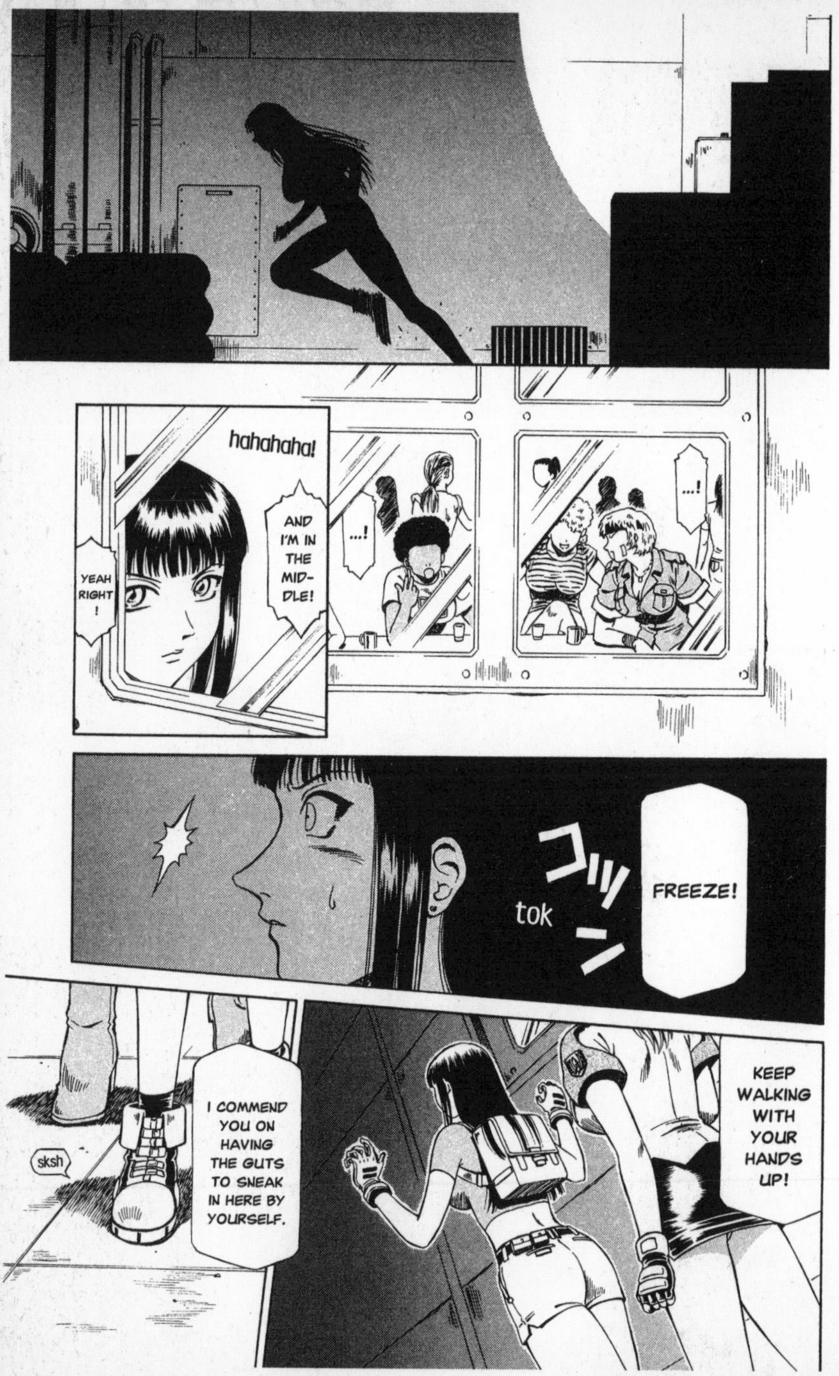

hahahaha!
AND I'M IN THE MID-DLE!
YEAH RIGHT!
...!
...!
FREEZE!
コツーン
tok
KEEP WALKING WITH YOUR HANDS UP!
I COMMEND YOU ON HAVING THE GUTS TO SNEAK IN HERE BY YOURSELF.
sksh

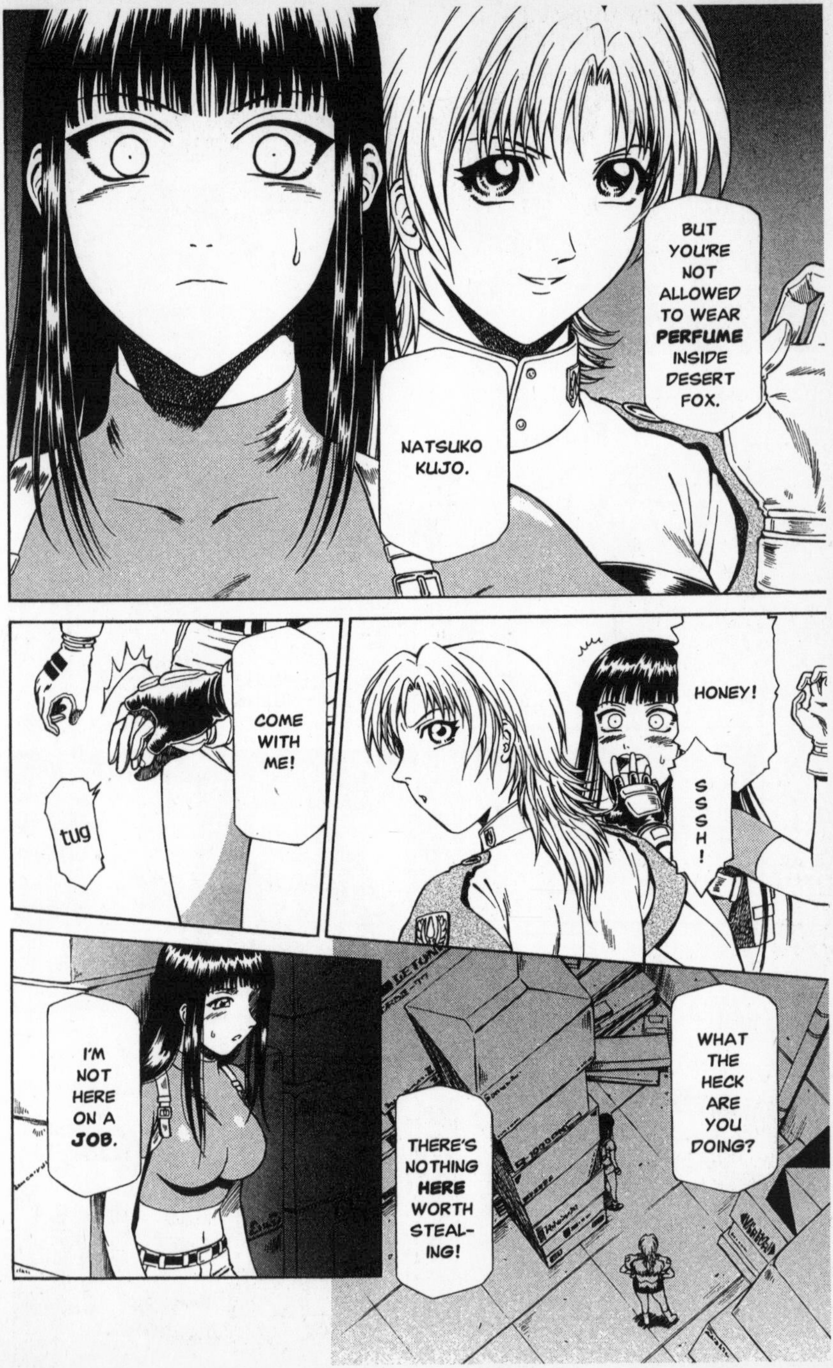
BUT YOU'RE NOT ALLOWED TO WEAR PERFUME INSIDE DESERT FOX.
NATSUKO KUJO.
HONEY!
SSSH!
COME WITH ME!
tug
WHAT THE HECK ARE YOU DOING?
THERE'S NOTHING HERE WORTH STEAL-ING!
I'M NOT HERE ON A JOB.

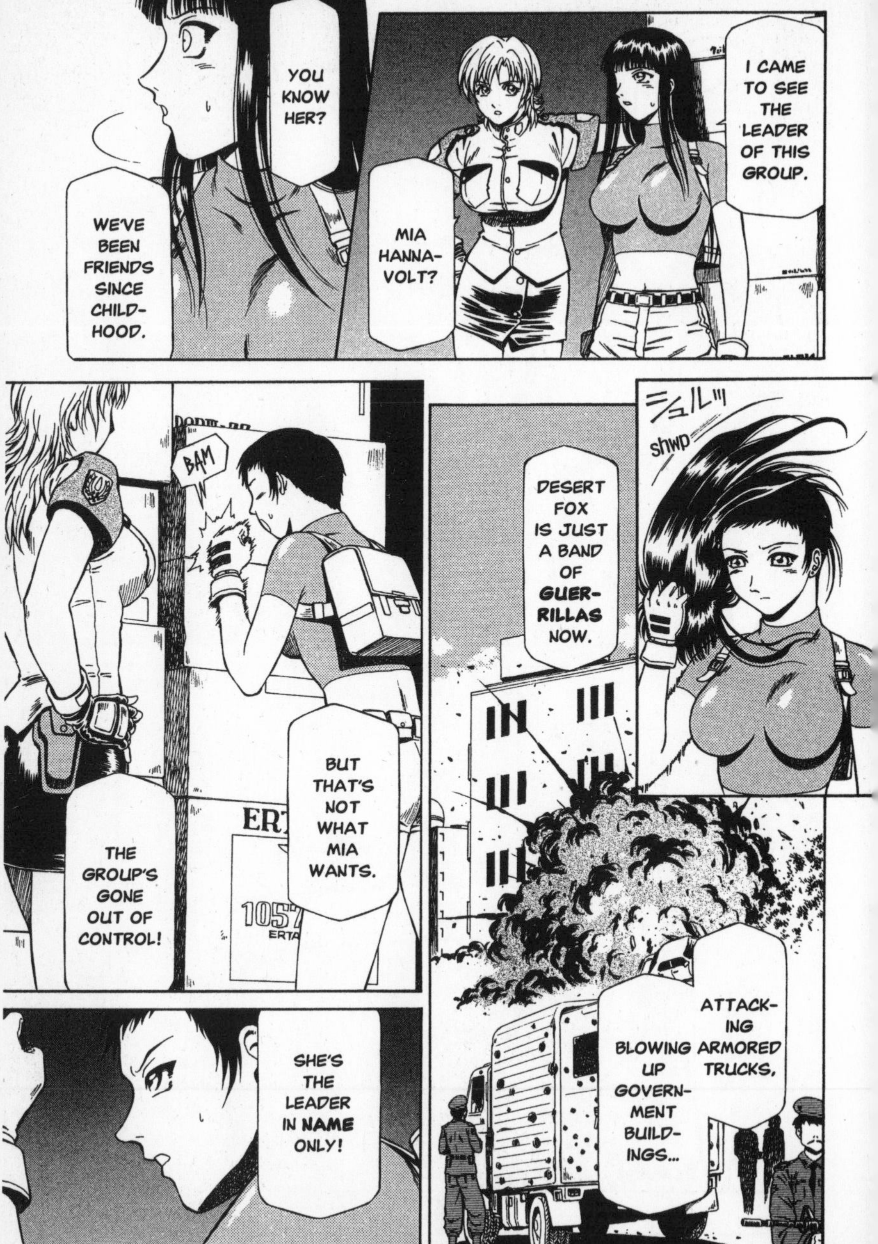
I CAME TO SEE THE LEADER OF THIS GROUP.
MIA HANNA-VOLT?
YOU KNOW HER?
WE'VE BEEN FRIENDS SINCE CHILDHOOD.
シュルッ
shwp
DESERT FOX IS JUST A BAND OF GUERRILLAS NOW.
BAM
BUT THAT'S NOT WHAT MIA WANTS.
THE GROUP'S GONE OUT OF CONTROL!
ATTACKING ARMORED TRUCKS,
BLOWING UP GOVERNMENT BUILDINGS...
SHE'S THE LEADER IN NAME ONLY!

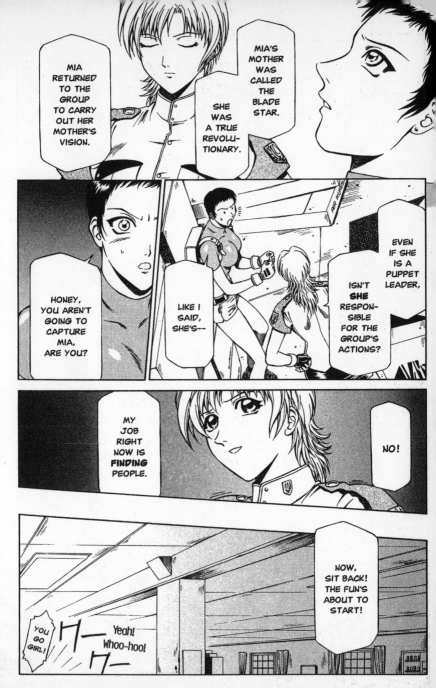

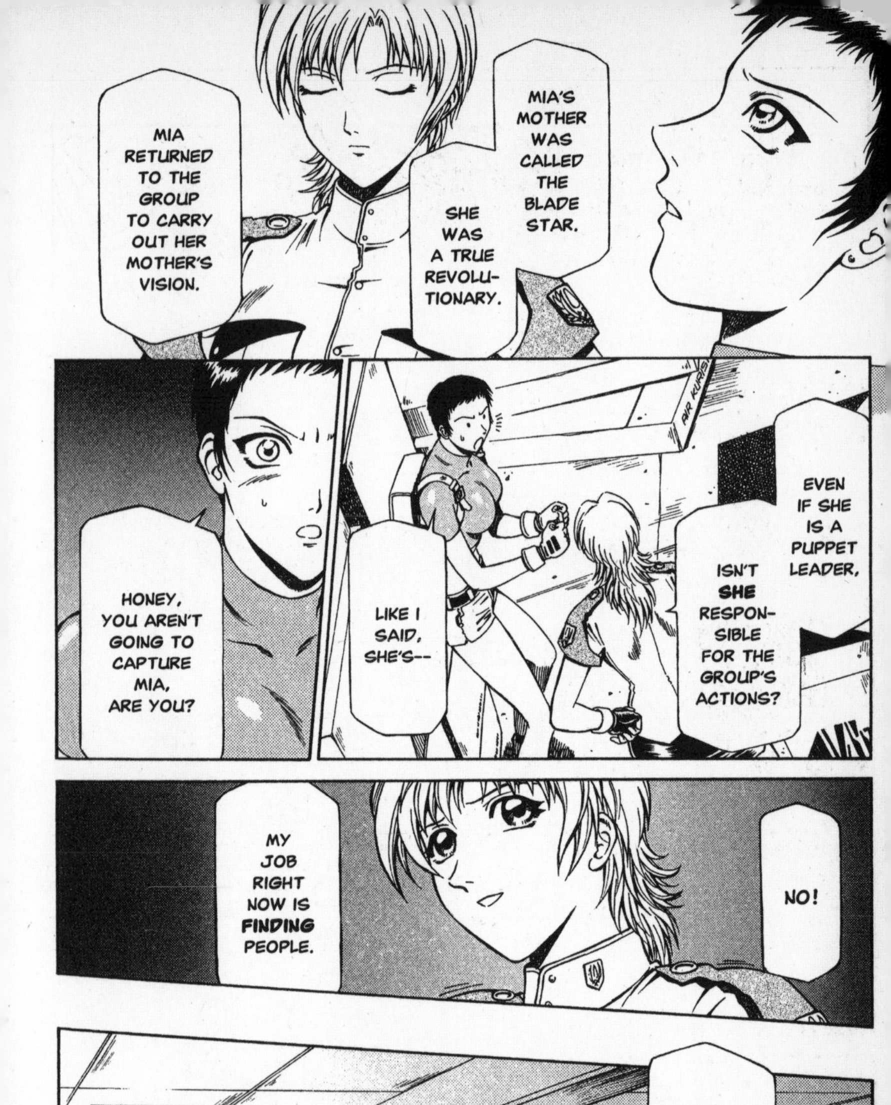
MIA'S MOTHER WAS CALLED THE BLADE STAR.
SHE WAS A TRUE REVOLUTIONARY.
MIA RETURNED TO THE GROUP TO CARRY OUT HER MOTHER'S VISION.
EVEN IF SHE IS A PUPPET LEADER,
ISN'T **SHE** RESPONSIBLE FOR THE GROUP'S ACTIONS?
LIKE I SAID, SHE'S--
HONEY, YOU AREN'T GOING TO CAPTURE MIA, ARE YOU?
NO!
MY JOB RIGHT NOW IS **FINDING** PEOPLE.
NOW, SIT BACK! THE FUN'S ABOUT TO START!
Yeah! Whoo-hoo!
YOU GO GIRL!

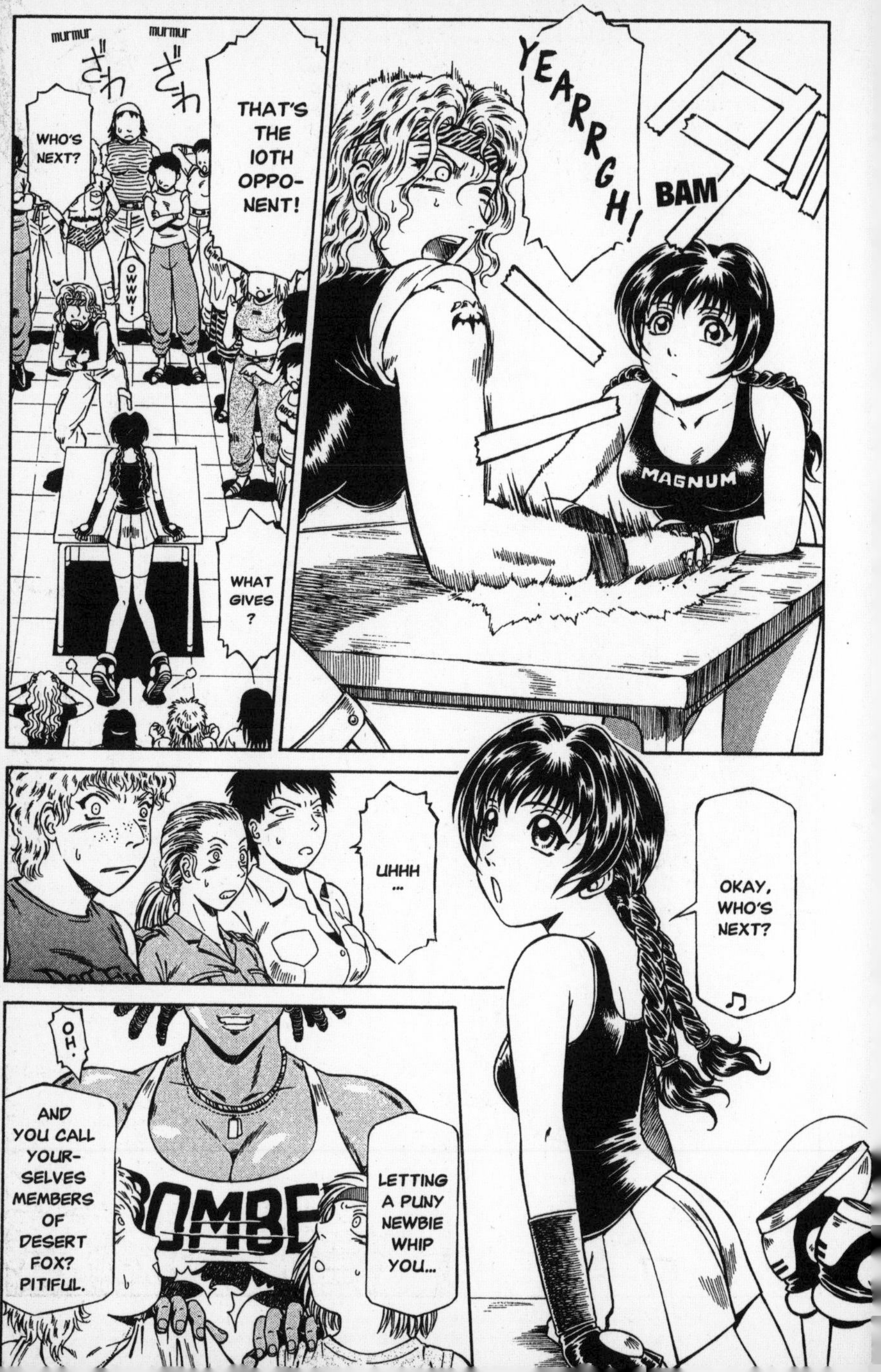
YEARRGH!
BAM
MAGNUM
murmur murmur
ざわ ざわ
THAT'S THE 10TH OPPONENT!
WHO'S NEXT?
OWWW!
WHAT GIVES?
OKAY, WHO'S NEXT? ♪
UHHH...
OH.
LETTING A PUNY NEWBIE WHIP YOU...
AND YOU CALL YOURSELVES MEMBERS OF DESERT FOX? PITIFUL.
BOMBE

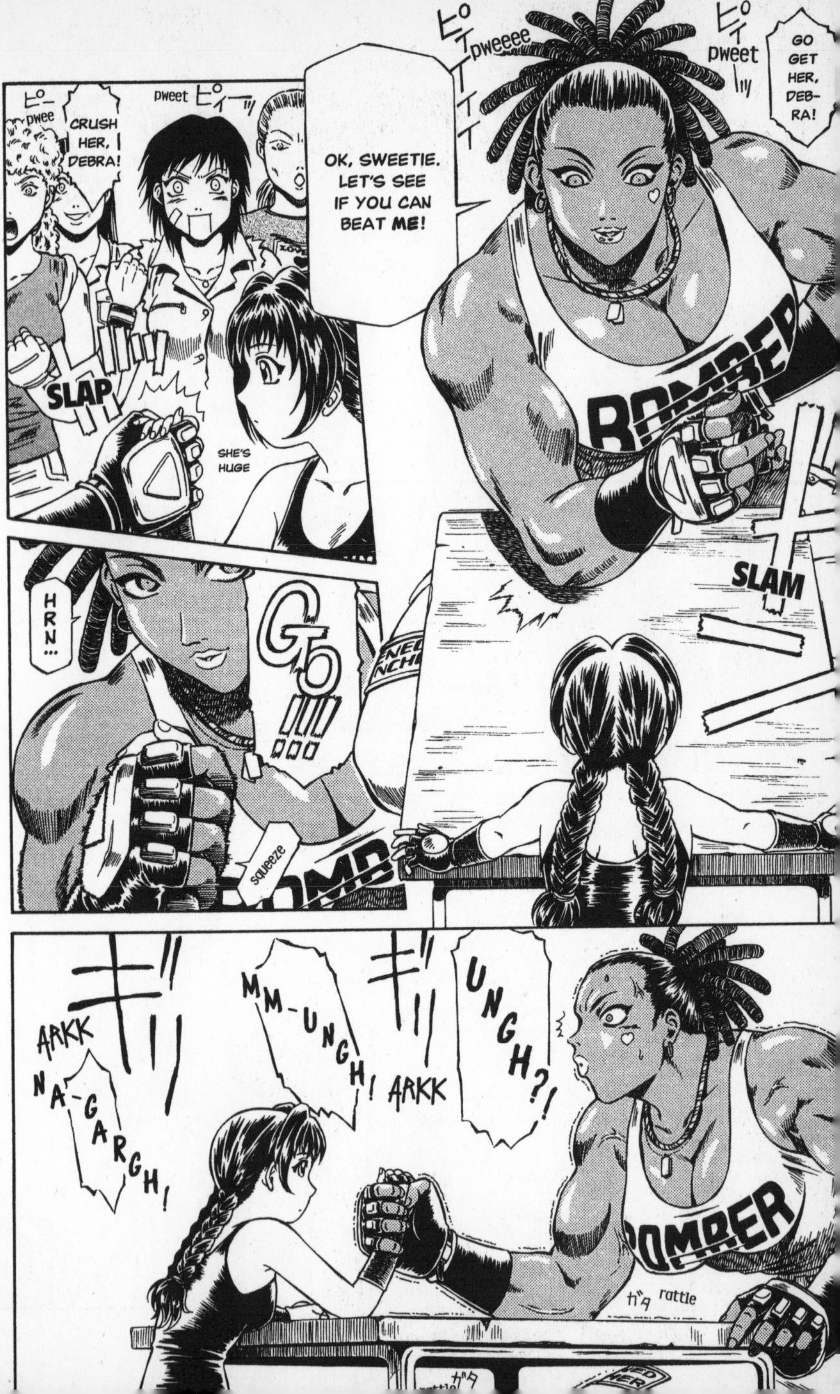
ピィ pweet ッ
GO GET HER, DEBRA!
ピィイイイ pweeee
OK, SWEETIE. LET'S SEE IF YOU CAN BEAT ME!
pweet ピイーッ
CRUSH HER, DEBRA!
ピー pwee
SLAP
SHE'S HUGE
SLAM
HRN...
GO
squeeze
UNGH?!
ARKK
MM-UNGH!
ARKK
NA-GARGH!
ガタ rattle

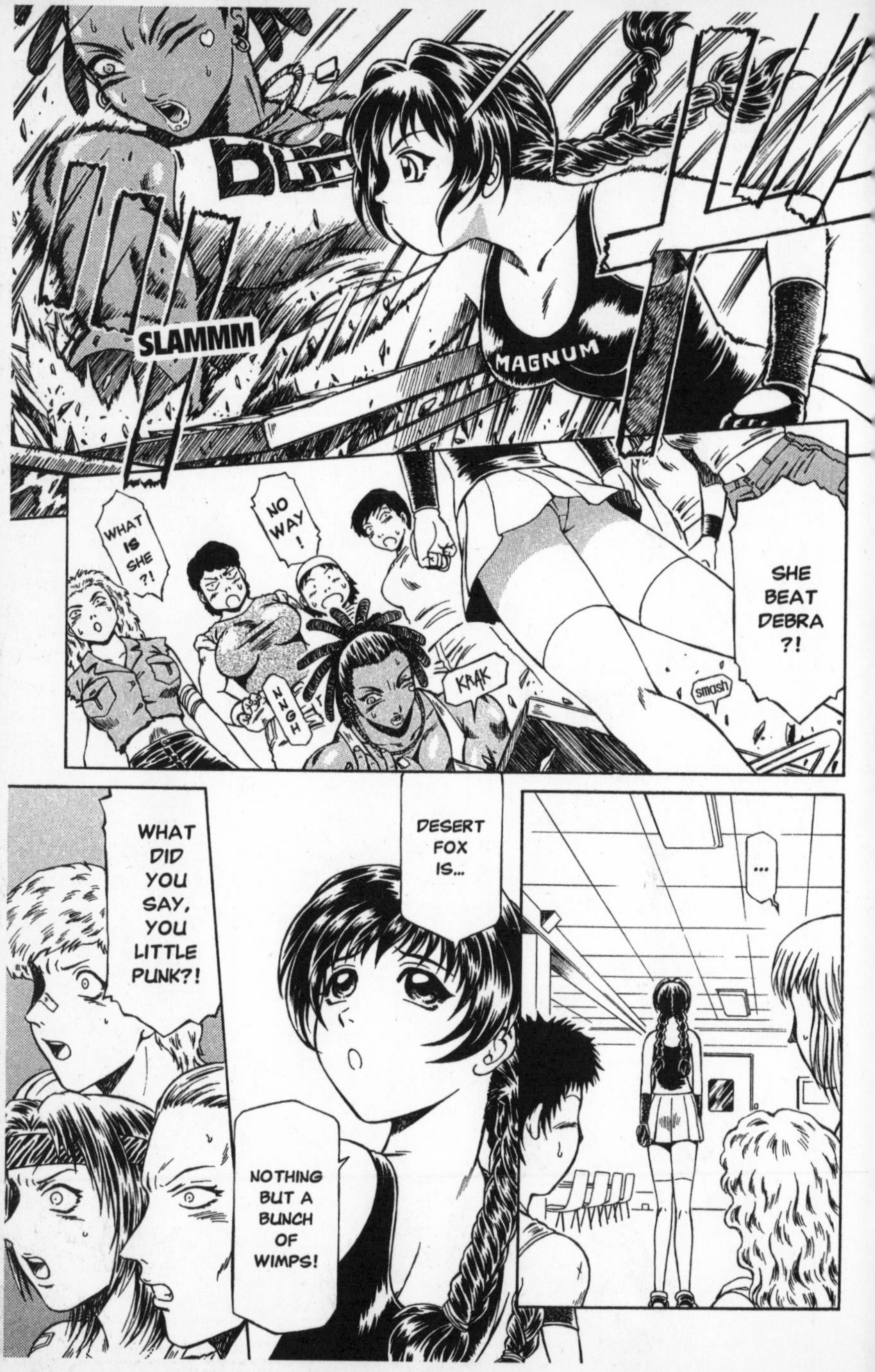
SLAMMM
MAGNUM
WHAT IS SHE ?!
NO WAY !
NNGH
KRAK
smash
SHE BEAT DEBRA ?!
DESERT FOX IS...
NOTHING BUT A BUNCH OF WIMPS!
WHAT DID YOU SAY, YOU LITTLE PUNK?!
...

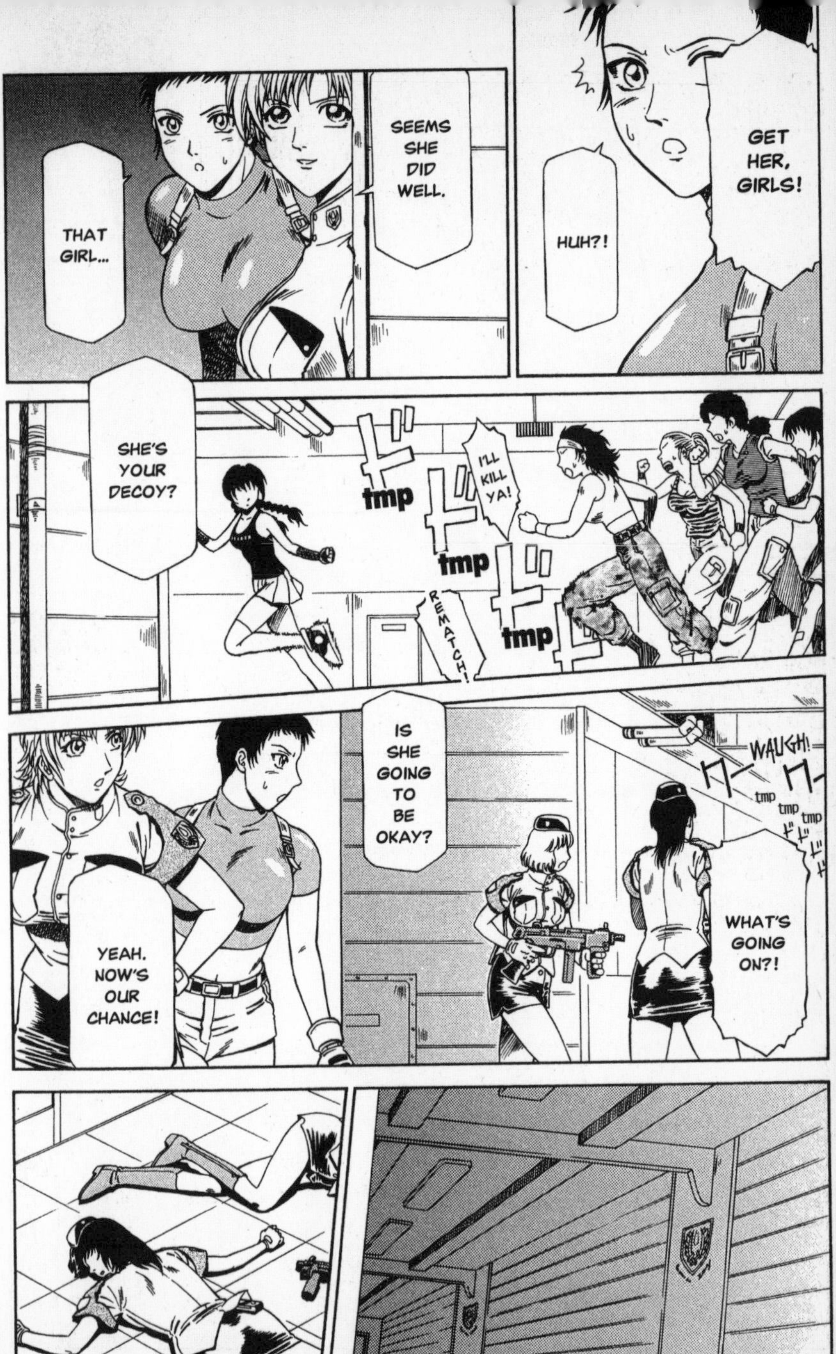

THAT GIRL...
SEEMS SHE DID WELL.
HUH?!
GET HER, GIRLS!
SHE'S YOUR DECOY?
tmp
tmp
tmp
I'LL KILL YA!
REMATCH!
IS SHE GOING TO BE OKAY?
YEAH. NOW'S OUR CHANCE!
WAUGH!
tmp tmp tmp
WHAT'S GOING ON?!

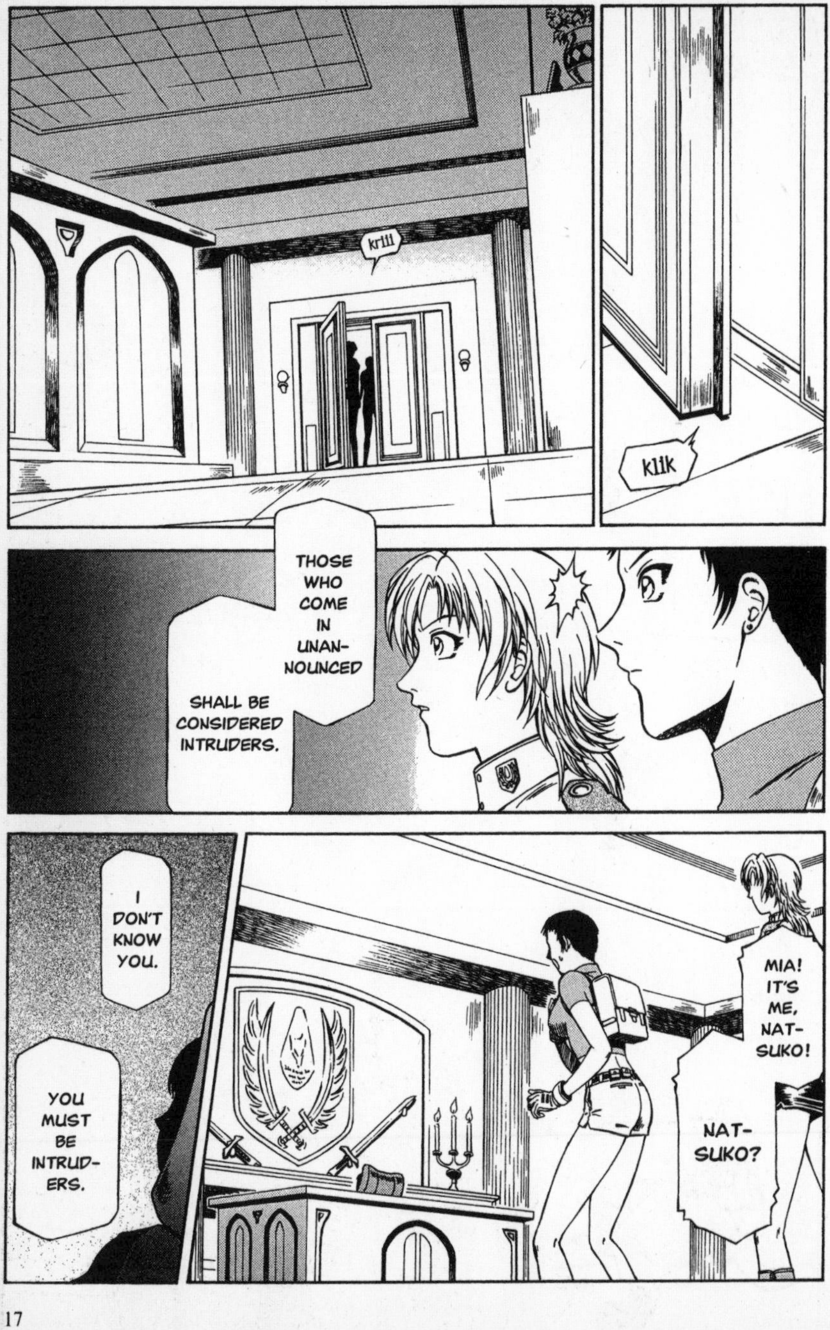
kriii
klik
THOSE WHO COME IN UNAN-NOUNCED
SHALL BE CONSIDERED INTRUDERS.
I DON'T KNOW YOU.
YOU MUST BE INTRUD-ERS.
MIA! IT'S ME, NAT-SUKO!
NAT-SUKO?

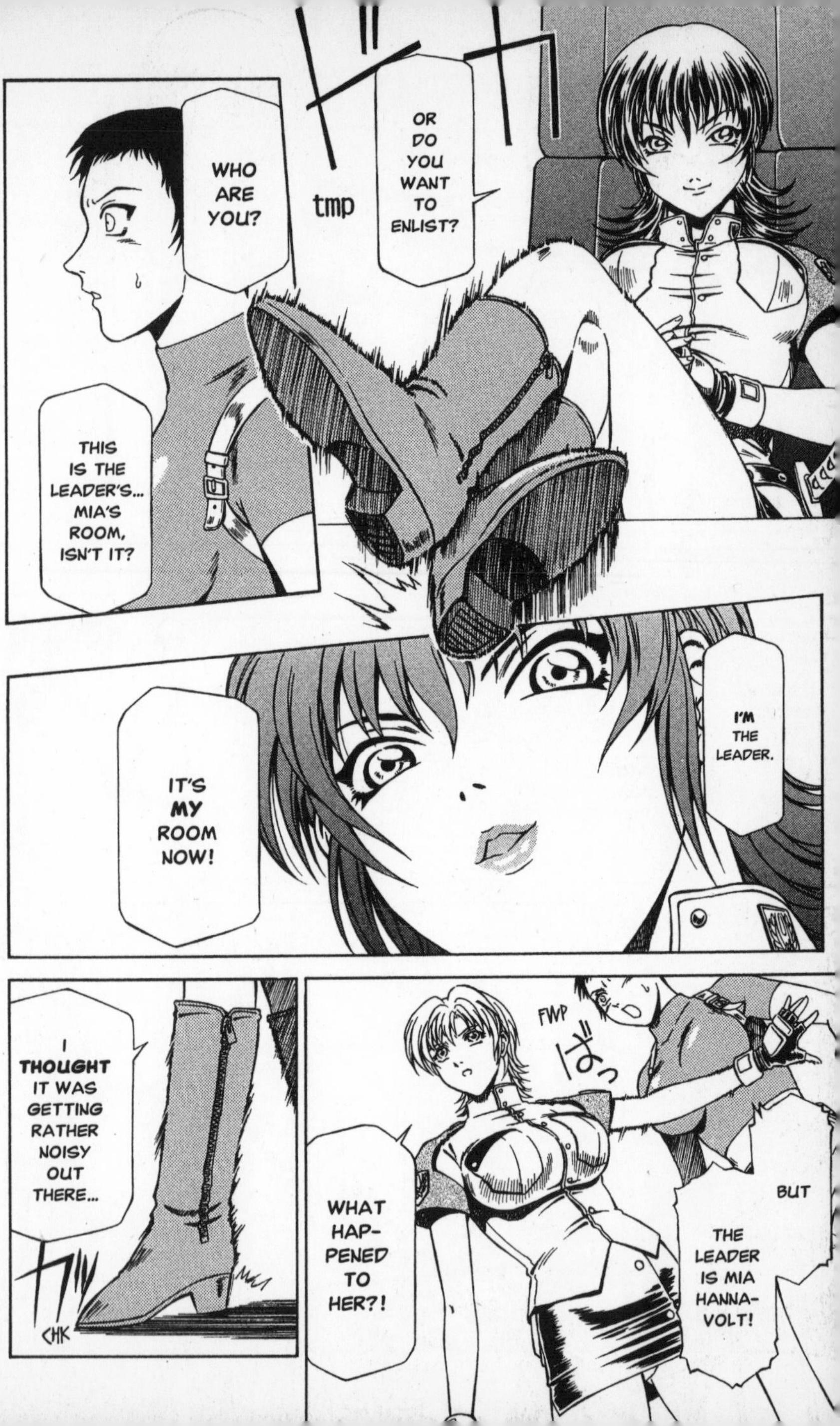

WHO ARE YOU?
tmp
OR DO YOU WANT TO ENLIST?
THIS IS THE LEADER'S... MIA'S ROOM, ISN'T IT?
IT'S MY ROOM NOW!
I'M THE LEADER.
I THOUGHT IT WAS GETTING RATHER NOISY OUT THERE...
CHK
FWP
ばっ
BUT THE LEADER IS MIA HANNA-VOLT!
WHAT HAP-PENED TO HER?!

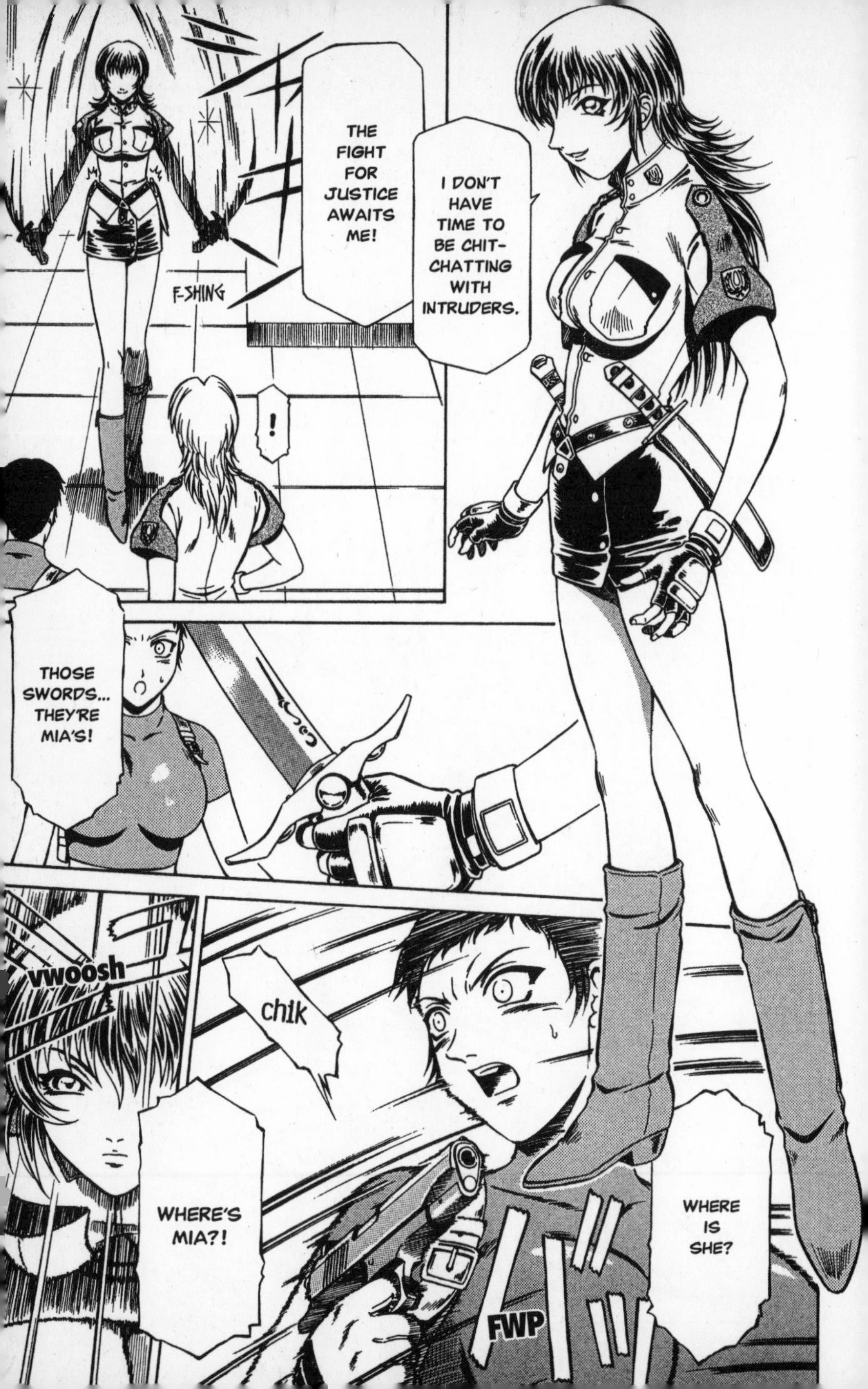
THE FIGHT FOR JUSTICE AWAITS ME!
I DON'T HAVE TIME TO BE CHIT-CHATTING WITH INTRUDERS.
F-SHING
!
THOSE SWORDS... THEY'RE MIA'S!
WHERE IS SHE?
chik
vwoosh
WHERE'S MIA?!
FWP

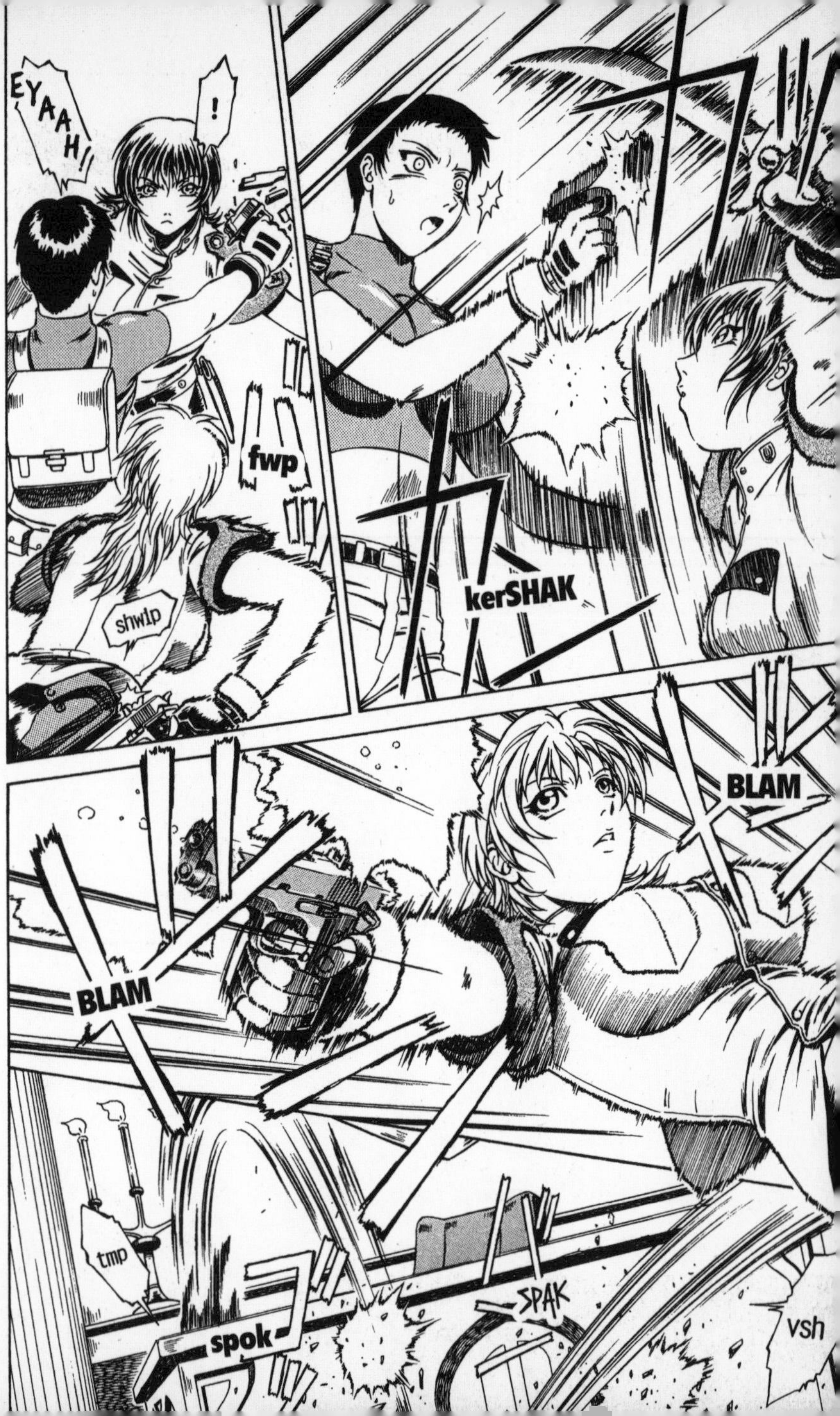
EYAAAH!!
!
fwp
shwip
kerSHAK
BLAM
BLAM
tmp
spok
SPAK
vsh

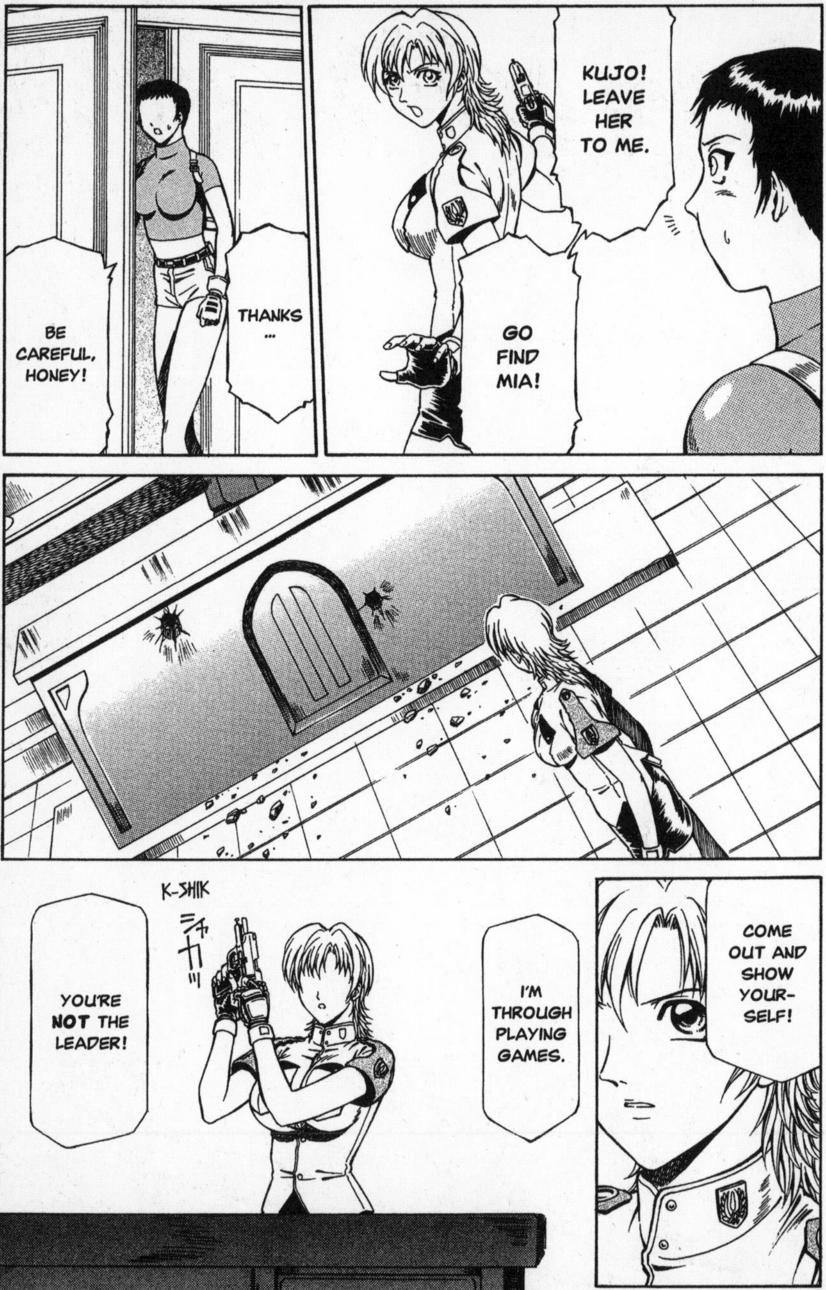
KUJO! LEAVE HER TO ME.
GO FIND MIA!
THANKS ...
BE CAREFUL, HONEY!
COME OUT AND SHOW YOUR-SELF!
I'M THROUGH PLAYING GAMES.
K-SHIK
シャカッ
YOU'RE **NOT** THE LEADER!

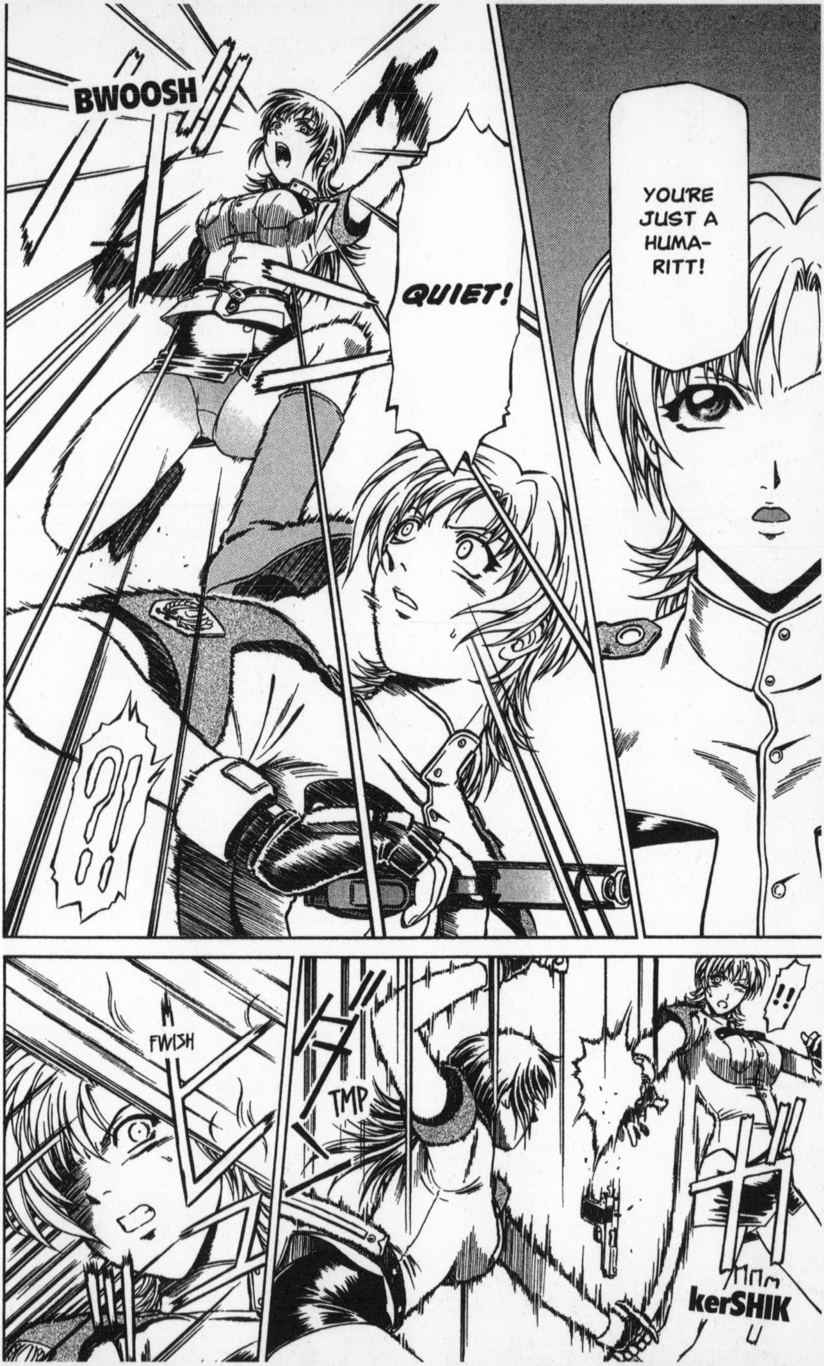
YOU'RE JUST A HUMA-RITT!
QUIET!
BWOOSH
?!
!!
FWISH
TMP
kerSHIK

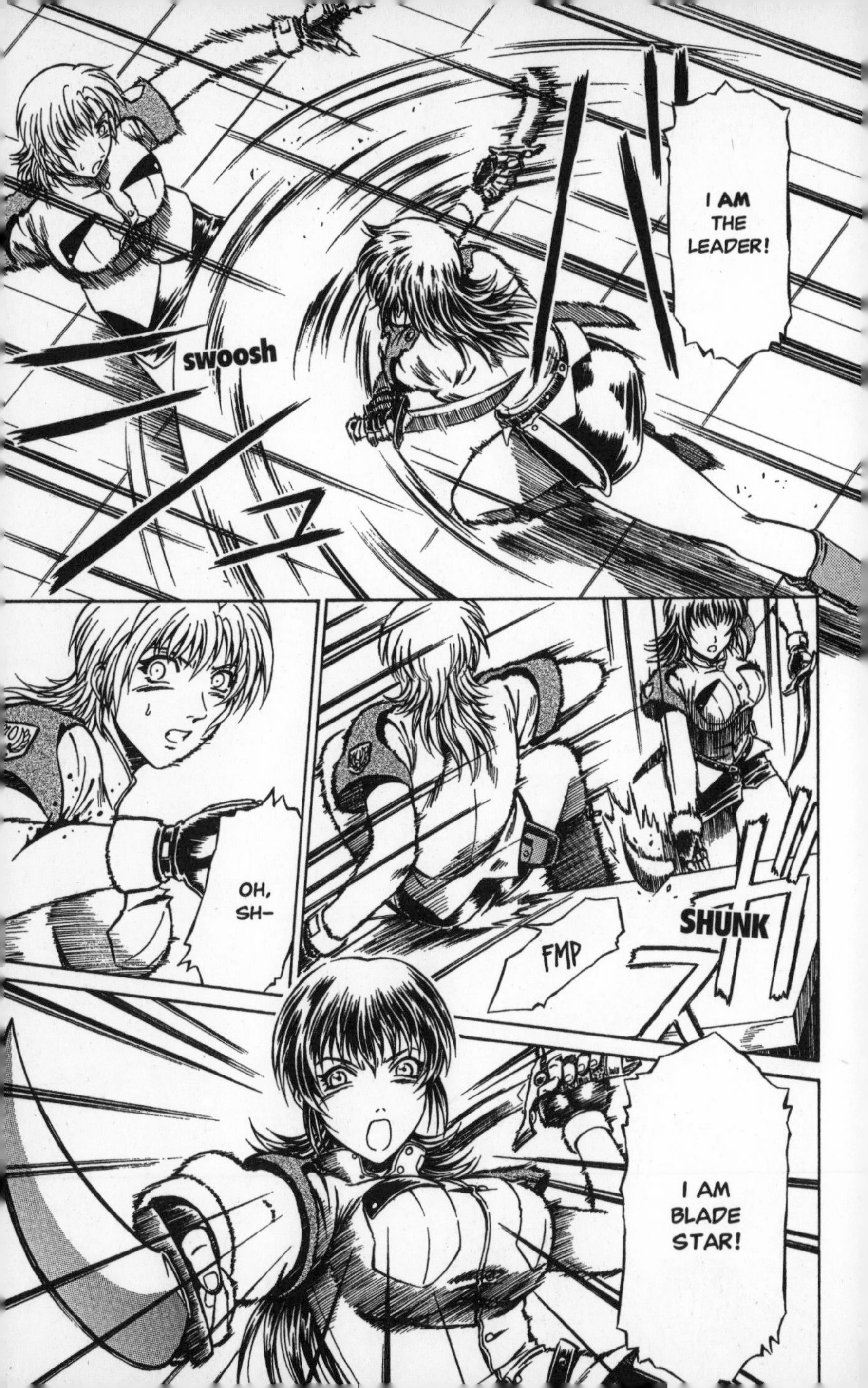
I AM THE LEADER!
swoosh
OH, SH-
FMP
SHUNK
I AM BLADE STAR!

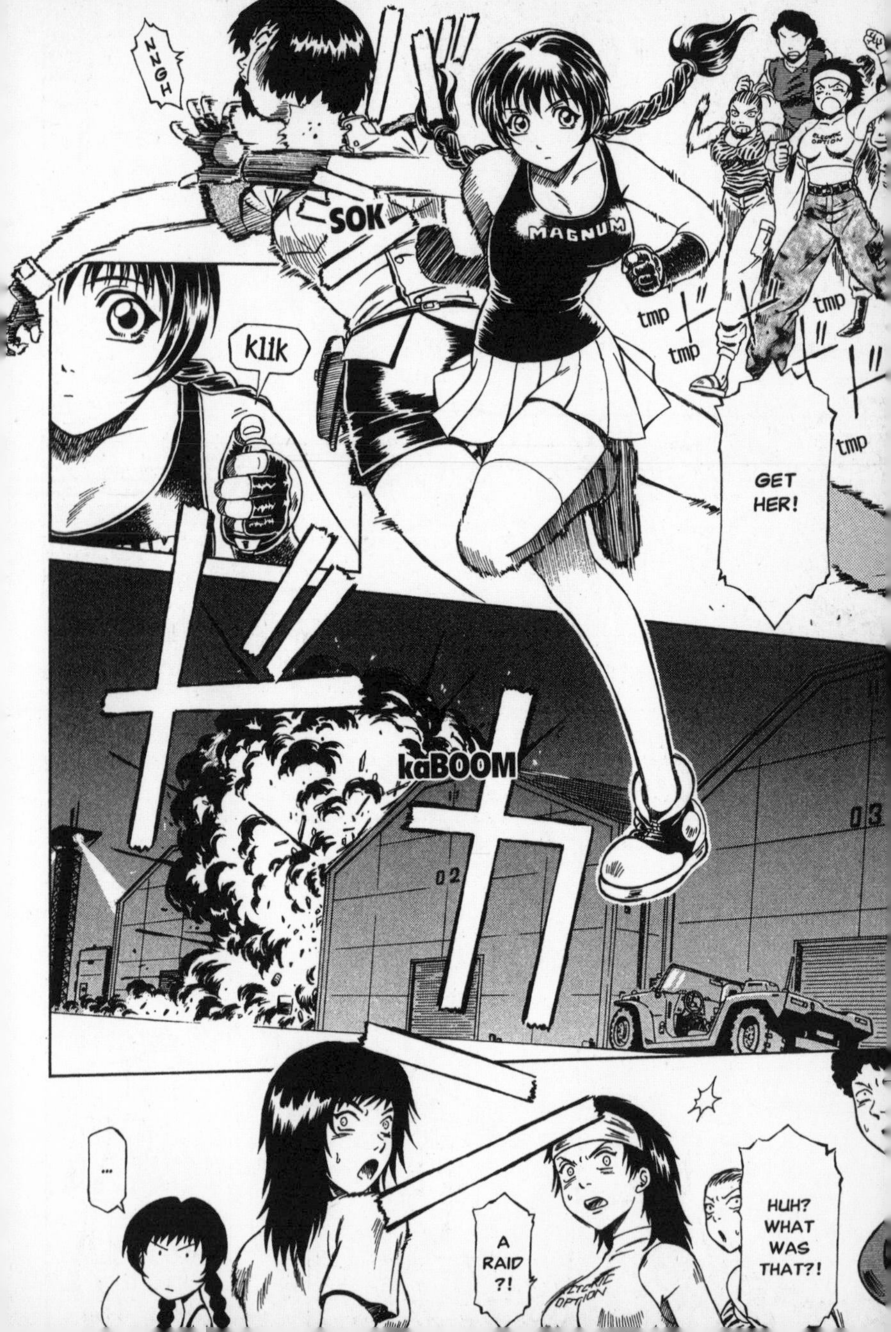
NNGH
SOK
MAGNUM
klik
tmp
tmp
tmp
tmp
GET HER!
kaBOOM
HUH? WHAT WAS THAT?!
A RAID ?!
...

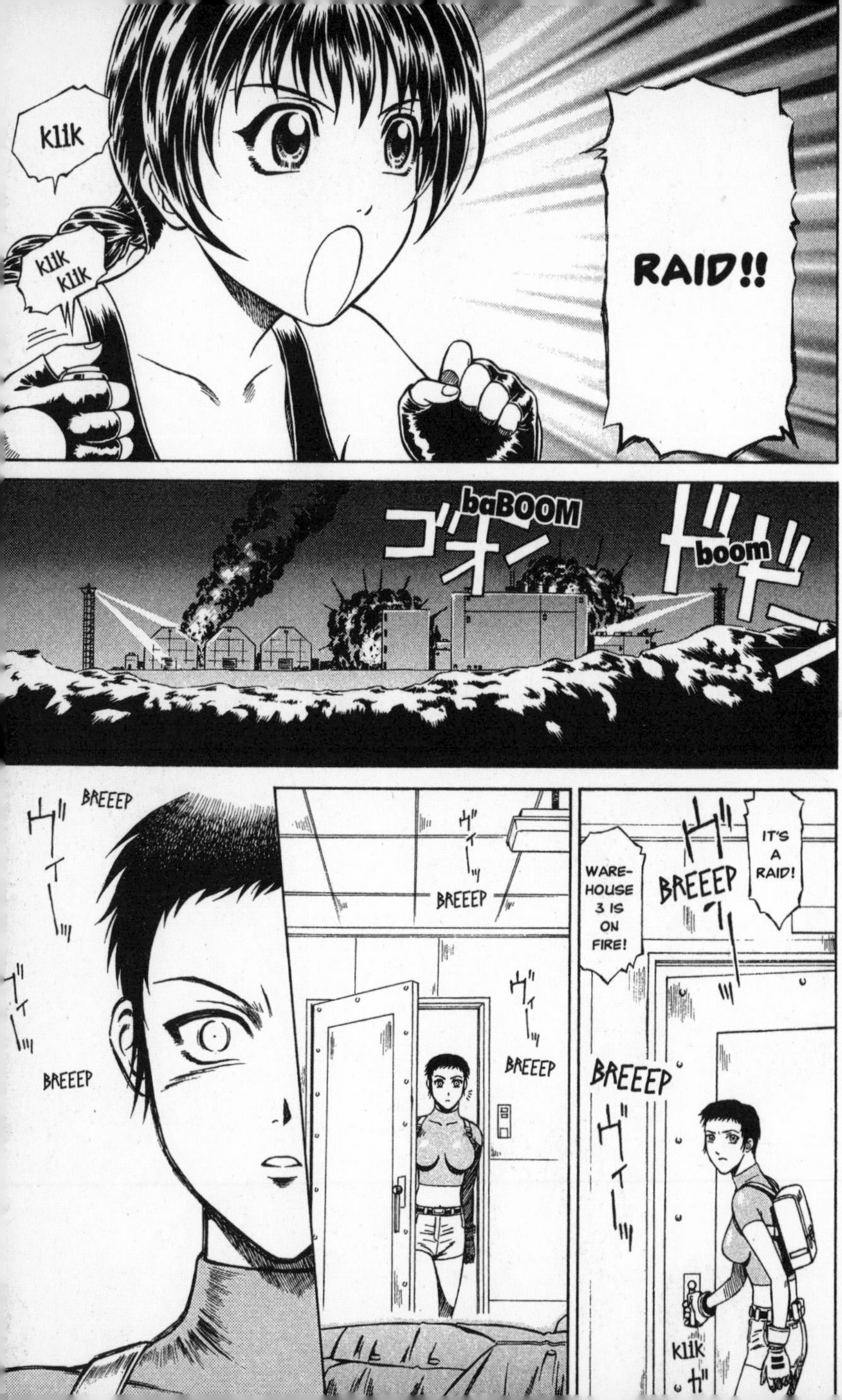
RAID!!
klik
klik klik
ゴオン baBOOM
ドドド boom
BREEEP
BREEEP
IT'S A RAID!
WARE-HOUSE 3 IS ON FIRE!
BREEEP
BREEEP
BREEEP
BREEEP
klik

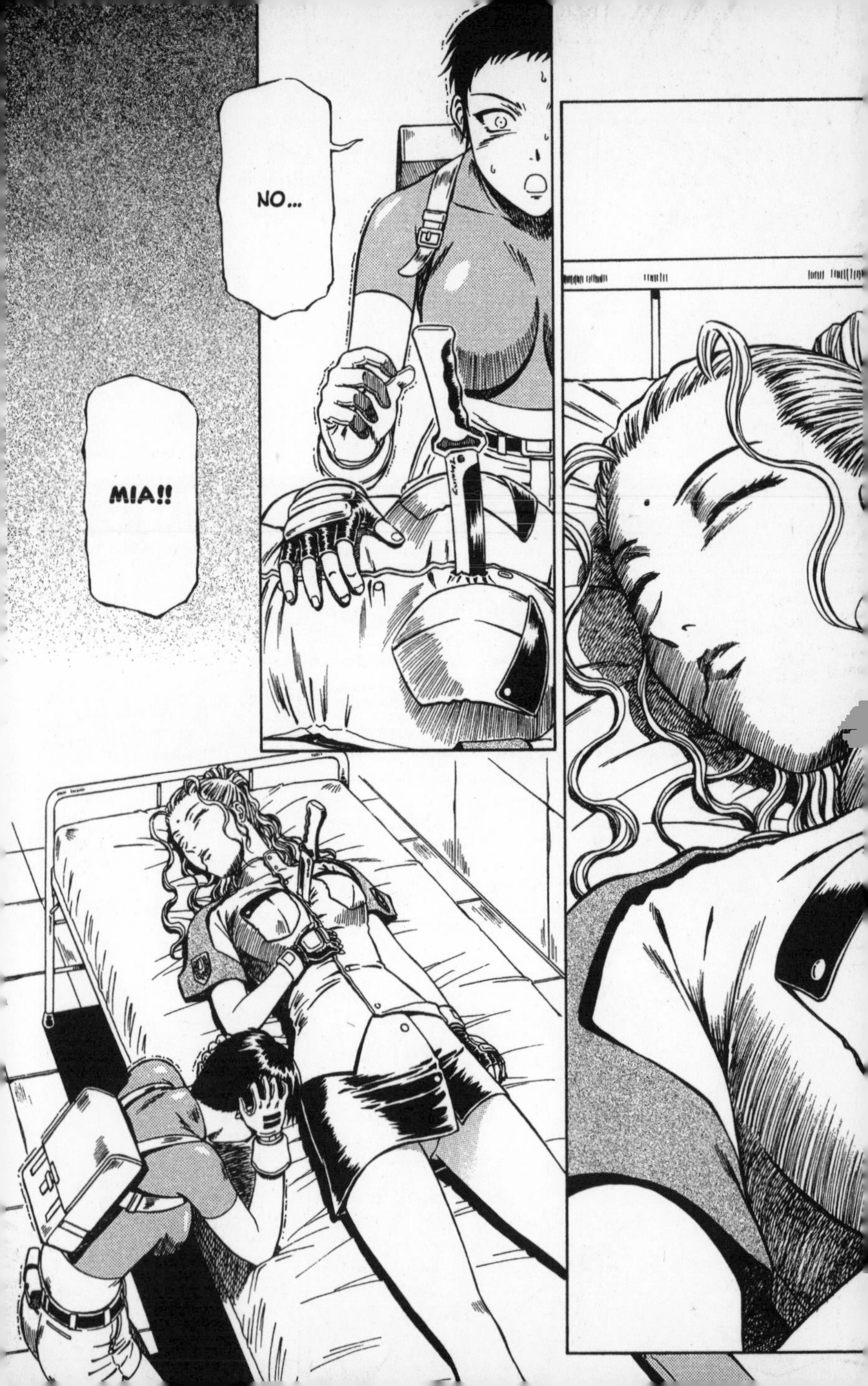
NO...
MIA!!

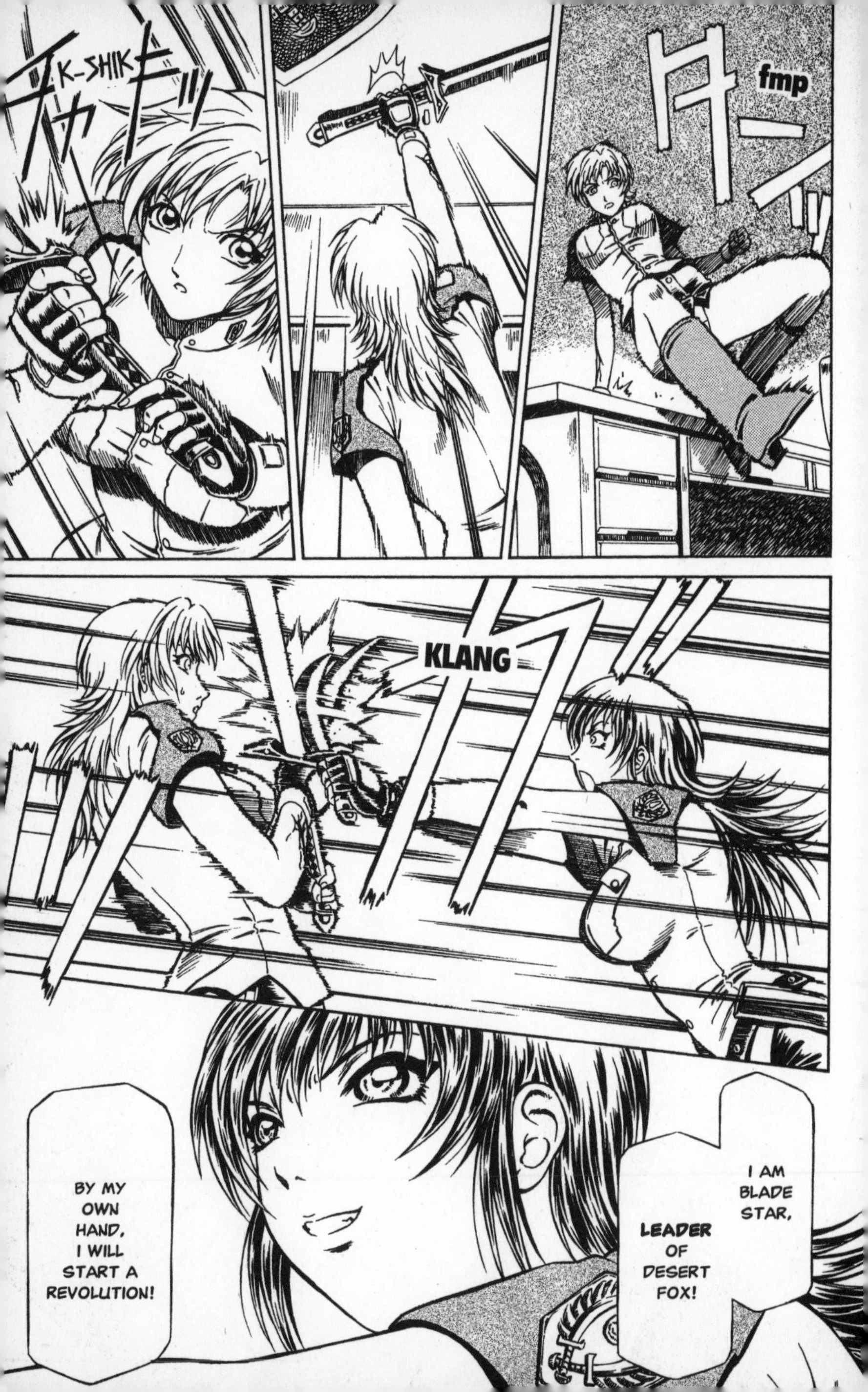
K-SHIK
fmp
KLANG
I AM BLADE STAR,
LEADER OF DESERT FOX!
BY MY OWN HAND, I WILL START A REVOLUTION!

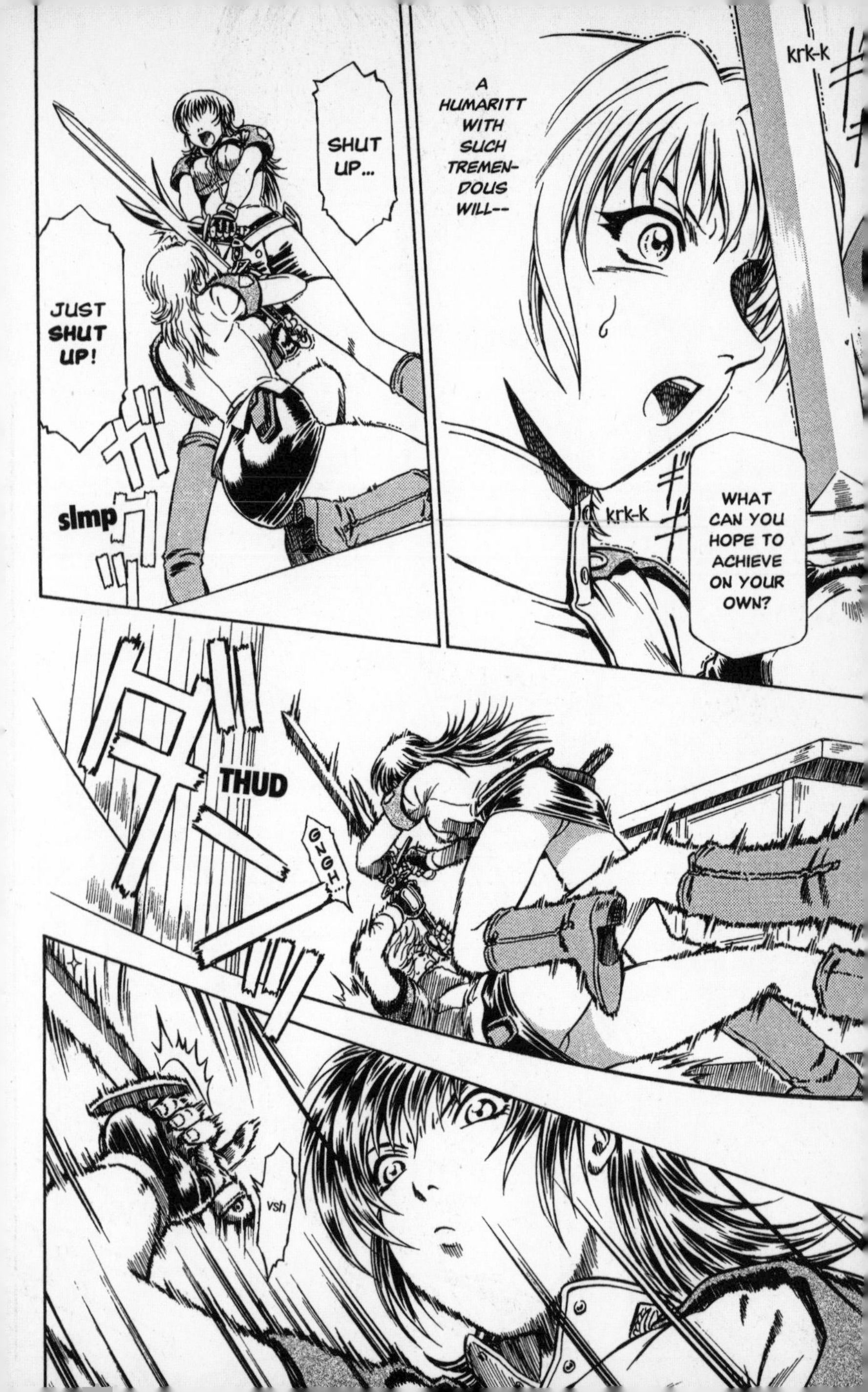
krk-k
A HUMARITT WITH SUCH TREMENDOUS WILL--
krk-k
WHAT CAN YOU HOPE TO ACHIEVE ON YOUR OWN?
SHUT UP...
JUST SHUT UP!
slmp
THUD
GNGH...
vsh

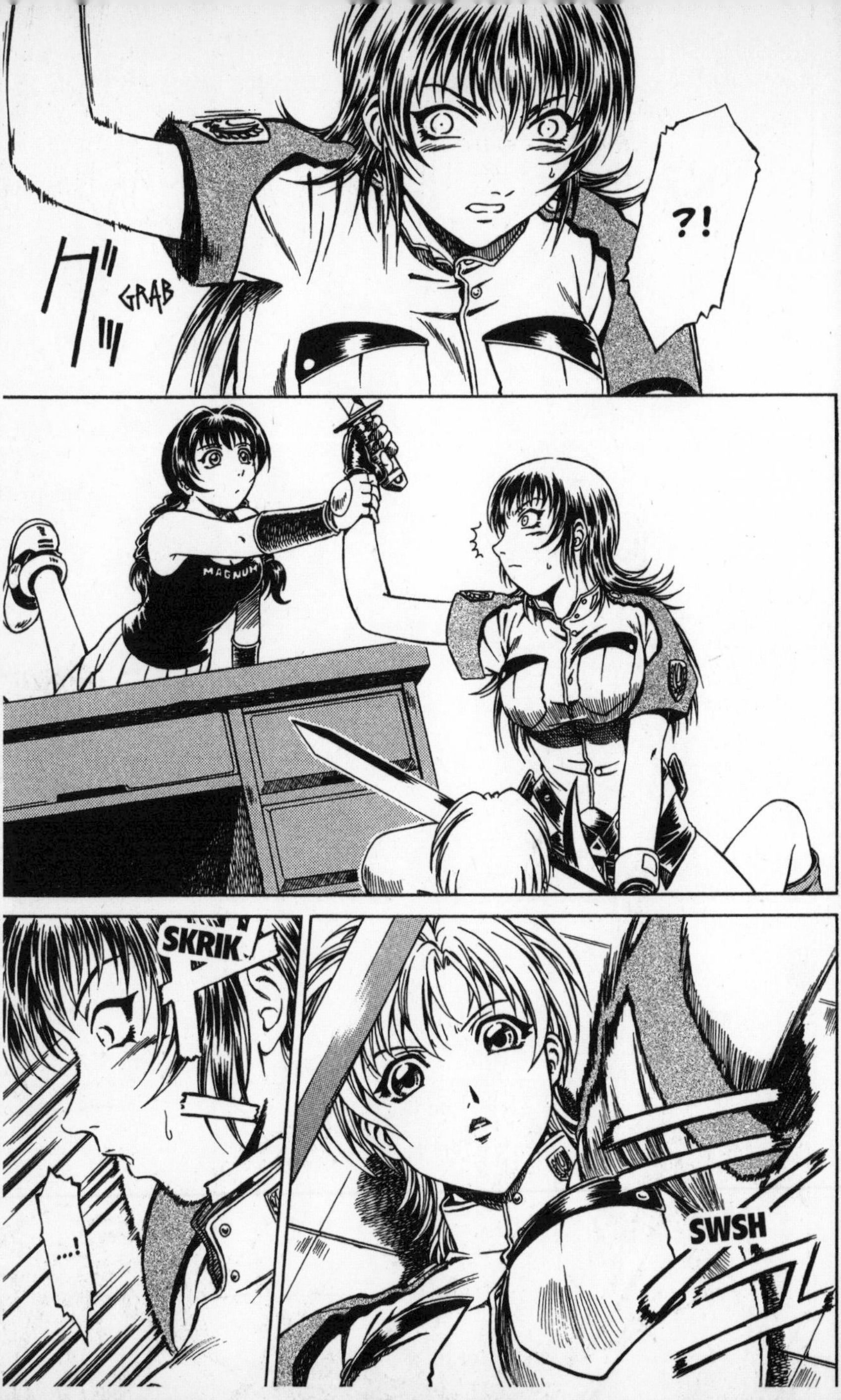

?!
GRAB
SKRIK
SWSH
...!

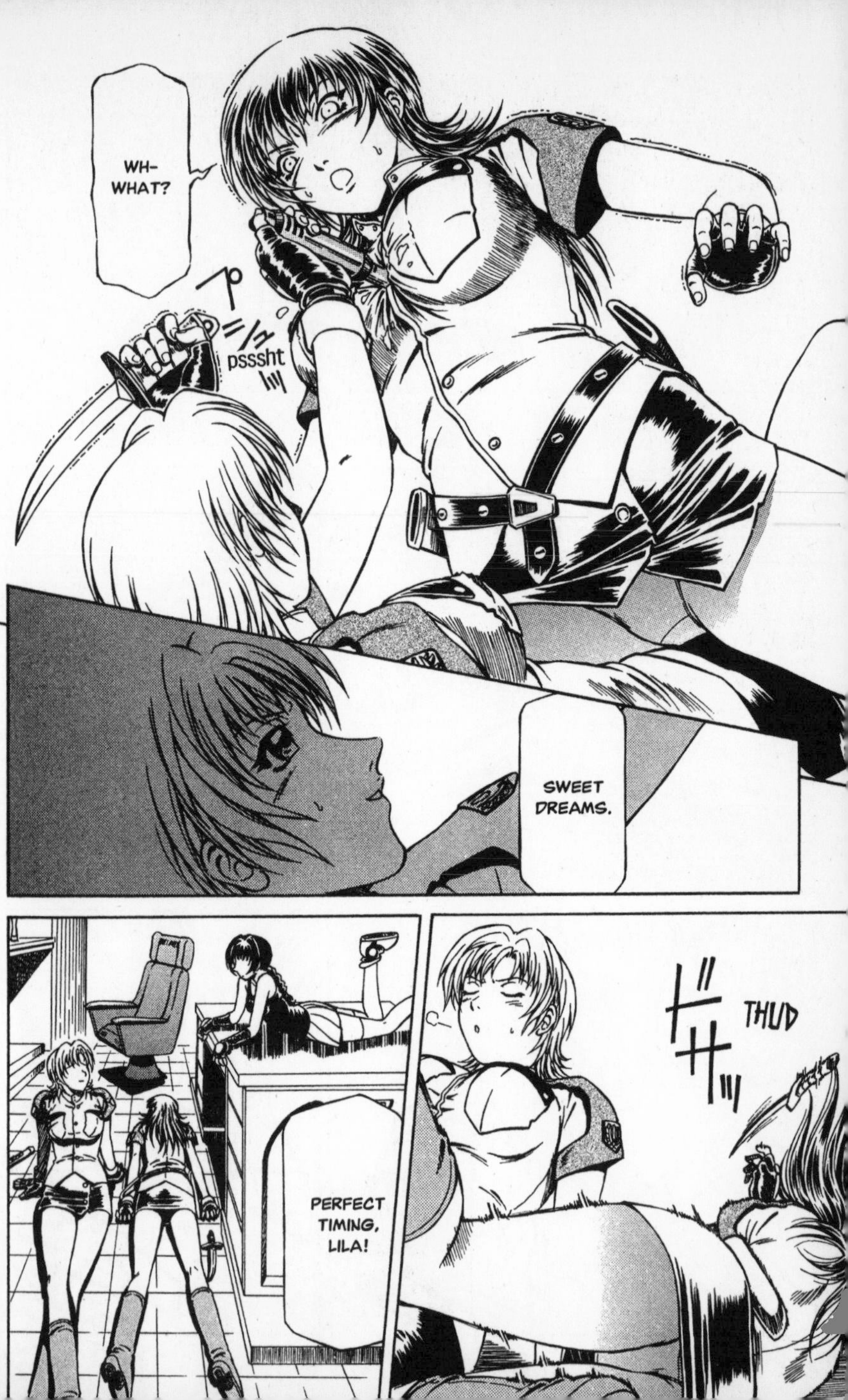
WH- WHAT?
pssht
SWEET DREAMS.
THUD
PERFECT TIMING, LILA!

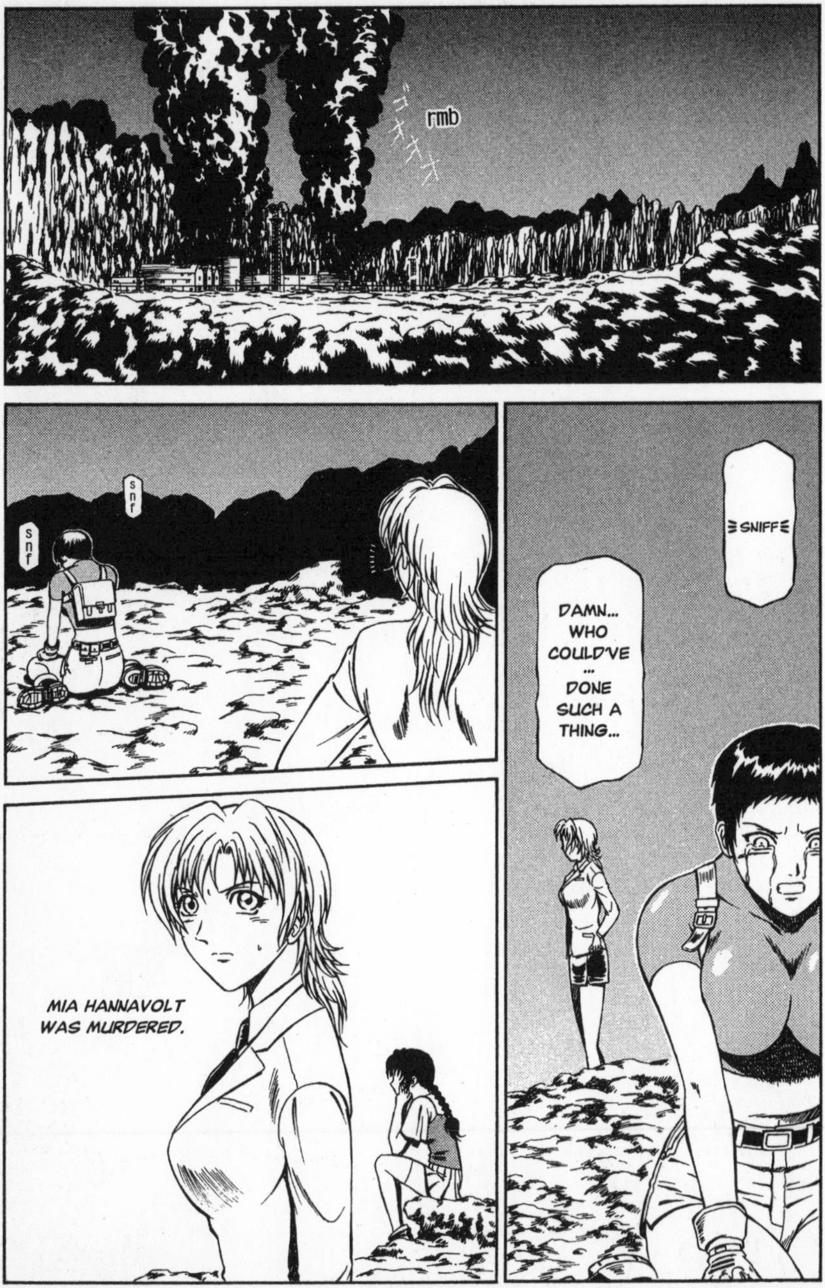
rmb
snf
snf
MIA HANNAVOLT WAS MURDERED.
SNIFF
DAMN... WHO COULD'VE ... DONE SUCH A THING...

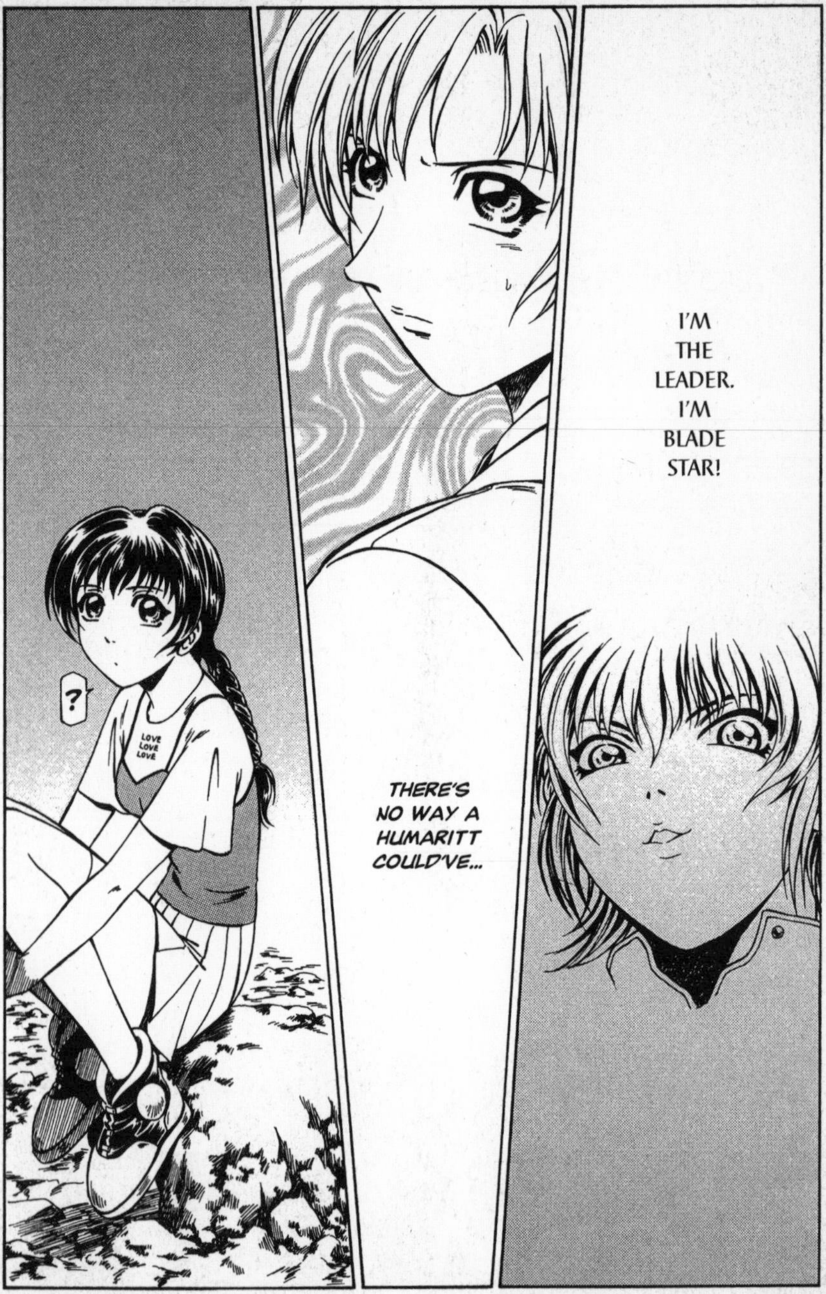
I'M THE LEADER. I'M BLADE STAR!
THERE'S NO WAY A HUMARITT COULD'VE...
?

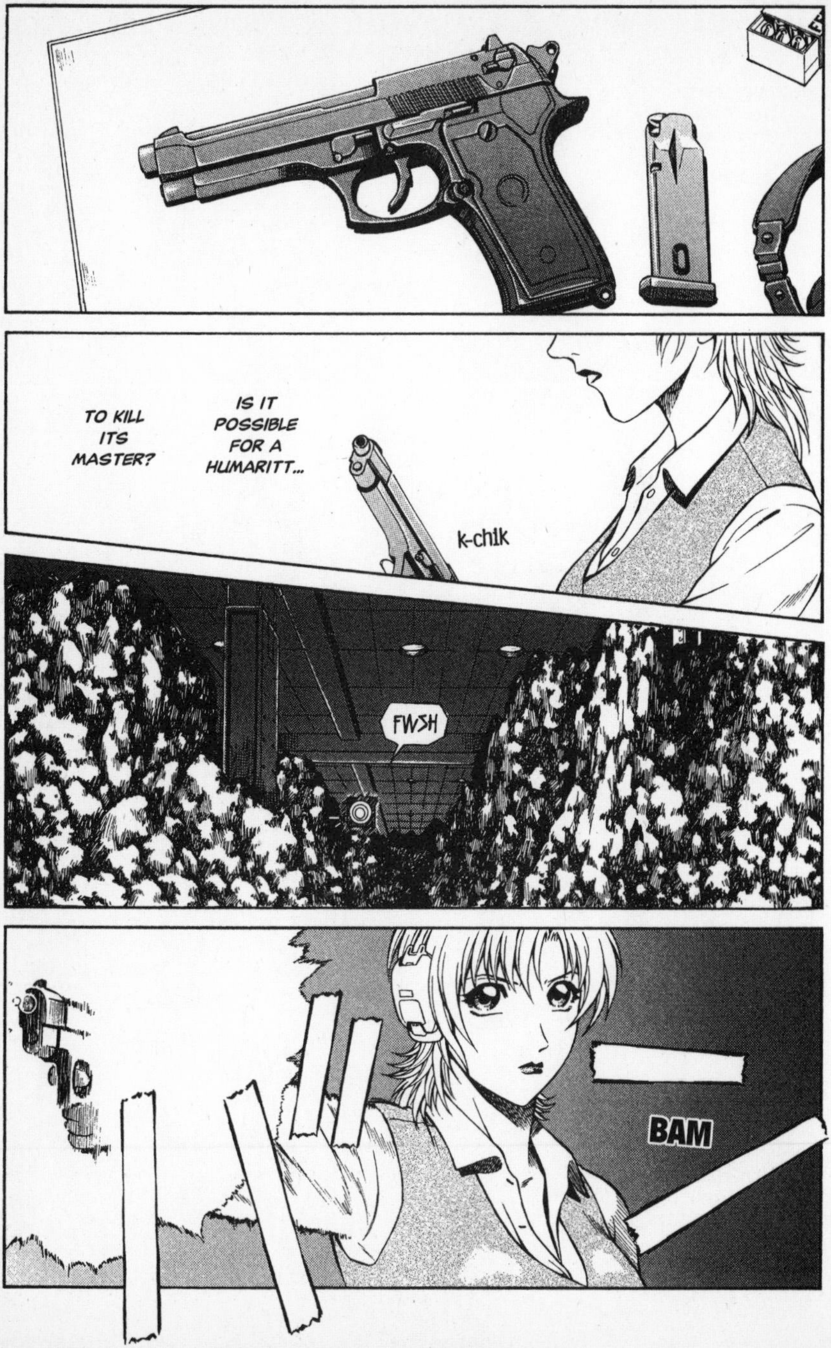
IS IT POSSIBLE FOR A HUMARITT...
TO KILL ITS MASTER?
k-chik
FWSH
BAM

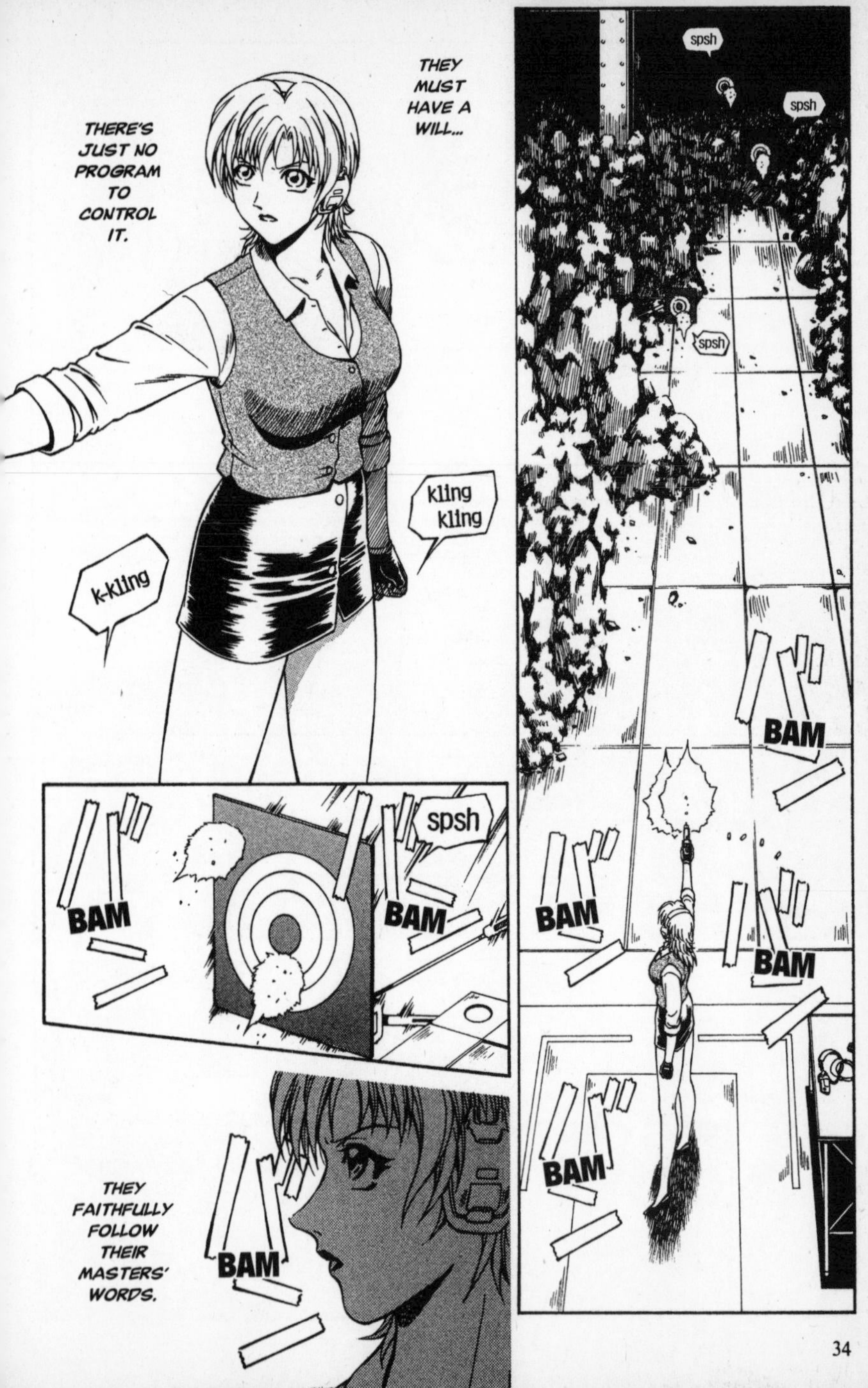
THEY MUST HAVE A WILL...
THERE'S JUST NO PROGRAM TO CONTROL IT.
spsh
spsh
spsh
kling kling
k-kling
BAM
spsh
BAM
BAM
BAM
BAM
BAM
THEY FAITHFULLY FOLLOW THEIR MASTERS' WORDS.
BAM

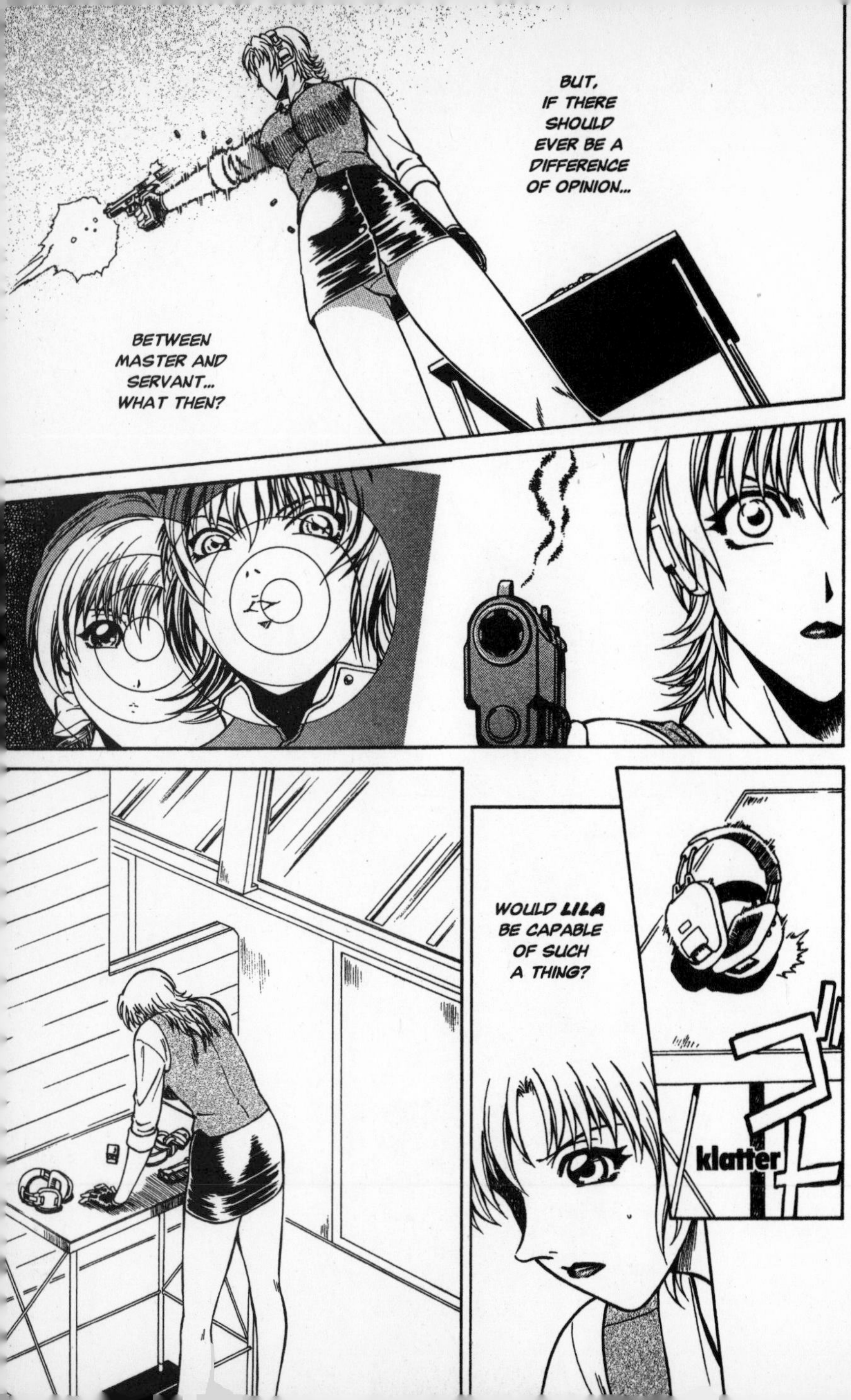
BUT, IF THERE SHOULD EVER BE A DIFFERENCE OF OPINION...
BETWEEN MASTER AND SERVANT... WHAT THEN?
WOULD LILA BE CAPABLE OF SUCH A THING?
klatter

Operation. 14
THE INTERLUDE

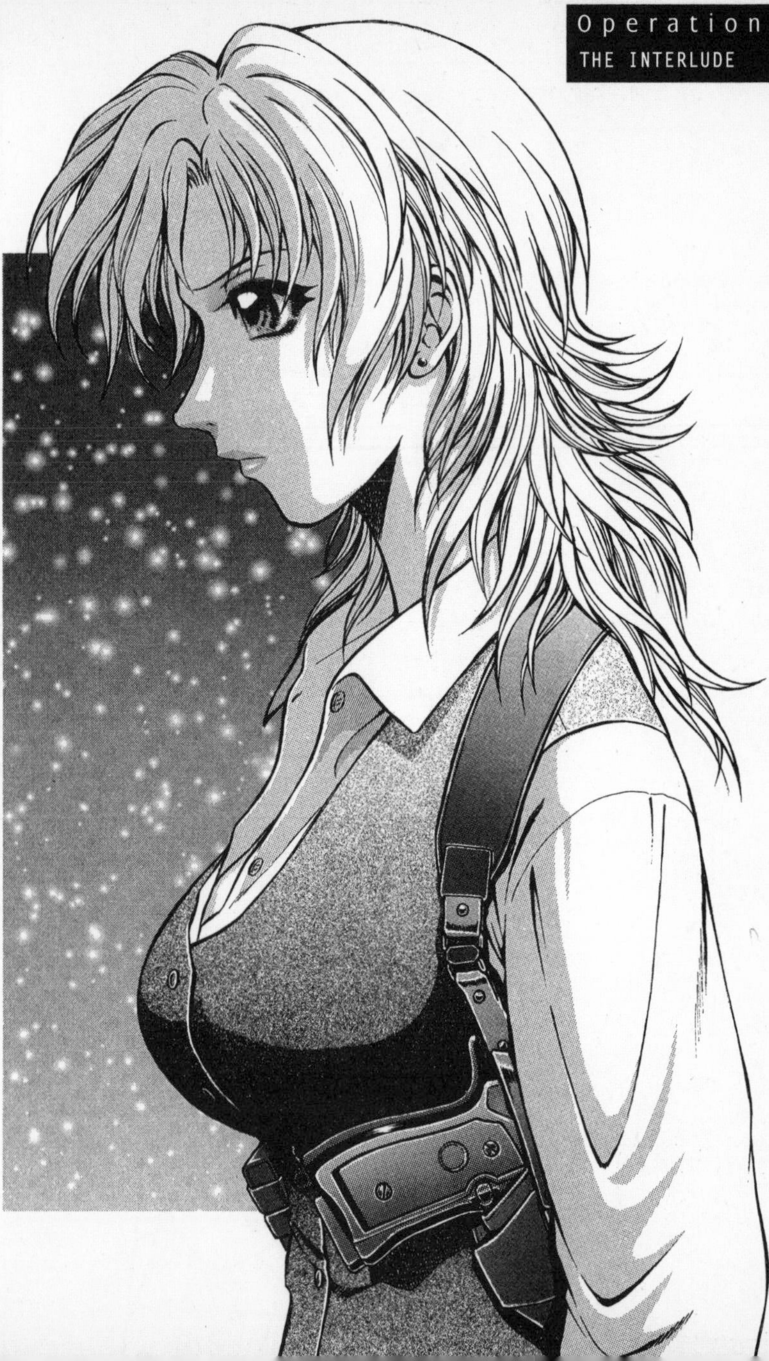

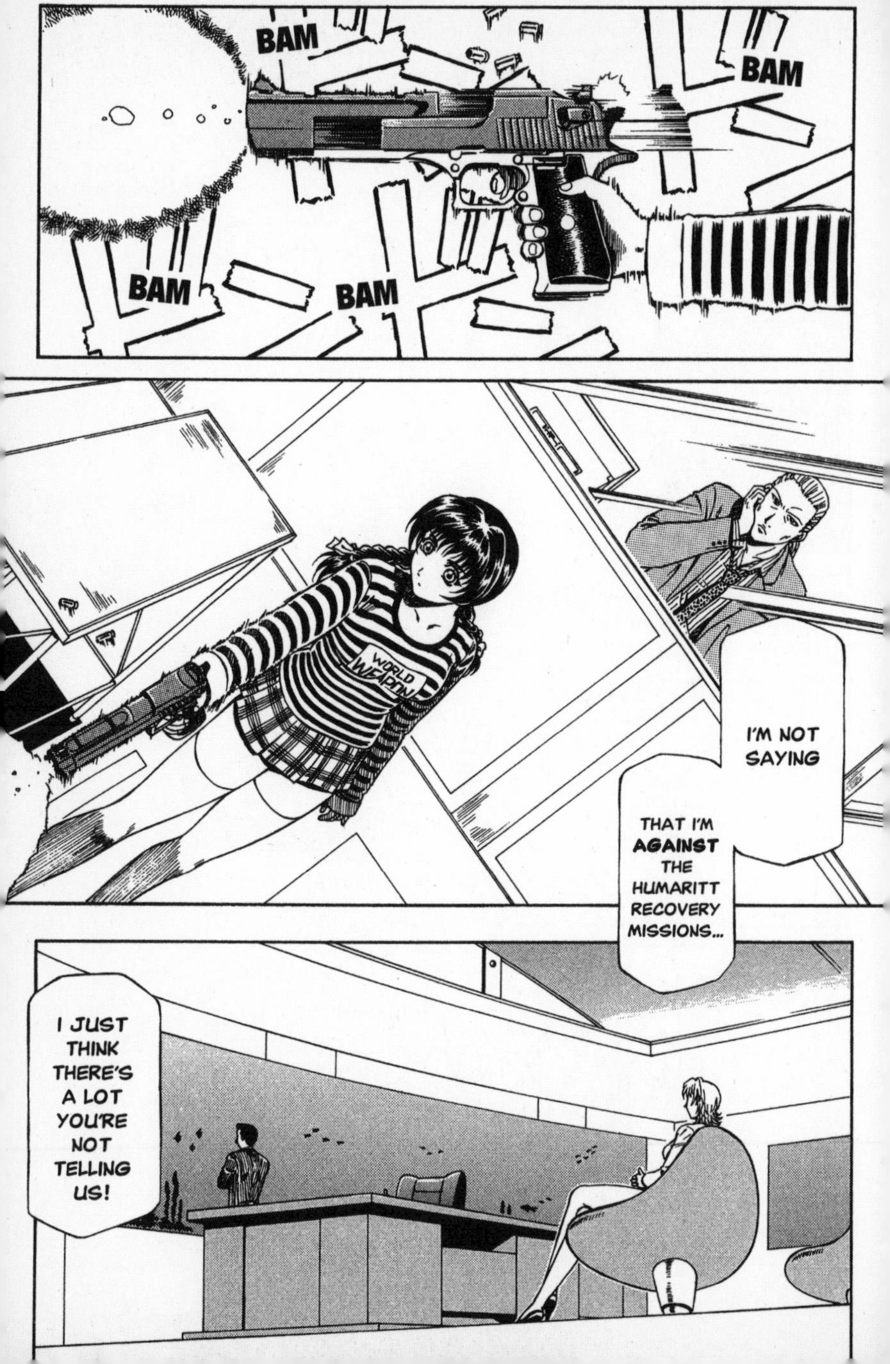
BAM
BAM
BAM
BAM
WORLD WEAPON
I'M NOT SAYING
THAT I'M AGAINST THE HUMARITT RECOVERY MISSIONS...
I JUST THINK THERE'S A LOT YOU'RE NOT TELLING US!

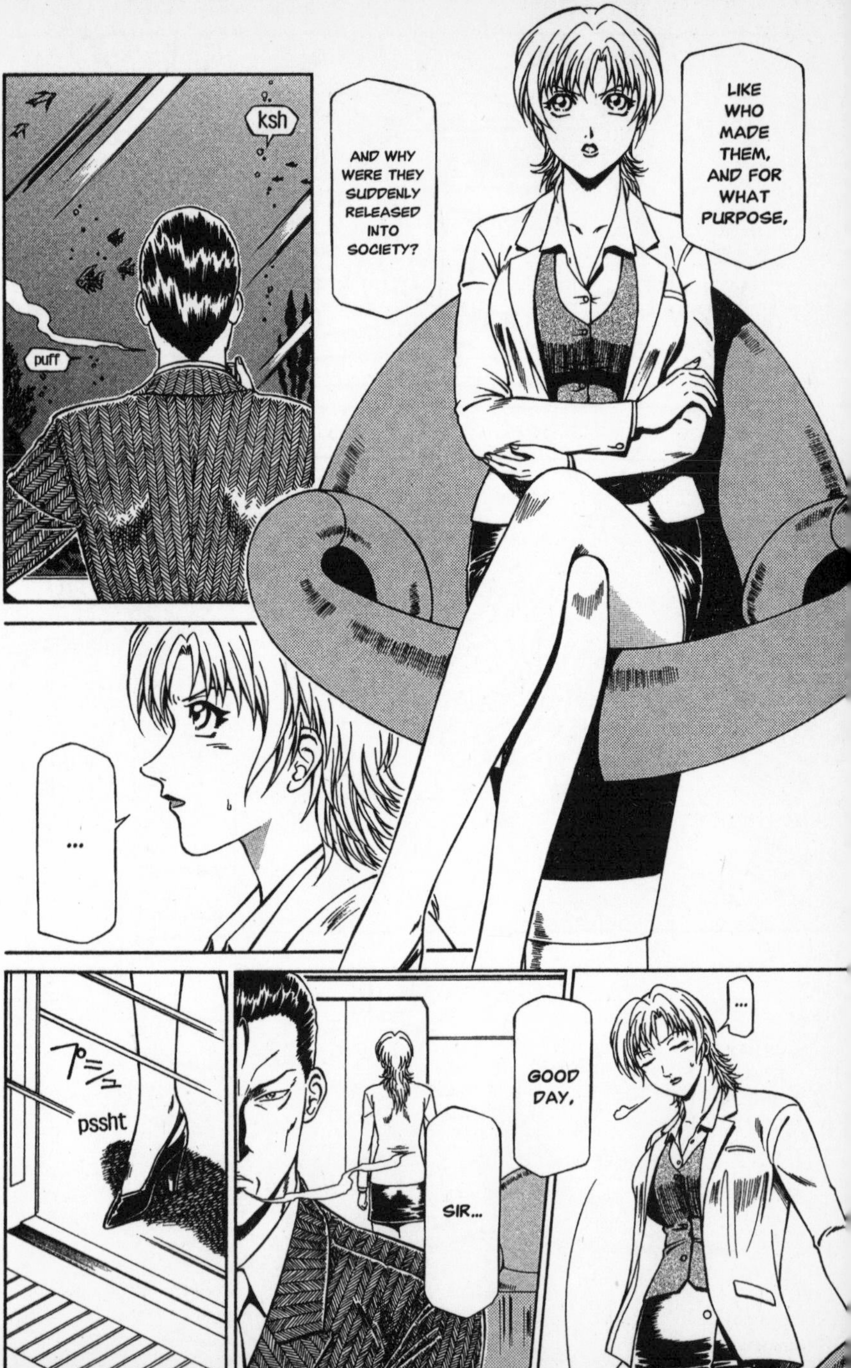
LIKE WHO MADE THEM, AND FOR WHAT PURPOSE,
AND WHY WERE THEY SUDDENLY RELEASED INTO SOCIETY?
ksh
puff
...
...
GOOD DAY,
SIR...
pssht

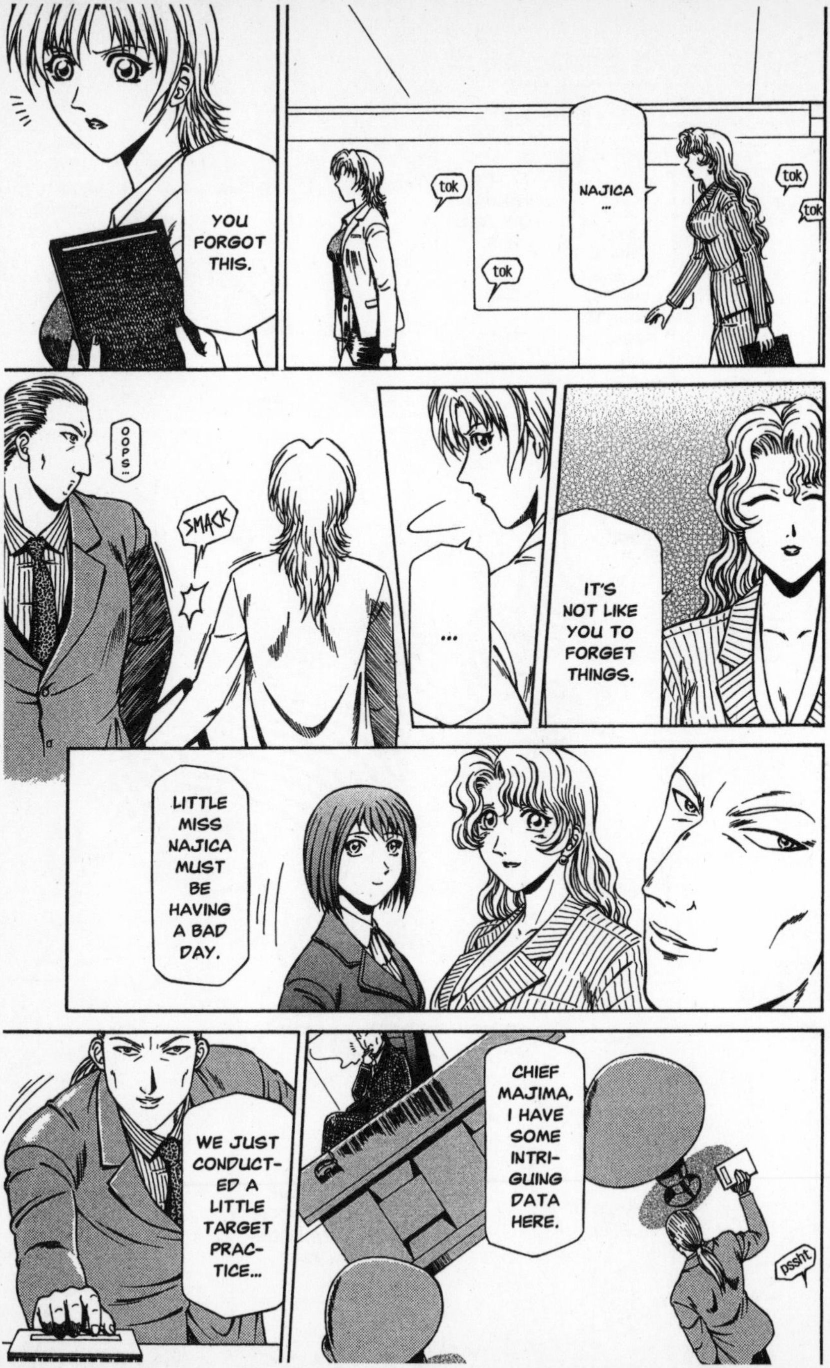
YOU FORGOT THIS.
tok
NAJICA ...
tok
tok
tok
OOPS...
SMACK
...
IT'S NOT LIKE YOU TO FORGET THINGS.
LITTLE MISS NAJICA MUST BE HAVING A BAD DAY.
WE JUST CONDUCTED A LITTLE TARGET PRACTICE...
CHIEF MAJIMA, I HAVE SOME INTRIGUING DATA HERE.
psssht

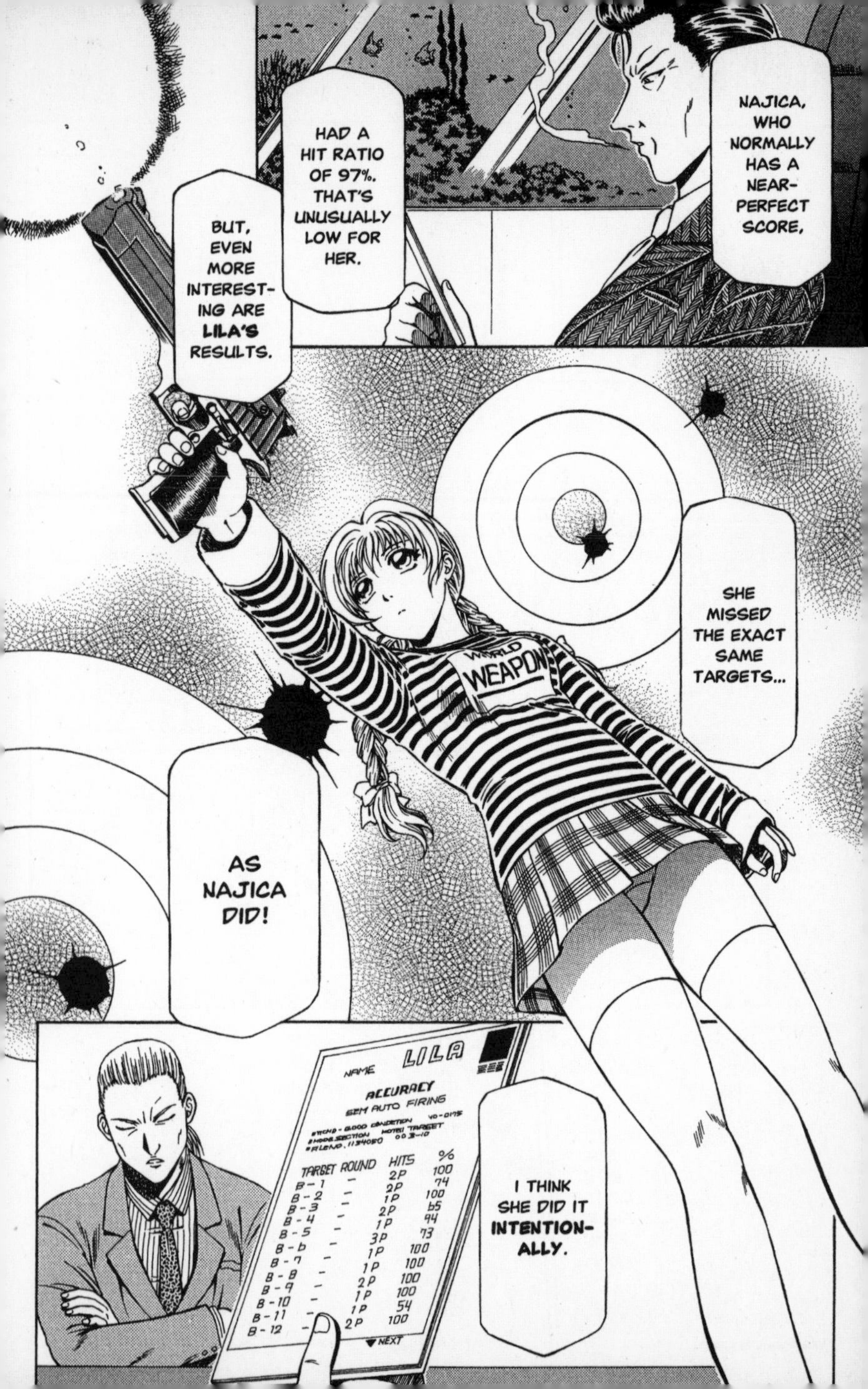
NAJICA, WHO NORMALLY HAS A NEAR-PERFECT SCORE,
HAD A HIT RATIO OF 97%. THAT'S UNUSUALLY LOW FOR HER.
BUT, EVEN MORE INTEREST-ING ARE **LILA'S** RESULTS.
SHE MISSED THE EXACT SAME TARGETS...
AS NAJICA DID!
WORLD WEAPON
NAME LILA
ACCURACY
SEMI AUTO FIRING
TARGET ROUND HITS %
B-1 - 2P 100
B-2 - 2P 74
B-3 - 1P 100
B-4 - 2P 65
B-5 - 1P 94
B-6 - 3P 73
B-7 - 1P 100
B-8 - 1P 100
B-9 - 2P 100
B-10 - 1P 100
B-11 - 1P 54
B-12 - 2P 100
NEXT
I THINK SHE DID IT **INTENTION-ALLY**.

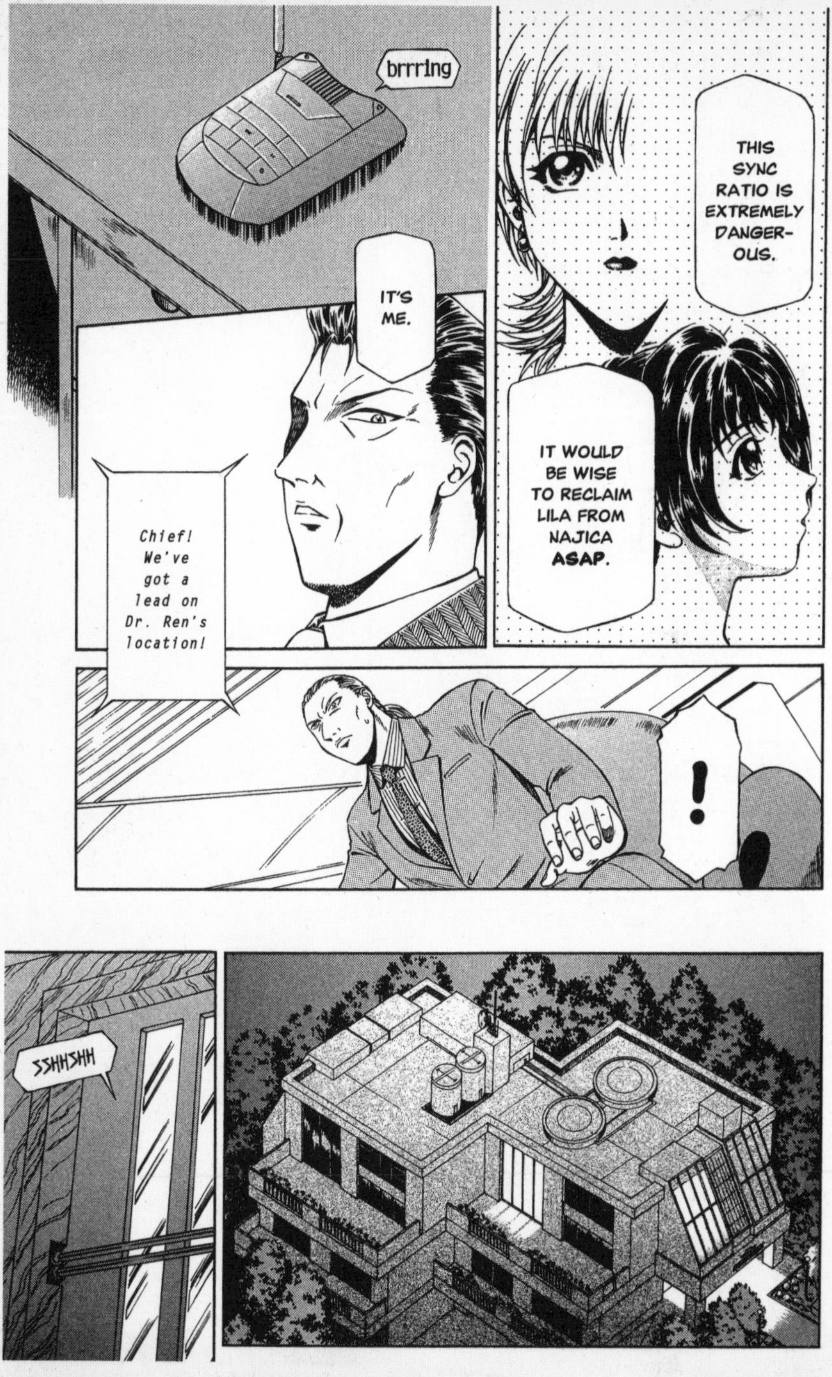
brrring
IT'S ME.
THIS SYNC RATIO IS EXTREMELY DANGER-OUS.
IT WOULD BE WISE TO RECLAIM LILA FROM NAJICA ASAP.
Chief! We've got a lead on Dr. Ren's location!
!

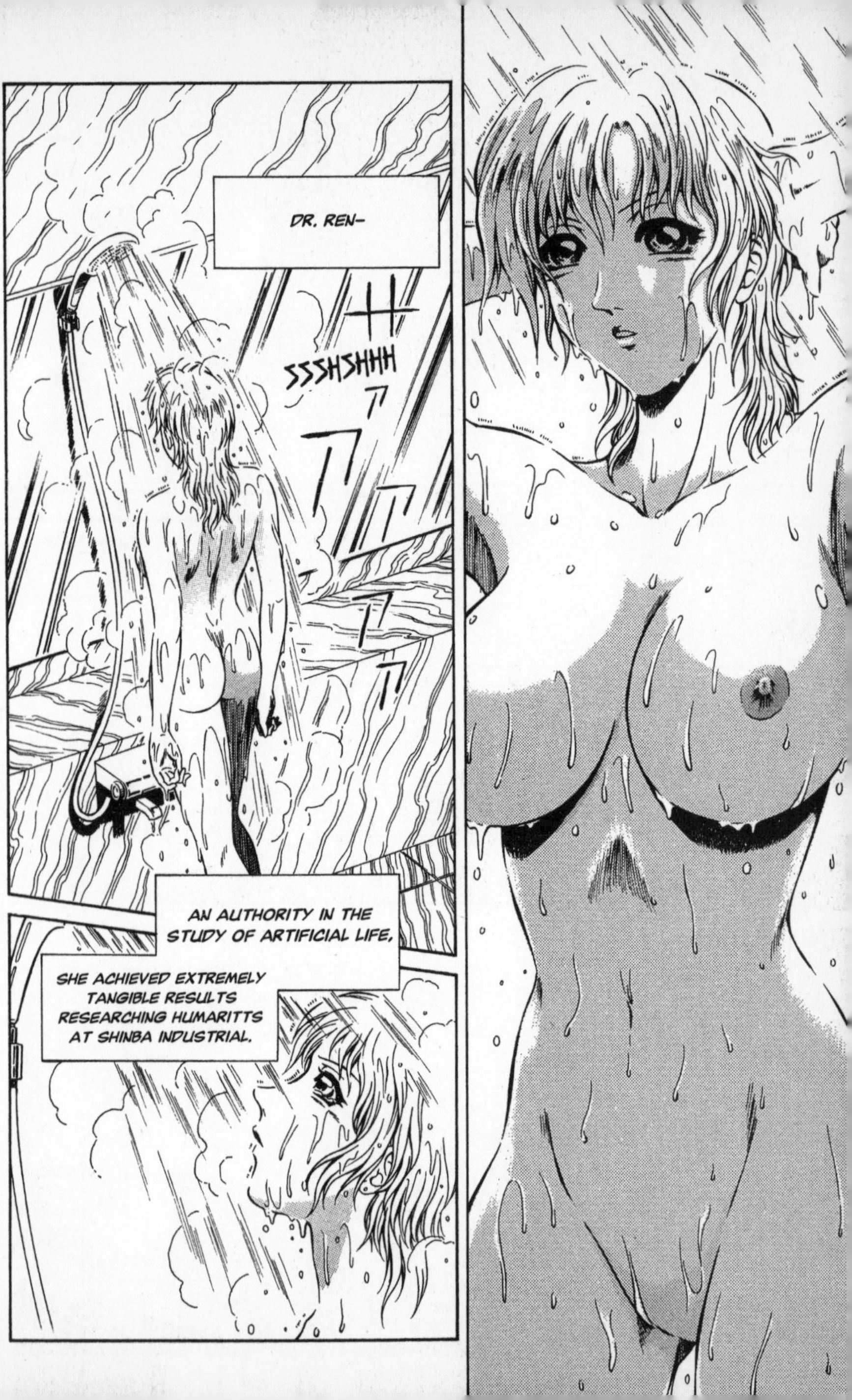
DR. REN-
SSSHSHHH
AN AUTHORITY IN THE STUDY OF ARTIFICIAL LIFE,
SHE ACHIEVED EXTREMELY TANGIBLE RESULTS RESEARCHING HUMARITTS AT SHINBA INDUSTRIAL.

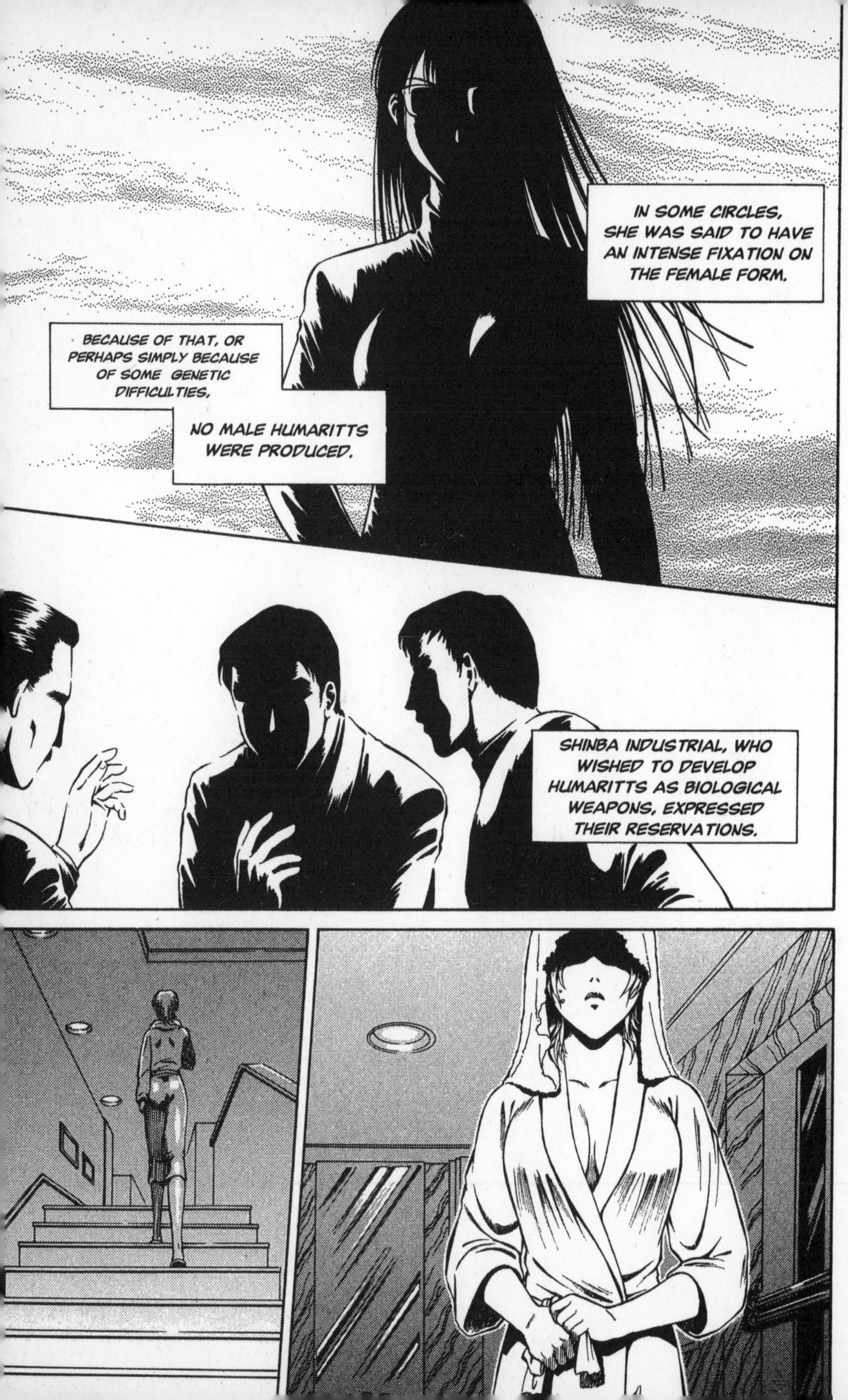
IN SOME CIRCLES, SHE WAS SAID TO HAVE AN INTENSE FIXATION ON THE FEMALE FORM.
BECAUSE OF THAT, OR PERHAPS SIMPLY BECAUSE OF SOME GENETIC DIFFICULTIES,
NO MALE HUMARITTS WERE PRODUCED.
SHINBA INDUSTRIAL, WHO WISHED TO DEVELOP HUMARITTS AS BIOLOGICAL WEAPONS, EXPRESSED THEIR RESERVATIONS.

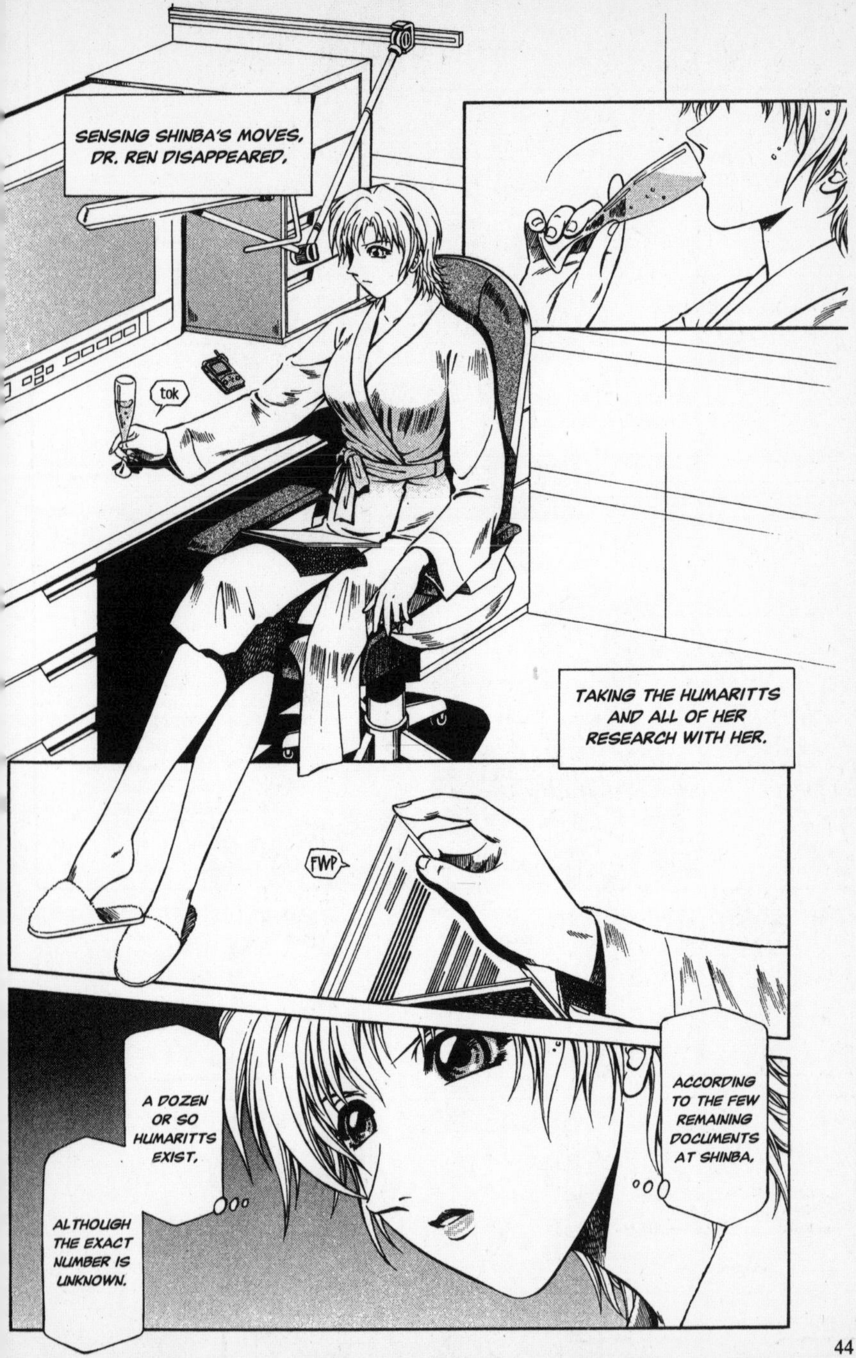
SENSING SHINBA'S MOVES, DR. REN DISAPPEARED,
tok
TAKING THE HUMARITTS AND ALL OF HER RESEARCH WITH HER.
FWP
ACCORDING TO THE FEW REMAINING DOCUMENTS AT SHINBA,
A DOZEN OR SO HUMARITTS EXIST,
ALTHOUGH THE EXACT NUMBER IS UNKNOWN.

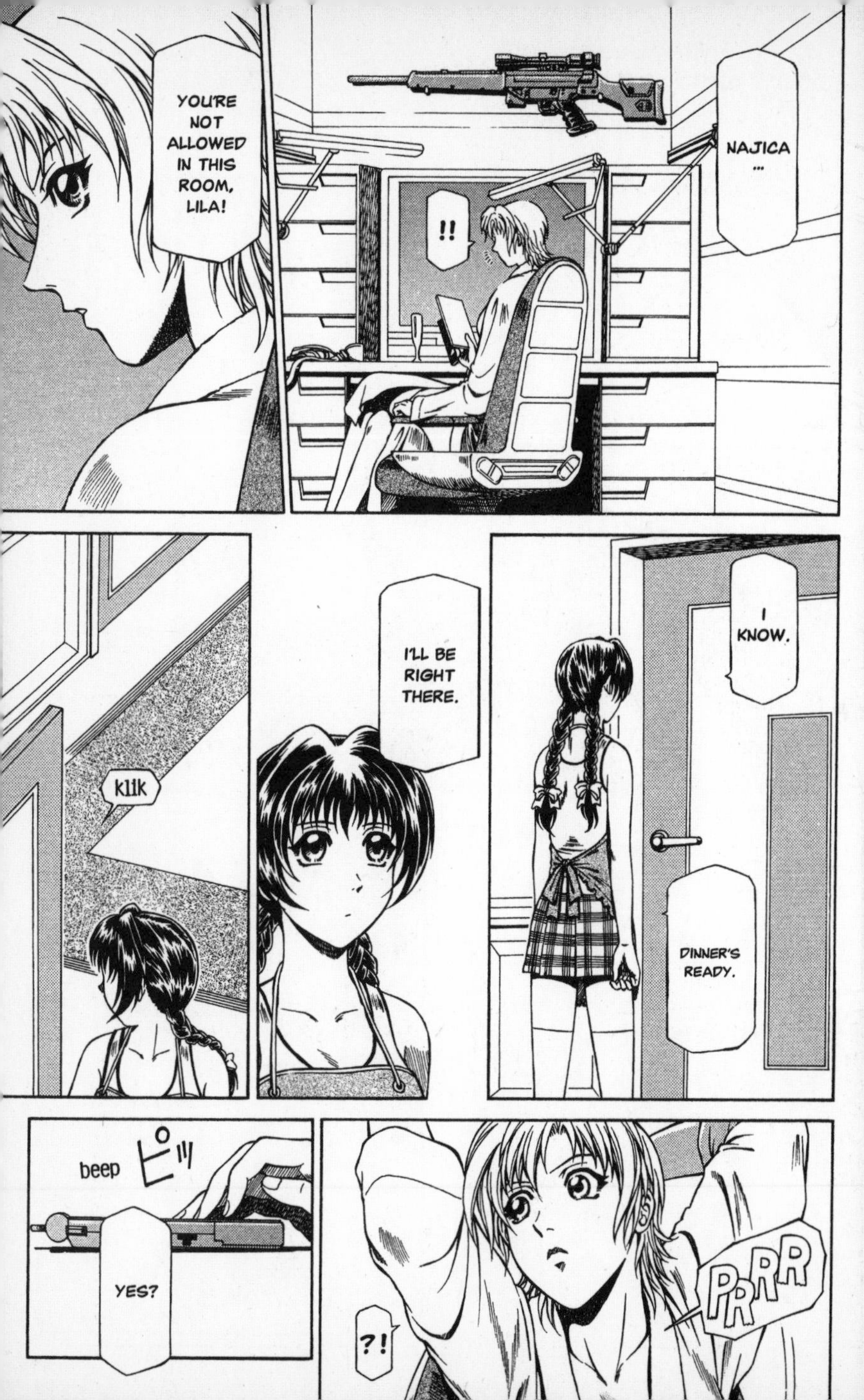

NAJICA ...
!!
YOU'RE NOT ALLOWED IN THIS ROOM, LILA!
I KNOW.
DINNER'S READY.
I'LL BE RIGHT THERE.
klik
PRRR
?!
beep ピッ
YES?

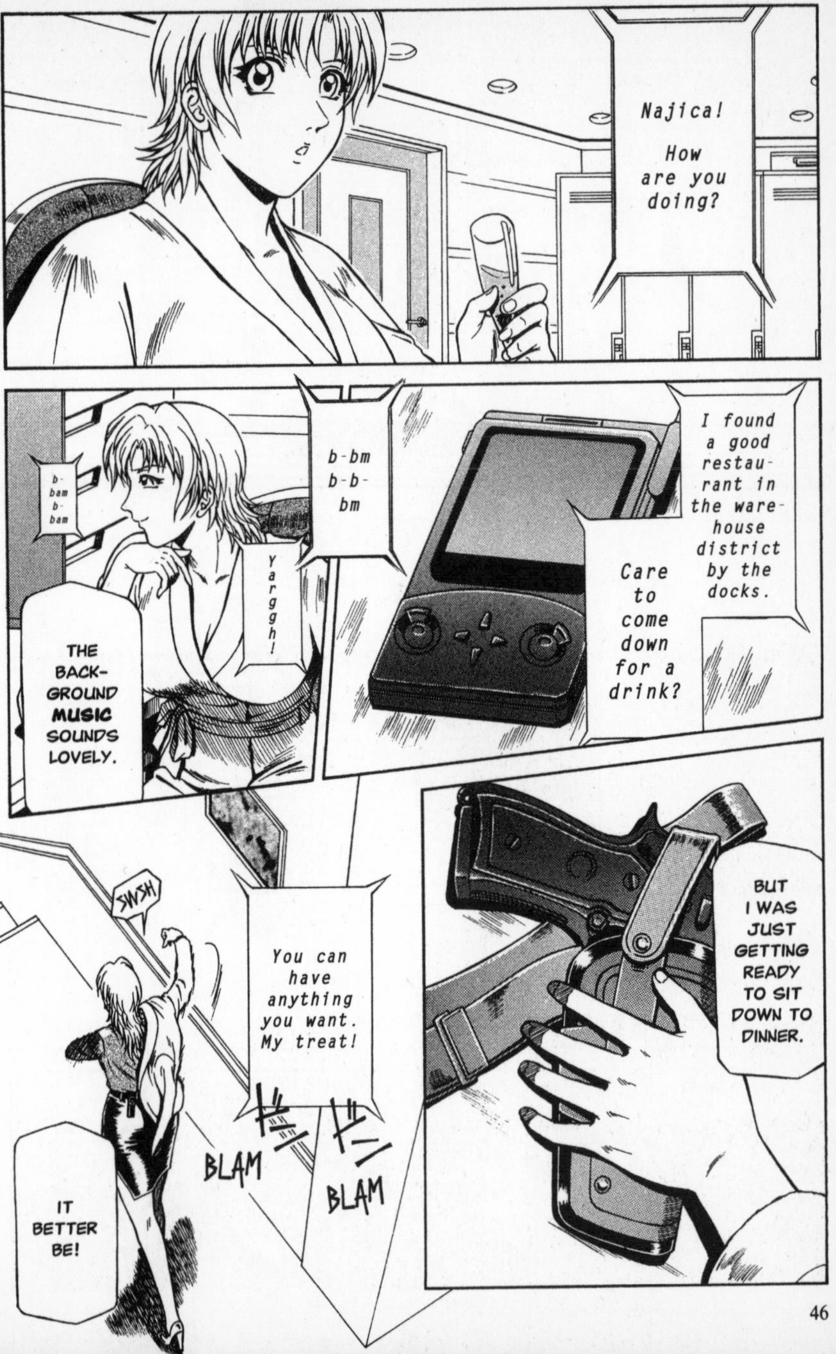
Najica!
How are you doing?
b-bam b-bam
b-bm b-b-bm
Yarggh!
THE BACK-GROUND MUSIC SOUNDS LOVELY.
I found a good restau-rant in the ware-house district by the docks.
Care to come down for a drink?
BUT I WAS JUST GETTING READY TO SIT DOWN TO DINNER.
SWSH
You can have anything you want. My treat!
BLAM
BLAM
IT BETTER BE!

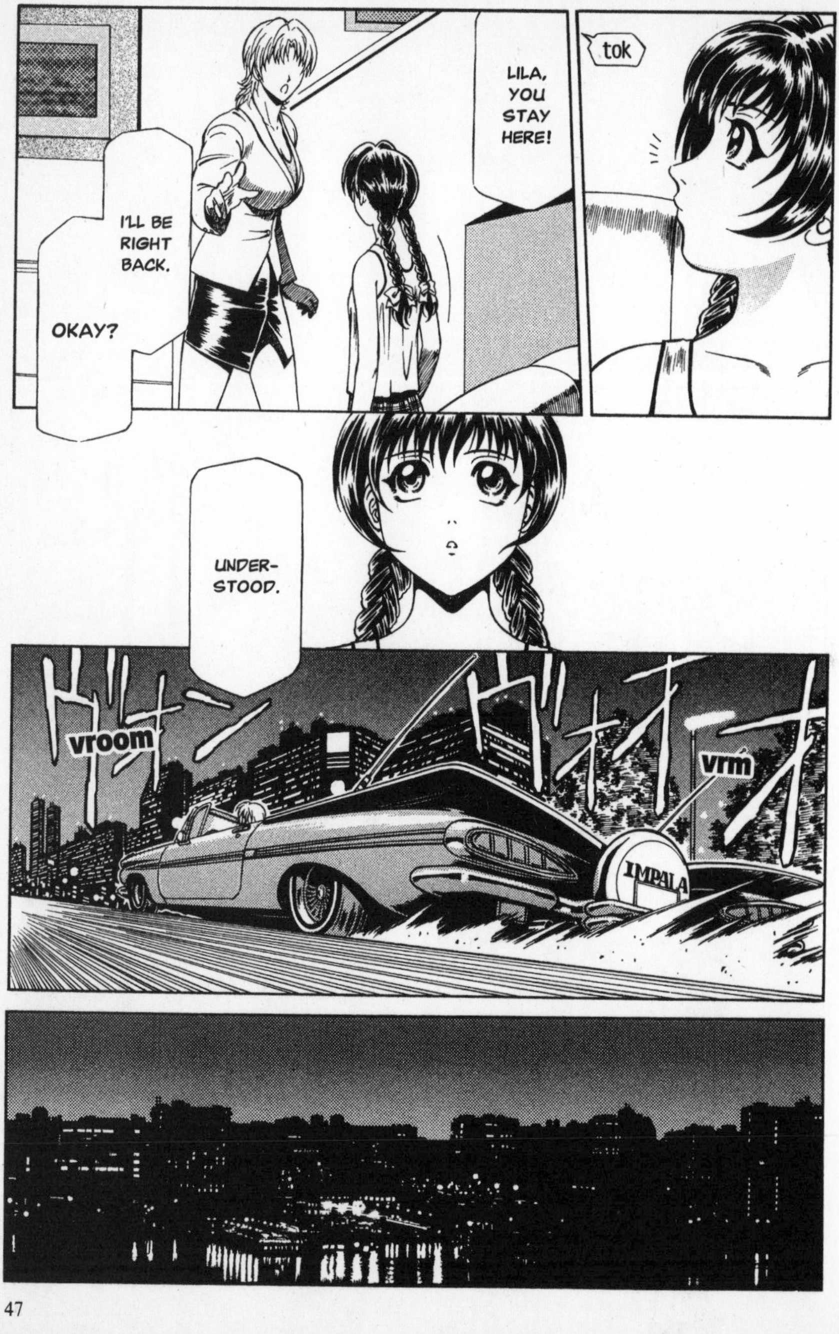

tok
LILA, YOU STAY HERE!
I'LL BE RIGHT BACK.
OKAY?
UNDER-STOOD.
vroom
vrm
IMPALA

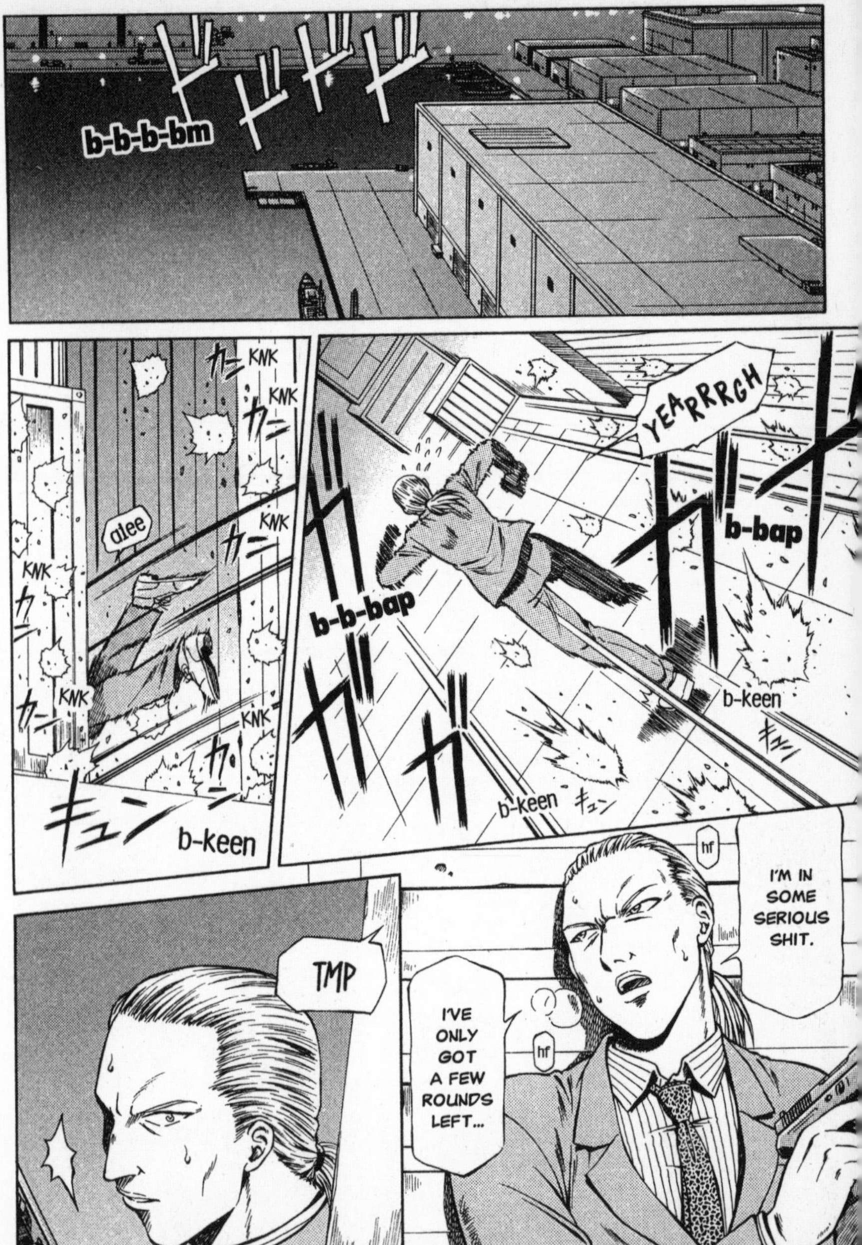
b-b-b-bm
YEARRRGH
b-bap
b-b-bap
b-keen
b-keen
KNK
KNK
aiee
KNK
KNK
KNK
KNK
b-keen
hf
I'M IN SOME SERIOUS SHIT.
hf
I'VE ONLY GOT A FEW ROUNDS LEFT...
TMP

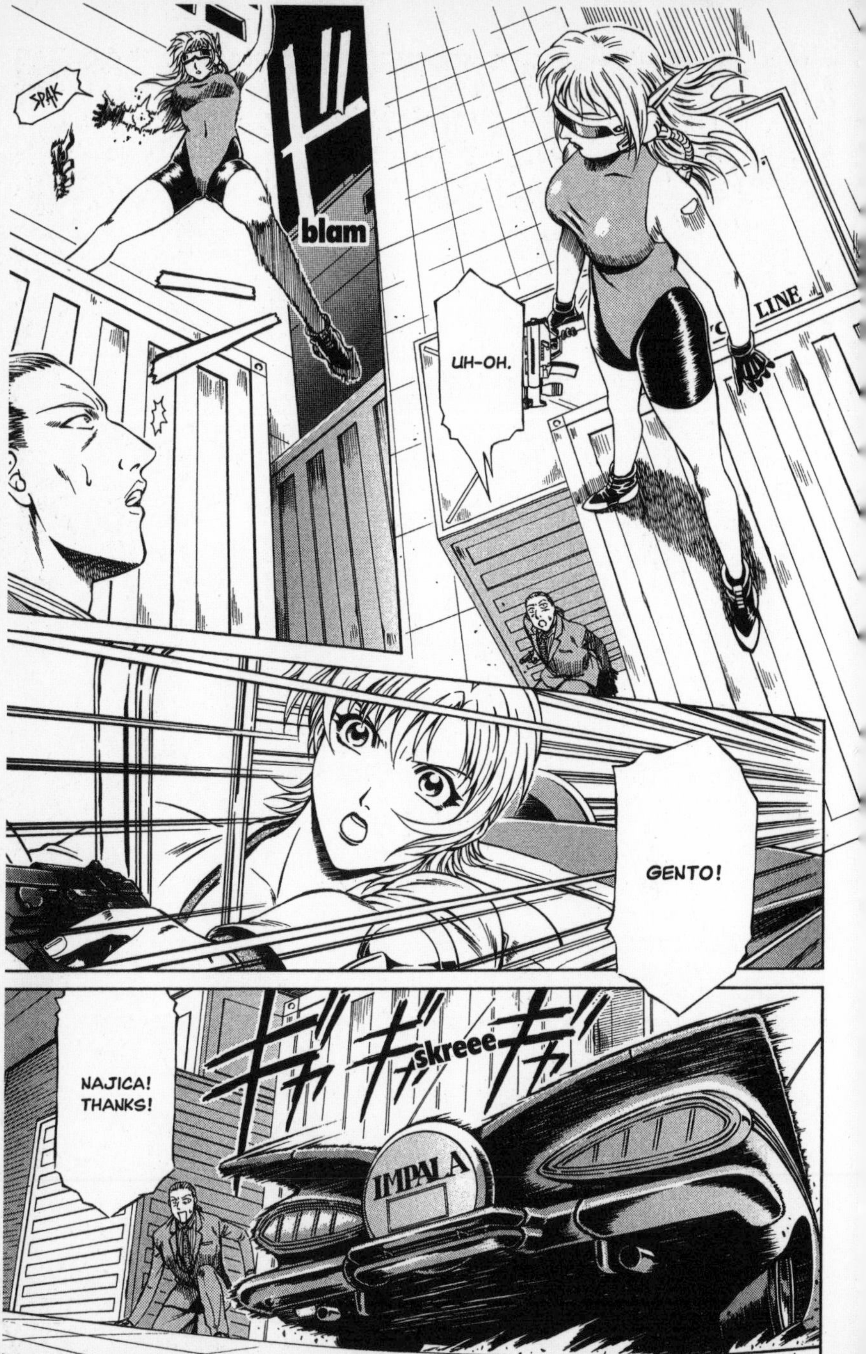
LINE
UH-OH.
SPAK
blam
GENTO!
skreee
NAJICA! THANKS!
IMPALA

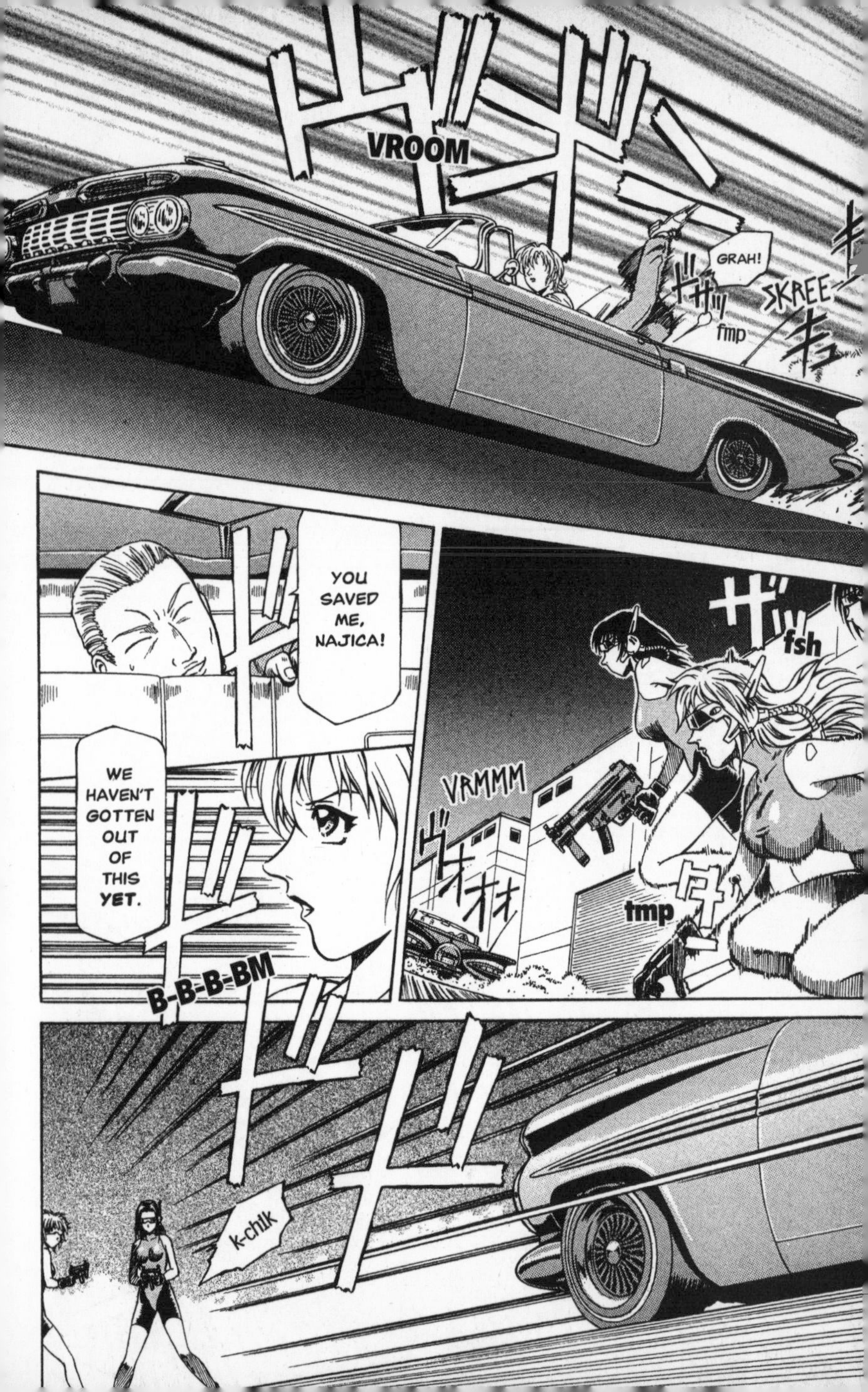

VROOM
GRAH!
fmp
SKREE
YOU SAVED ME, NAJICA!
WE HAVEN'T GOTTEN OUT OF THIS YET.
fsh
VRMMM
tmp
B-B-B-BM
k-chik

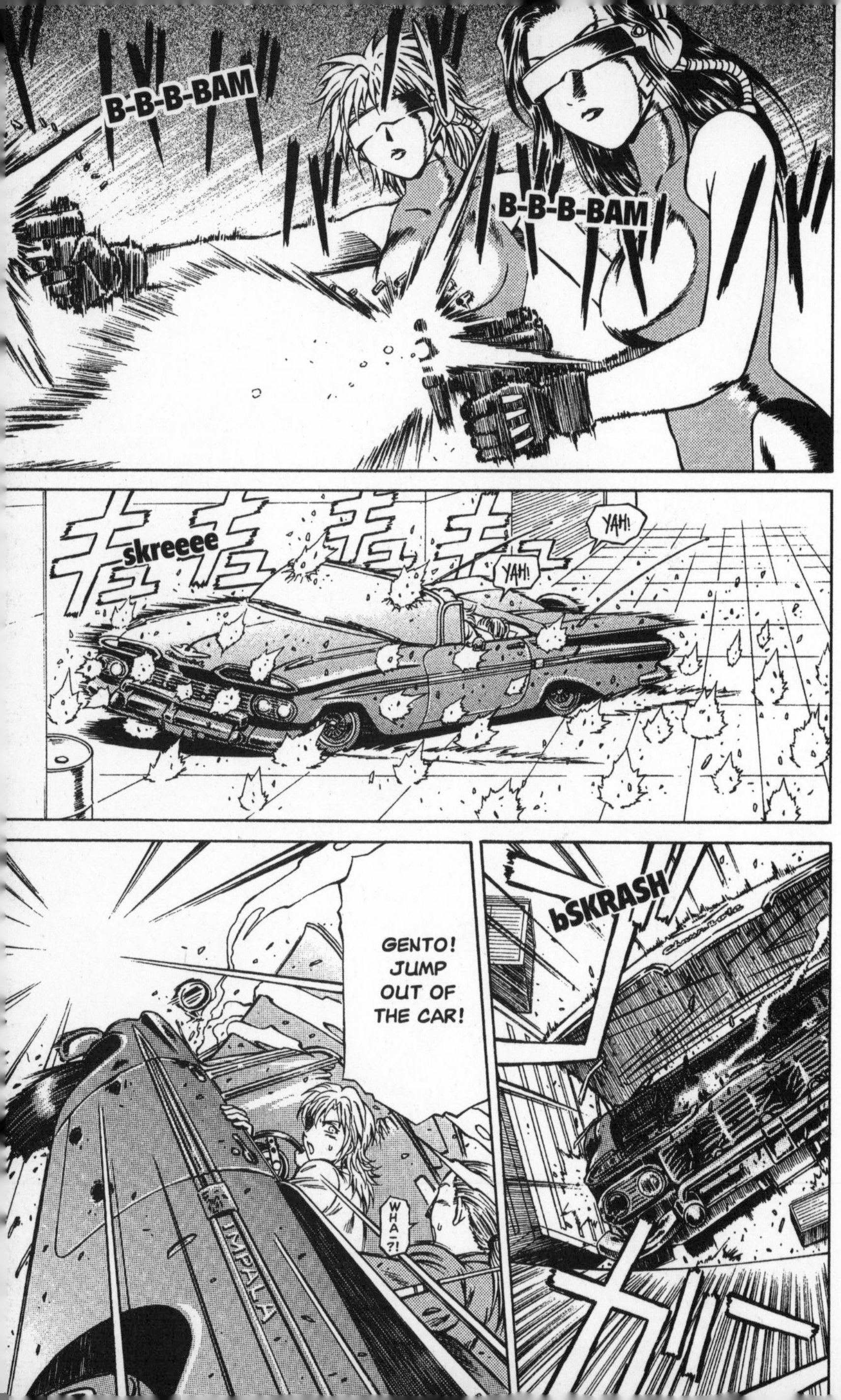
B-B-B-BAM
B-B-B-BAM
skreeee
YAH!
YAH!
GENTO! JUMP OUT OF THE CAR!
WHA-?!
IMPALA
bSKRASH

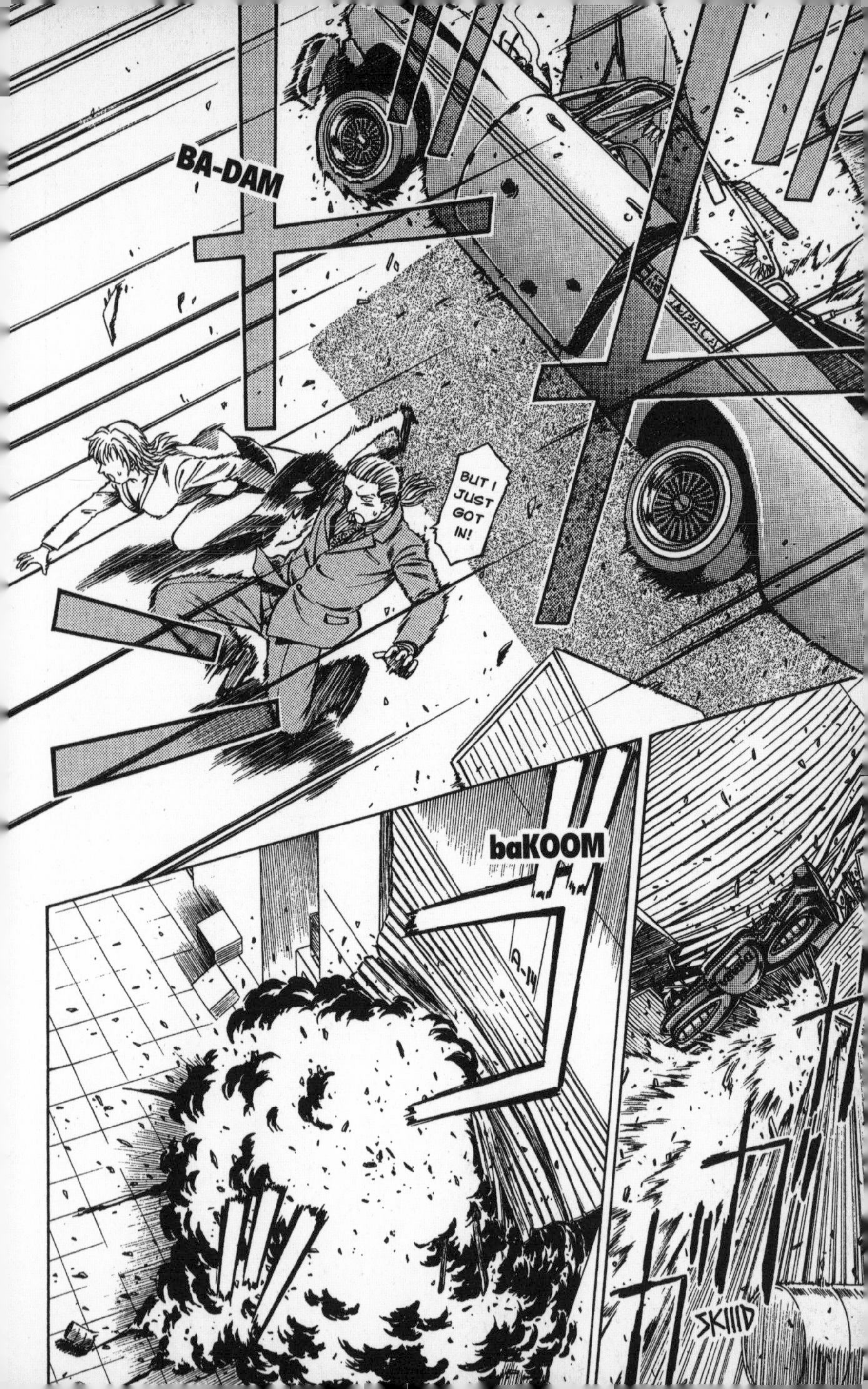
BA-DAM
BUT I JUST GOT IN!
baKOOM
SKIIID

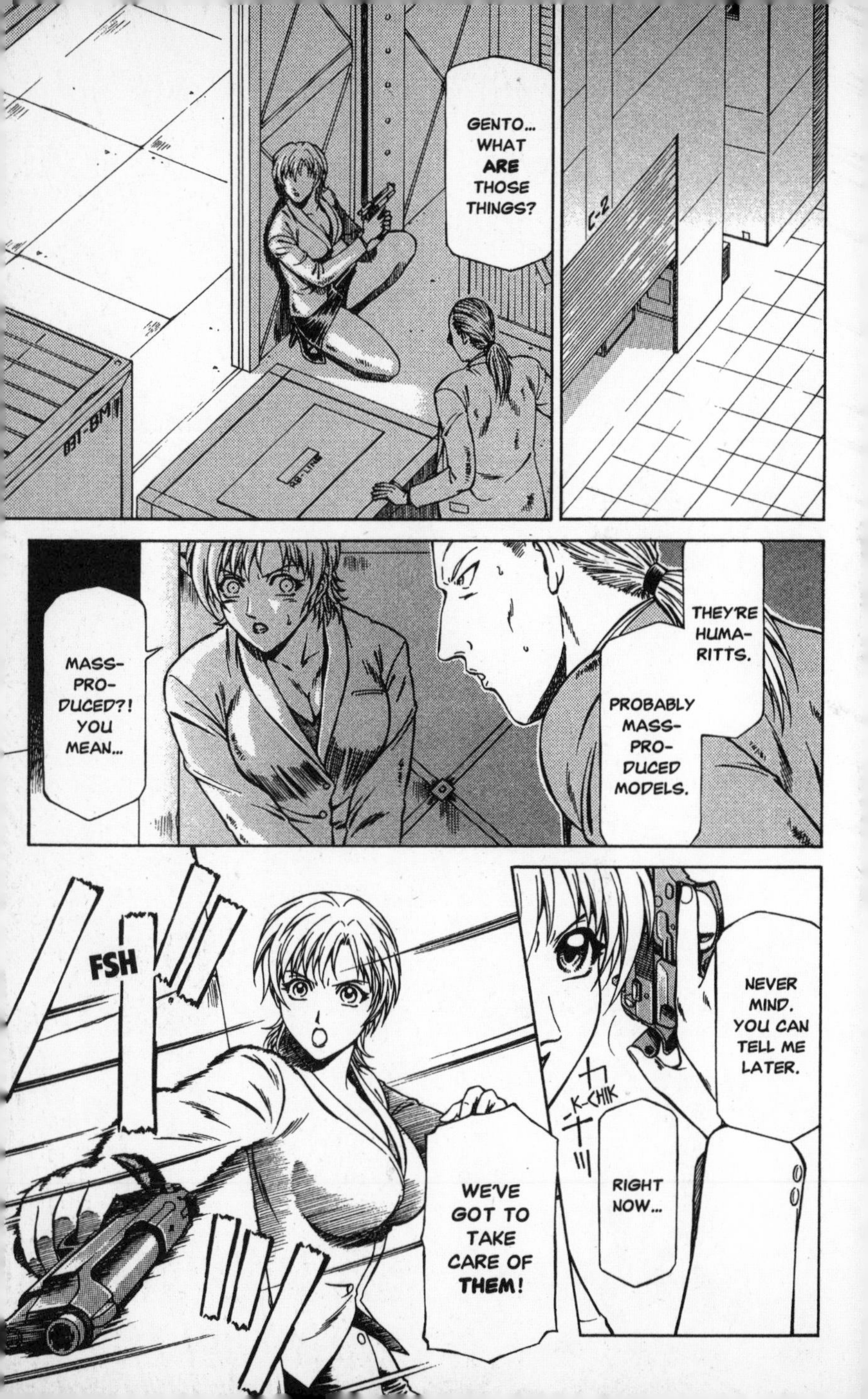
GENTO... WHAT ARE THOSE THINGS?
THEY'RE HUMA-RITTS.
PROBABLY MASS-PRO-DUCED MODELS.
MASS-PRO-DUCED?! YOU MEAN...
NEVER MIND. YOU CAN TELL ME LATER.
K-CHIK
RIGHT NOW...
WE'VE GOT TO TAKE CARE OF THEM!
FSH

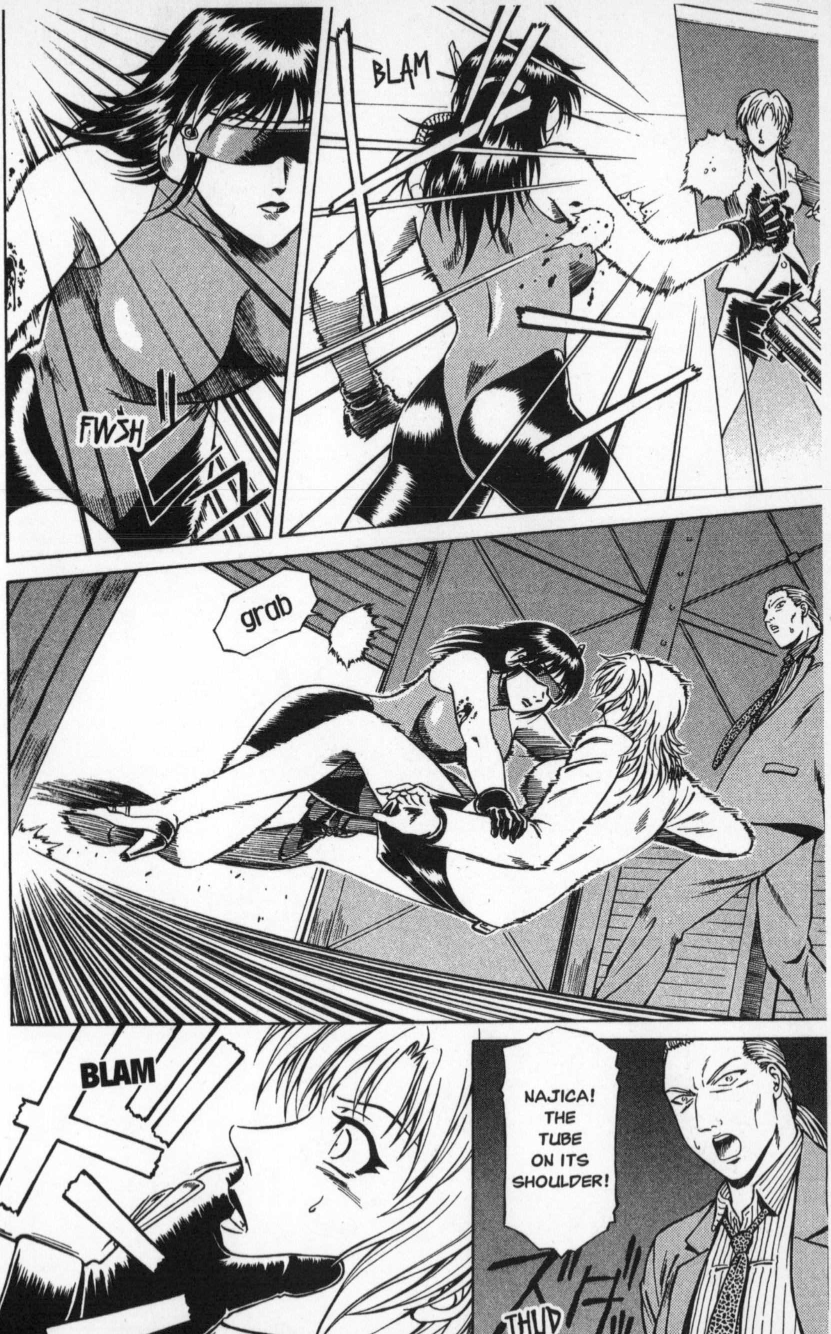
BLAM
FWSH
grab
BLAM
NAJICA! THE TUBE ON ITS SHOULDER!
THUD

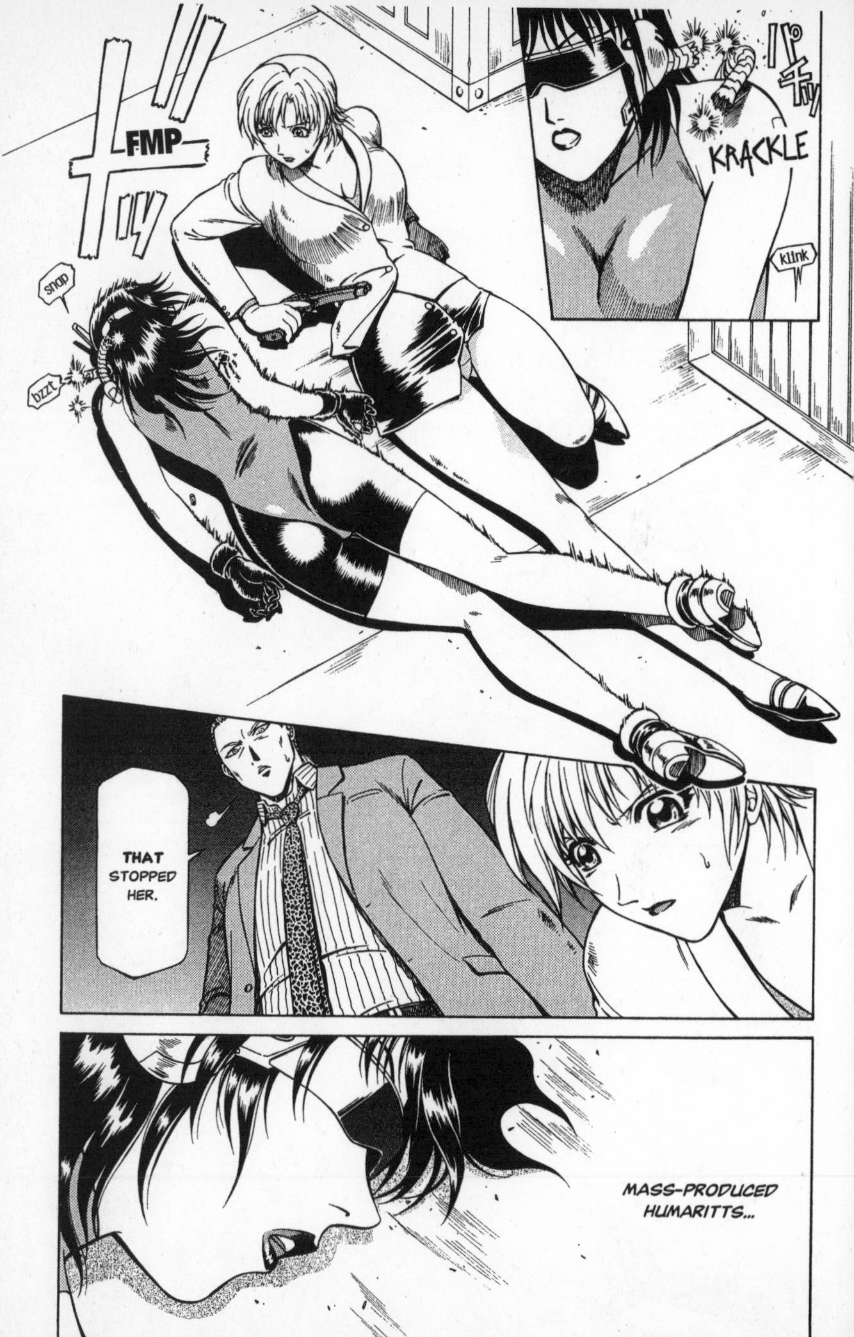

KRACKLE
klink
FMP
snap
bzzt
THAT STOPPED HER.
MASS-PRODUCED HUMARITTS...

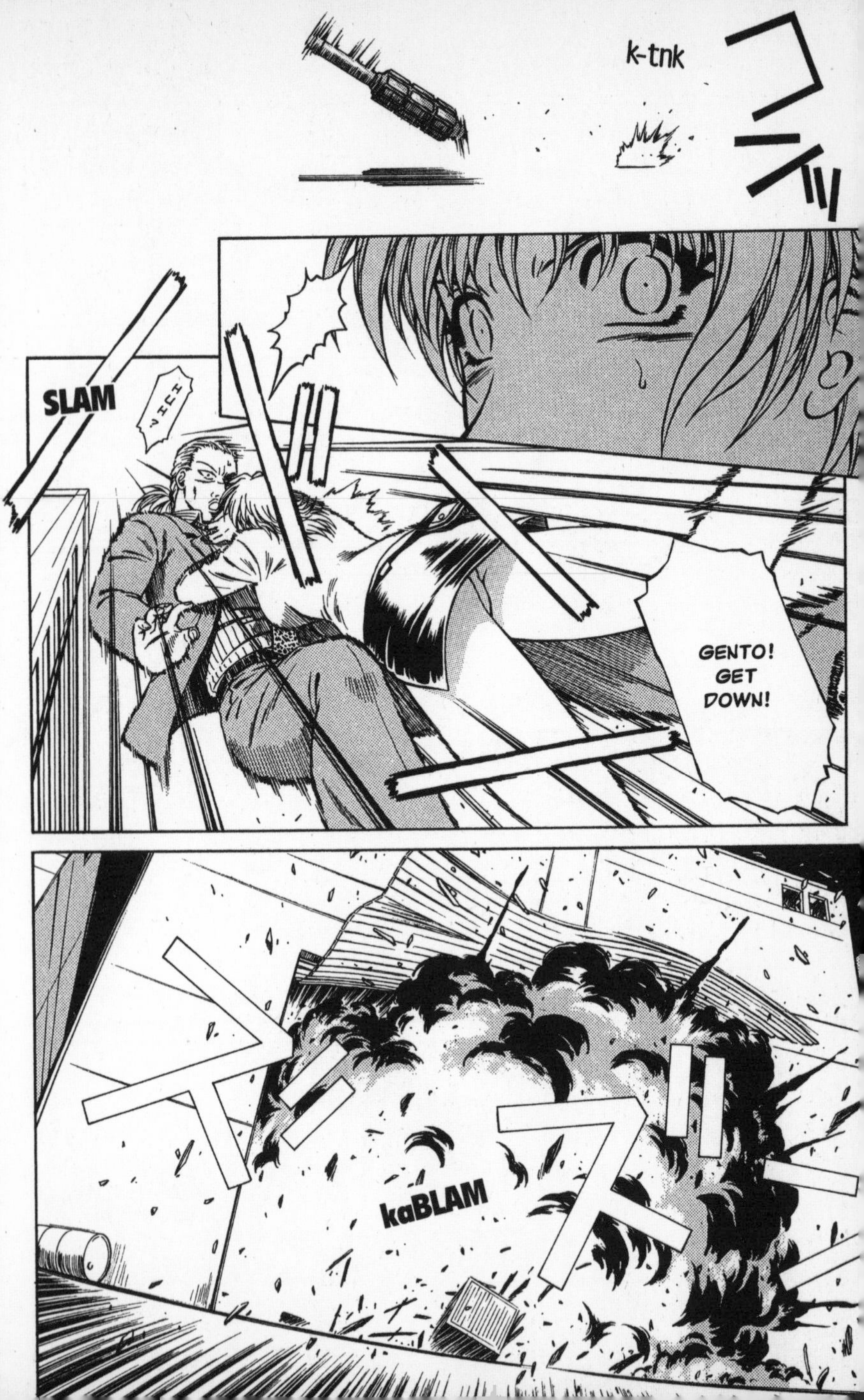

k-tnk
SLAM
GENTO! GET DOWN!
kaBLAM

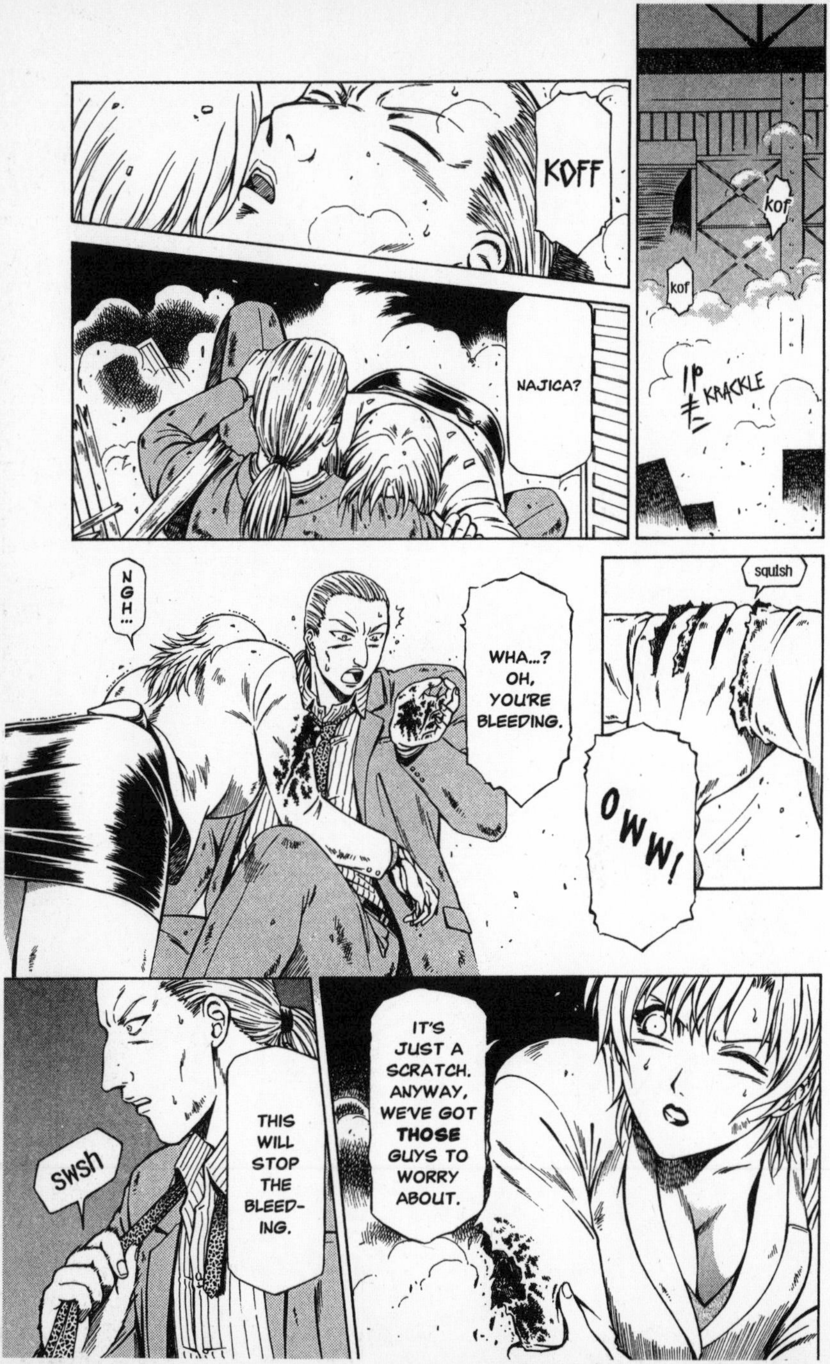

kof
kof
KRACKLE
KOFF
NAJICA?
squish
OWW!
WHA...? OH, YOU'RE BLEEDING.
NGH...
IT'S JUST A SCRATCH. ANYWAY, WE'VE GOT **THOSE** GUYS TO WORRY ABOUT.
THIS WILL STOP THE BLEED-ING.
swsh

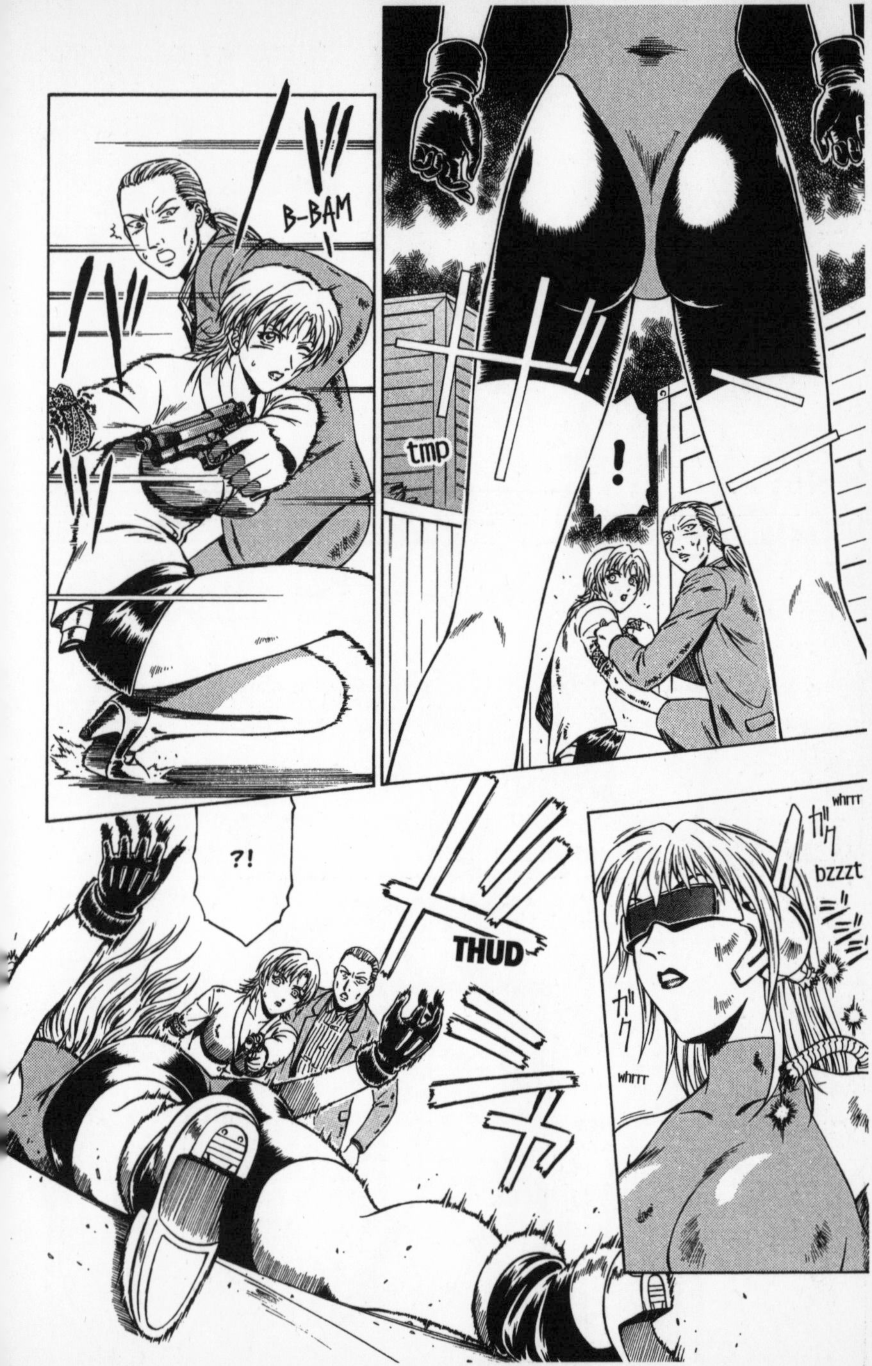
tmp
!
B-BAM
whrrr
ガク
bzzzt
ジジジ
ガク
whrrr
?!
THUD

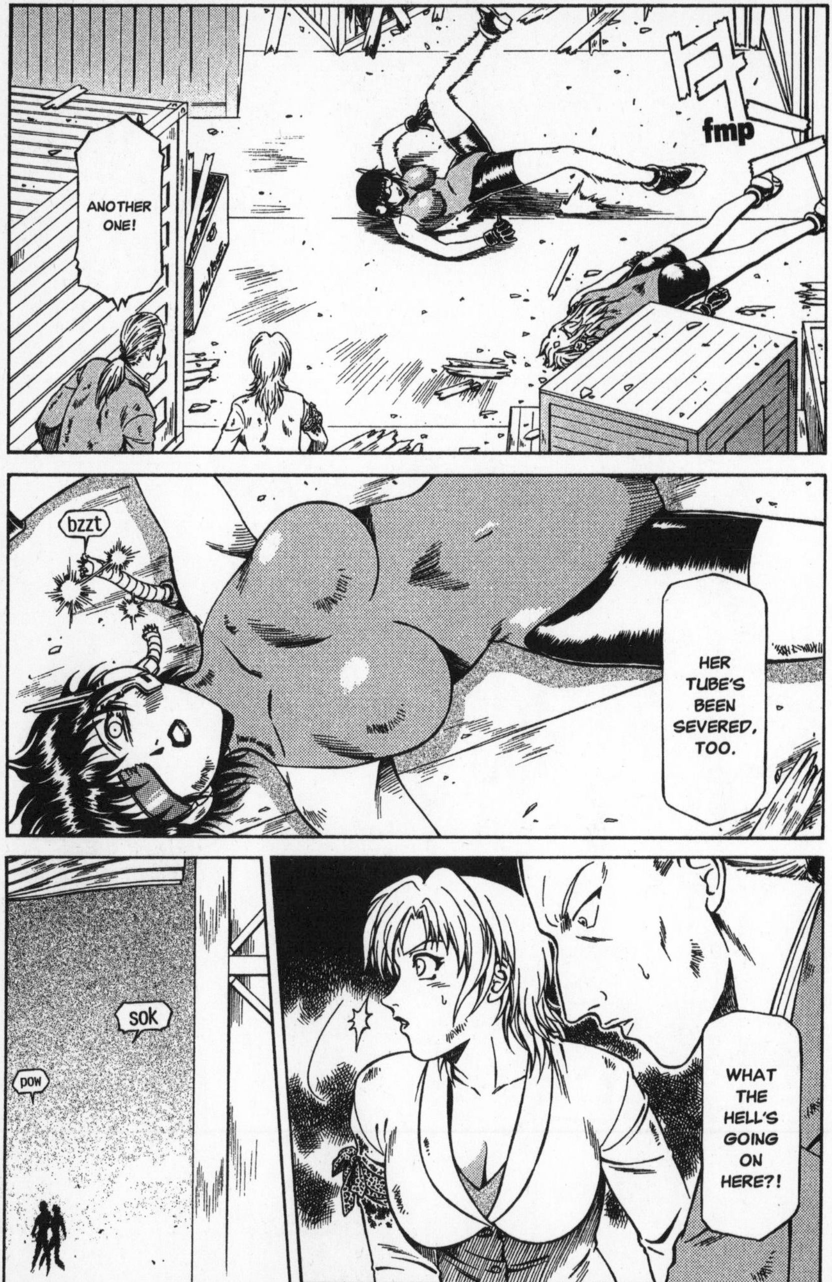

ANOTHER ONE!
fmp
bzzt
HER TUBE'S BEEN SEVERED, TOO.
sok
pow
WHAT THE HELL'S GOING ON HERE?!

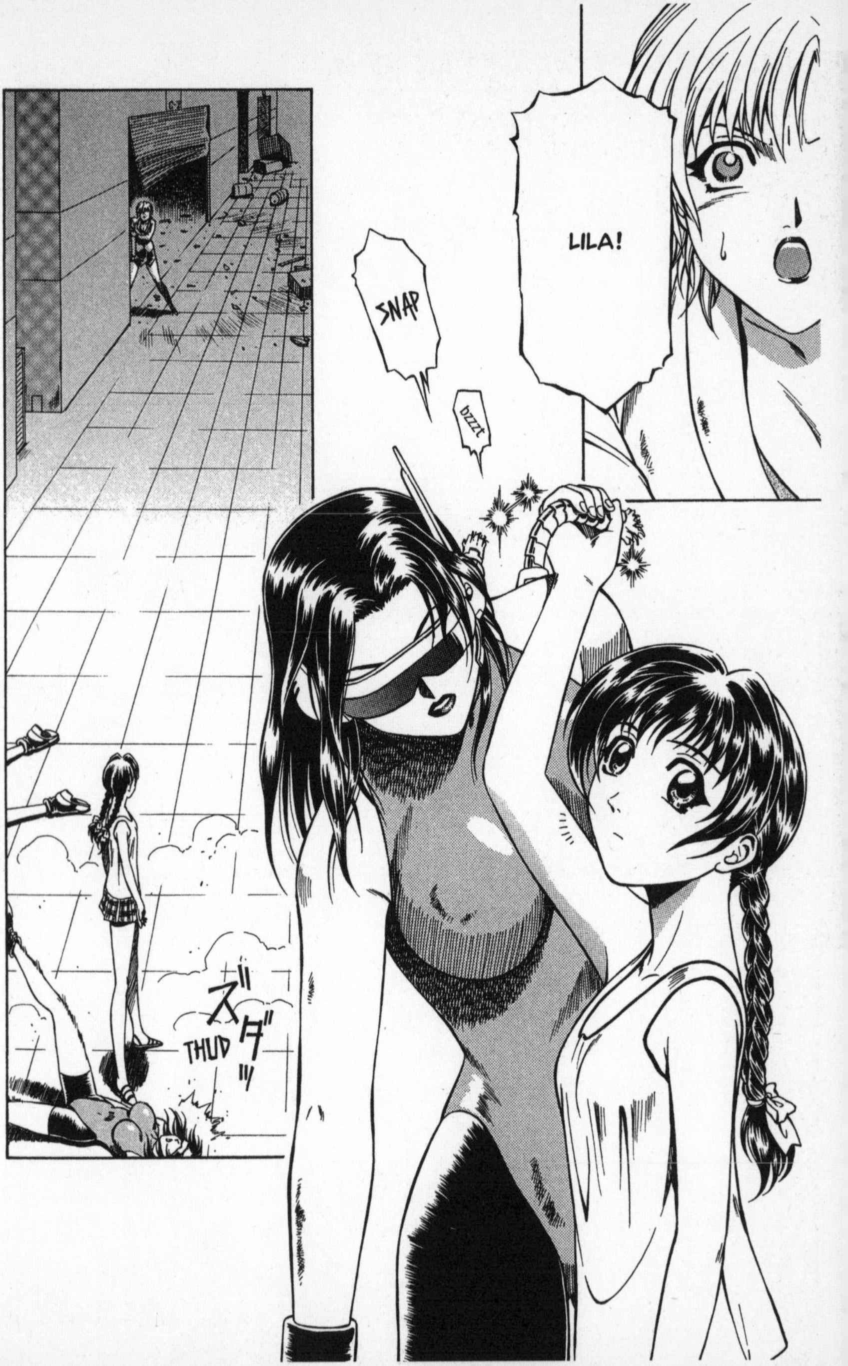
LILA!
SNAP
bzzzt
ズダッ
THUD

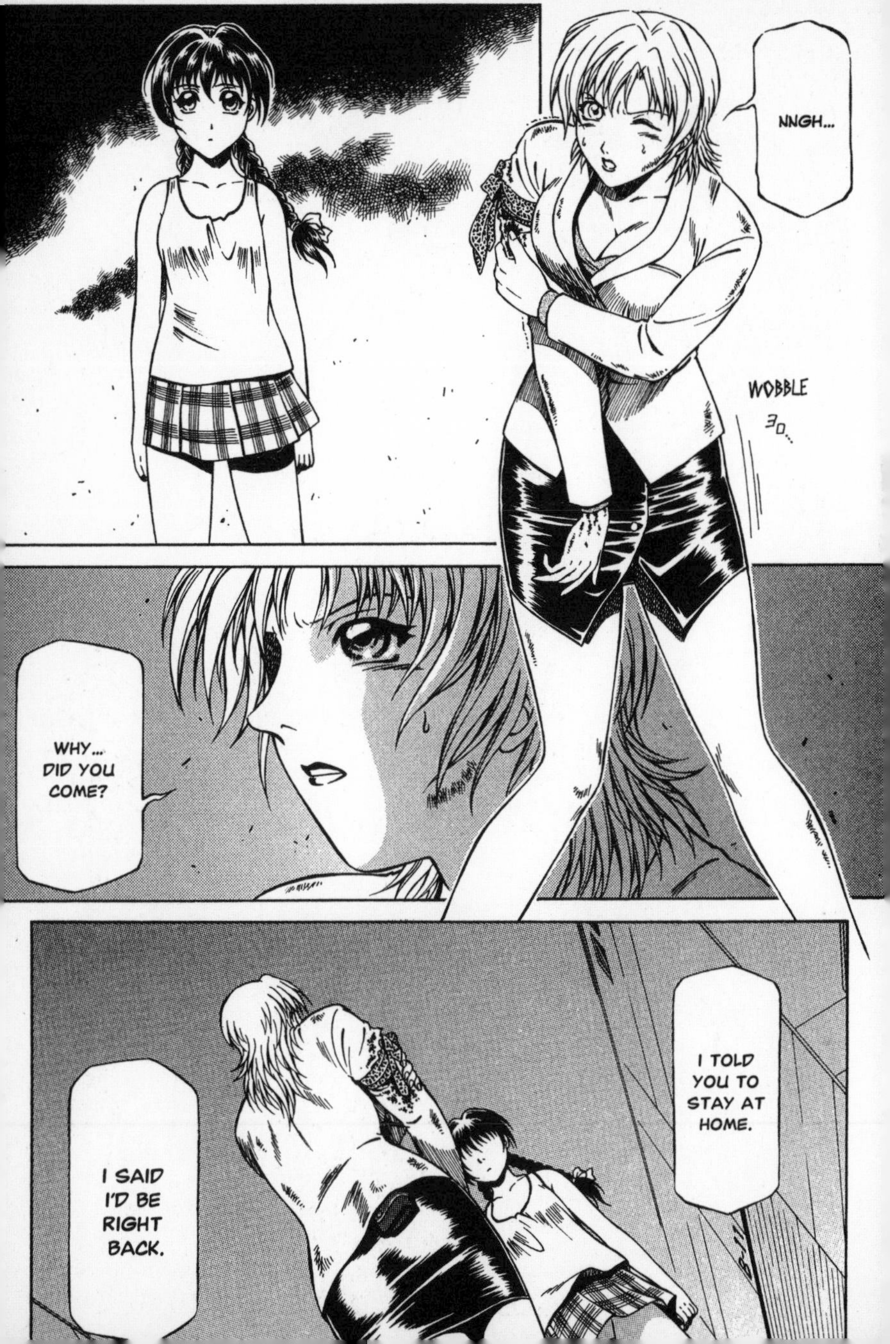

NNGH...
WOBBLE
WHY... DID YOU COME?
I TOLD YOU TO STAY AT HOME.
I SAID I'D BE RIGHT BACK.

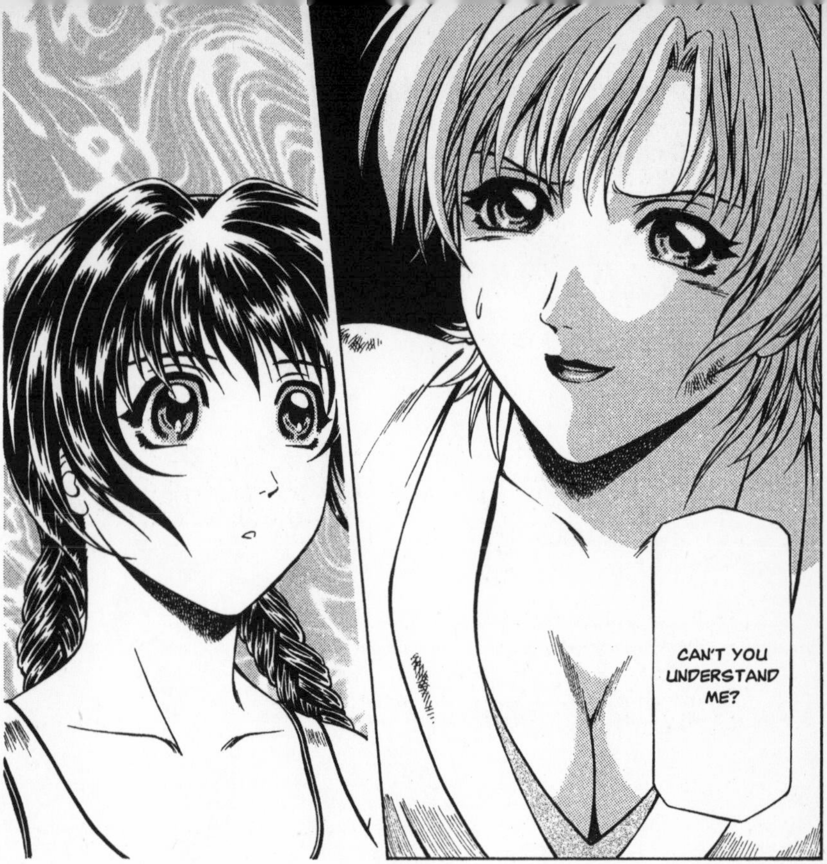
CAN'T YOU UNDERSTAND ME?

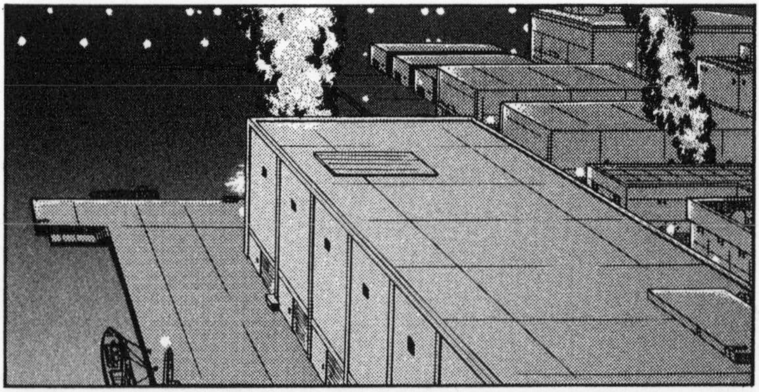

Operation. 15
BLITZ TACTICS PART 1

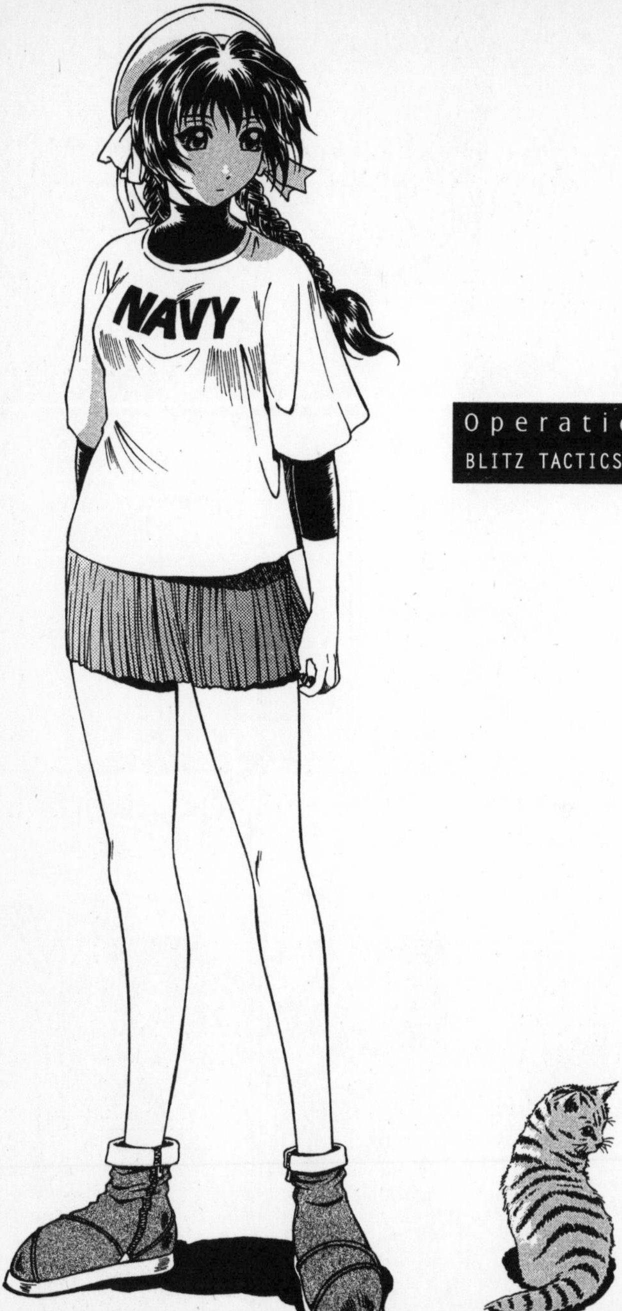
NAVY

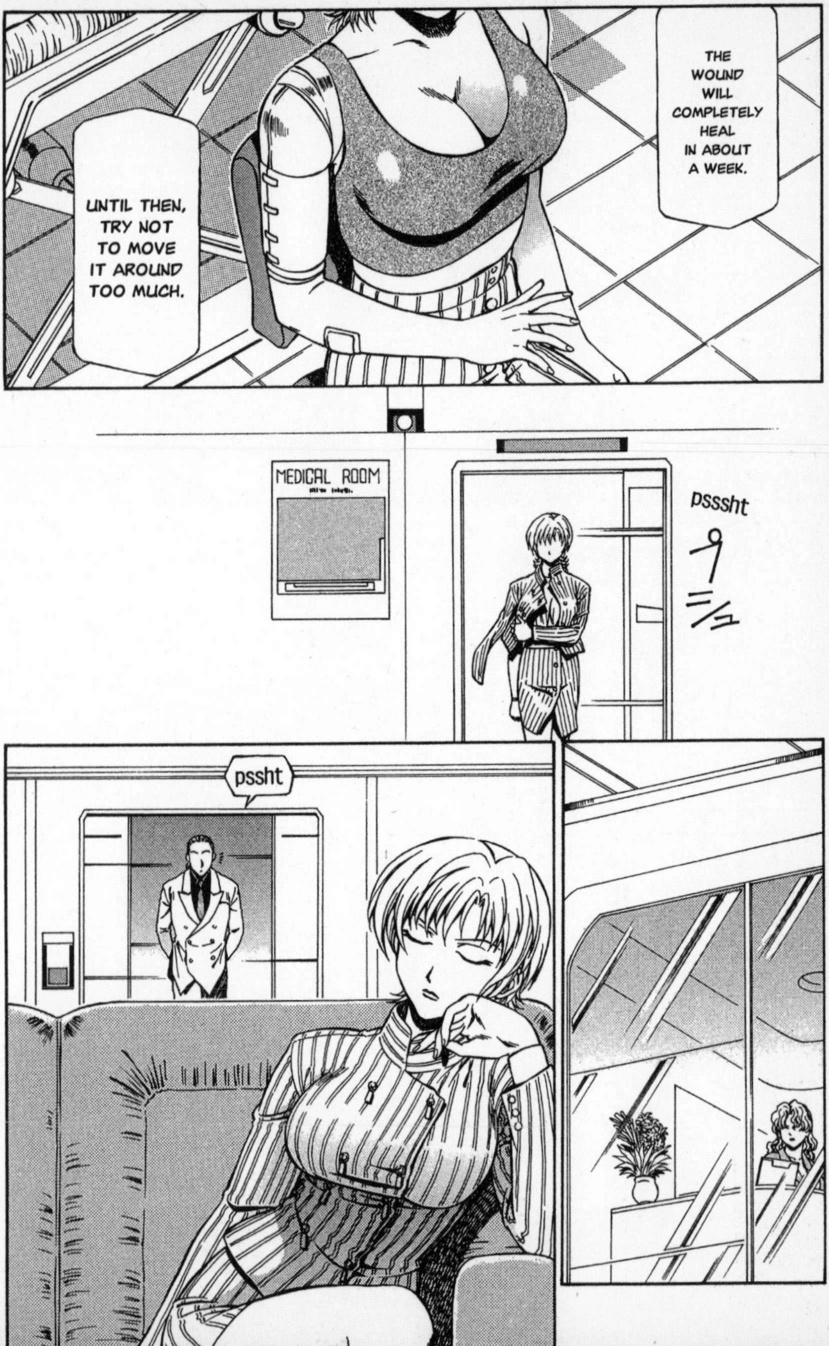
THE WOUND WILL COMPLETELY HEAL IN ABOUT A WEEK.
UNTIL THEN, TRY NOT TO MOVE IT AROUND TOO MUCH.
MEDICAL ROOM
psssht
pssht

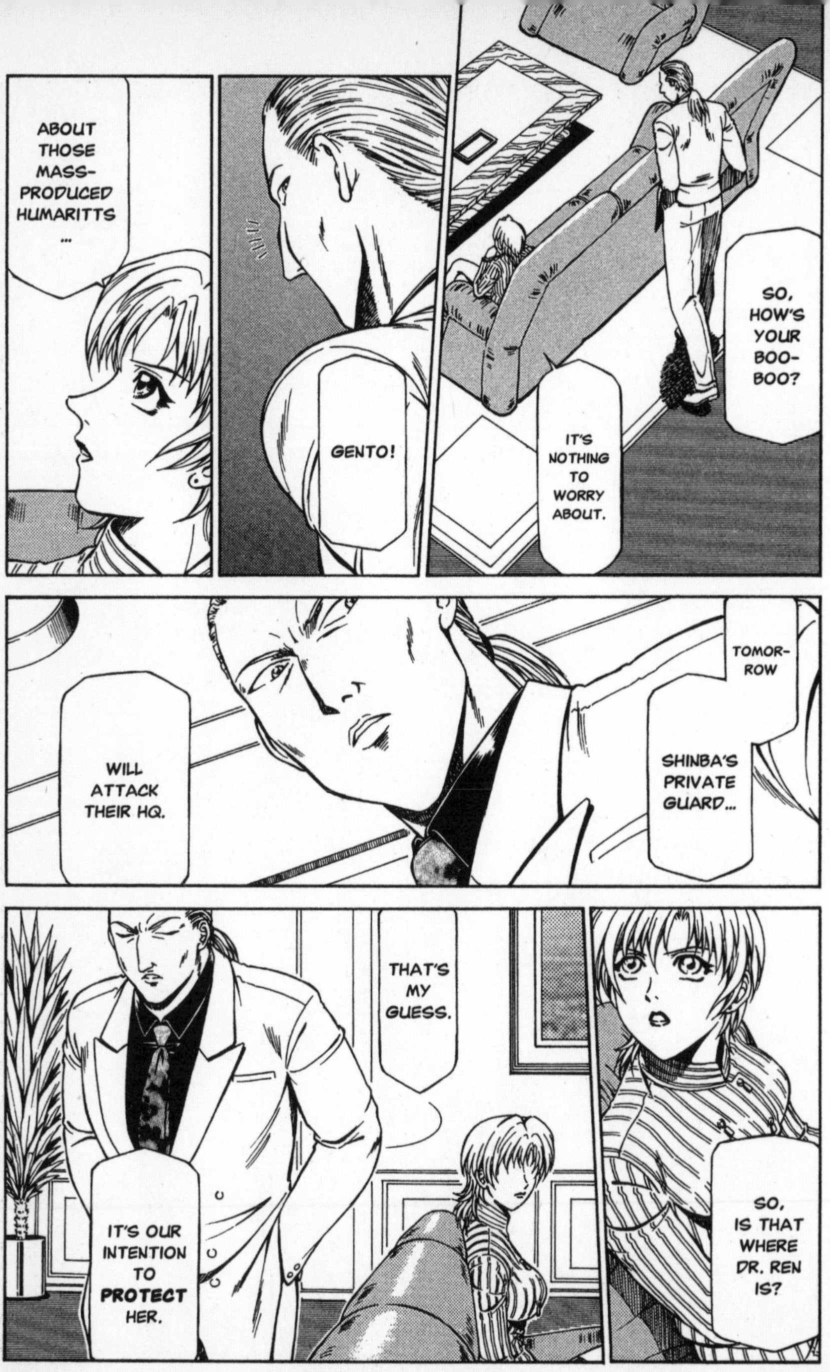
SO, HOW'S YOUR BOO-BOO?
IT'S NOTHING TO WORRY ABOUT.
GENTO!
ABOUT THOSE MASS-PRODUCED HUMARITTS ...
TOMORROW
SHINBA'S PRIVATE GUARD...
WILL ATTACK THEIR HQ.
SO, IS THAT WHERE DR. REN IS?
THAT'S MY GUESS.
IT'S OUR INTENTION TO PROTECT HER.

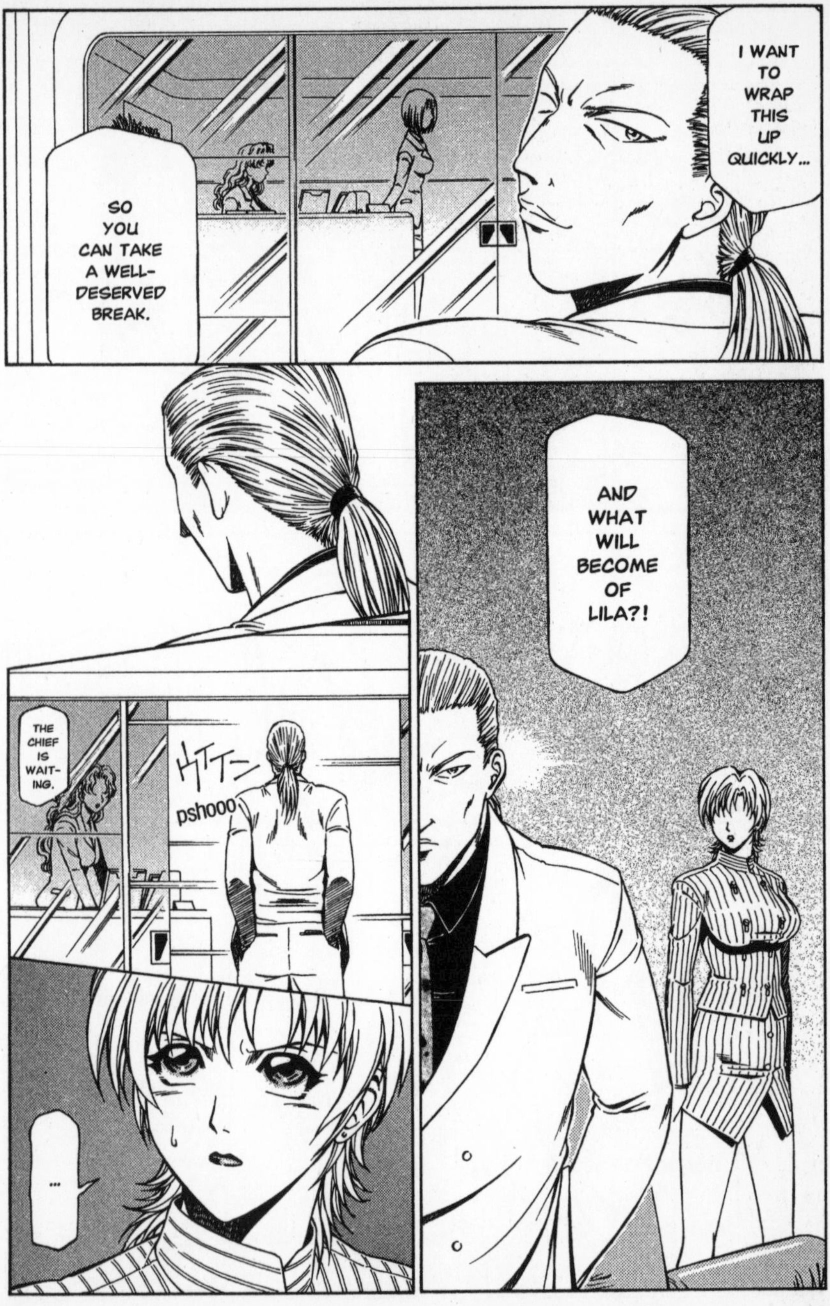
I WANT TO WRAP THIS UP QUICKLY...
SO YOU CAN TAKE A WELL-DESERVED BREAK.
AND WHAT WILL BECOME OF LILA?!
THE CHIEF IS WAIT-ING.
pshooo
...

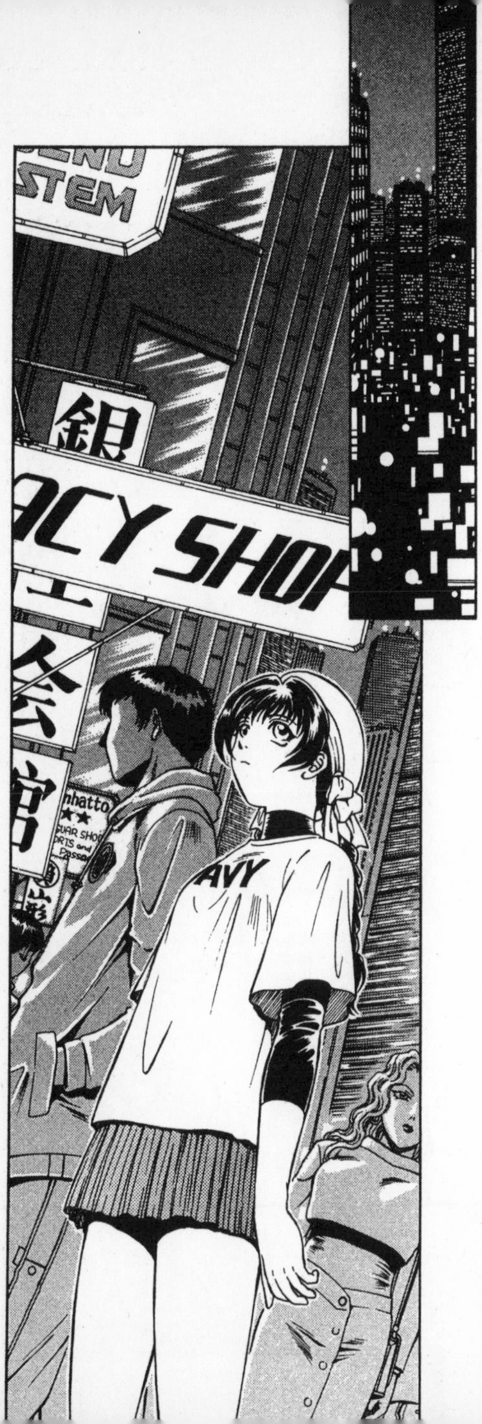
STEM
銀
ACY SHOP
AVY
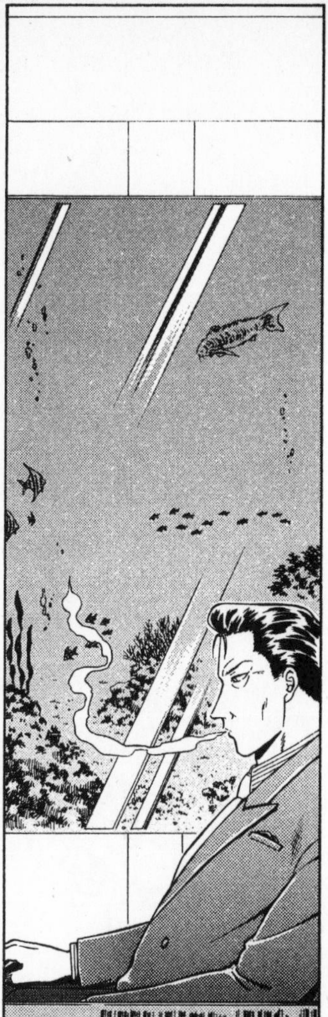

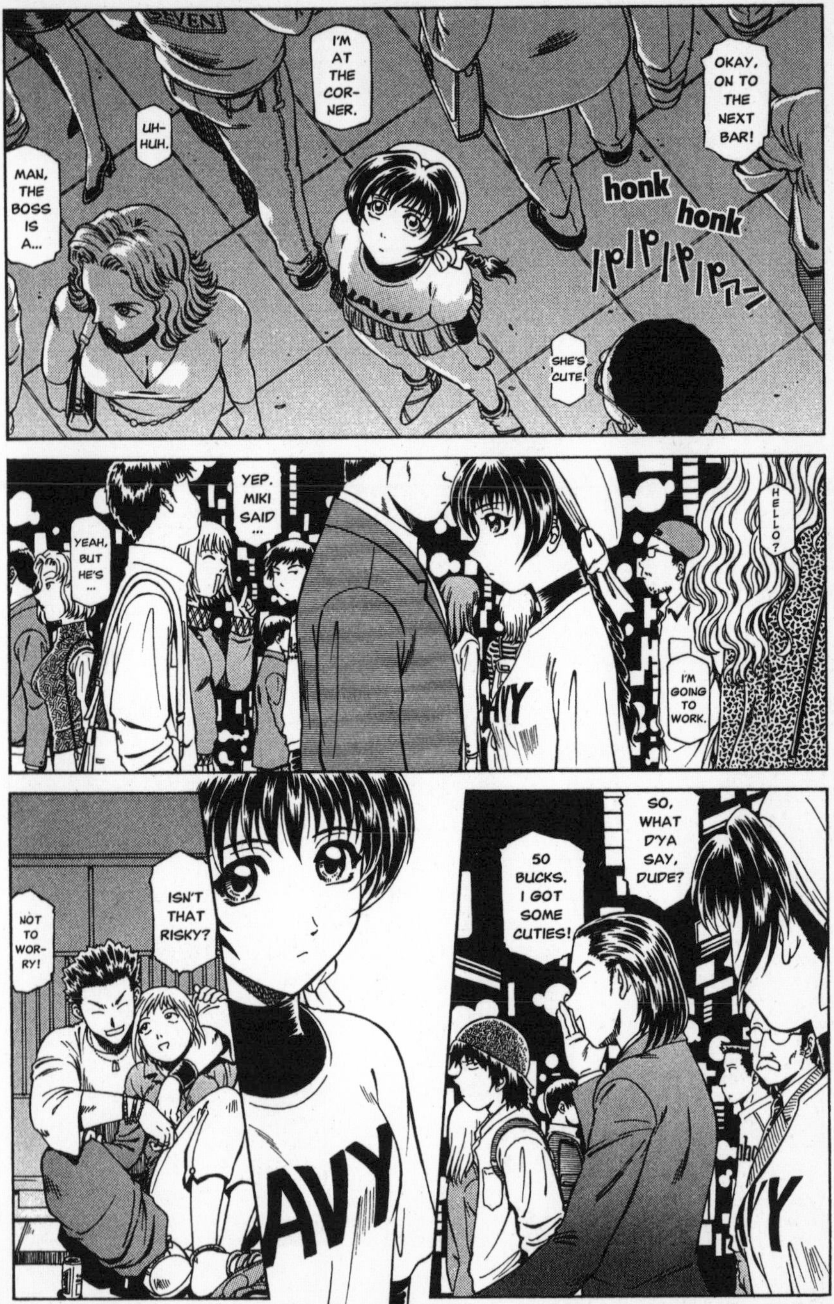
OKAY, ON TO THE NEXT BAR!
I'M AT THE CORNER.
UH-HUH.
MAN, THE BOSS IS A...
honk
honk
SHE'S CUTE!
HELLO?
I'M GOING TO WORK.
YEP. MIKI SAID ...
YEAH, BUT HE'S ...
SO, WHAT D'YA SAY, DUDE?
50 BUCKS. I GOT SOME CUTIES!
ISN'T THAT RISKY?
NOT TO WORRY!

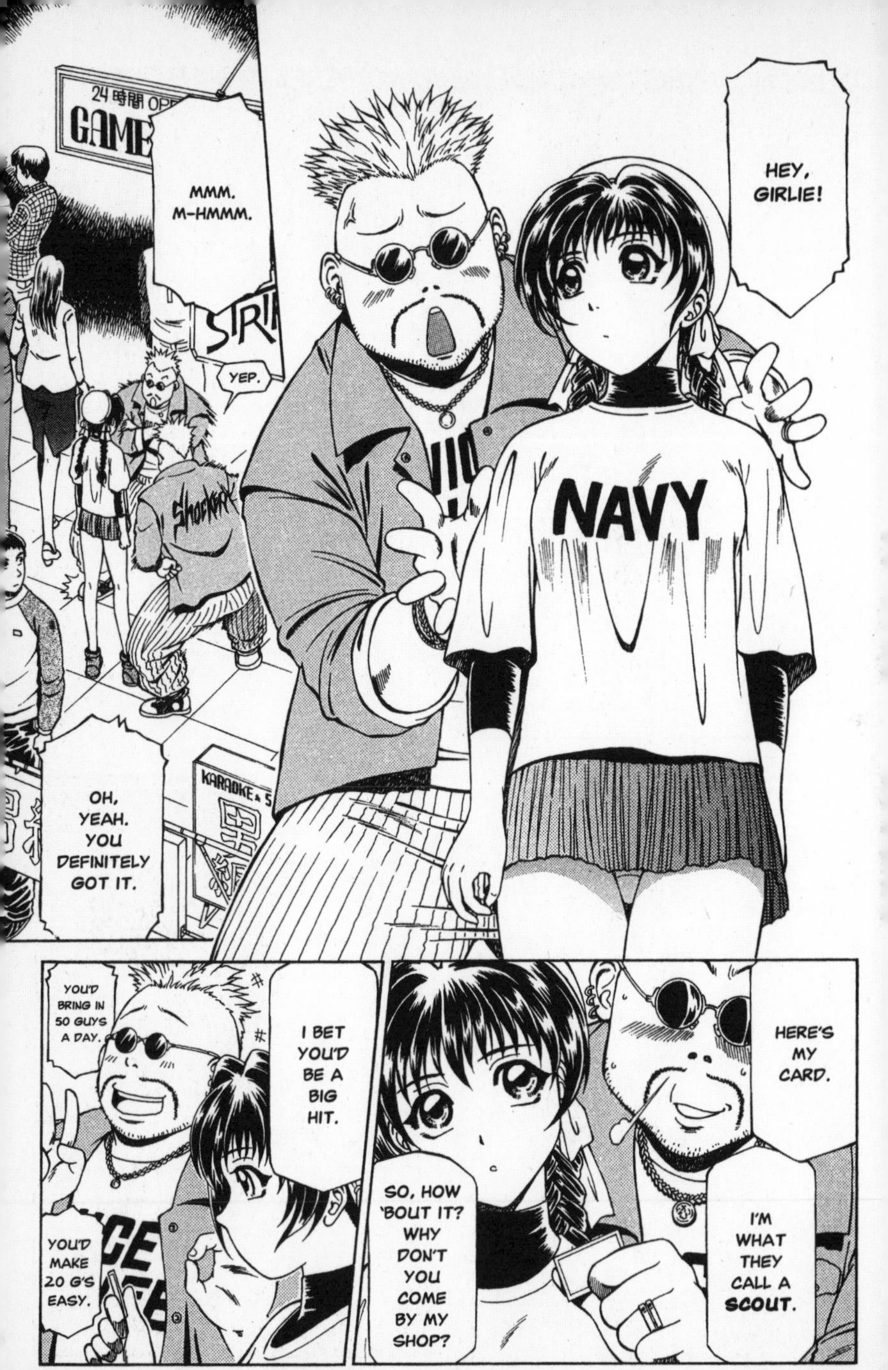
HEY, GIRLIE!
MMM. M-HMMM.
YEP.
OH, YEAH. YOU DEFINITELY GOT IT.
NAVY
HERE'S MY CARD.
I'M WHAT THEY CALL A **SCOUT**.
SO, HOW 'BOUT IT? WHY DON'T YOU COME BY MY SHOP?
I BET YOU'D BE A BIG HIT.
YOU'D BRING IN 50 GUYS A DAY.
YOU'D MAKE 20 G'S EASY.

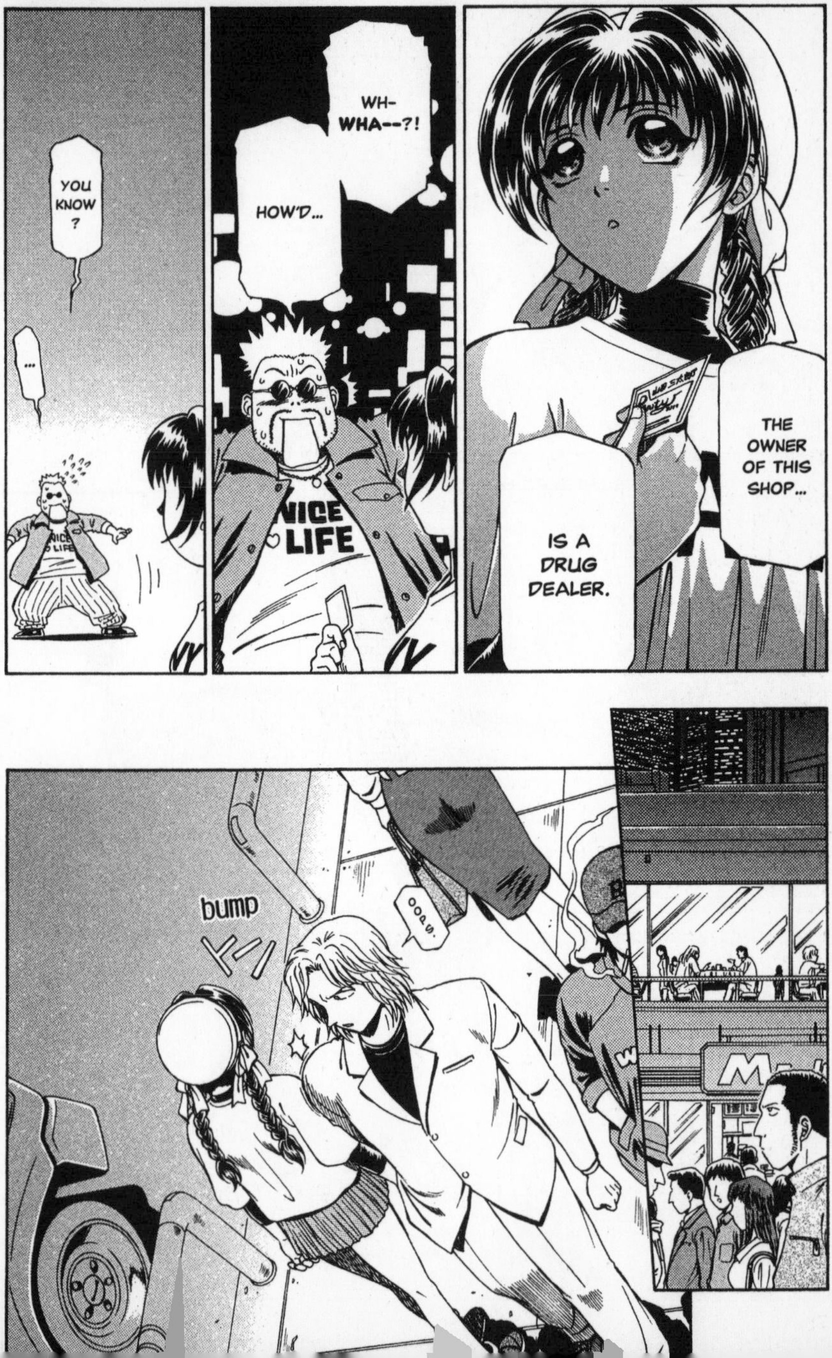
THE OWNER OF THIS SHOP...
IS A DRUG DEALER.
WH- WHA--?!
HOW'D...
NICE LIFE
YOU KNOW?
...
OOPS.
bump

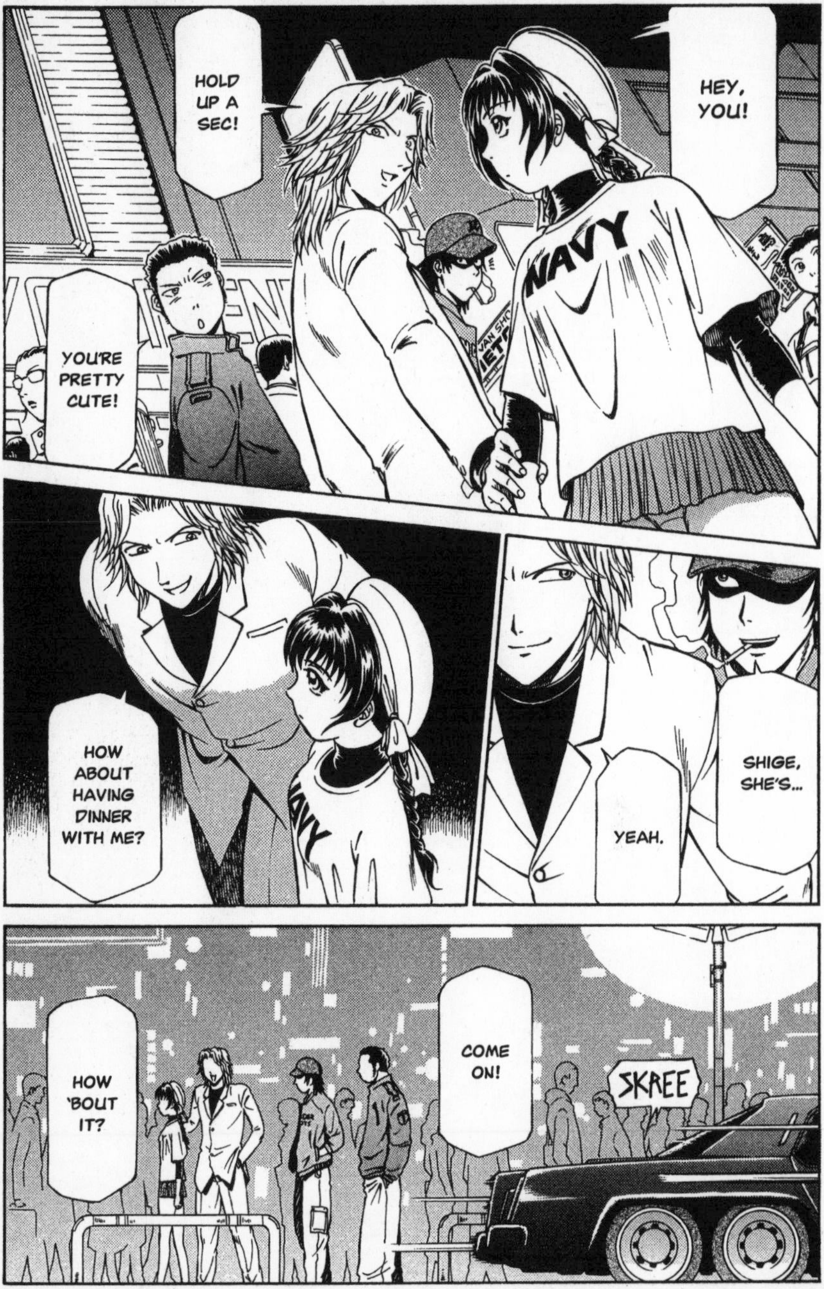
HEY, YOU!
HOLD UP A SEC!
YOU'RE PRETTY CUTE!
HOW ABOUT HAVING DINNER WITH ME?
SHIGE, SHE'S...
YEAH.
HOW 'BOUT IT?
COME ON!
SKREE
NAVY

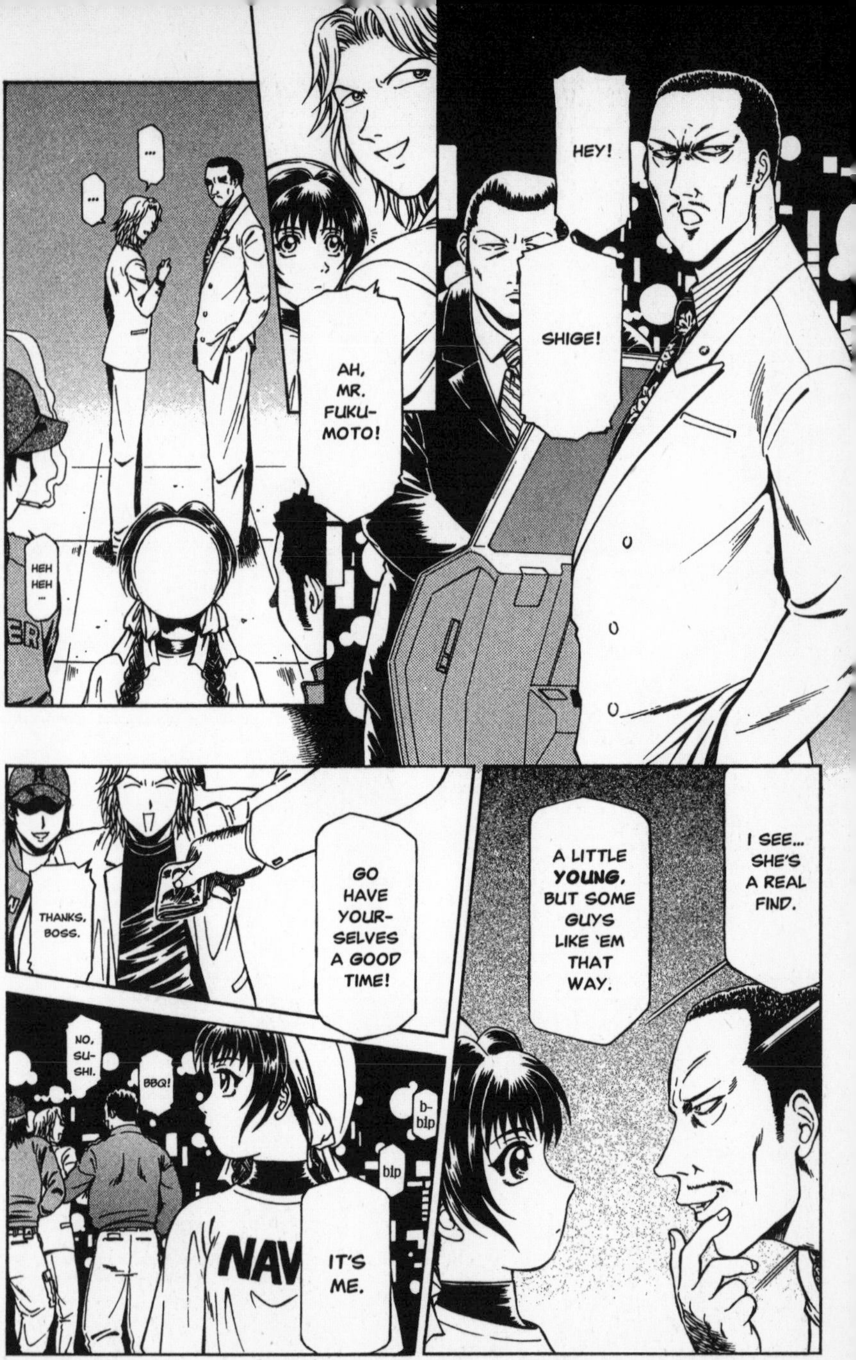
HEY!
SHIGE!
AH, MR. FUKU-MOTO!
...
...
HEH HEH ...
I SEE... SHE'S A REAL FIND.
A LITTLE **YOUNG**, BUT SOME GUYS LIKE 'EM THAT WAY.
GO HAVE YOUR-SELVES A GOOD TIME!
THANKS, BOSS.
IT'S ME.
b-bip
bip
BBQ!
NO, SU-SHI.

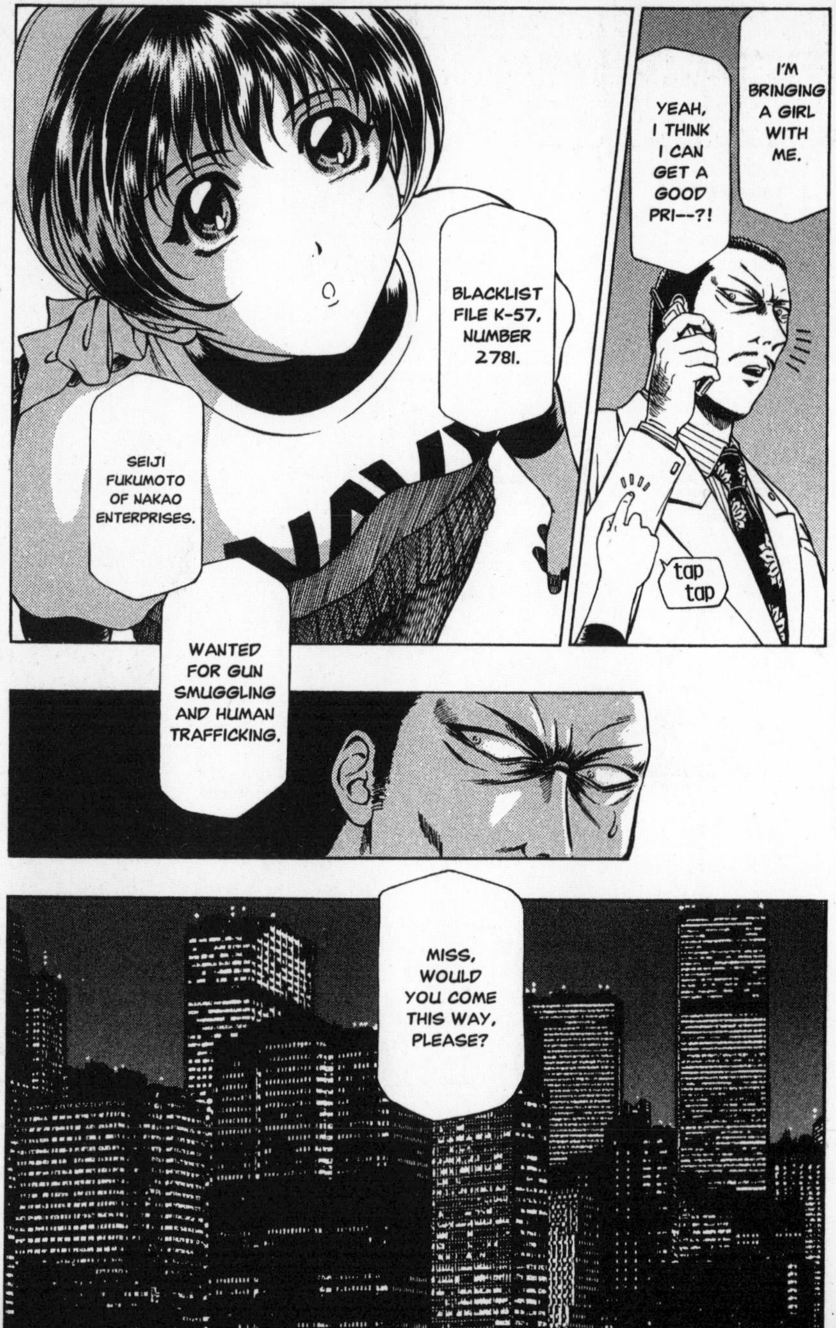
I'M BRINGING A GIRL WITH ME.
YEAH, I THINK I CAN GET A GOOD PRI--?!
tap tap
BLACKLIST FILE K-57, NUMBER 2781.
SEIJI FUKUMOTO OF NAKAO ENTERPRISES.
WANTED FOR GUN SMUGGLING AND HUMAN TRAFFICKING.
MISS, WOULD YOU COME THIS WAY, PLEASE?

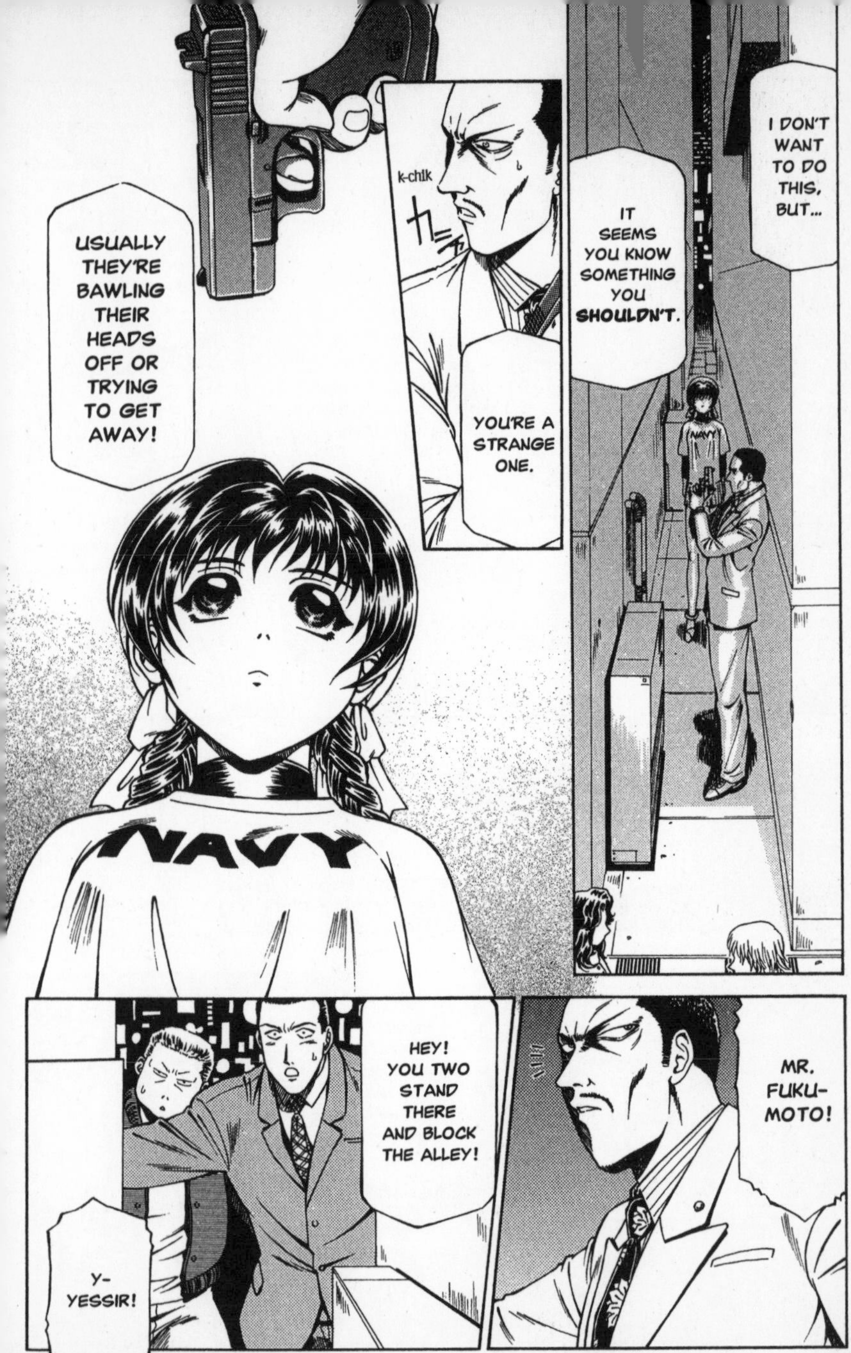
I DON'T WANT TO DO THIS, BUT...
IT SEEMS YOU KNOW SOMETHING YOU SHOULDN'T.
k-chik
YOU'RE A STRANGE ONE.
USUALLY THEY'RE BAWLING THEIR HEADS OFF OR TRYING TO GET AWAY!
NAVY
MR. FUKU-MOTO!
HEY! YOU TWO STAND THERE AND BLOCK THE ALLEY!
Y-YESSIR!

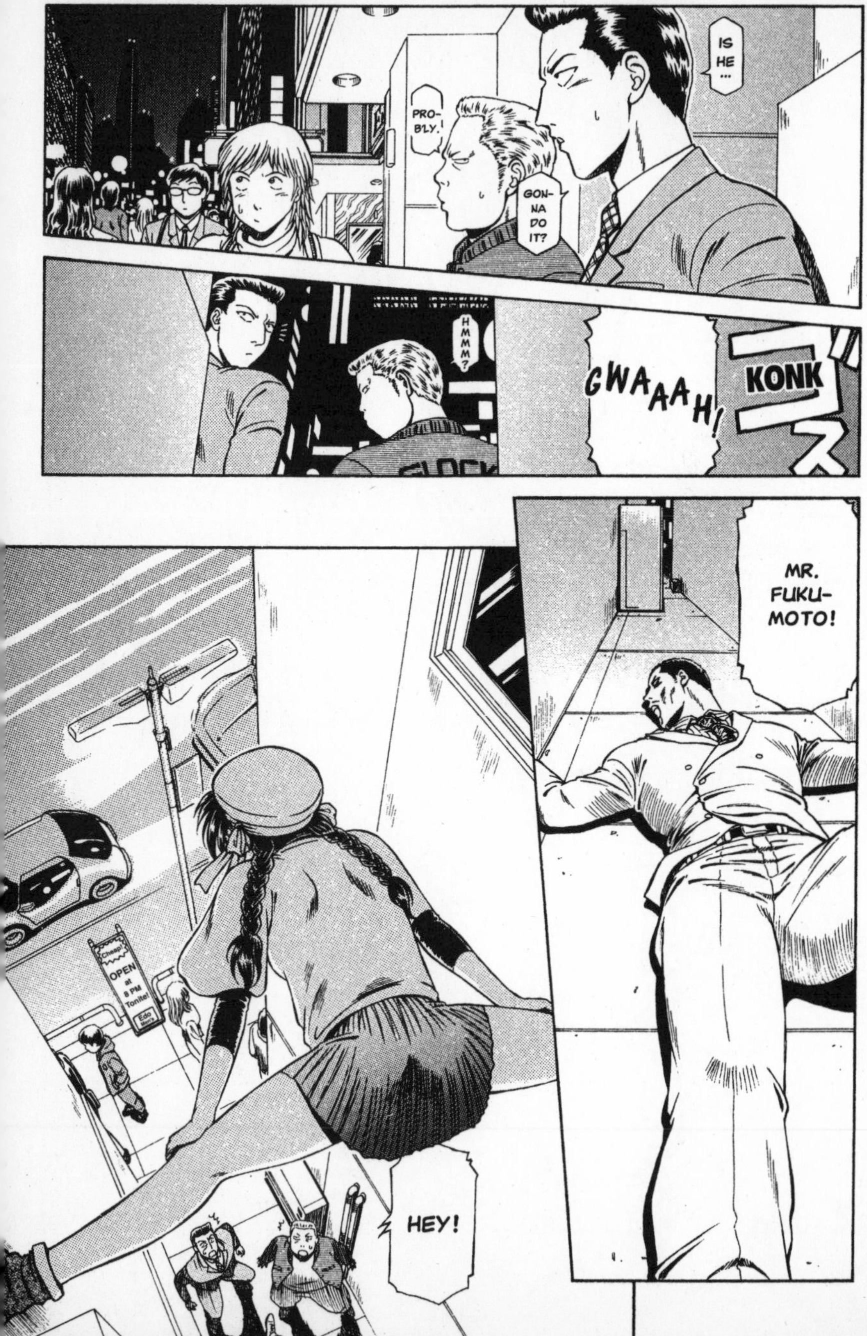
IS HE ...
GON-NA DO IT?
PRO-B'LY.
KONK
GWAAAH!
HMMM?
MR. FUKU-MOTO!
HEY!
Cheap!
OPEN at 8 PM Tonite!

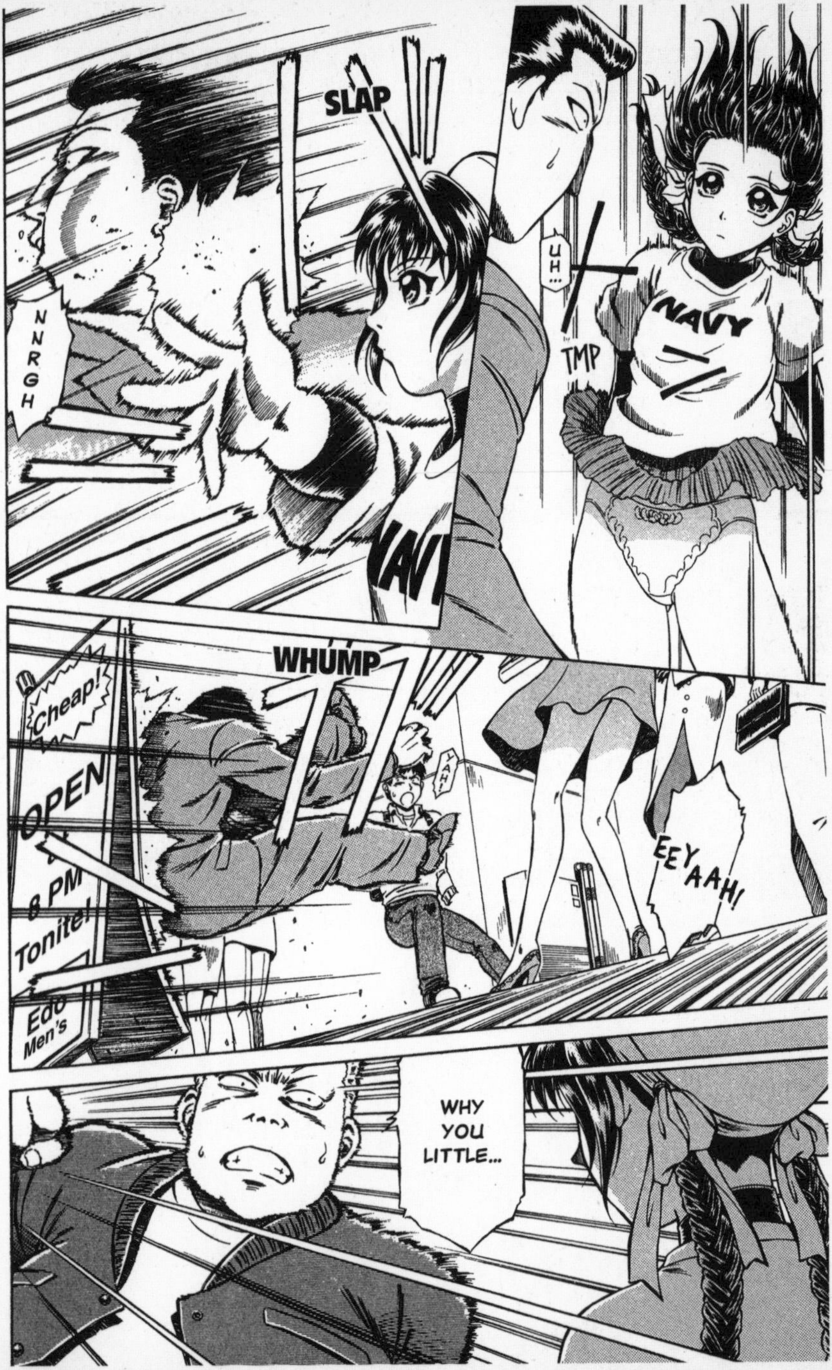
UH...
TMP
SLAP
NNRGH
EEYAAH!
WHUMP
YAAH!
Cheap!
OPEN
8 PM
Tonite!
Edo
Men's
WHY YOU LITTLE...

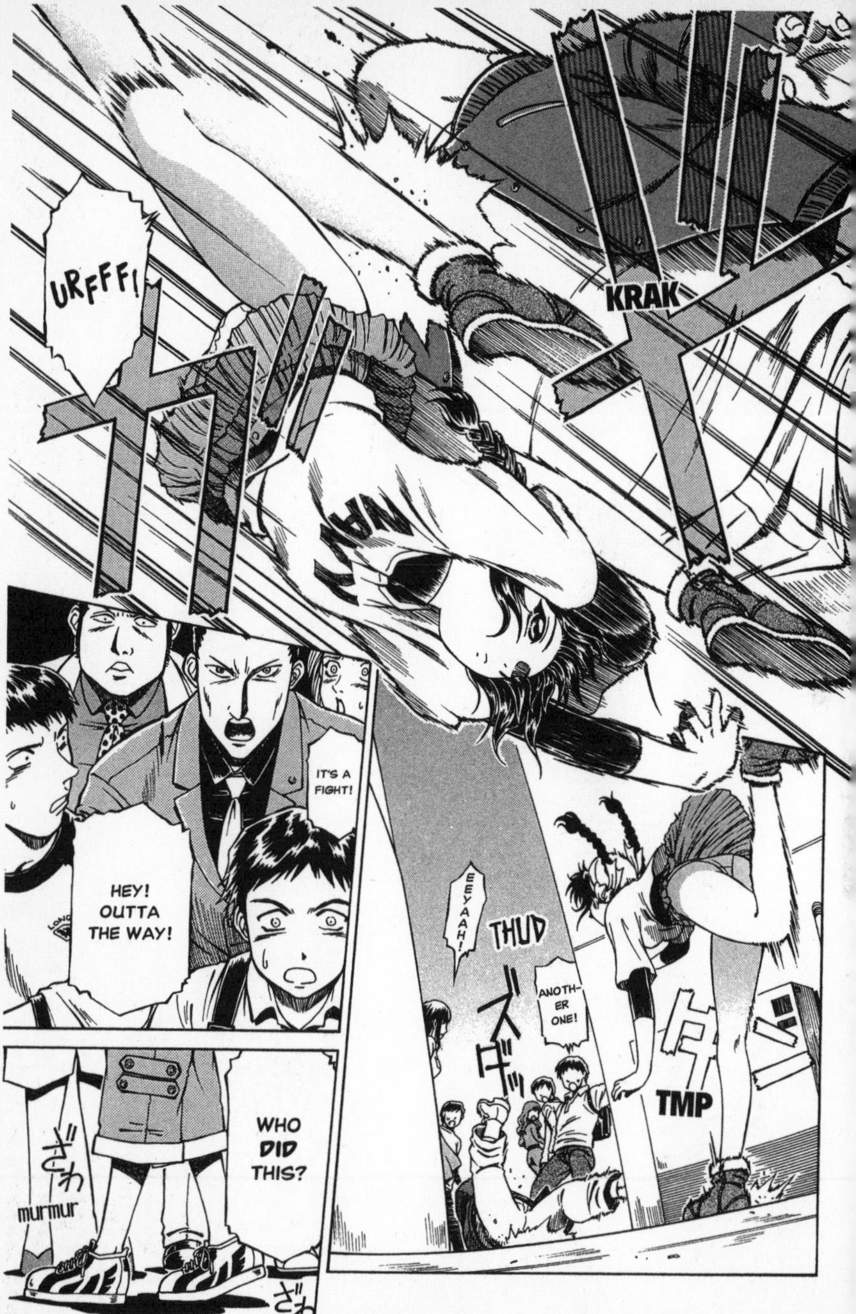
KRAK
URFFF!
IT'S A FIGHT!
HEY! OUTTA THE WAY!
TMP
ANOTHER-ER ONE!
EEYAAH!
THUD
WHO DID THIS?
ざわ
murmur
ざわ
murmur

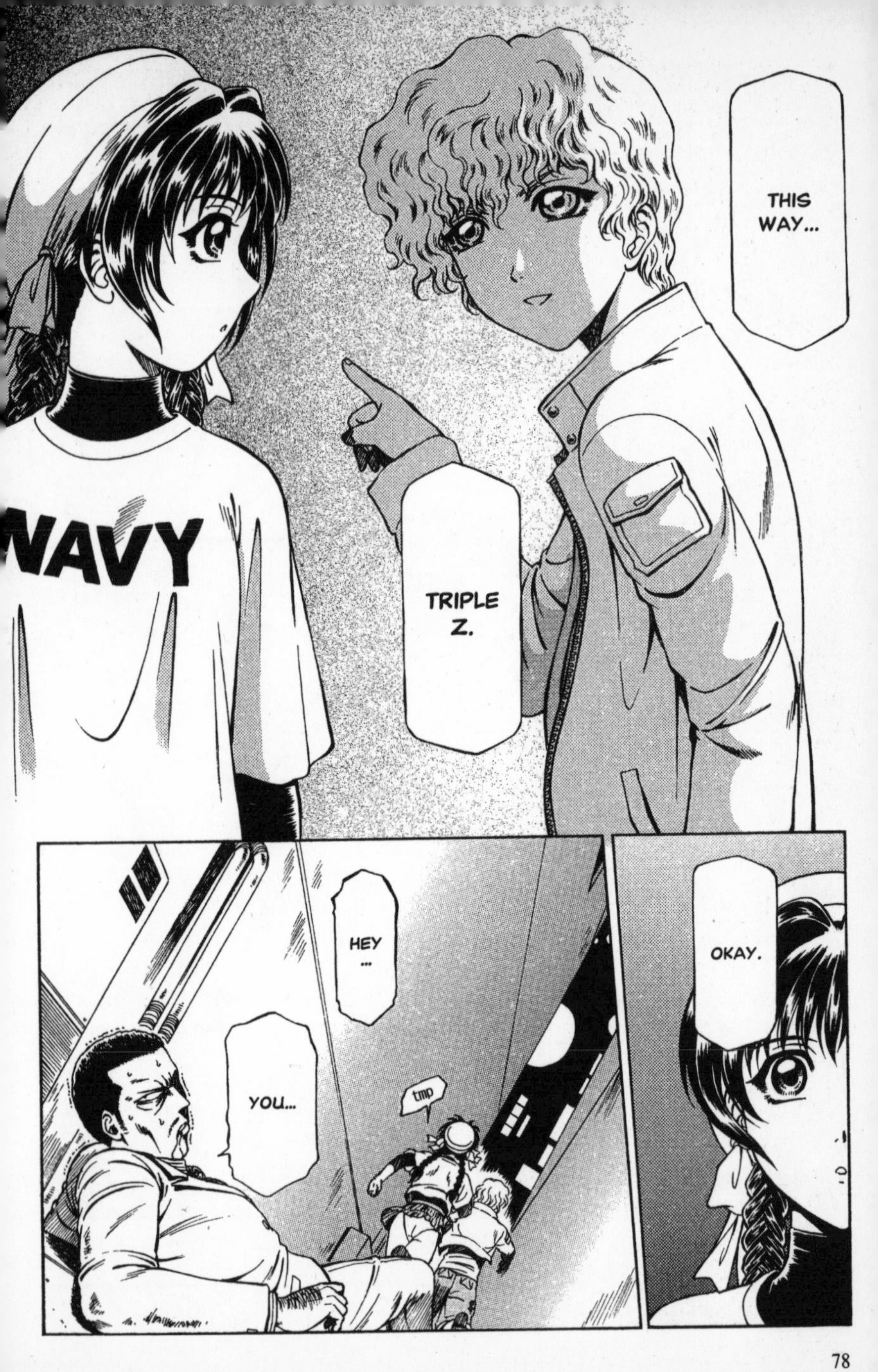
THIS WAY...
TRIPLE Z.
NAVY
OKAY.
HEY ...
YOU...
tmp

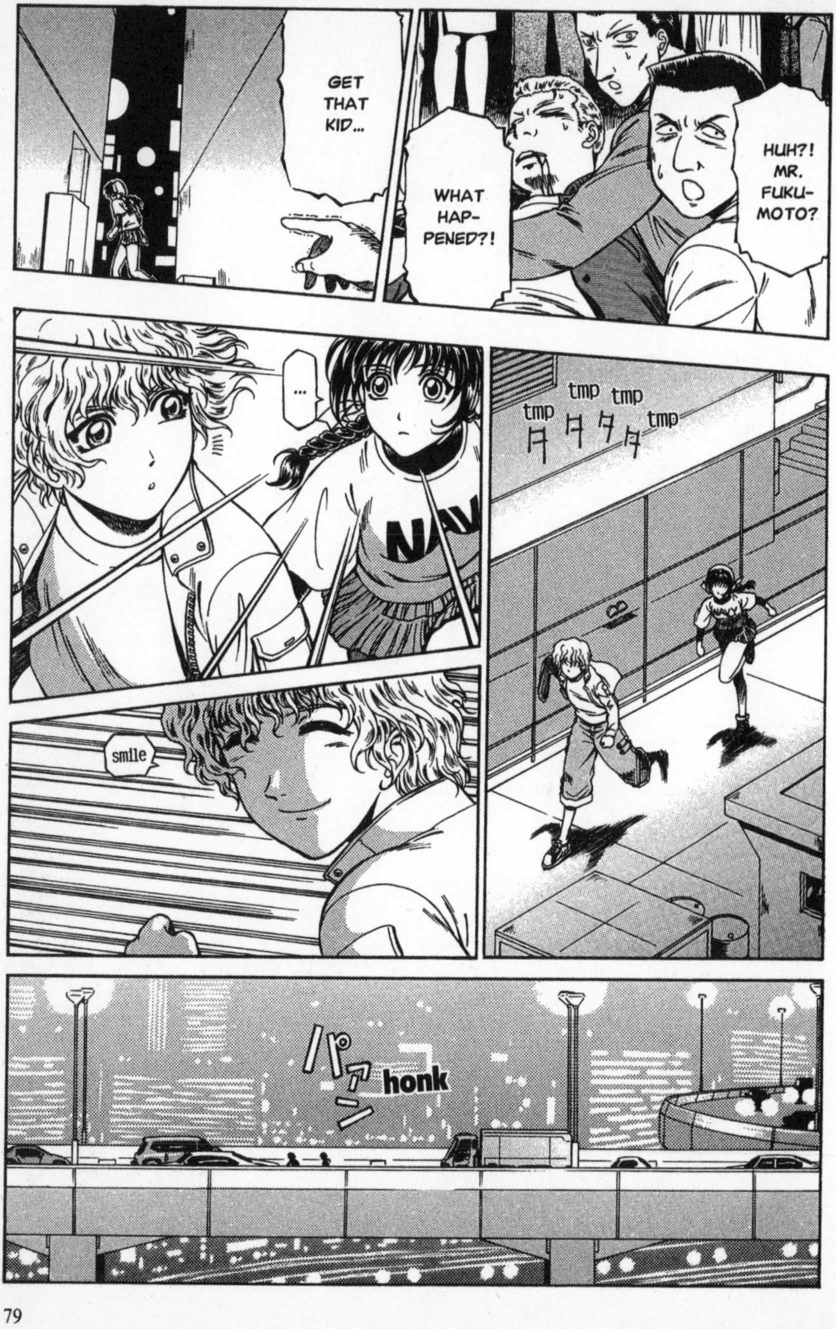
HUH?! MR. FUKU-MOTO?
WHAT HAP-PENED?!
GET THAT KID...
tmp tmp tmp tmp
タタタタ
...
smile
パァーン
honk

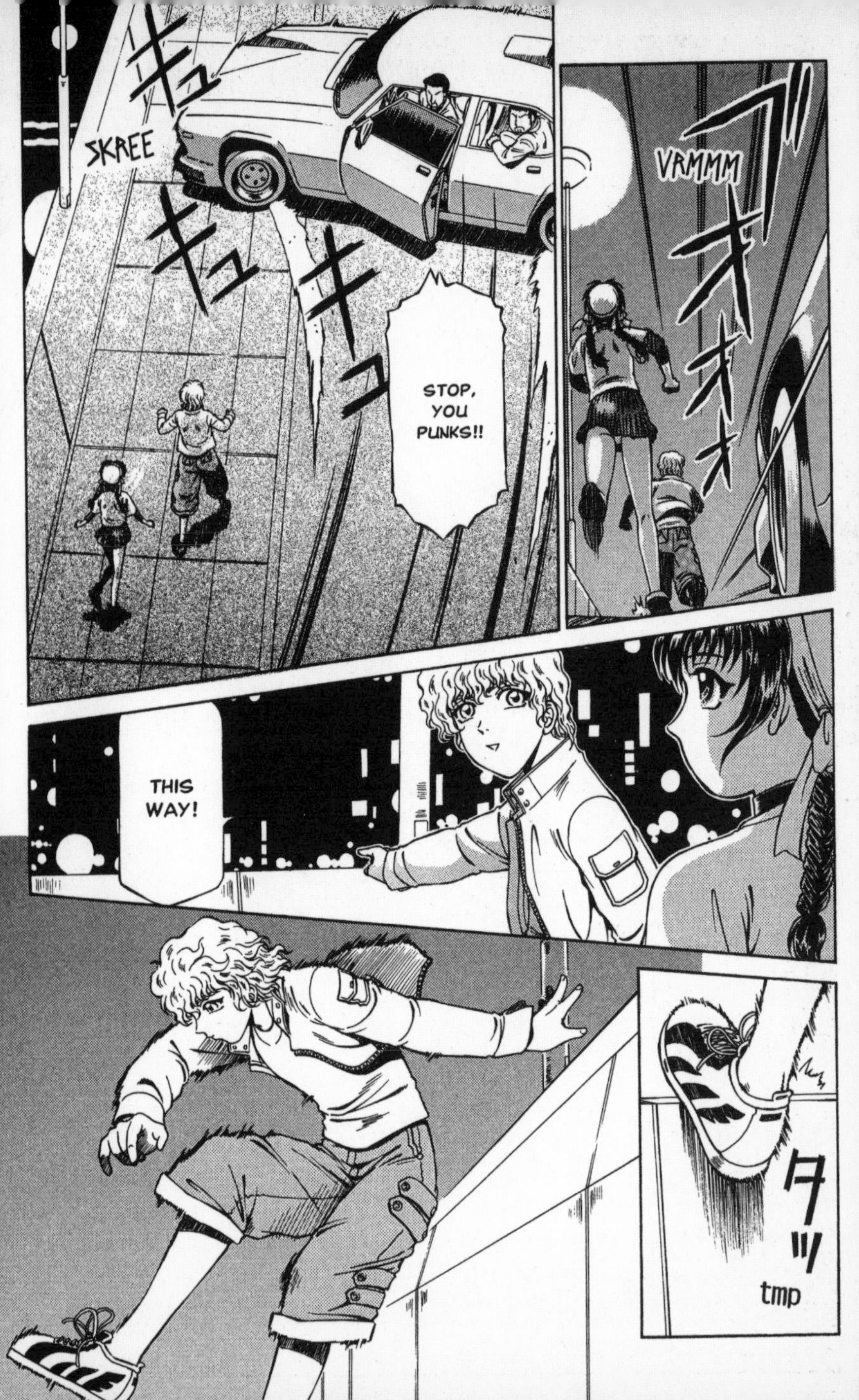
VRMMM
SKREE
STOP, YOU PUNKS!!
THIS WAY!
タッ
tmp

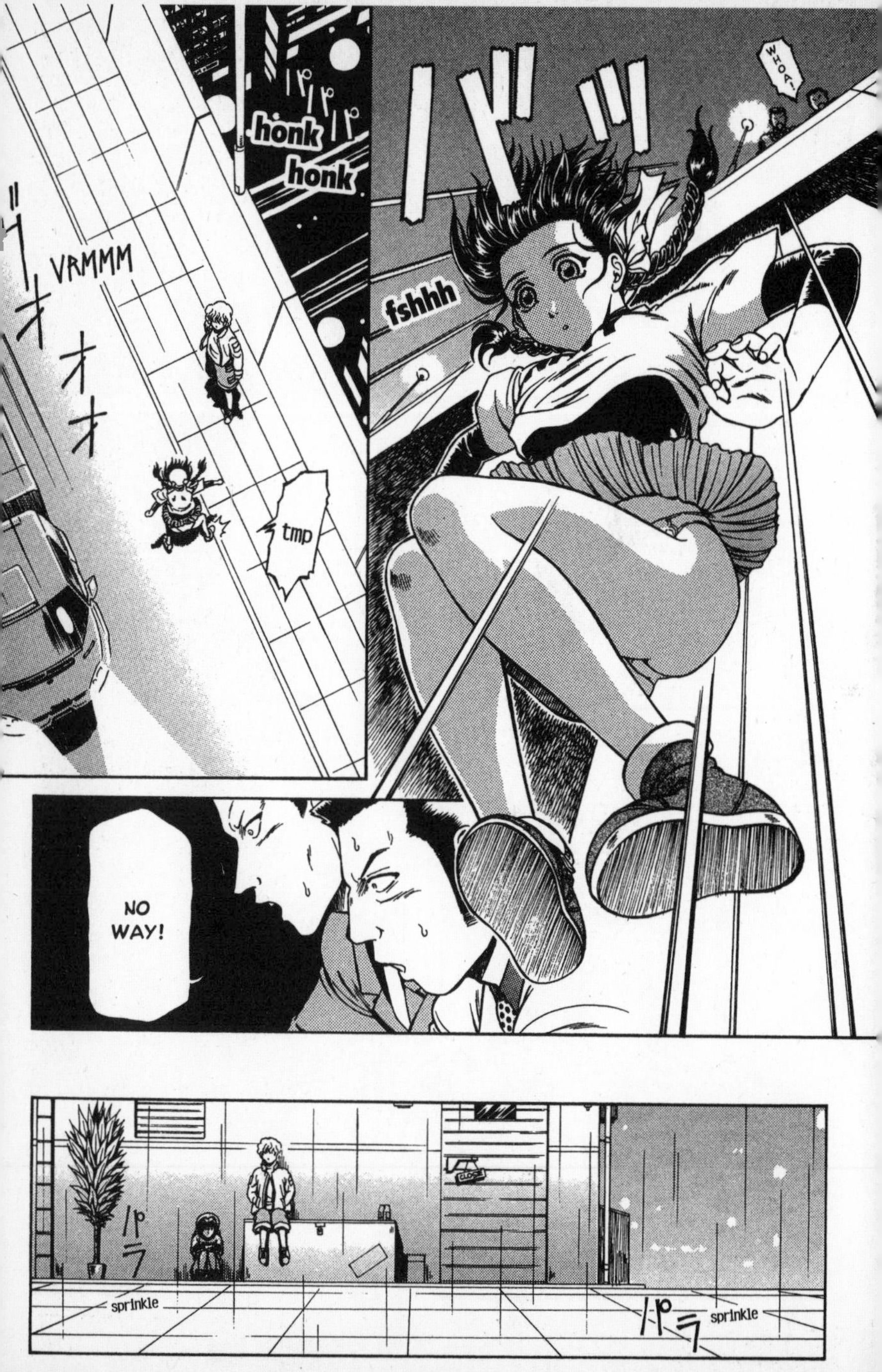
WHOA!
fshhh
honk
honk
VRMMM
tmp
NO WAY!
パラ
sprinkle
パラ
sprinkle

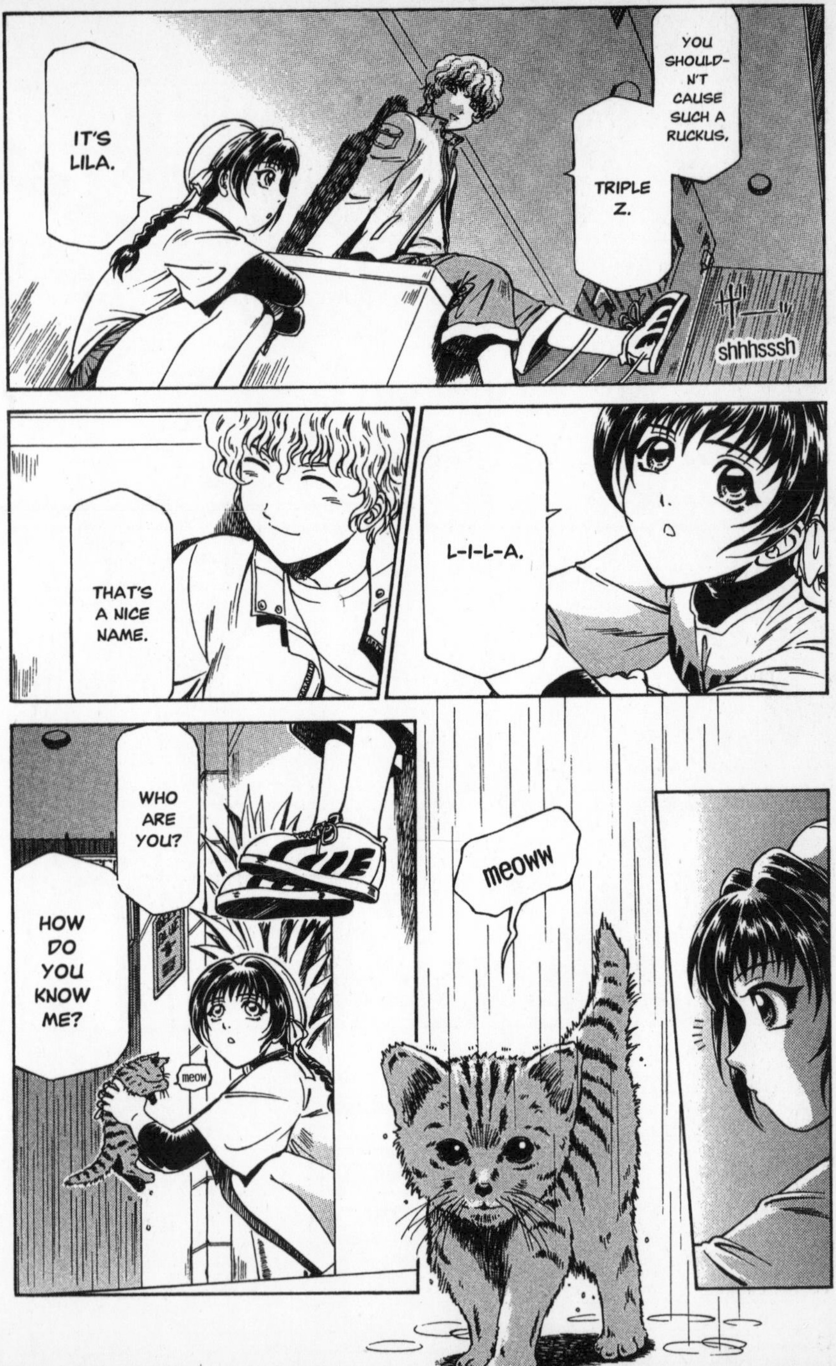
YOU SHOULDN'T CAUSE SUCH A RUCKUS,
TRIPLE Z.
shhhsssh
IT'S LILA.
L-I-L-A.
THAT'S A NICE NAME.
meoww
WHO ARE YOU?
HOW DO YOU KNOW ME?
meow

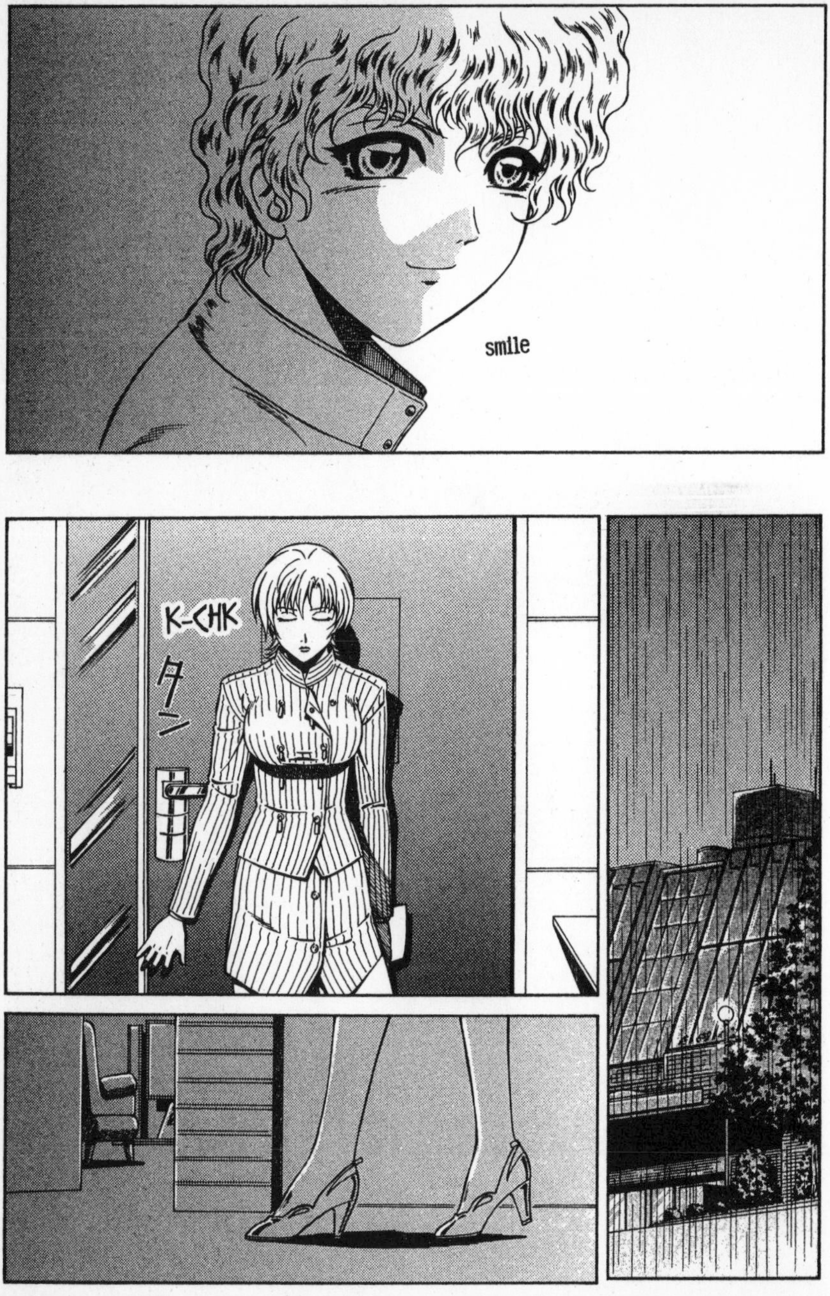
smile
K-CHK
タン

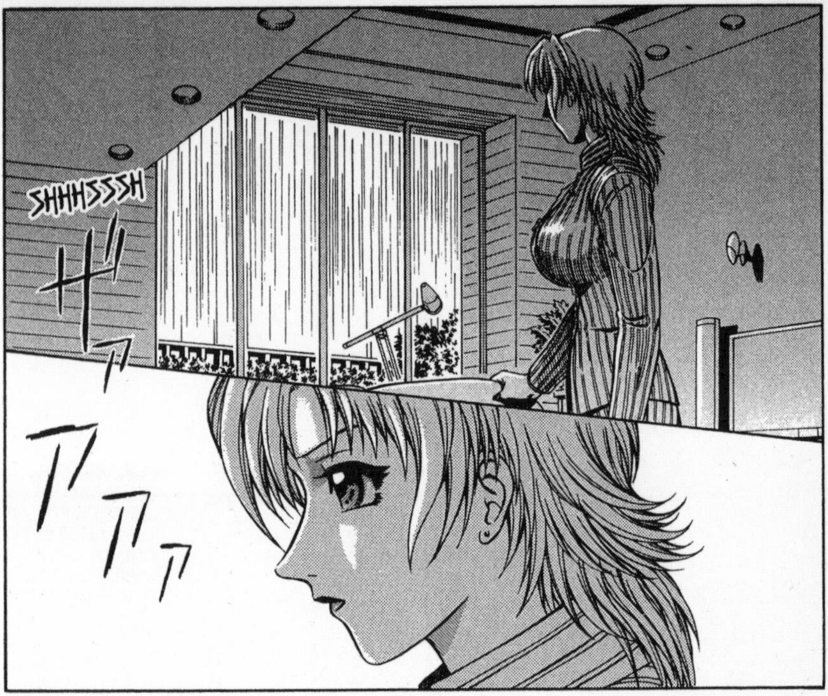
SHHHSSSH

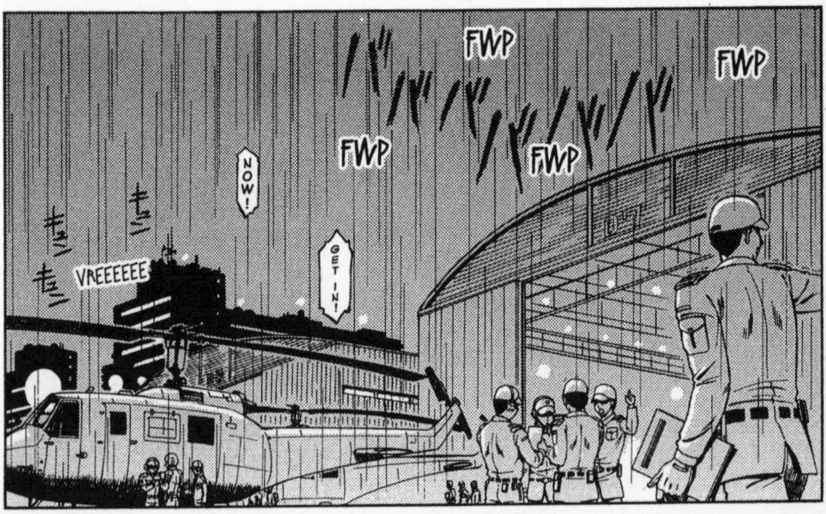
FWP
FWP
FWP
FWP
NOW!
GET IN!
VREEEEEE

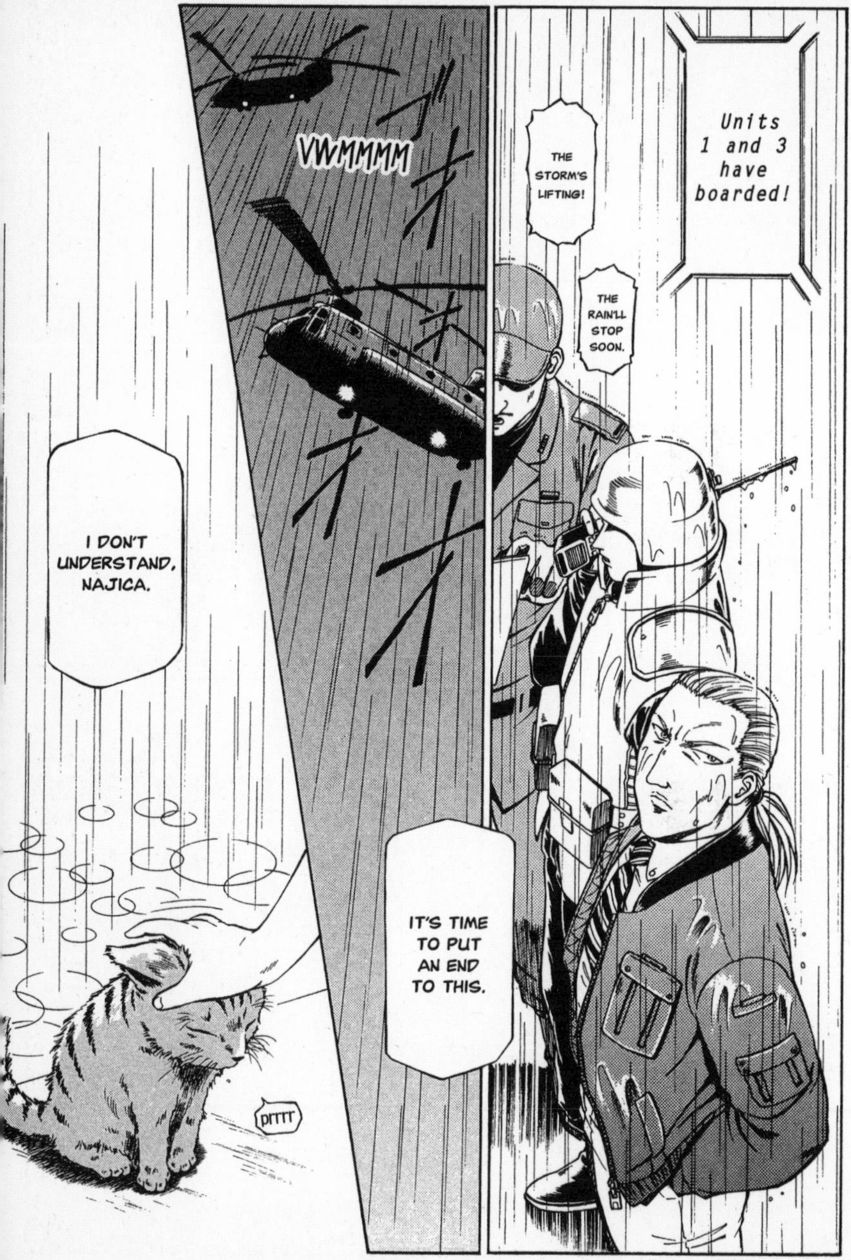
Units 1 and 3 have boarded!
THE STORM'S LIFTING!
THE RAIN'LL STOP SOON.
VWMMMM
I DON'T UNDERSTAND, NAJICA.
IT'S TIME TO PUT AN END TO THIS.
prrrr

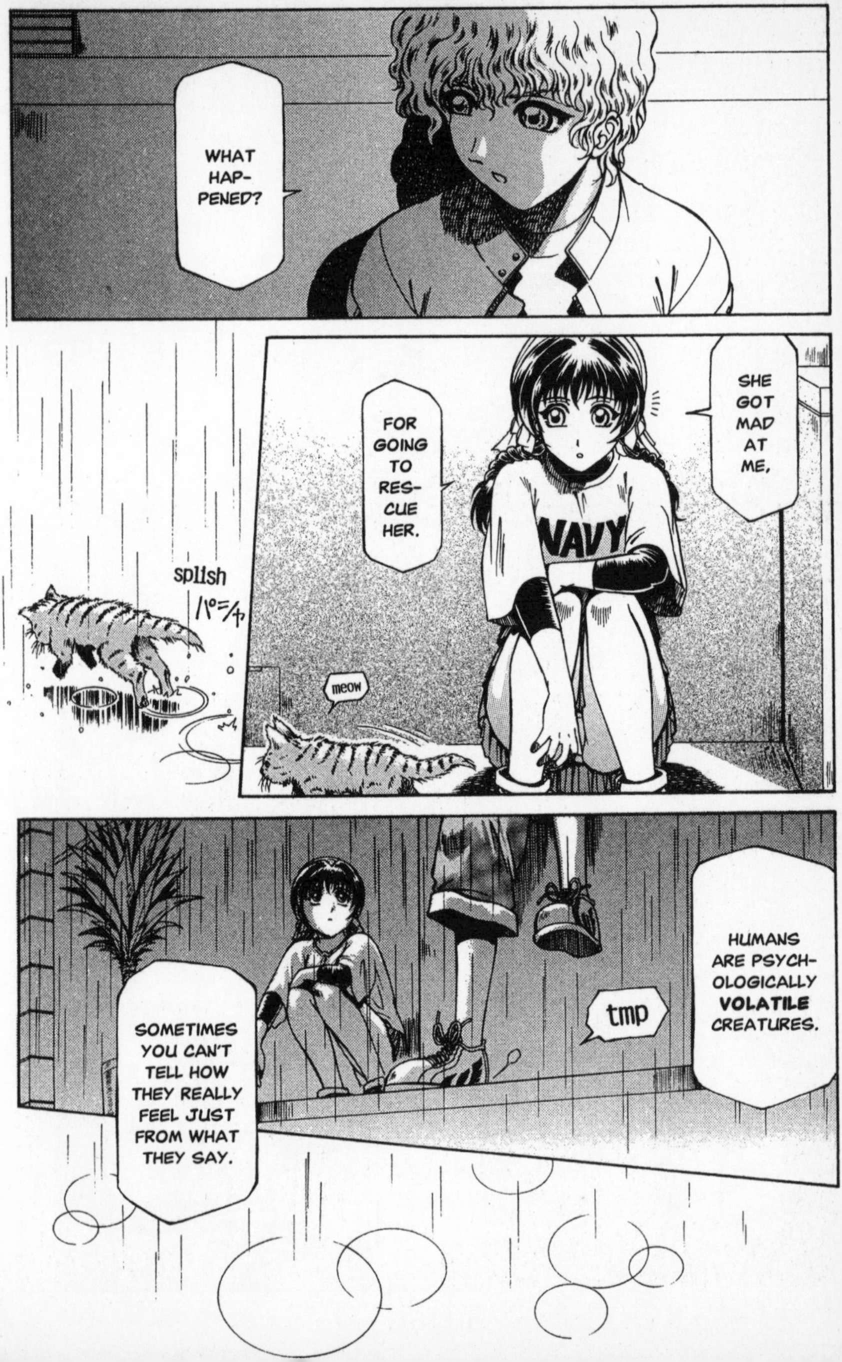
WHAT HAP-PENED?
SHE GOT MAD AT ME,
FOR GOING TO RES-CUE HER.
splish
パシャ
meow
HUMANS ARE PSYCH-OLOGICALLY **VOLATILE** CREATURES.
tmp
SOMETIMES YOU CAN'T TELL HOW THEY REALLY FEEL JUST FROM WHAT THEY SAY.

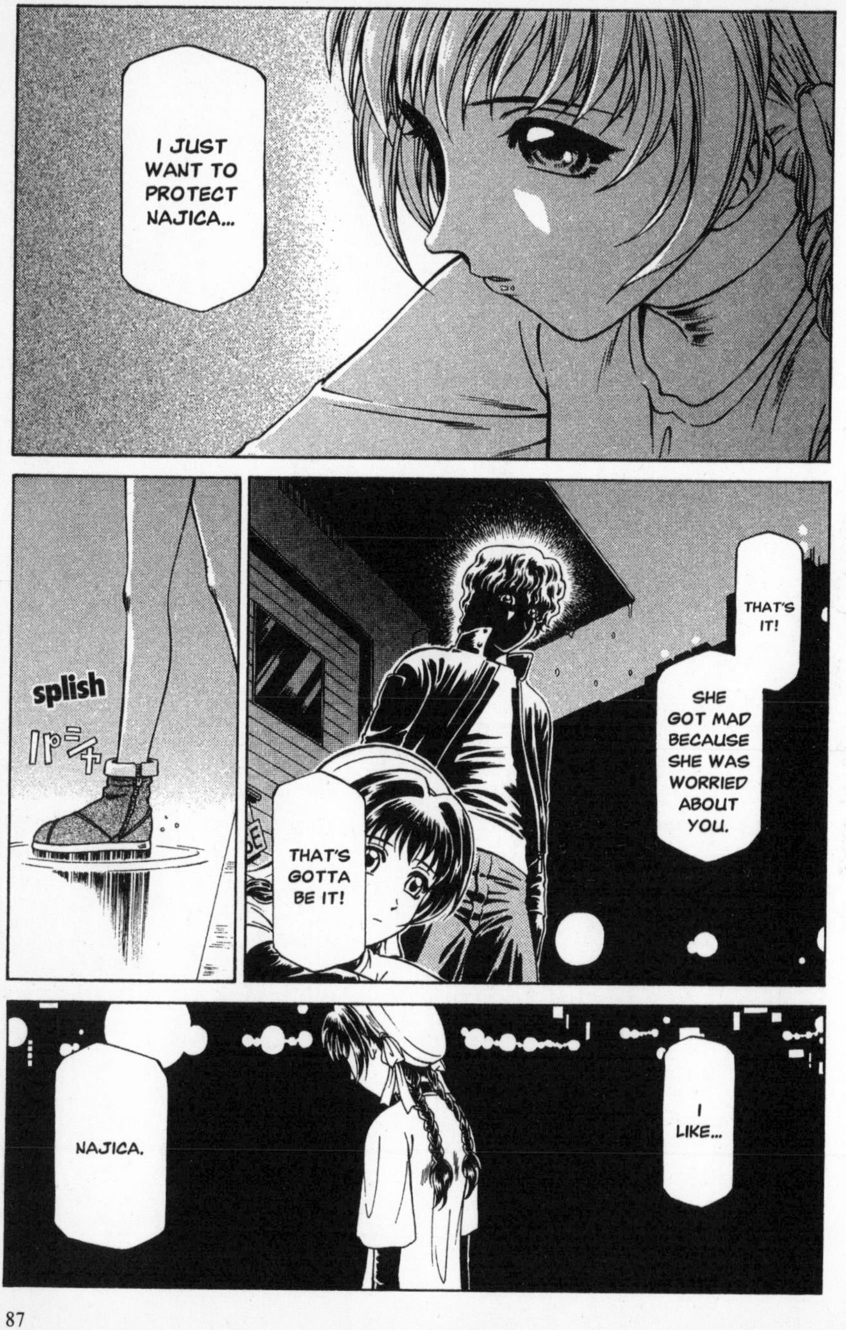
I JUST WANT TO PROTECT NAJICA...
THAT'S IT!
SHE GOT MAD BECAUSE SHE WAS WORRIED ABOUT YOU.
THAT'S GOTTA BE IT!
splish
パシャ
I LIKE...
NAJICA.

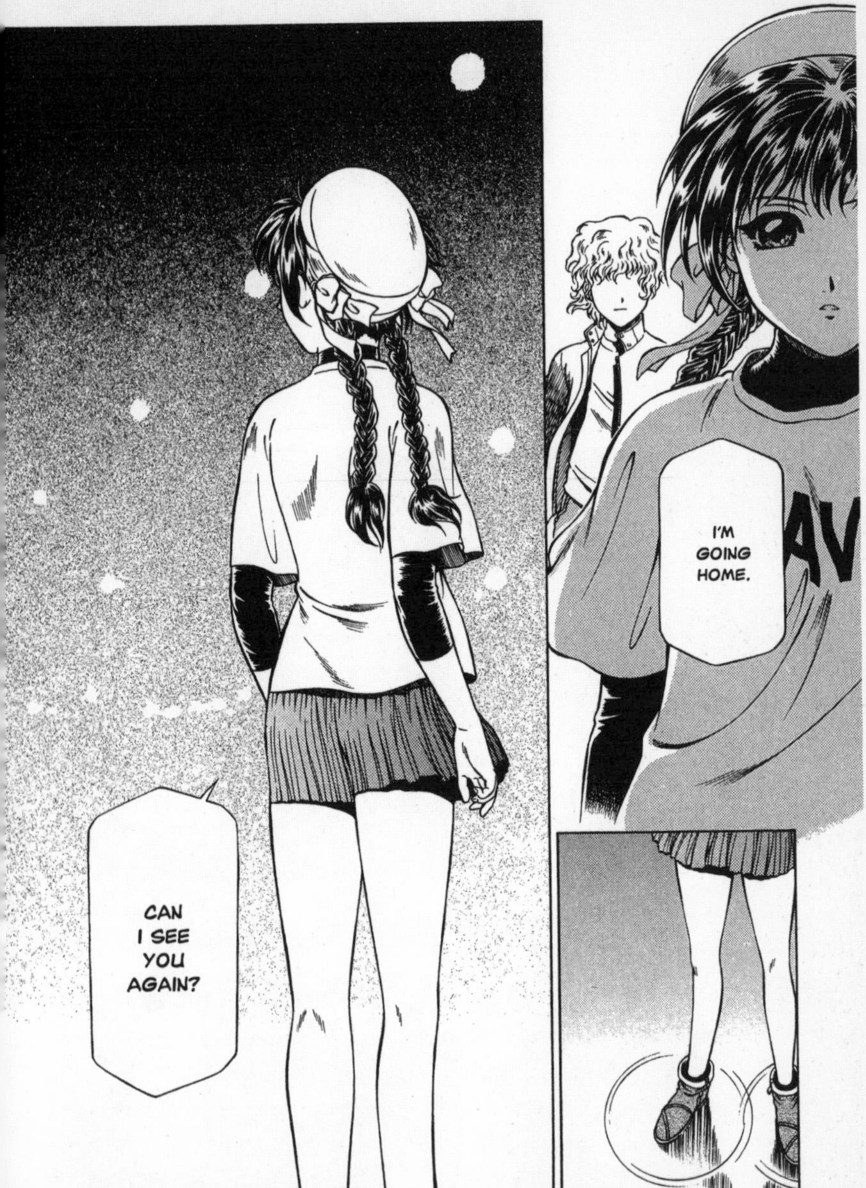
I'M GOING HOME.
CAN I SEE YOU AGAIN?

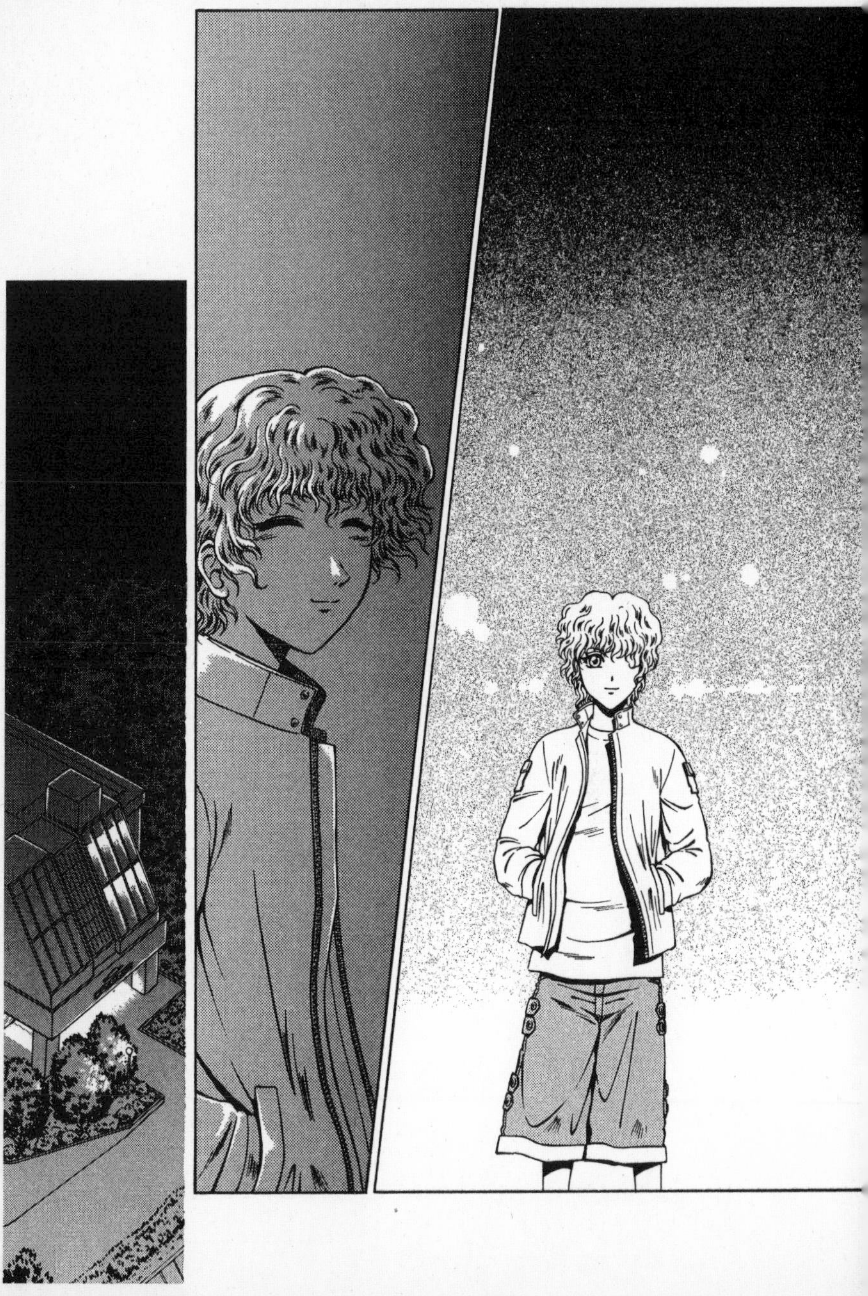

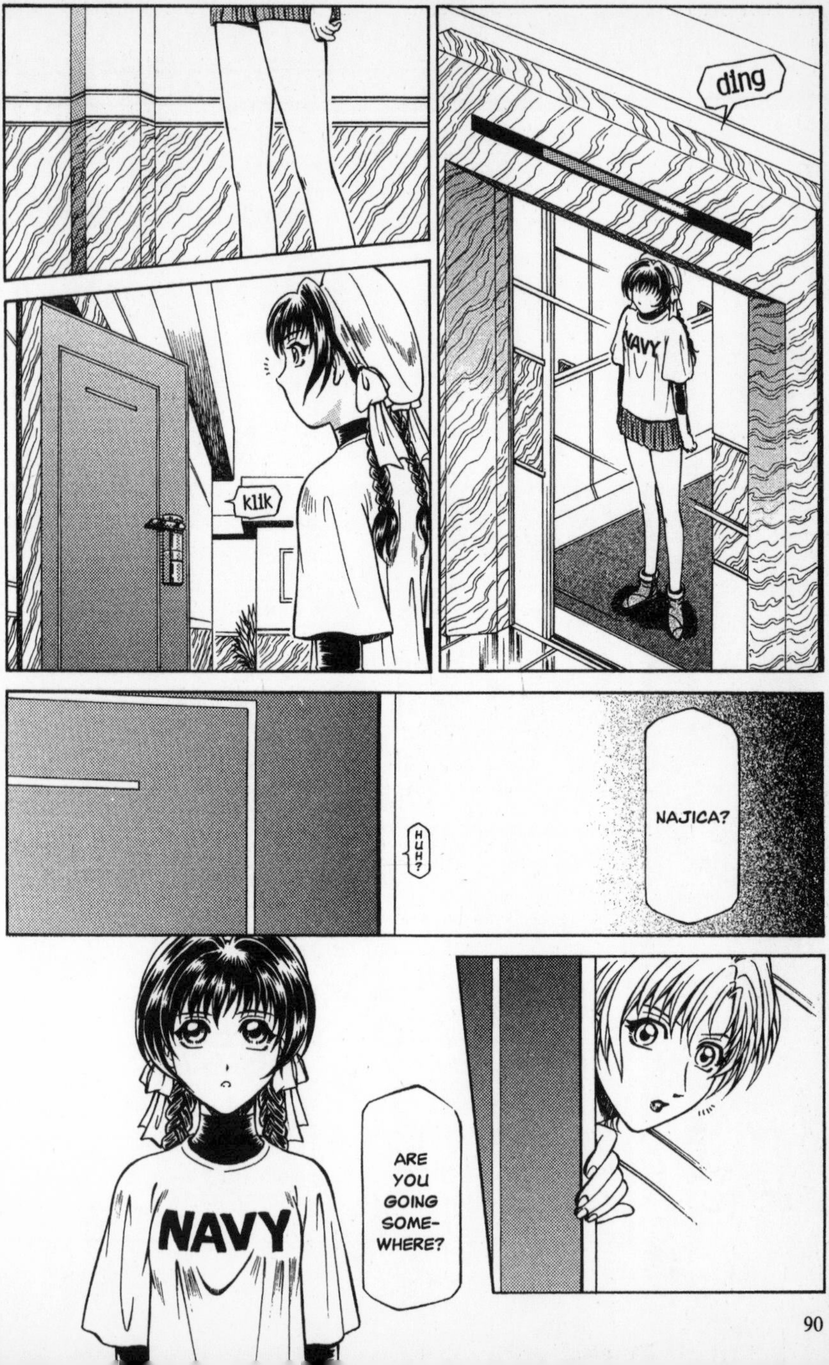
ding
klik
HUH?
NAJICA?
ARE YOU GOING SOME-WHERE?

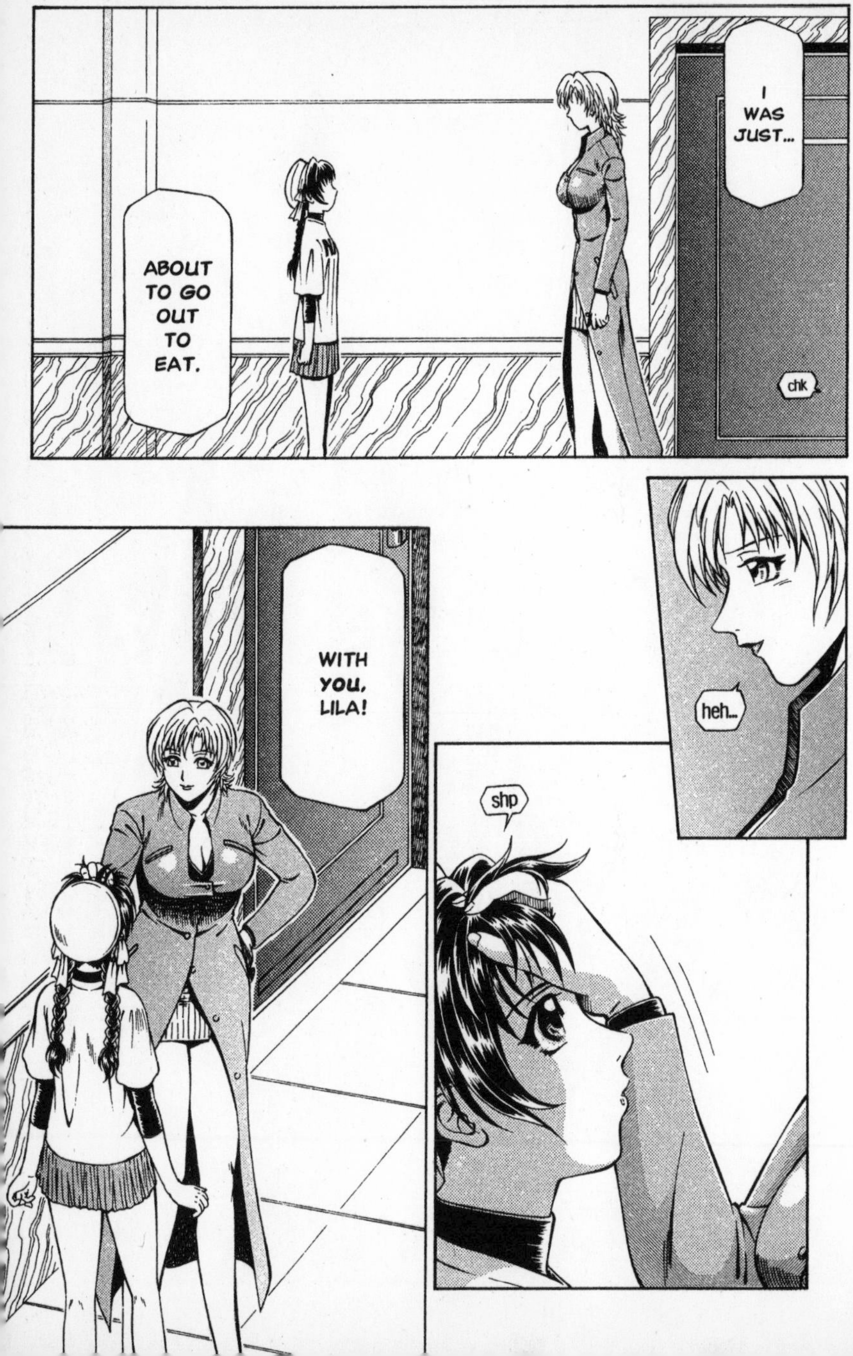

I WAS JUST...
ABOUT TO GO OUT TO EAT.
chk
heh...
WITH YOU, LILA!
shp

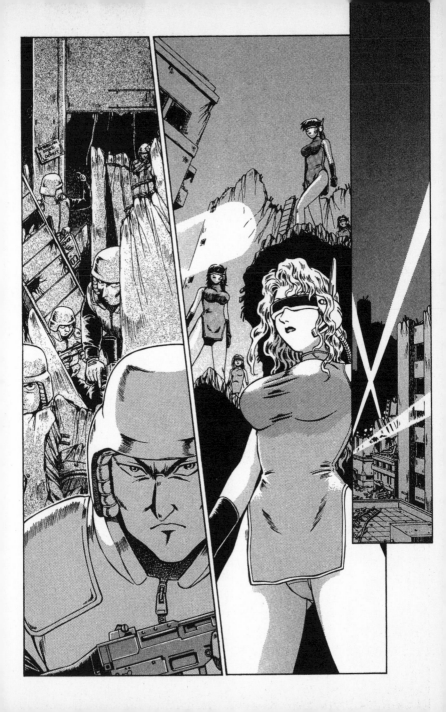

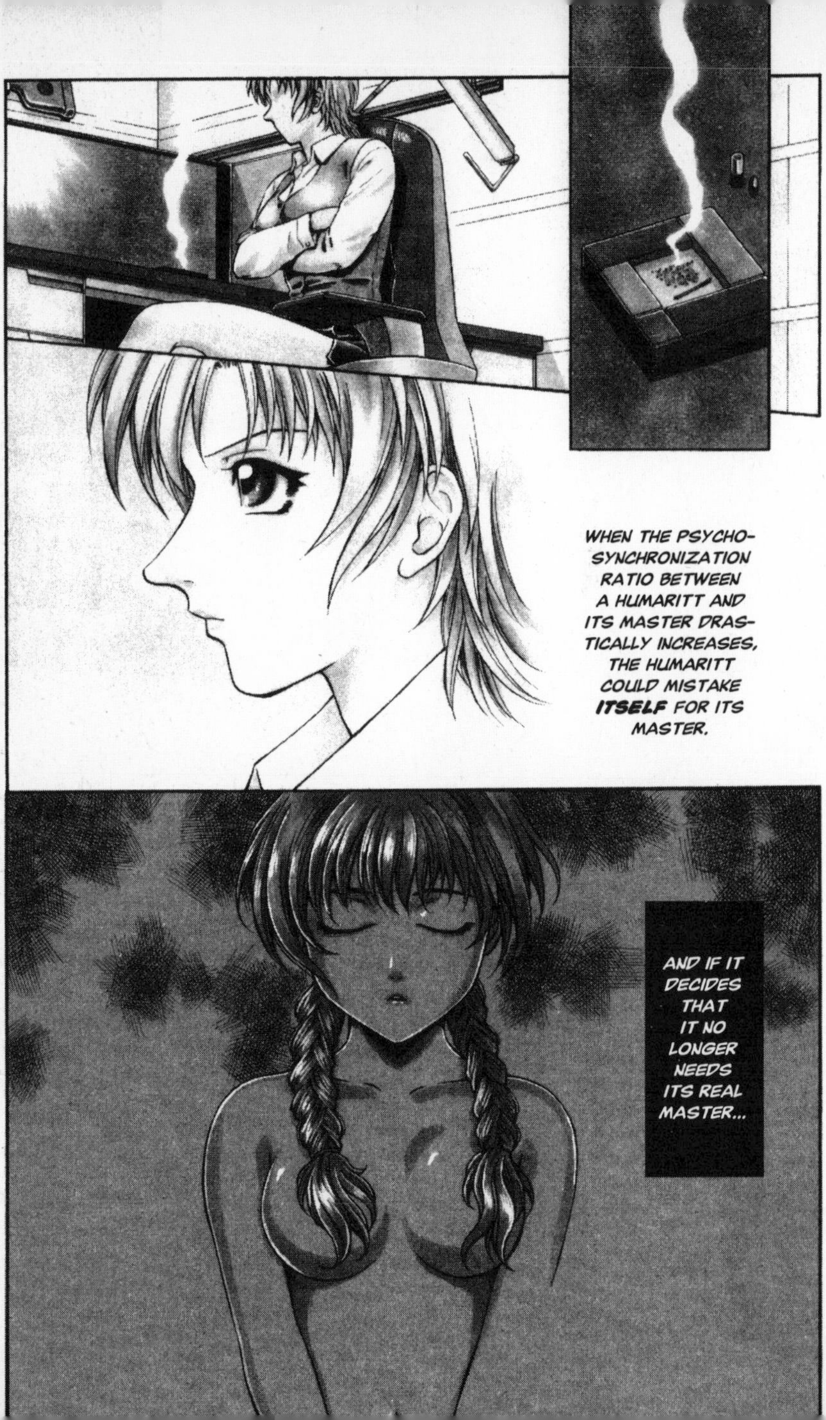
WHEN THE PSYCHO-SYNCHRONIZATION RATIO BETWEEN A HUMARITT AND ITS MASTER DRASTICALLY INCREASES, THE HUMARITT COULD MISTAKE **ITSELF** FOR ITS MASTER.
AND IF IT DECIDES THAT IT NO LONGER NEEDS ITS REAL MASTER...

Operation.16
BLITZ TACTICS PART 2

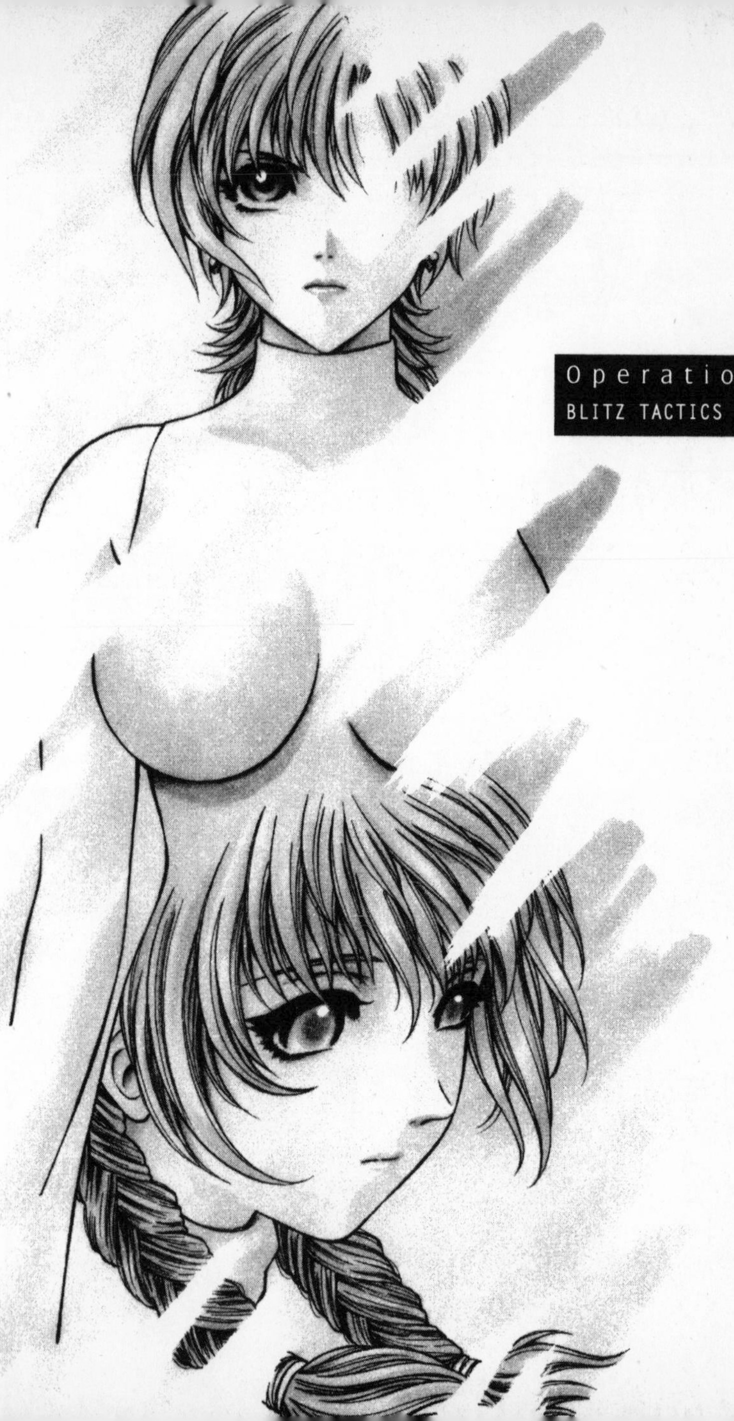

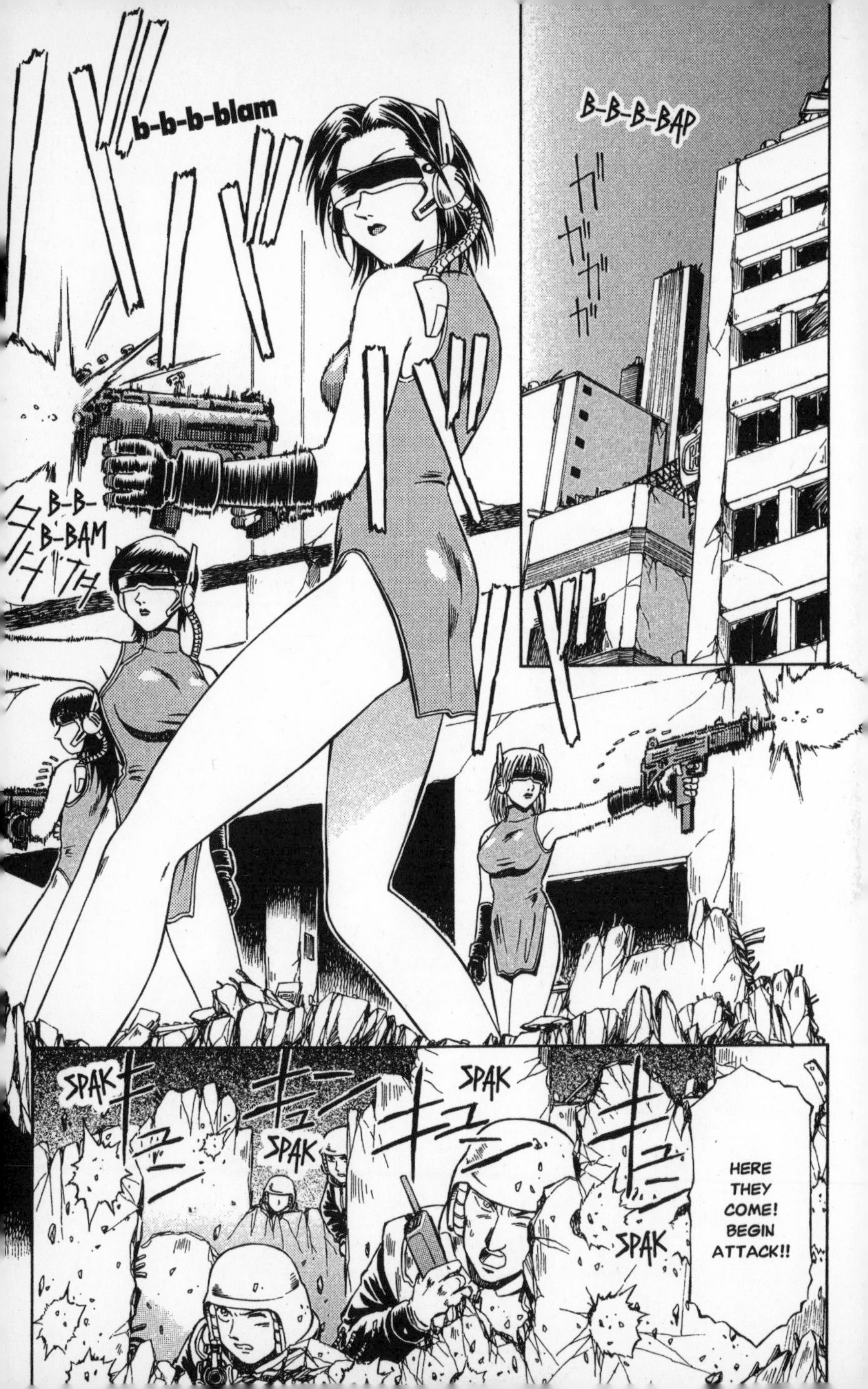
B-B-B-BAP
ガガガガ
b-b-b-blam
B-B-B-BAM
SPAK
SPAK
SPAK
SPAK
HERE THEY COME! BEGIN ATTACK!!

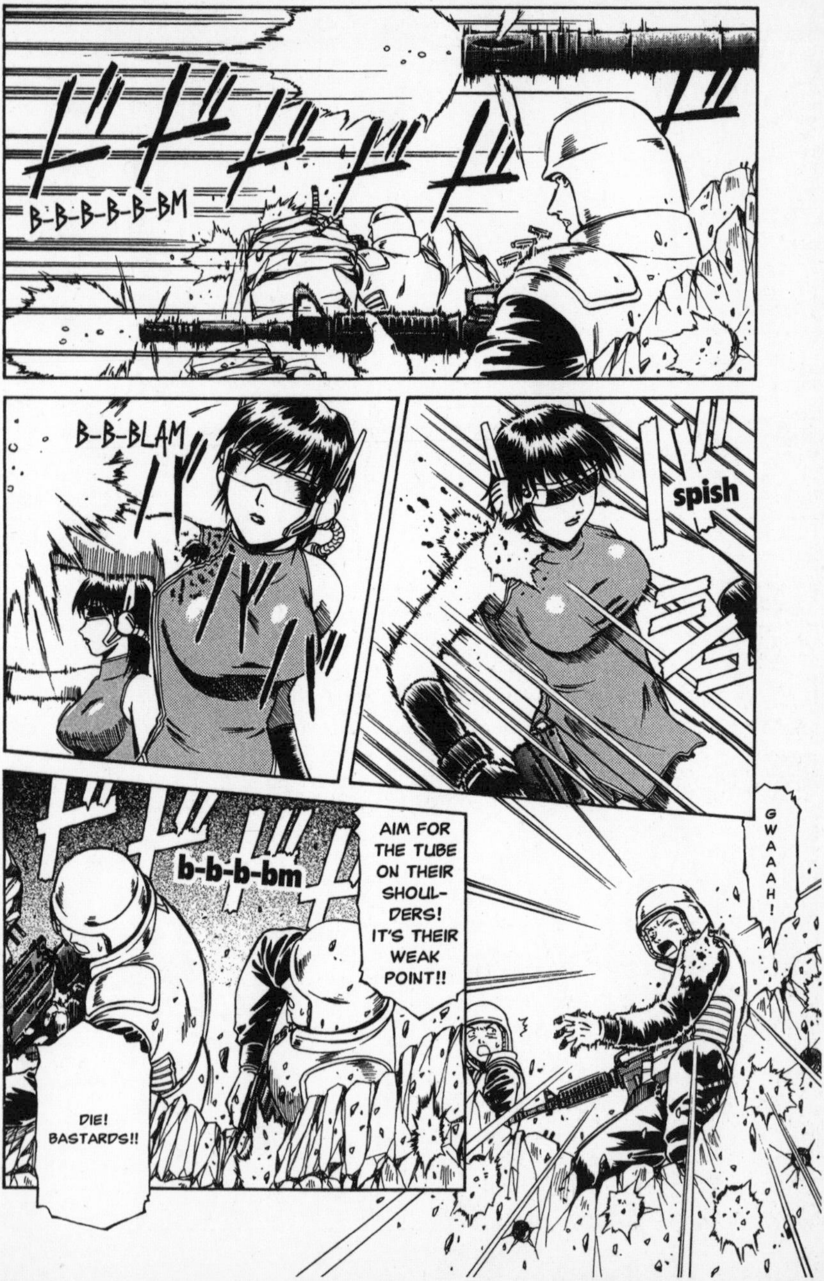

B-B-B-B-B-BM
B-B-BLAM
spish
b-b-b-bm
AIM FOR THE TUBE ON THEIR SHOULDERS! IT'S THEIR WEAK POINT!!
GWAAAAH!
DIE! BASTARDS!!

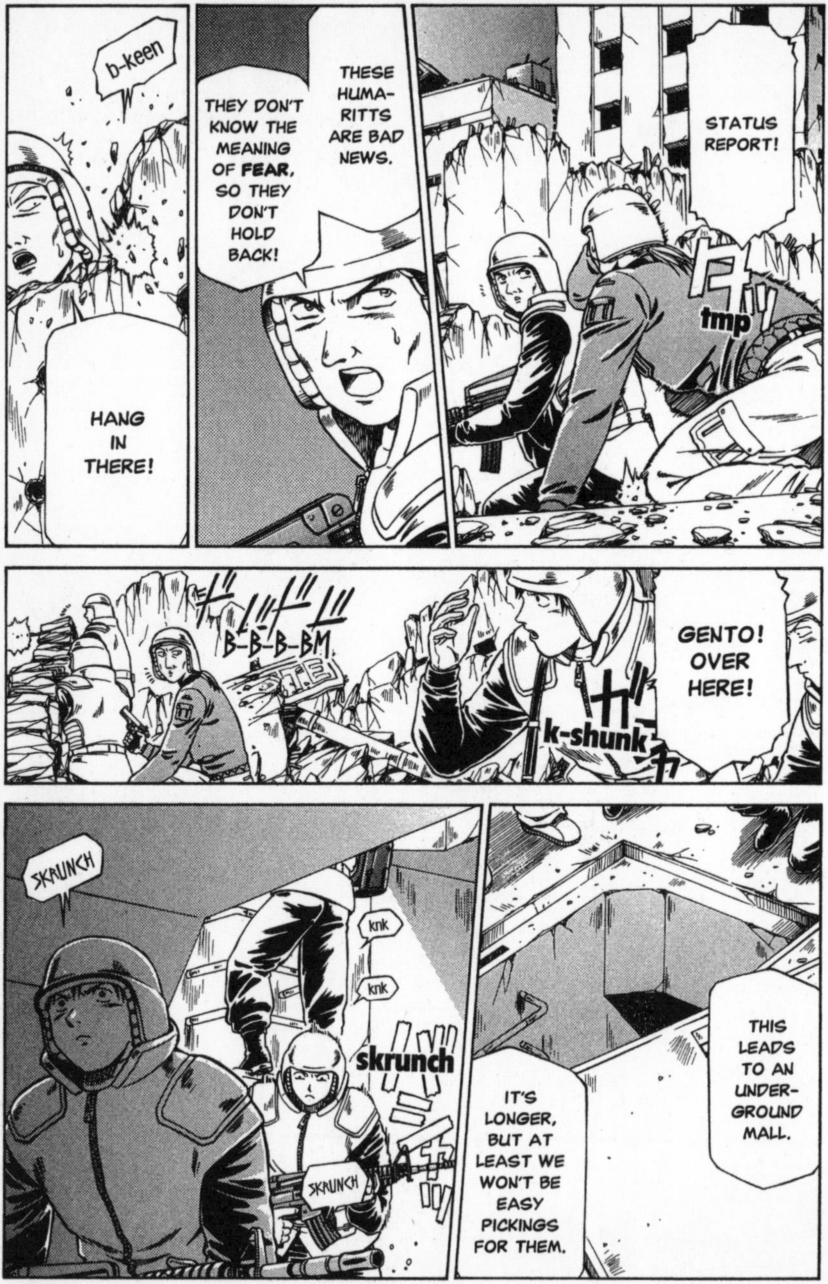
STATUS REPORT!
tmp
THESE HUMARITTS ARE BAD NEWS.
THEY DON'T KNOW THE MEANING OF **FEAR**, SO THEY DON'T HOLD BACK!
b-keen
HANG IN THERE!
GENTO! OVER HERE!
k-shunk
B-B-B-BM
THIS LEADS TO AN UNDERGROUND MALL.
IT'S LONGER, BUT AT LEAST WE WON'T BE EASY PICKINGS FOR THEM.
knk
knk
skrunch
SKRUNCH
SKRUNCH

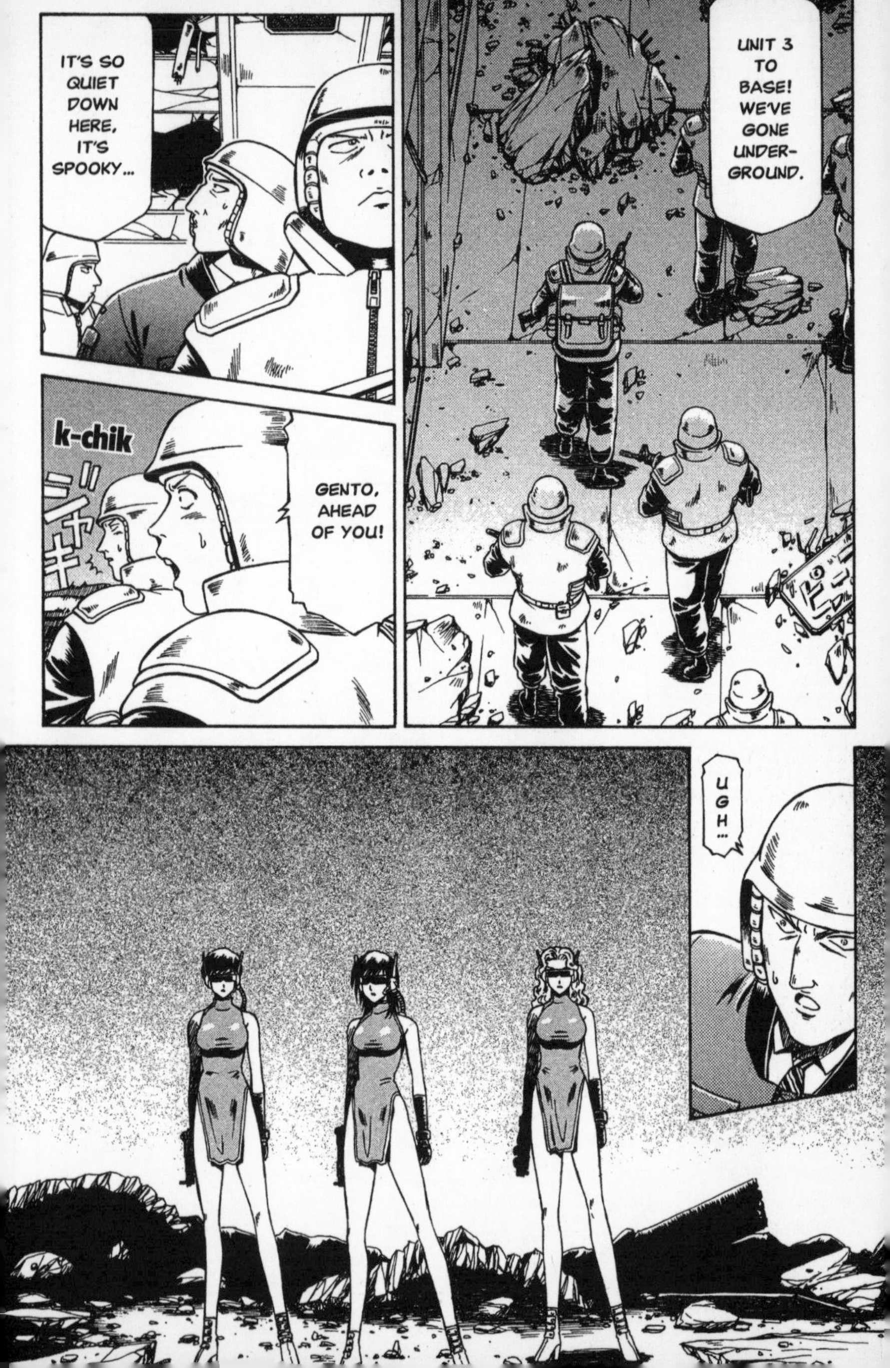
UNIT 3 TO BASE! WE'VE GONE UNDER-GROUND.
IT'S SO QUIET DOWN HERE, IT'S SPOOKY...
k-chik
GENTO, AHEAD OF YOU!
UGH...

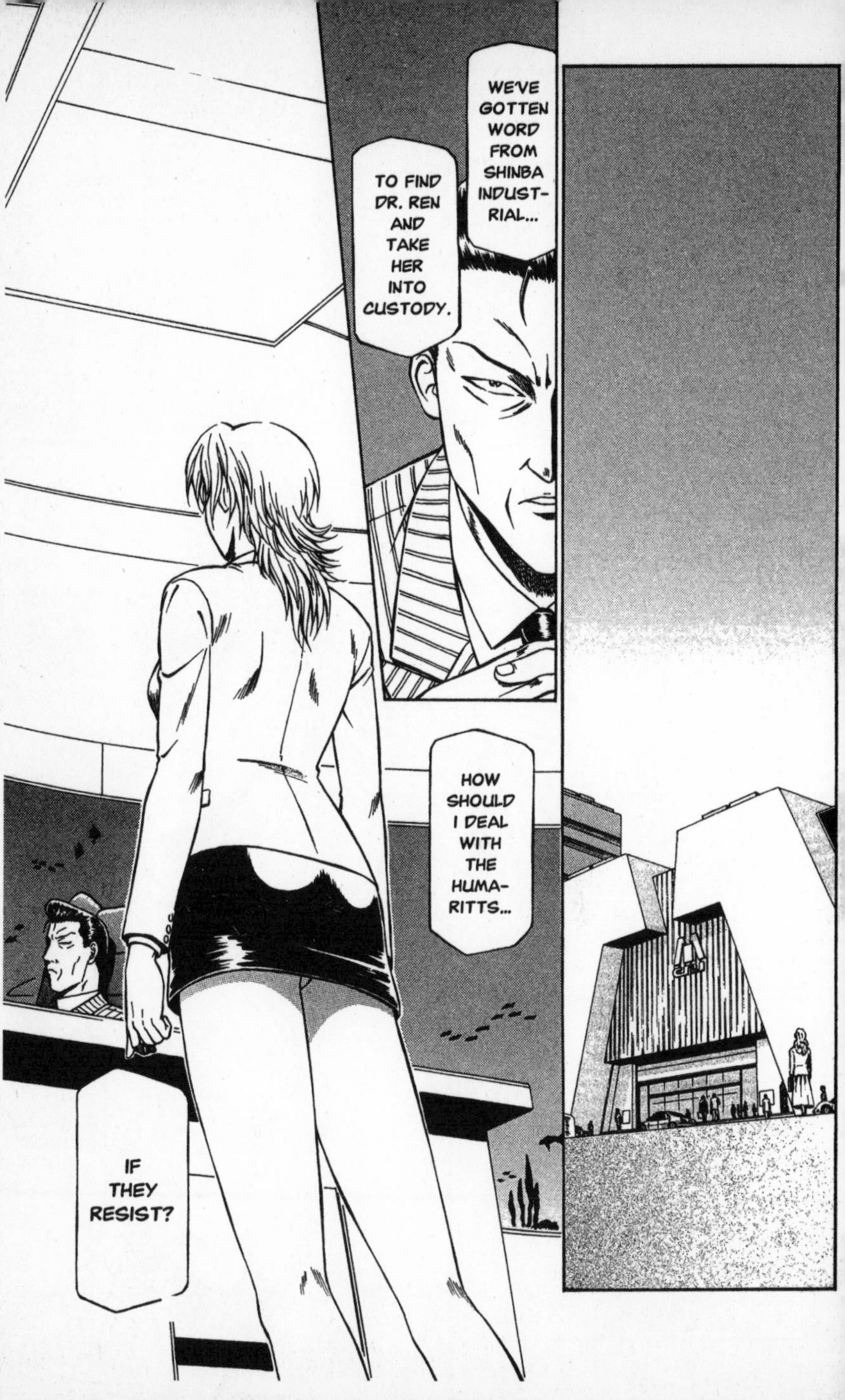
WE'VE GOTTEN WORD FROM SHINBA INDUST-RIAL...
TO FIND DR. REN AND TAKE HER INTO CUSTODY.
HOW SHOULD I DEAL WITH THE HUMA-RITTS...
IF THEY RESIST?

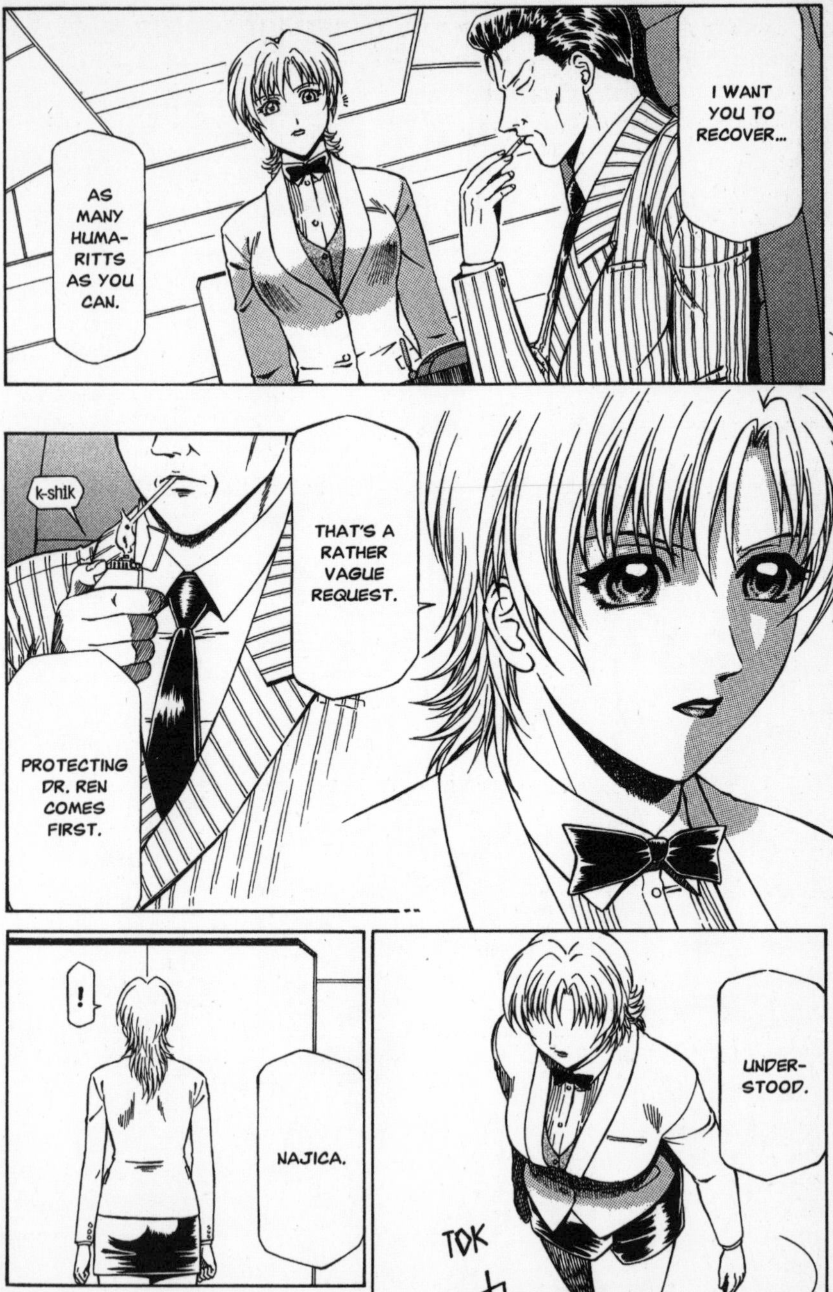
I WANT YOU TO RECOVER...
AS MANY HUMA-RITTS AS YOU CAN.
THAT'S A RATHER VAGUE REQUEST.
k-shik
PROTECTING DR. REN COMES FIRST.
UNDER-STOOD.
TOK
!
NAJICA.

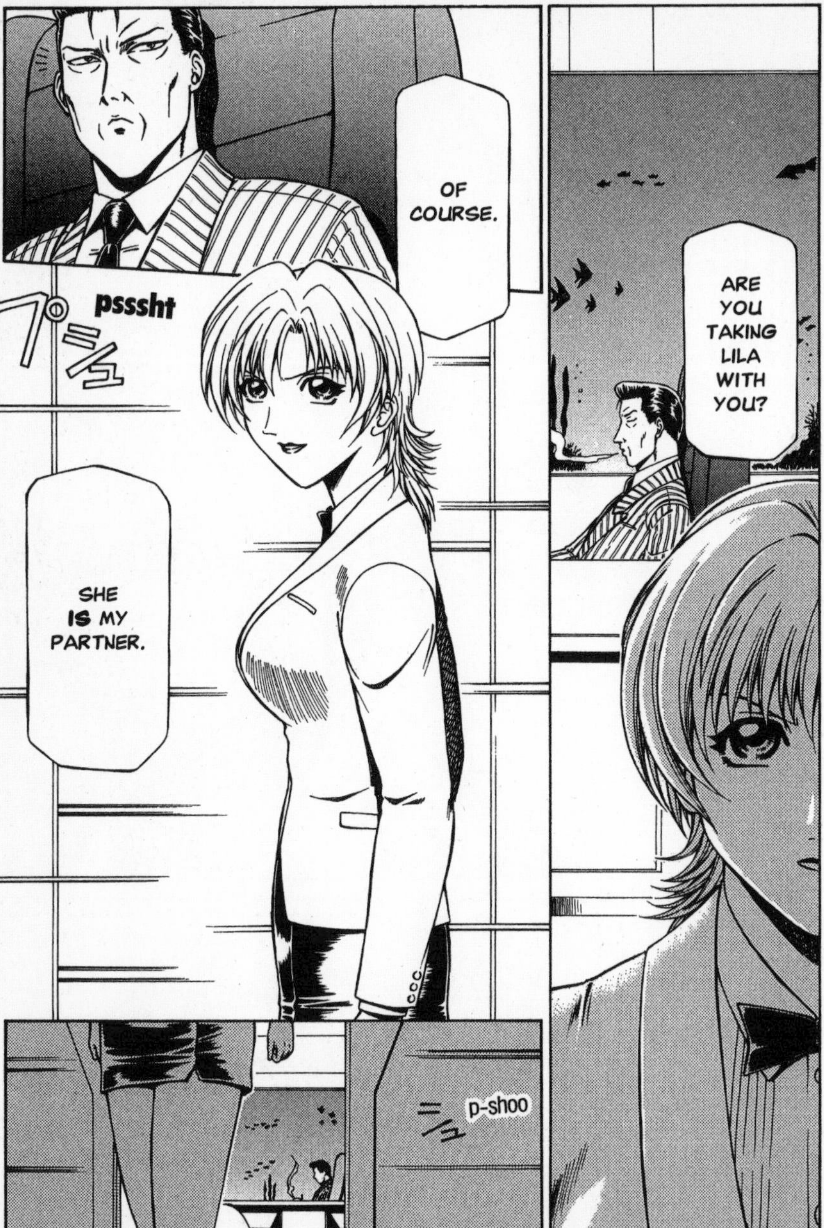
ARE YOU TAKING LILA WITH YOU?
OF COURSE.
プシュ
psssht
SHE **IS** MY PARTNER.
シュ
p-shoo

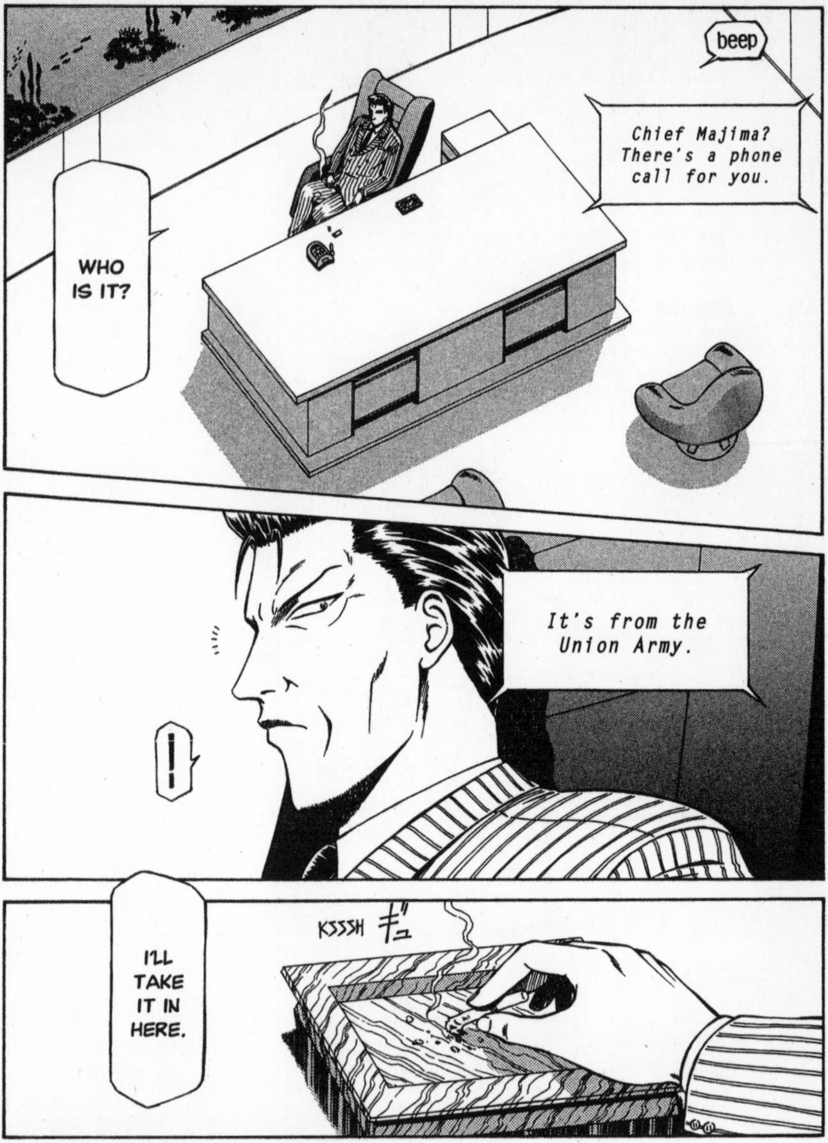
beep
Chief Majima? There's a phone call for you.
WHO IS IT?
It's from the Union Army.
!
KSSSH ギュ
I'LL TAKE IT IN HERE.

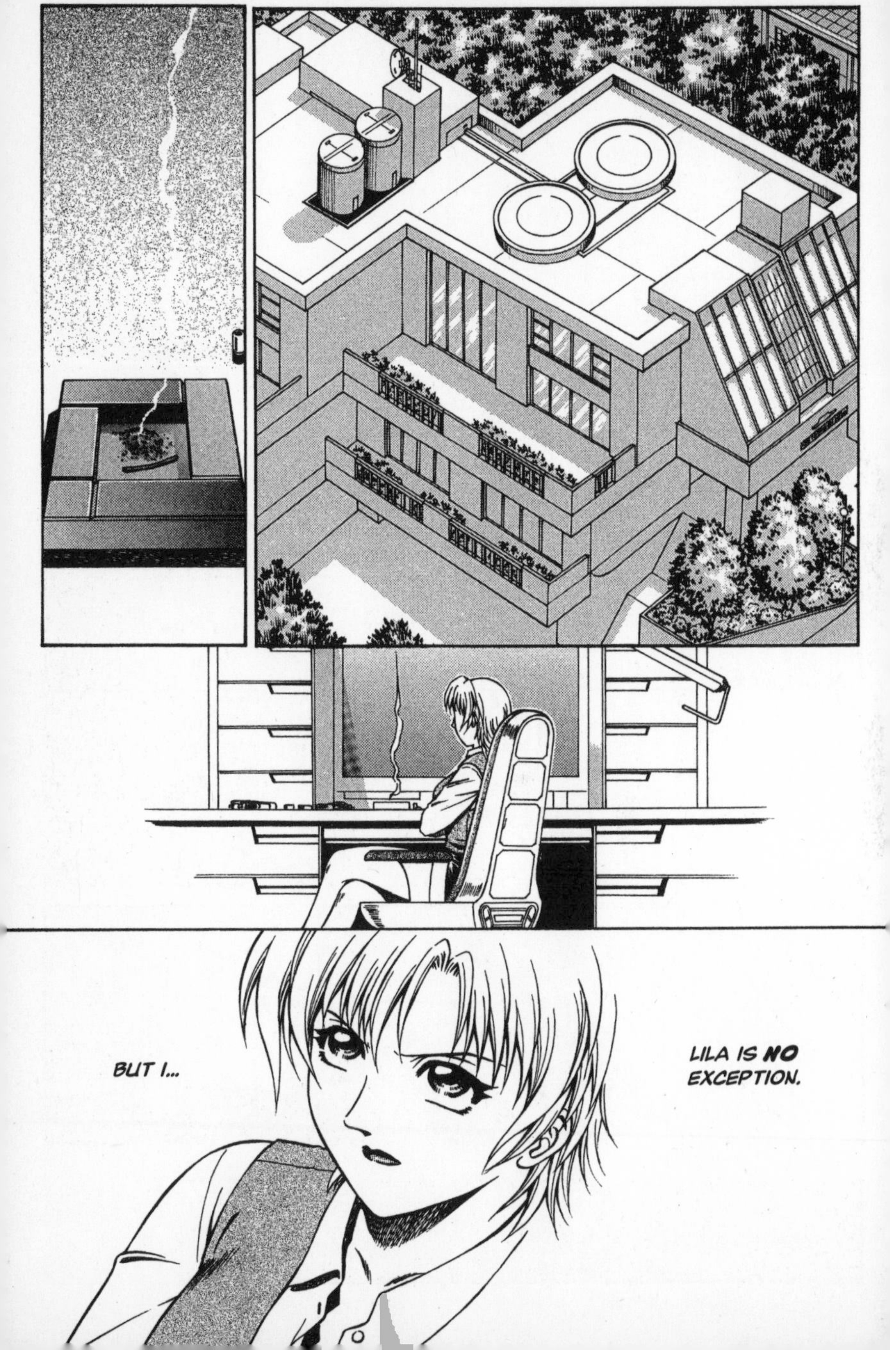
LILA IS **NO** EXCEPTION.
BUT I...

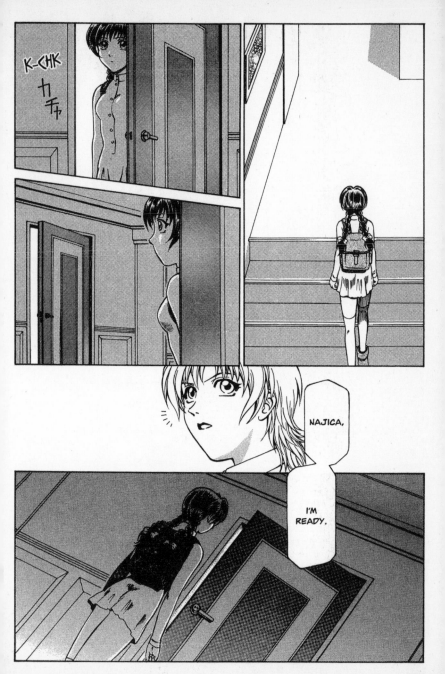

K-CHK

カチャ

NAJICA,

I'M READY.

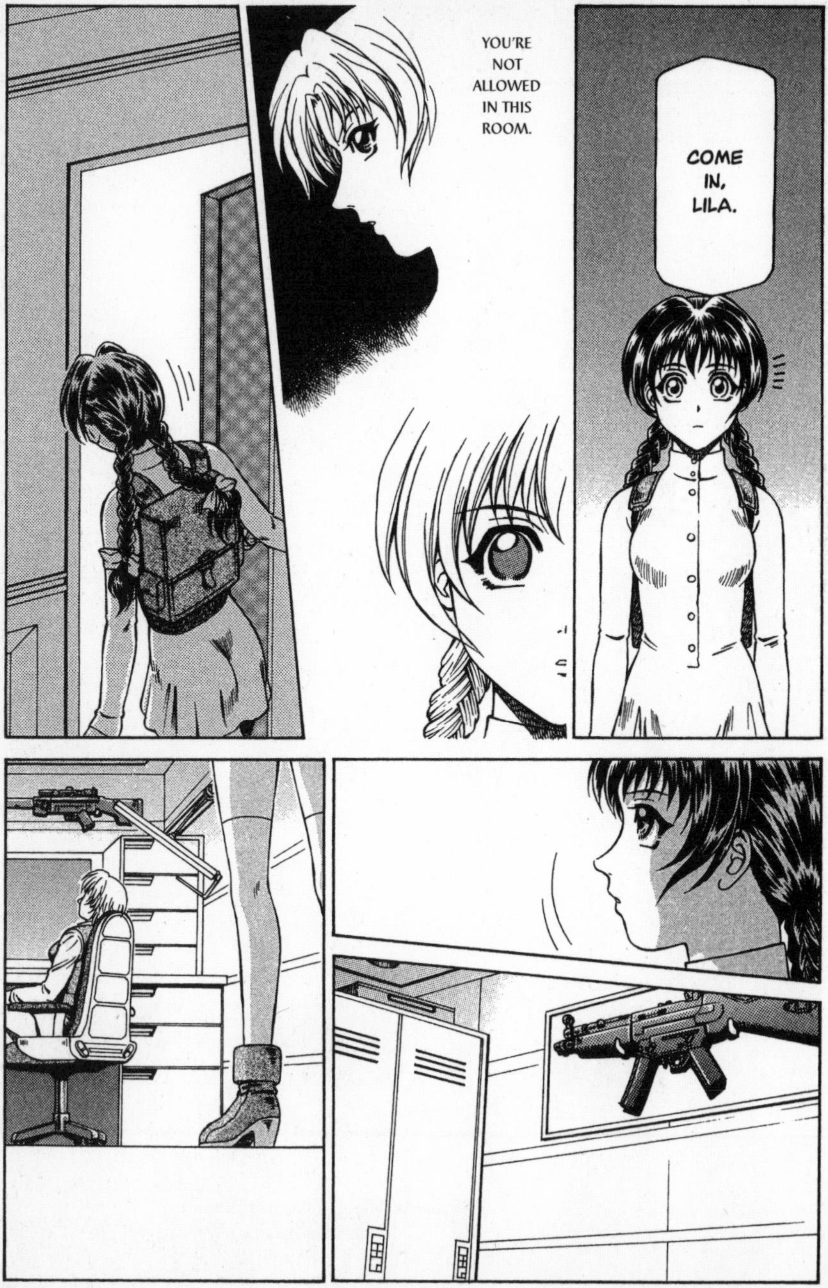
COME IN, LILA.
YOU'RE NOT ALLOWED IN THIS ROOM.

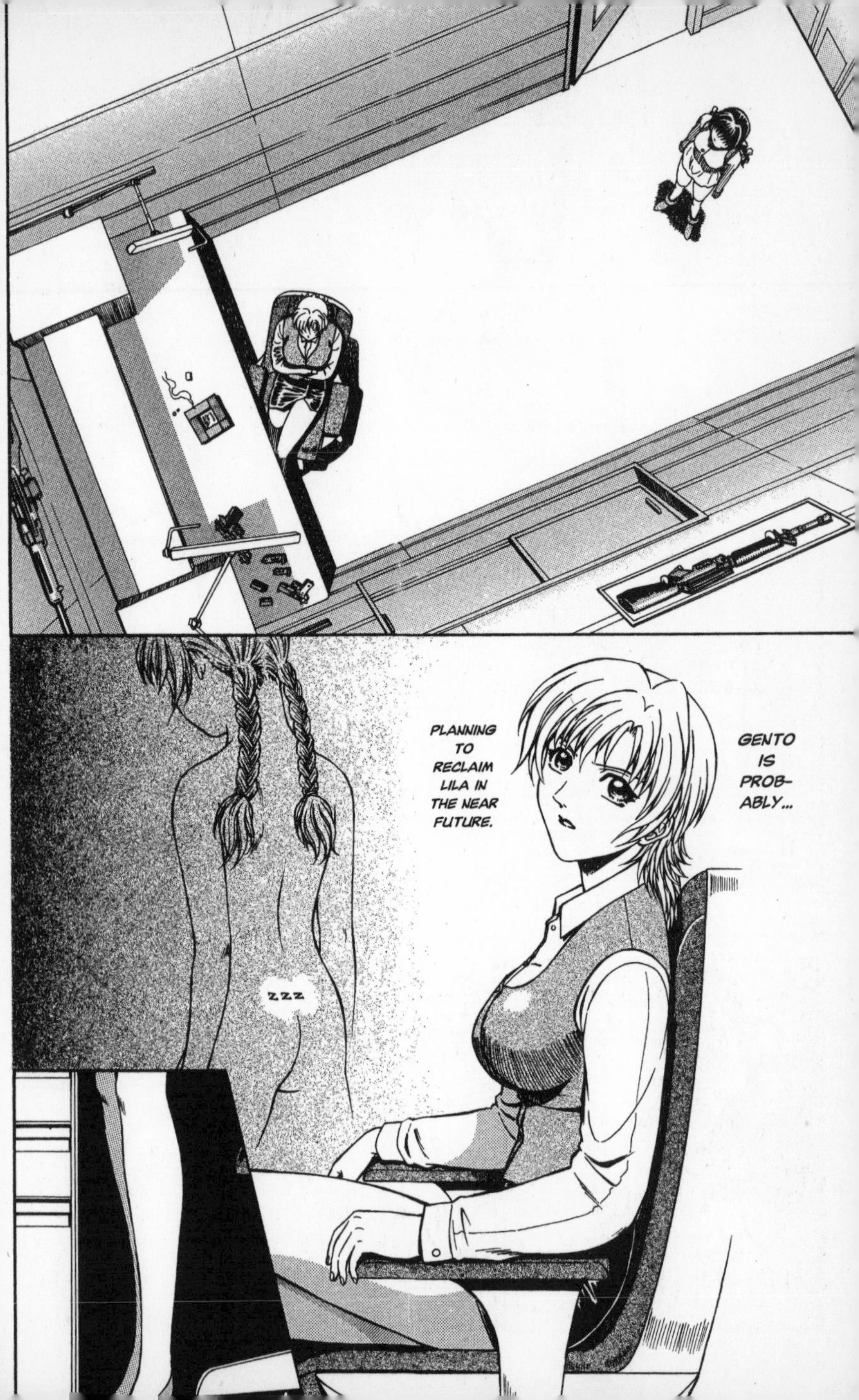
GENTO IS PROBABLY...
PLANNING TO RECLAIM LILA IN THE NEAR FUTURE.
ZZZ

AND THE PLACE WE'RE GOING TO INFILTRATE WILL PROBABLY BE LIKE A WALK DOWN MEMORY LANE FOR LILA.

IT MIGHT HAVE AN ADVERSE EFFECT.

I WANT TO BELIEVE IN HER.

BUT SHE'S MY PARTNER.

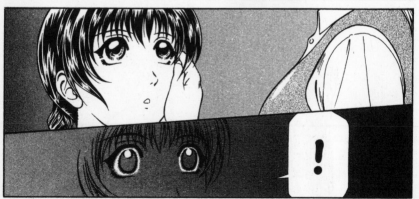

!

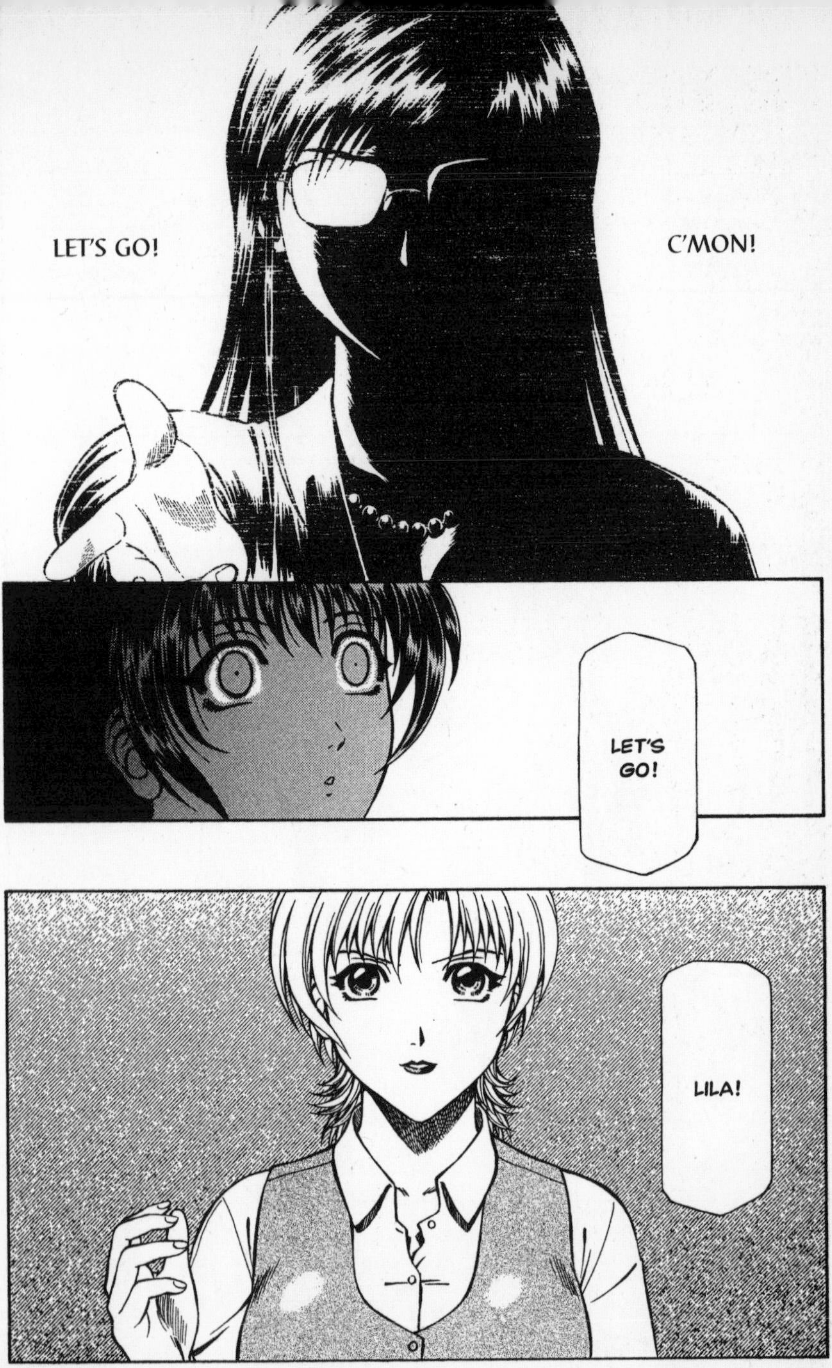
C'MON!
LET'S GO!
LET'S GO!
LILA!

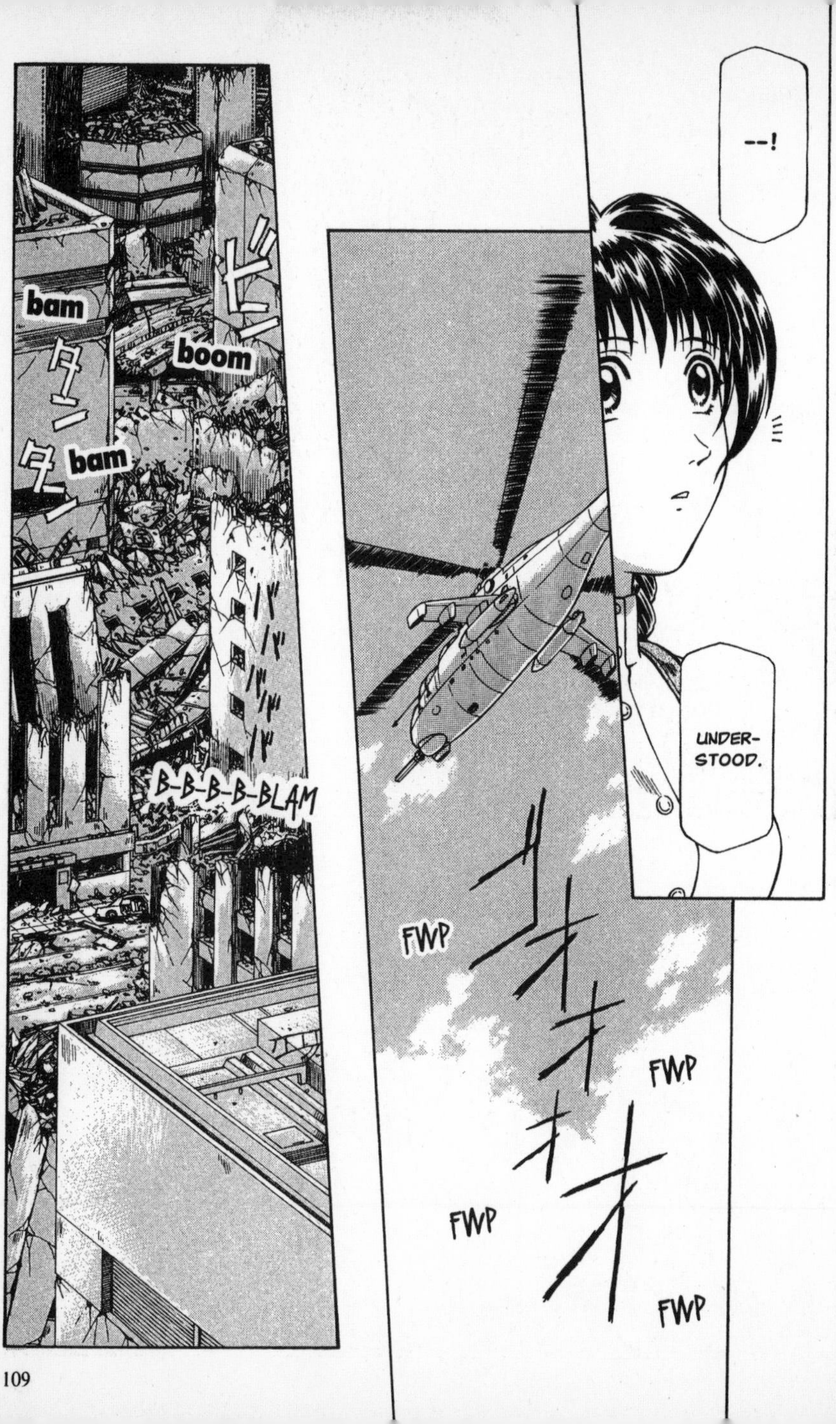
--!
bam
boom
bam
B-B-B-B-BLAM
UNDER-
STOOD.
FWP
FWP
FWP
FWP

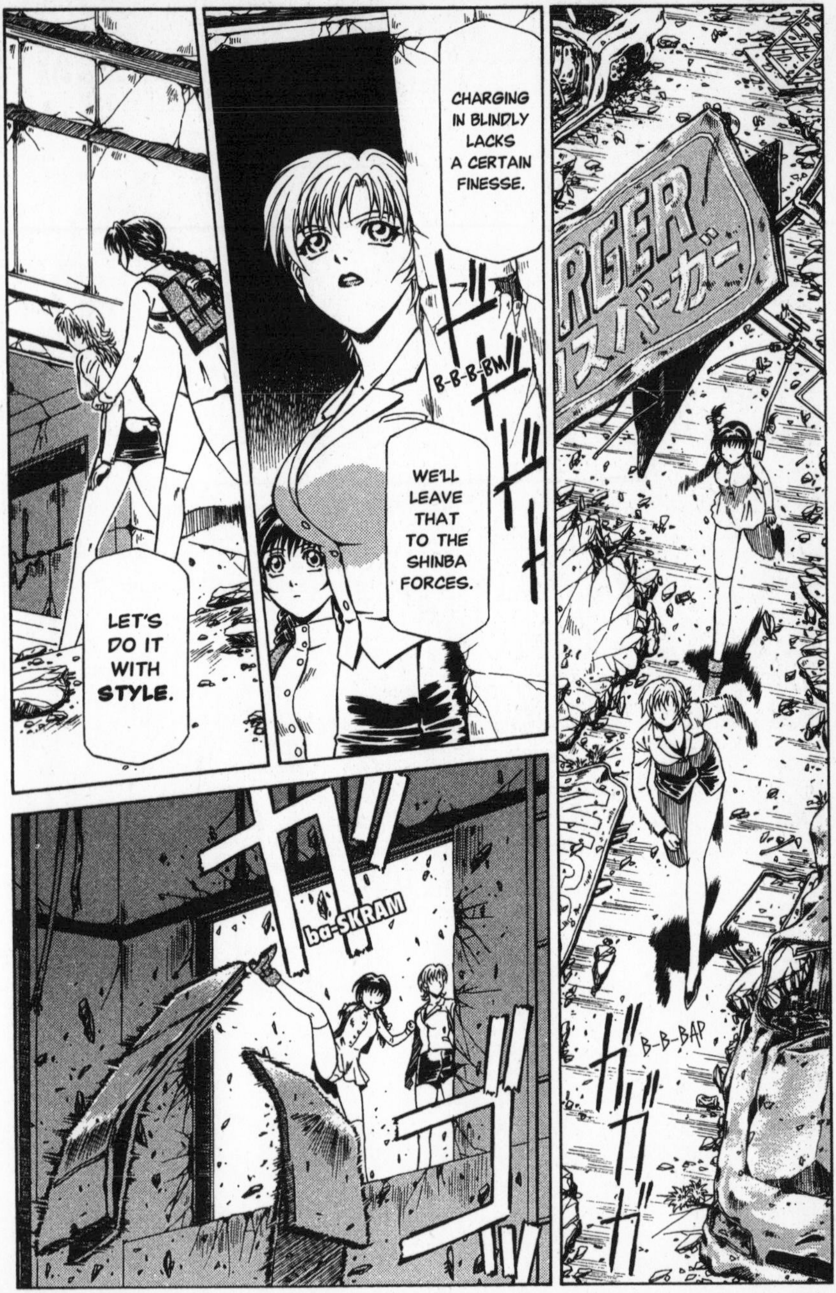
RGER
スバーガー
B-B-BAP
CHARGING IN BLINDLY LACKS A CERTAIN FINESSE.
B-B-B-BM
WE'LL LEAVE THAT TO THE SHINBA FORCES.
LET'S DO IT WITH STYLE.
ba-SKRAM

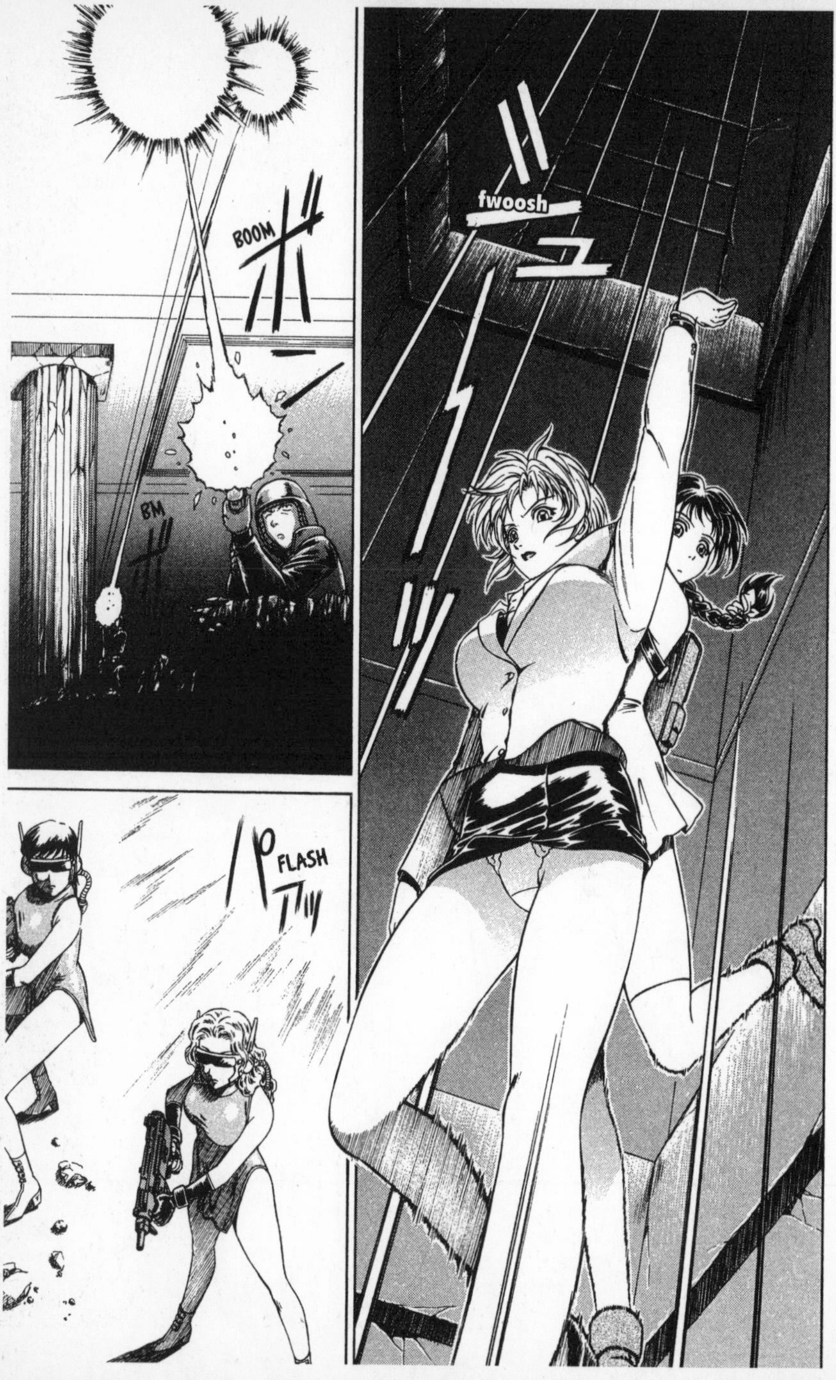
fwoosh
BOOM
BM
FLASH

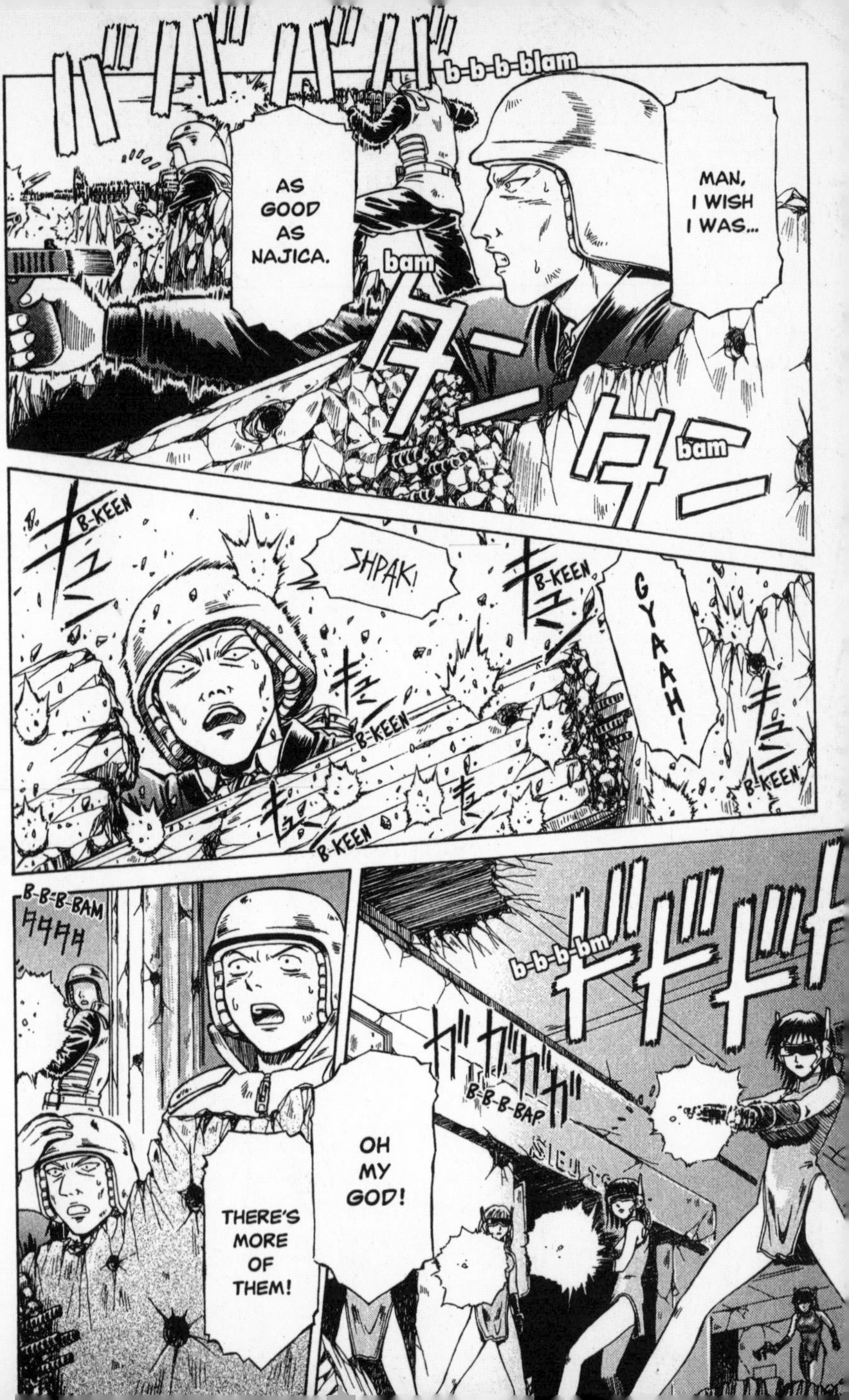
b-b-b-blam
MAN, I WISH I WAS...
AS GOOD AS NAJICA.
bam
bam
B-KEEN
GYAAH!
B-KEEN
SHPAK!
B-KEEN
B-KEEN
B-KEEN
B-KEEN
b-b-b-bm
B-B-B-BAP
OH MY GOD!
THERE'S MORE OF THEM!
B-B-B-BAM

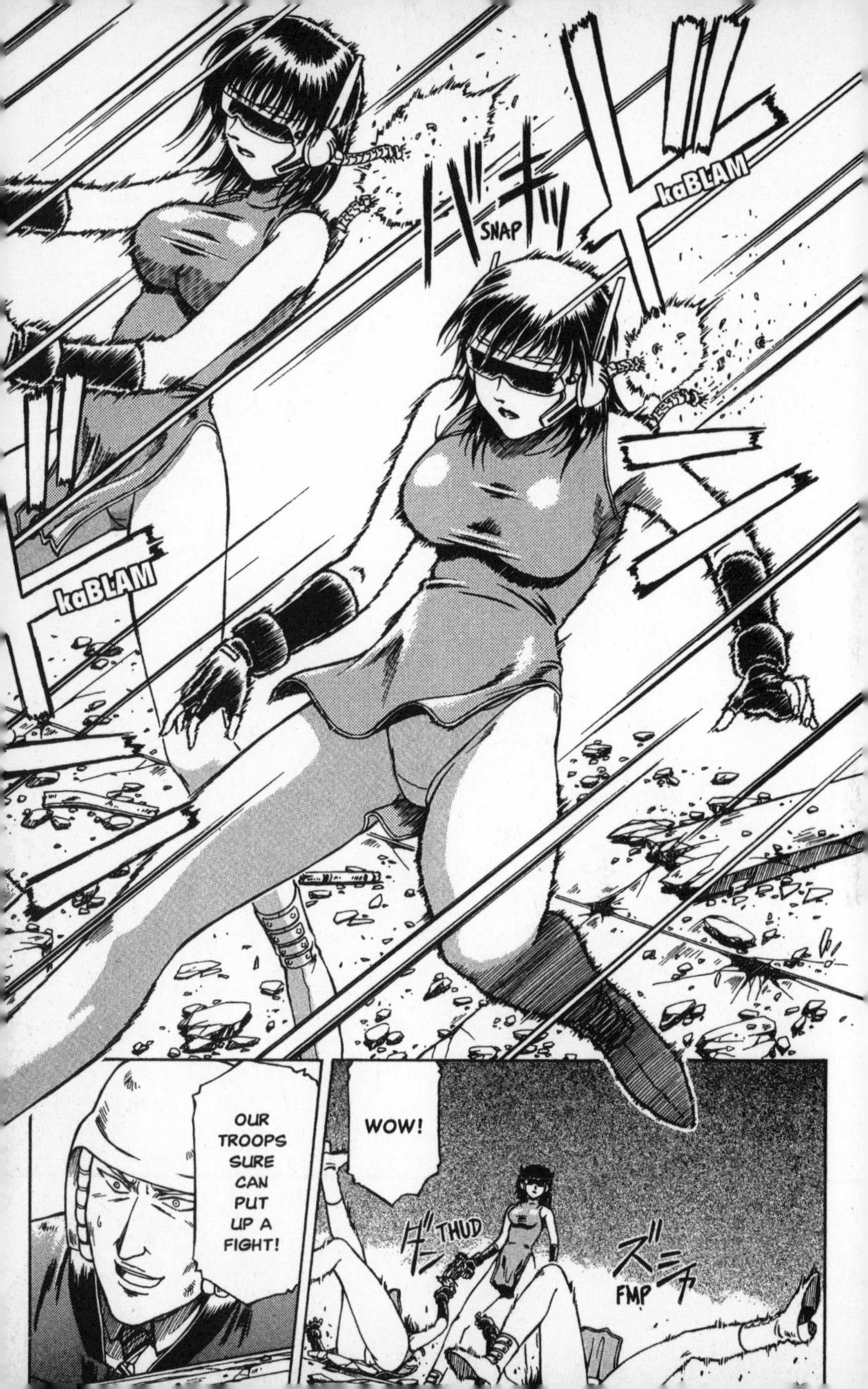

バキッ
SNAP
ドン
kaBLAM
kaBLAM
OUR TROOPS SURE CAN PUT UP A FIGHT!
WOW!
ザー
THUD
ズシャ
FMP

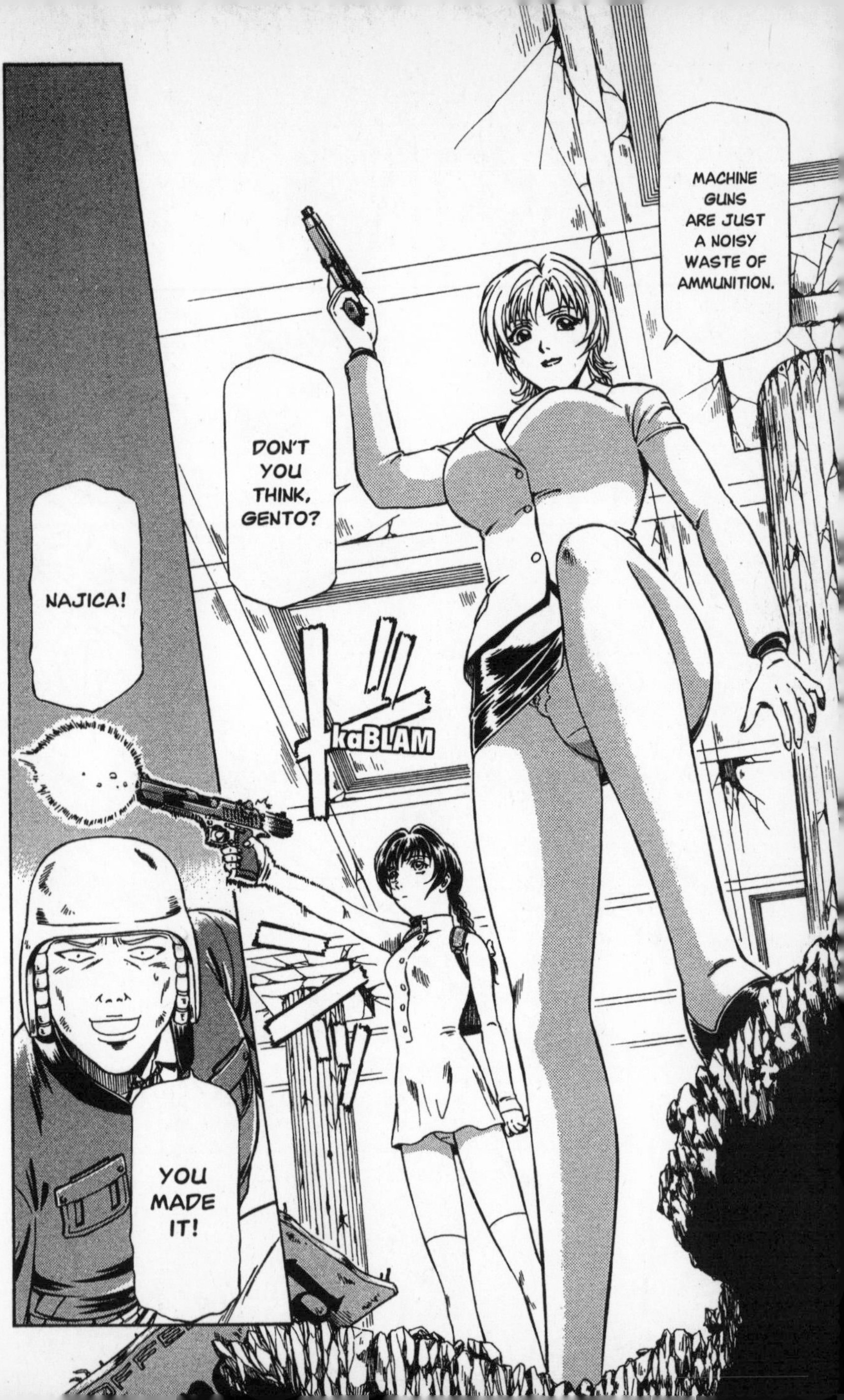
MACHINE GUNS ARE JUST A NOISY WASTE OF AMMUNITION.
DON'T YOU THINK, GENTO?
kaBLAM
NAJICA!
YOU MADE IT!

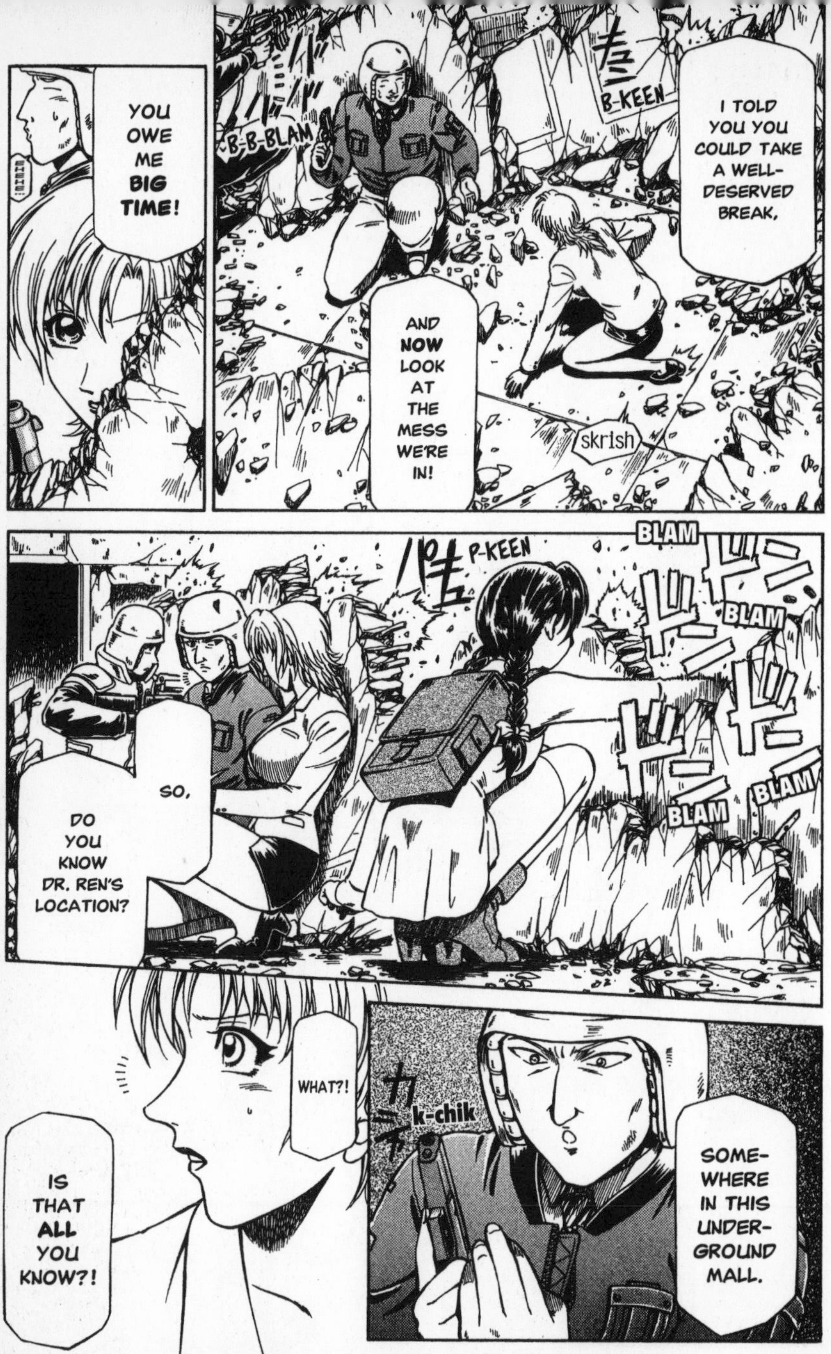

B-KEEN
I TOLD YOU YOU COULD TAKE A WELL-DESERVED BREAK,
B-B-BLAM
AND NOW LOOK AT THE MESS WE'RE IN!
skrish
YOU OWE ME BIG TIME!
BLAM
BLAM
P-KEEN
BLAM
BLAM
SO,
DO YOU KNOW DR. REN'S LOCATION?
k-chik
SOME-WHERE IN THIS UNDER-GROUND MALL.
WHAT?!
IS THAT ALL YOU KNOW?!

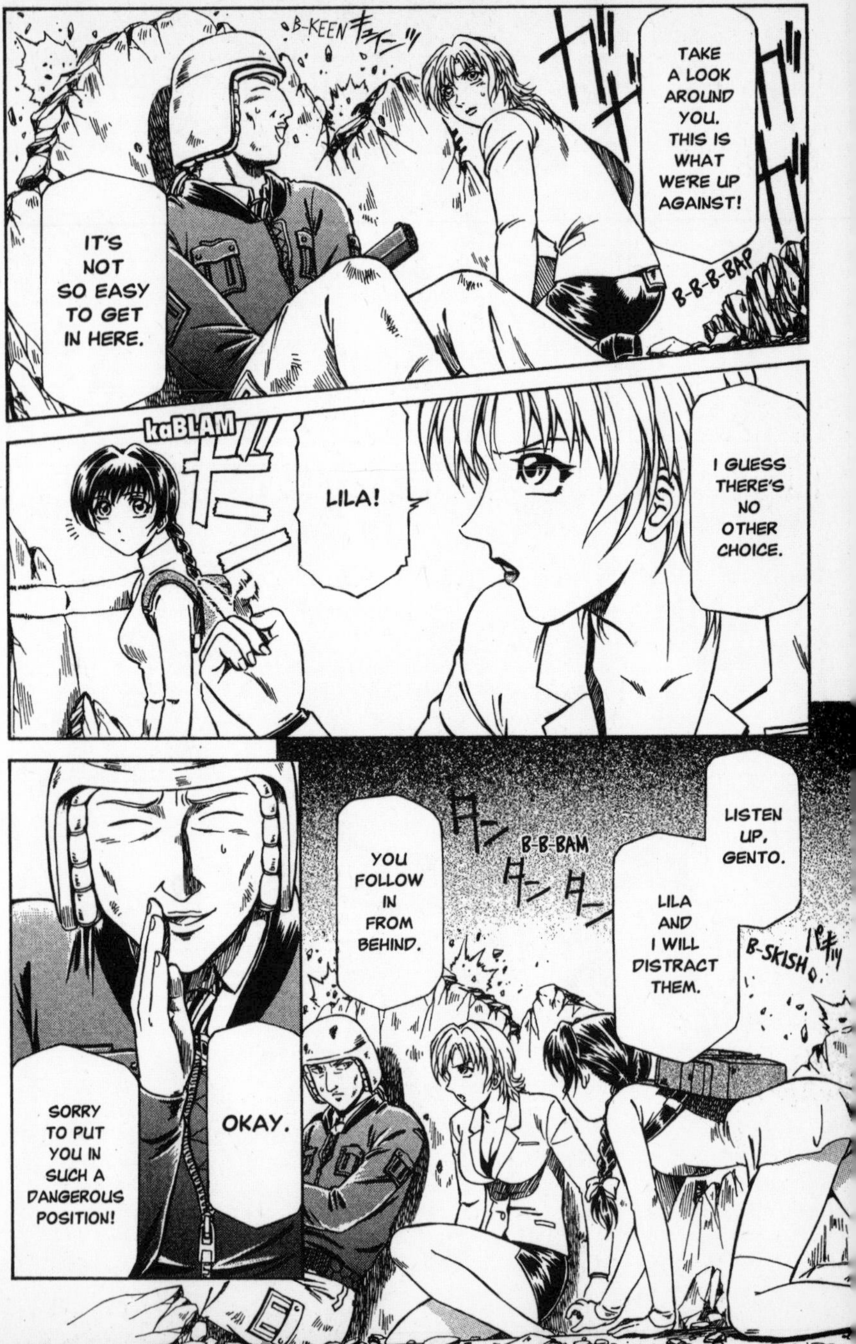

TAKE A LOOK AROUND YOU. THIS IS WHAT WE'RE UP AGAINST!
B-KEEN
B-B-B-BAP
IT'S NOT SO EASY TO GET IN HERE.
I GUESS THERE'S NO OTHER CHOICE.
LILA!
kaBLAM
LISTEN UP, GENTO.
LILA AND I WILL DISTRACT THEM.
B-SKISH
B-B-BAM
YOU FOLLOW IN FROM BEHIND.
OKAY.
SORRY TO PUT YOU IN SUCH A DANGEROUS POSITION!

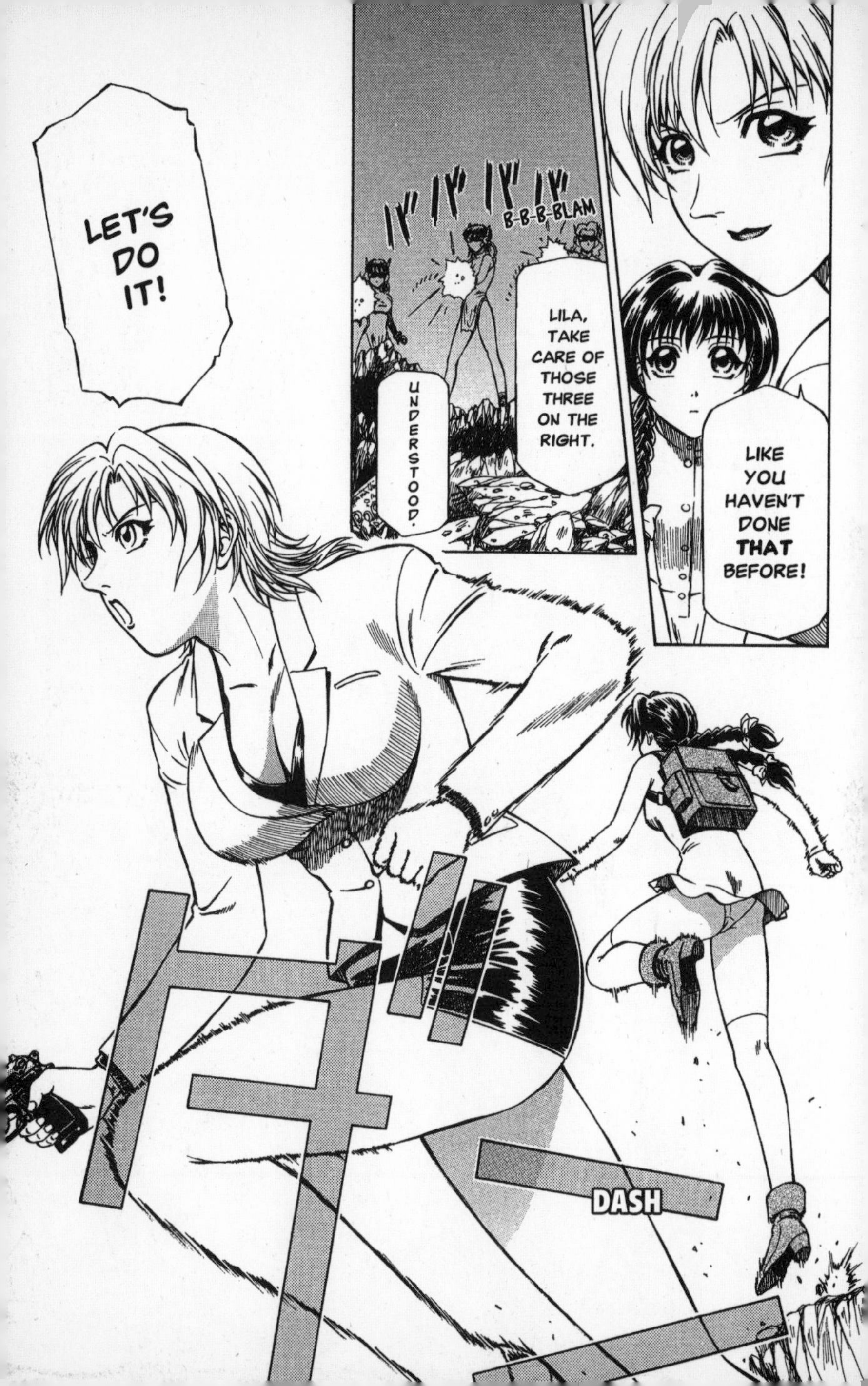
LIKE YOU HAVEN'T DONE THAT BEFORE!
LILA, TAKE CARE OF THOSE THREE ON THE RIGHT.
UNDERSTOOD.
B-B-B-BLAM
LET'S DO IT!
DASH

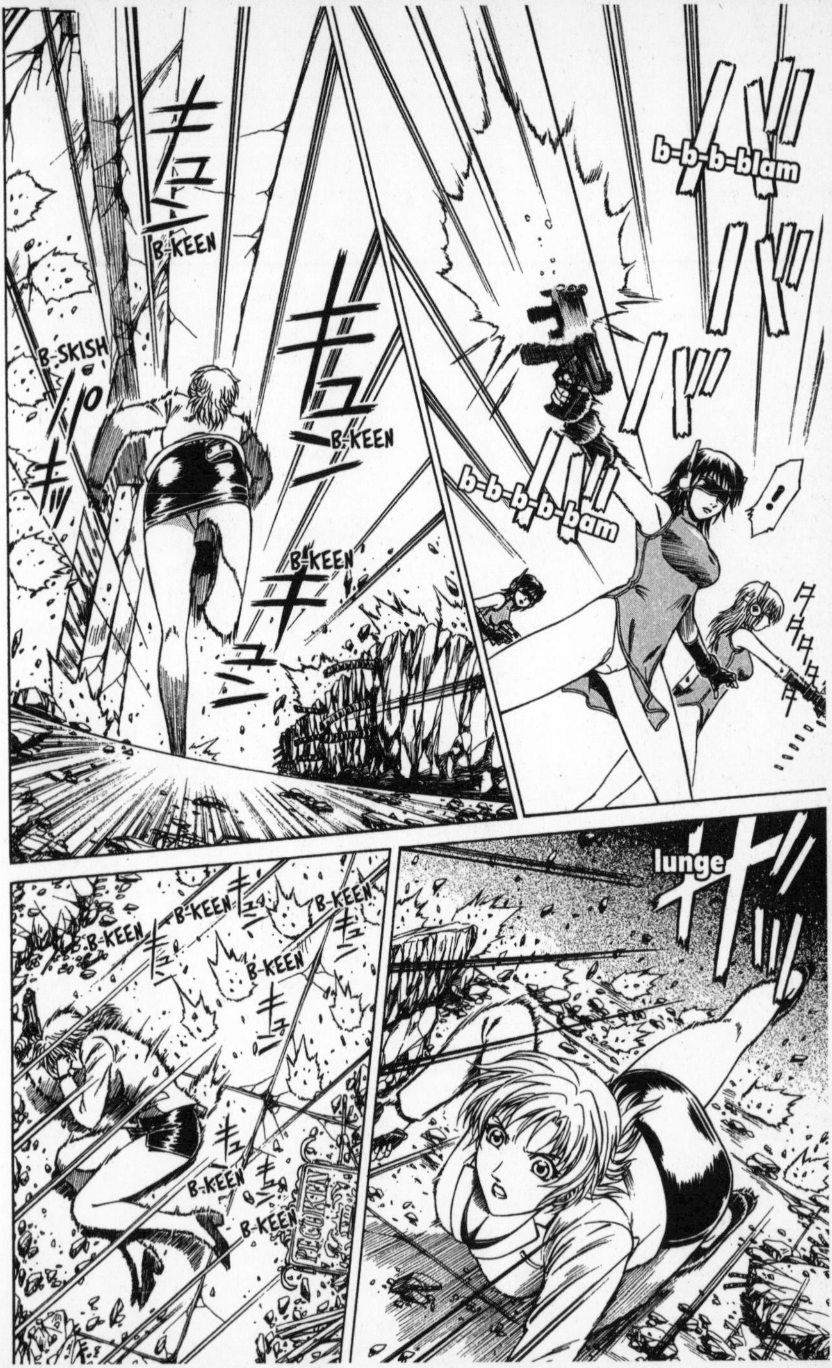
b-b-b-blam
b-b-b-b-bam
!
B-KEEN
B-KEEN
B-KEEN
B-SKISH
lunge
B-KEEN
B-KEEN
B-KEEN
B-KEEN
B-KEEN
B-KEEN

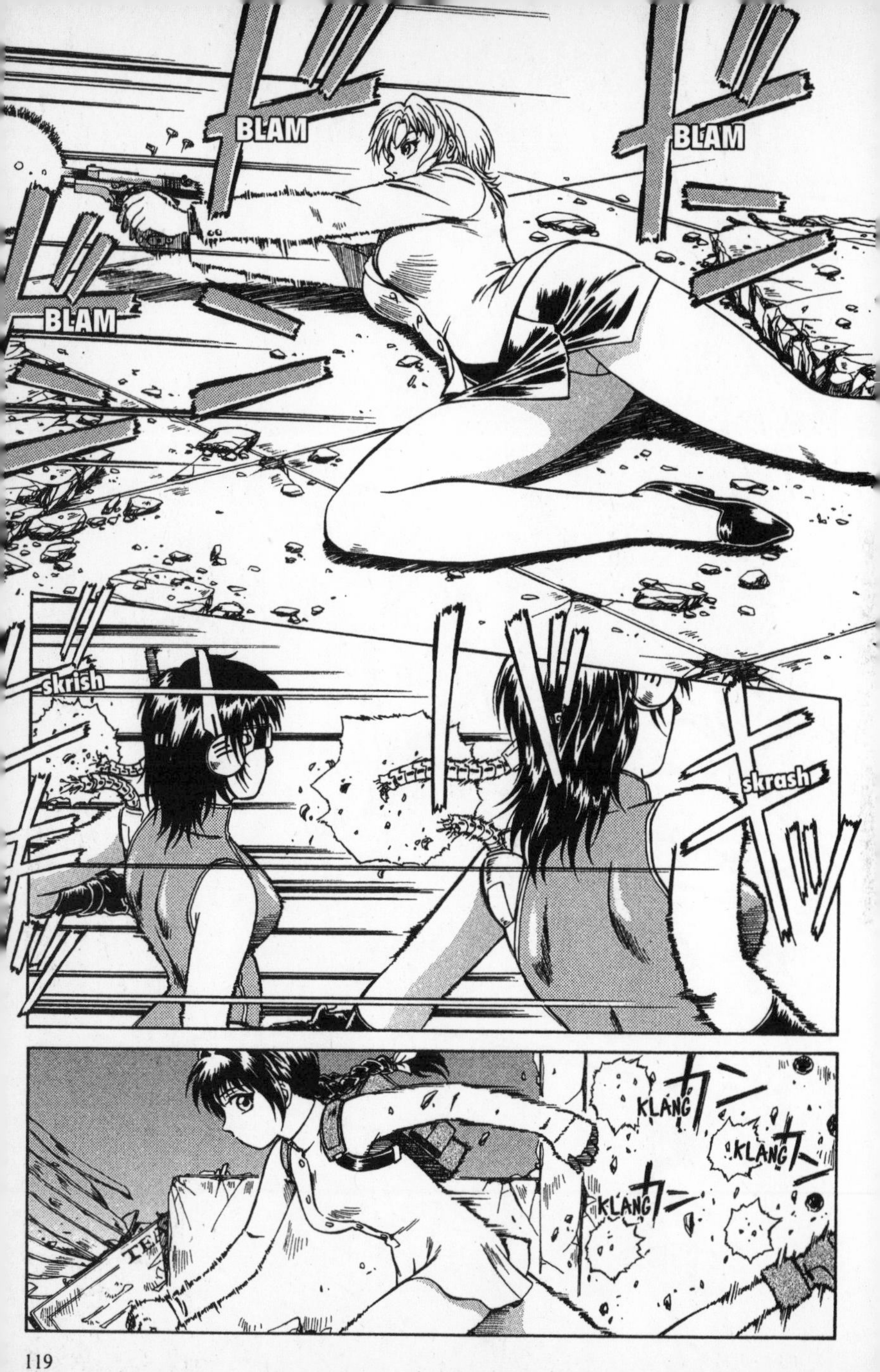
BLAM
BLAM
BLAM
skrish
skrash
KLANG
KLANG
KLANG

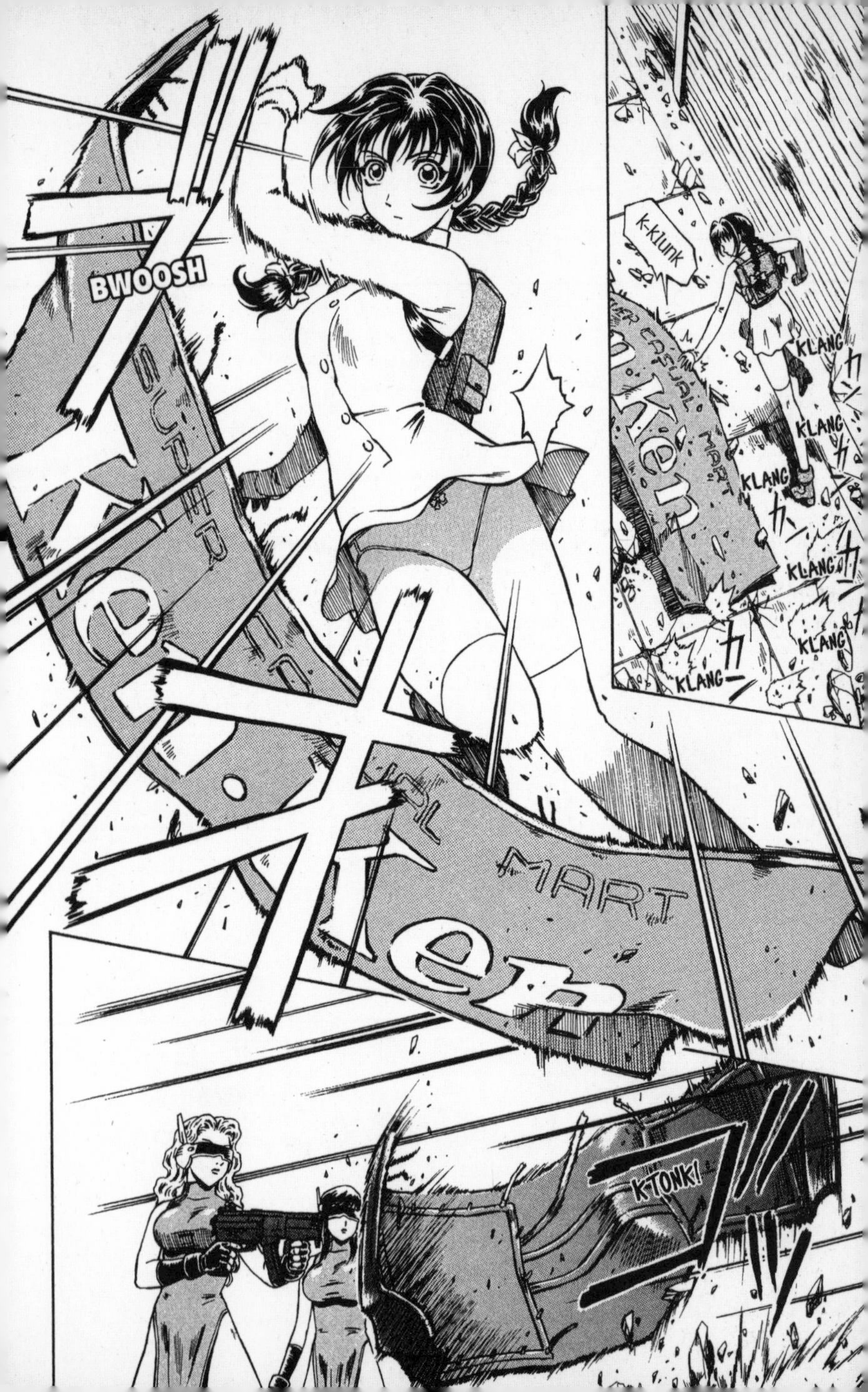
k-klunk
KLANG
KLANG
KLANG
KLANG
KLANG
KLANG
BWOOSH
SUPER
MART
K-TONK!

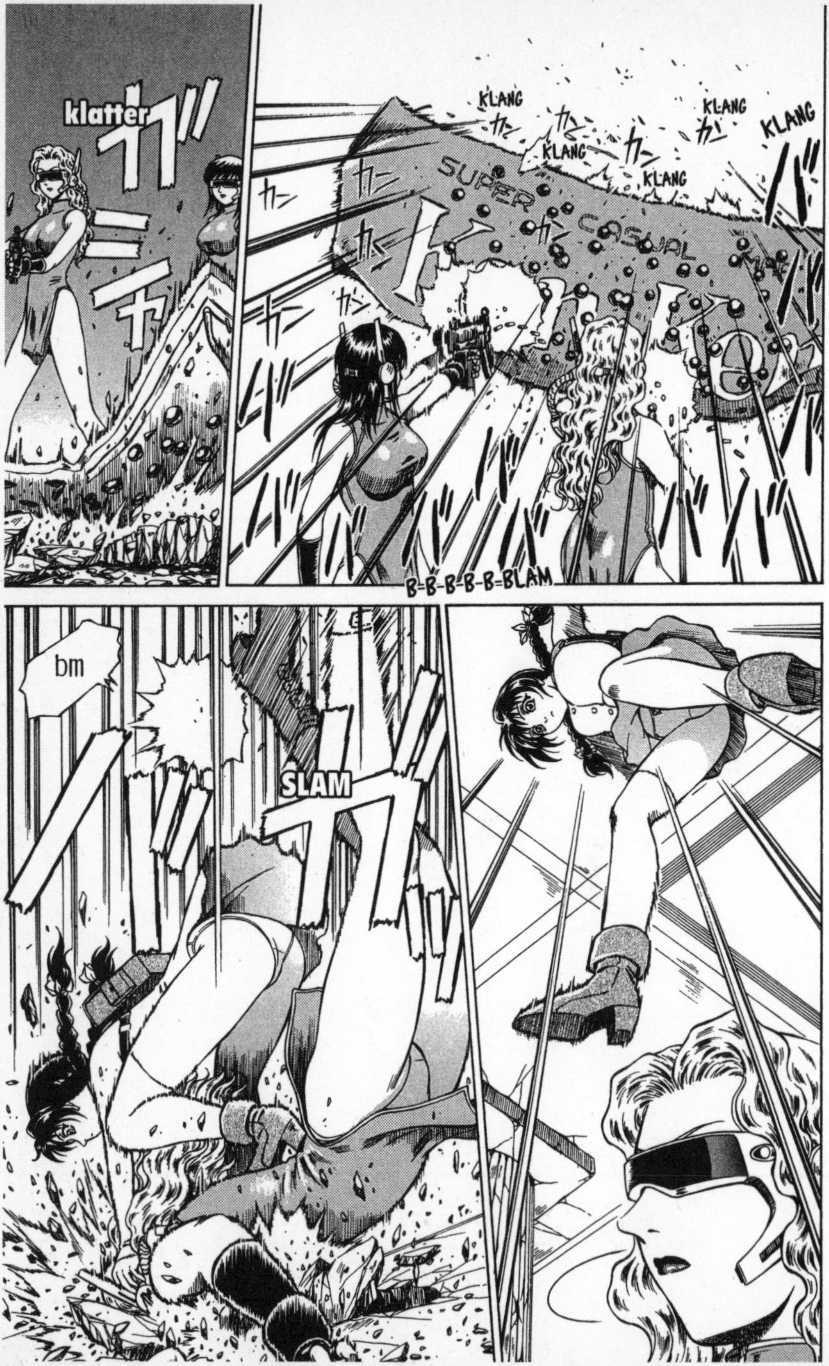

klatter
KLANG
KLANG
KLANG
KLANG
KLANG
SUPER CASUAL
B-B-B-B-B-BLAM
bm
SLAM

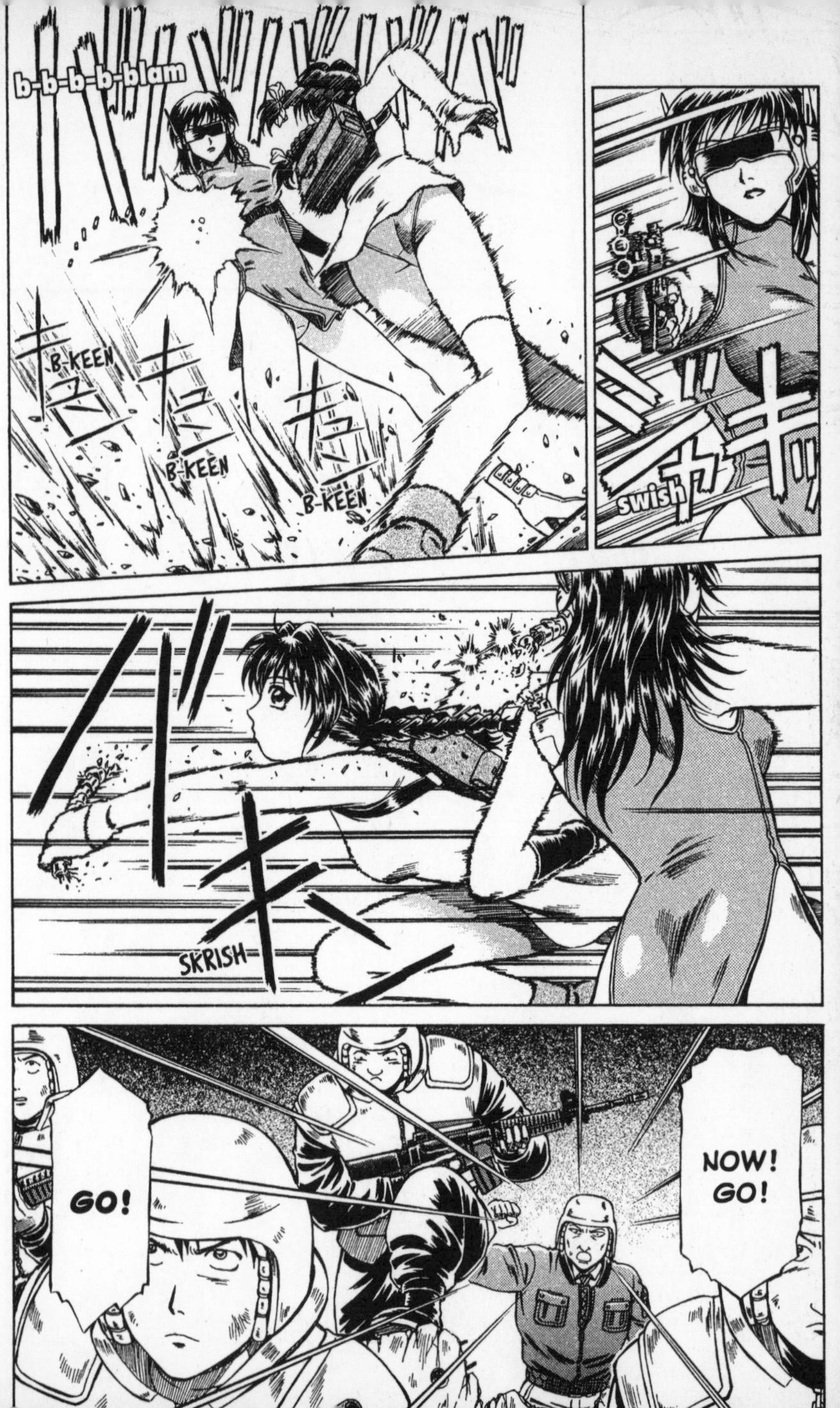

b-b-b-b-blam
B-KEEN
B-KEEN
B-KEEN
swish
SKRISH
NOW! GO!
GO!

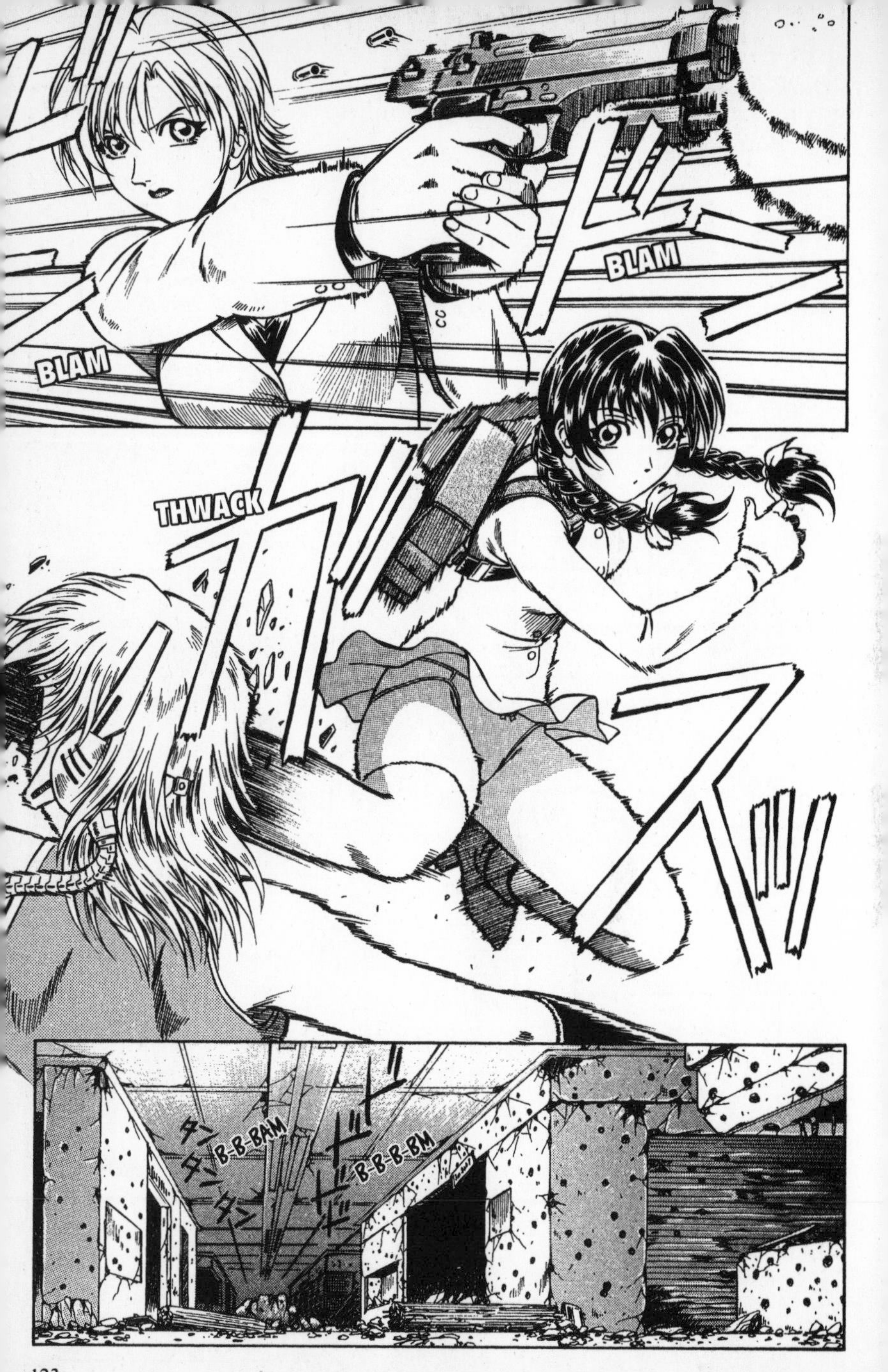
BLAM
BLAM
THWACK
B-B-B-BM
B-B-BAM
タン
タン
タン

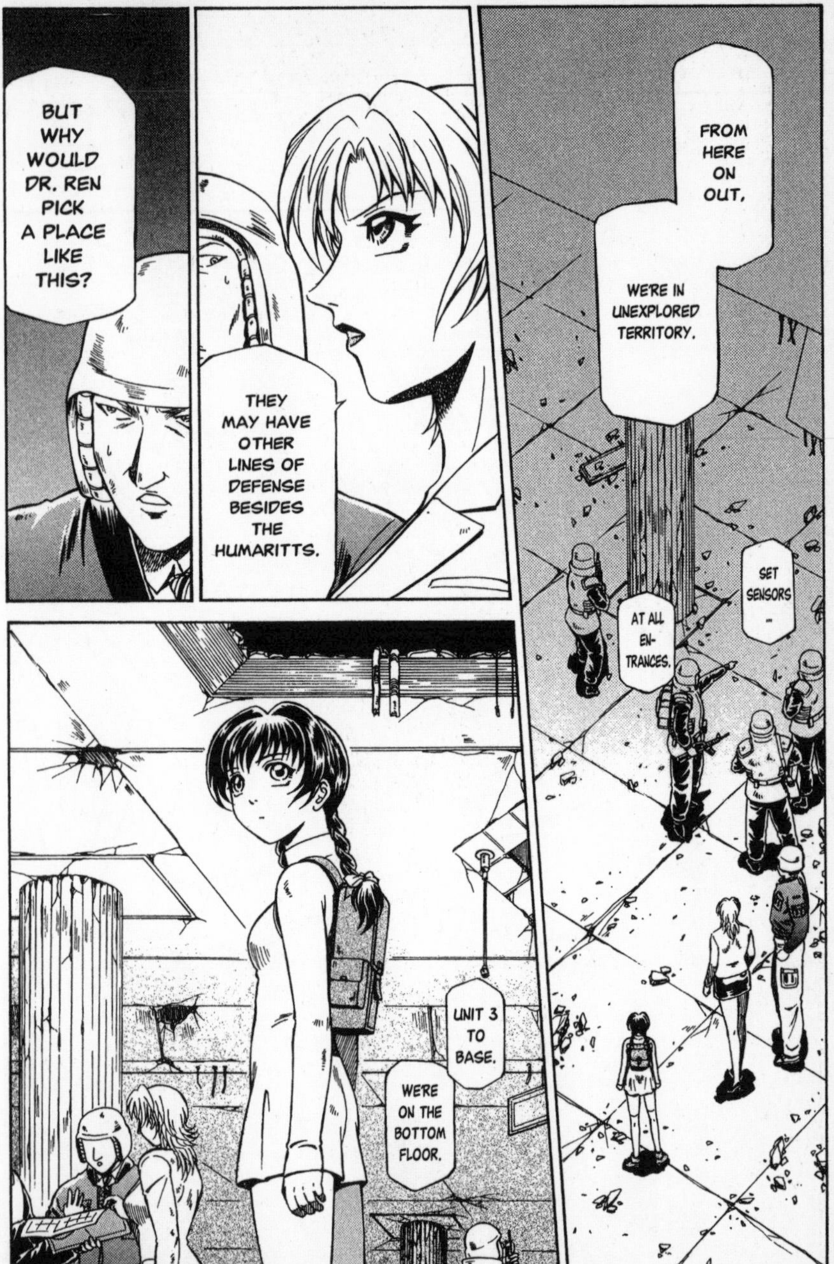

BUT WHY WOULD DR. REN PICK A PLACE LIKE THIS?
THEY MAY HAVE OTHER LINES OF DEFENSE BESIDES THE HUMARITTS.
FROM HERE ON OUT,
WE'RE IN UNEXPLORED TERRITORY.
SET SENSORS...
AT ALL EN-TRANCES.
UNIT 3 TO BASE.
WE'RE ON THE BOTTOM FLOOR.

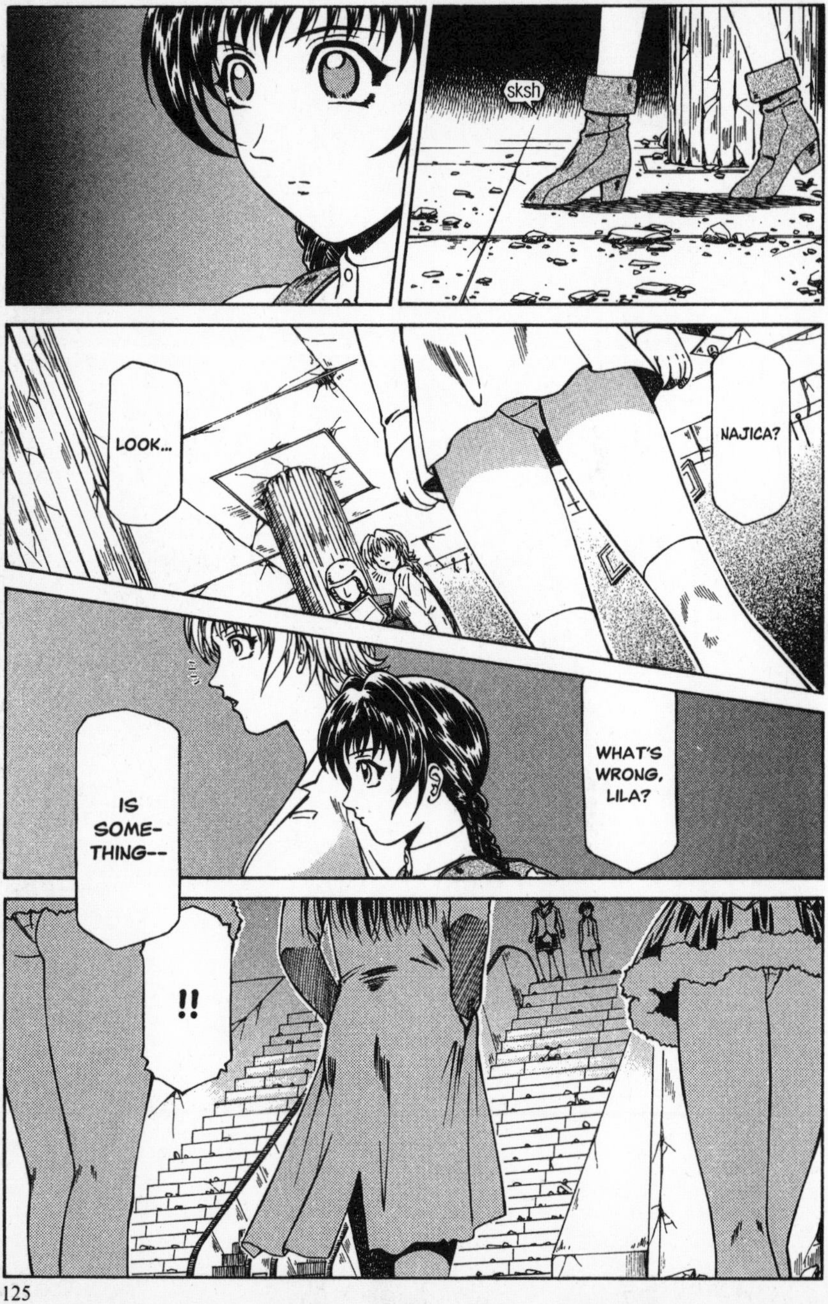
sksh
NAJICA?
LOOK...
WHAT'S WRONG, LILA?
IS SOMETHING--
!!

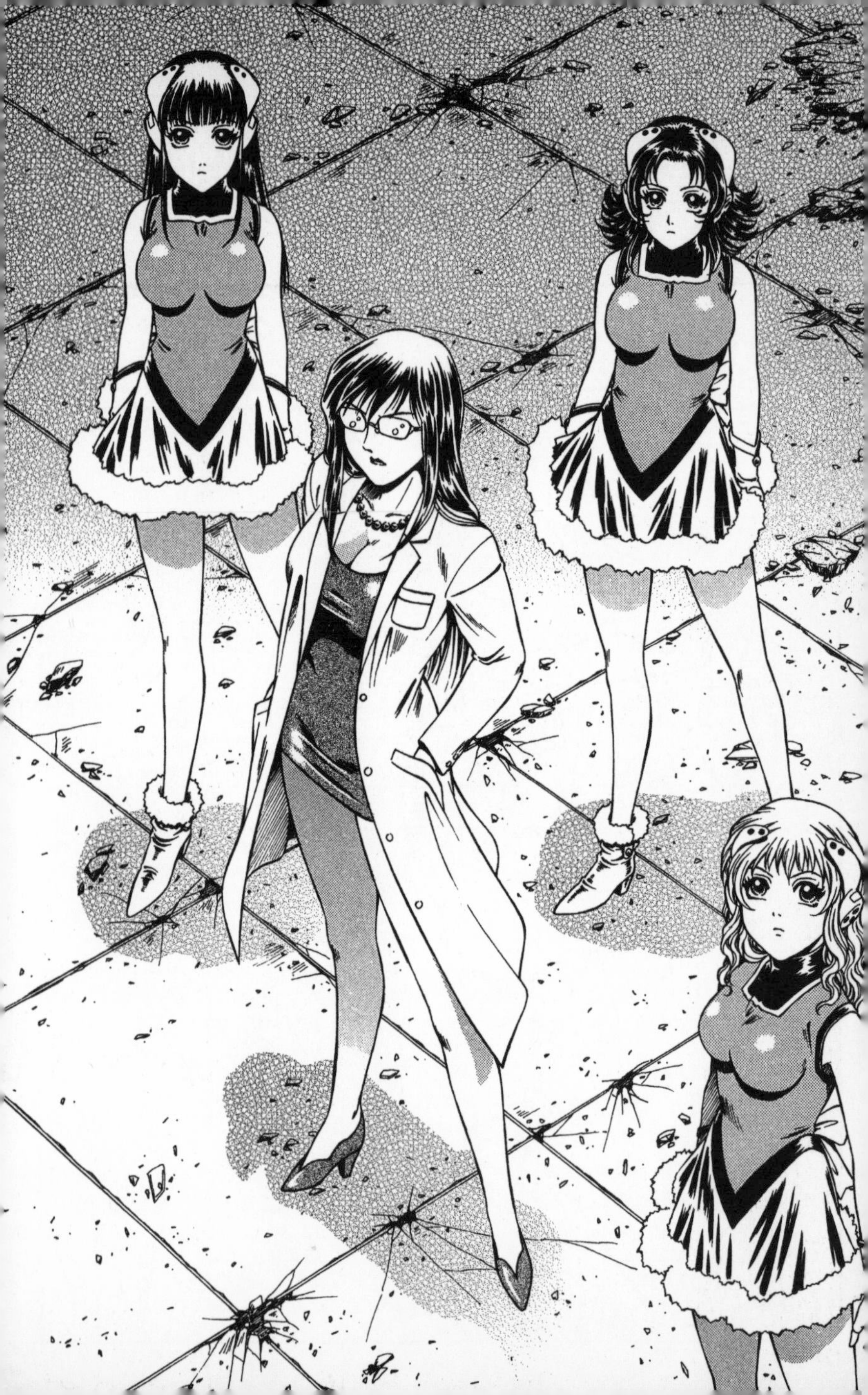

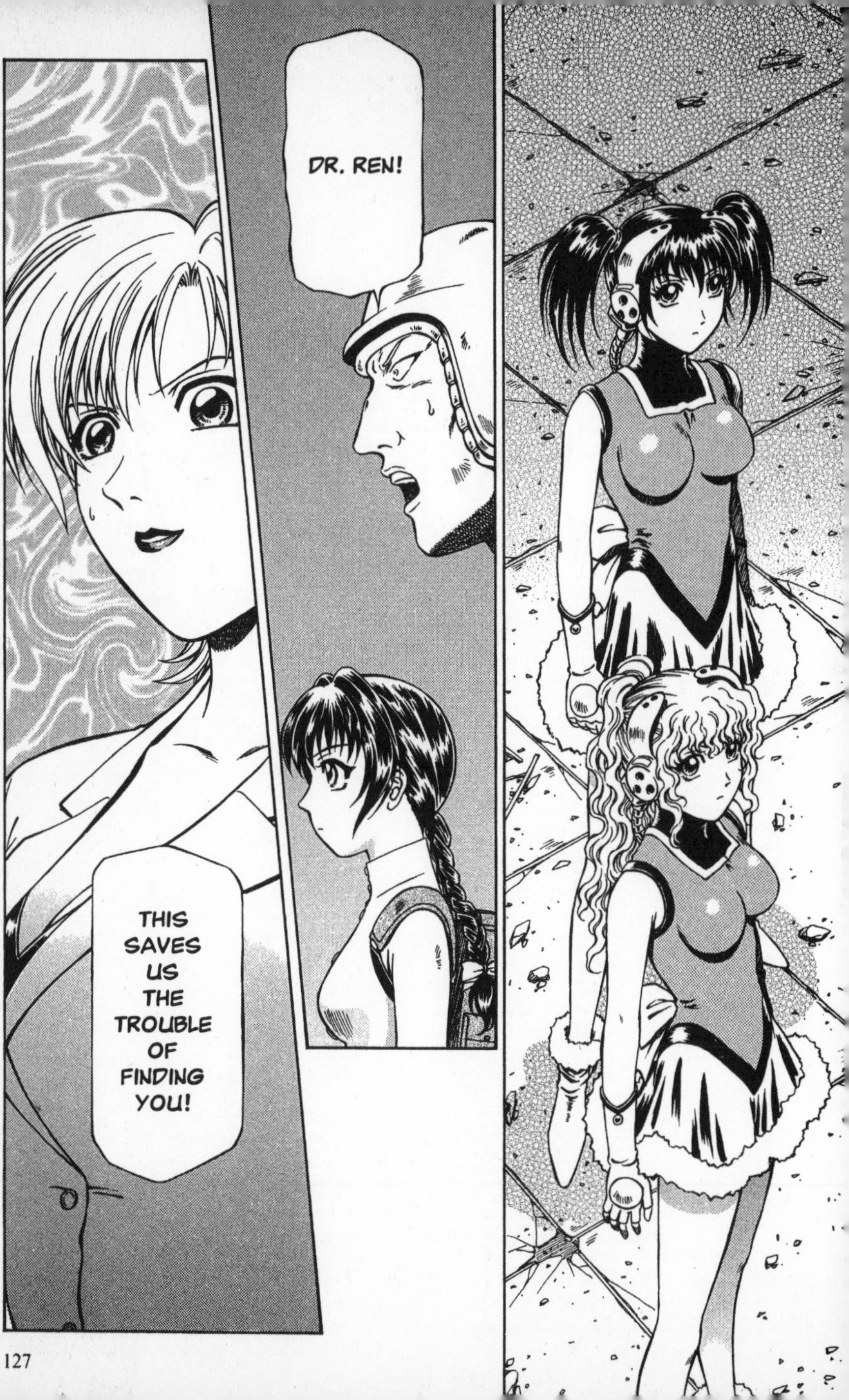

DR. REN!
THIS SAVES US THE TROUBLE OF FINDING YOU!

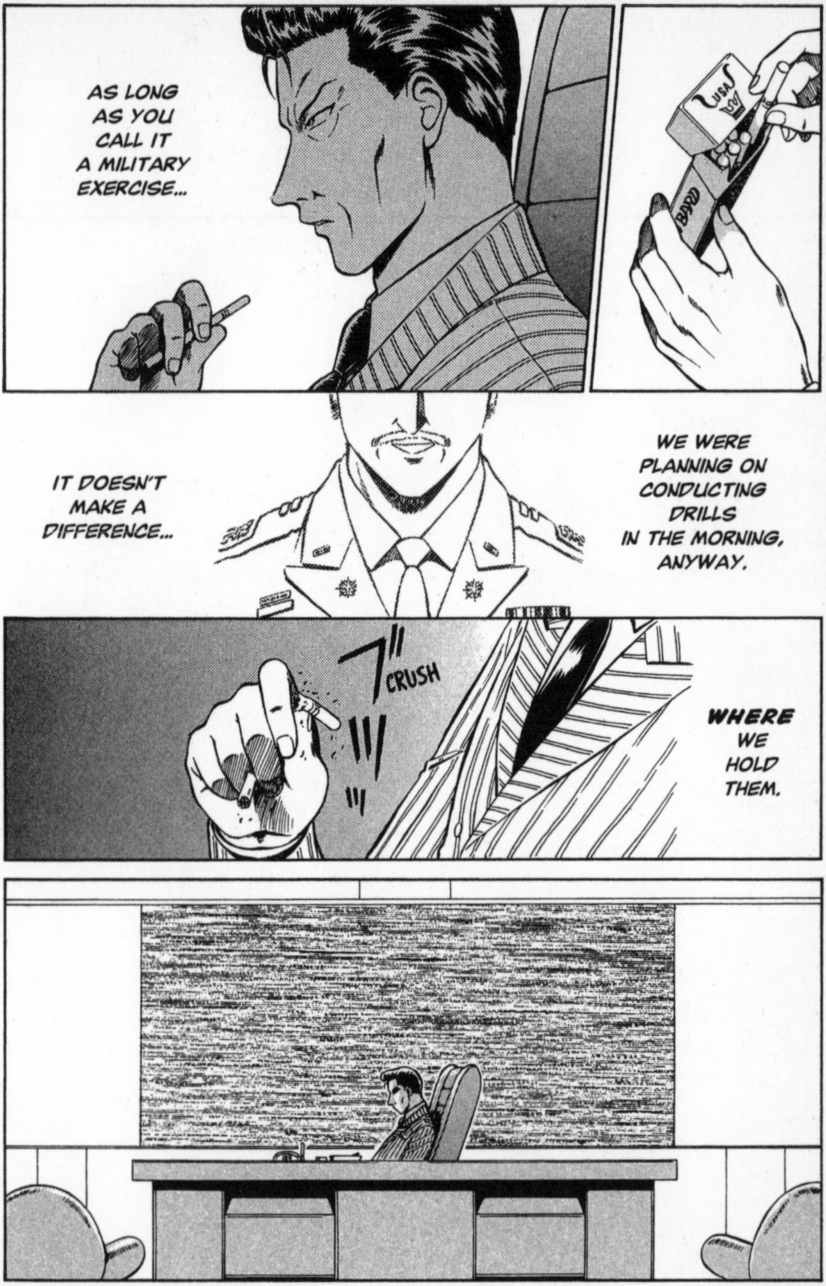
AS LONG AS YOU CALL IT A MILITARY EXERCISE...
USA
BARD
IT DOESN'T MAKE A DIFFERENCE...
WE WERE PLANNING ON CONDUCTING DRILLS IN THE MORNING, ANYWAY.
CRUSH
WHERE WE HOLD THEM.

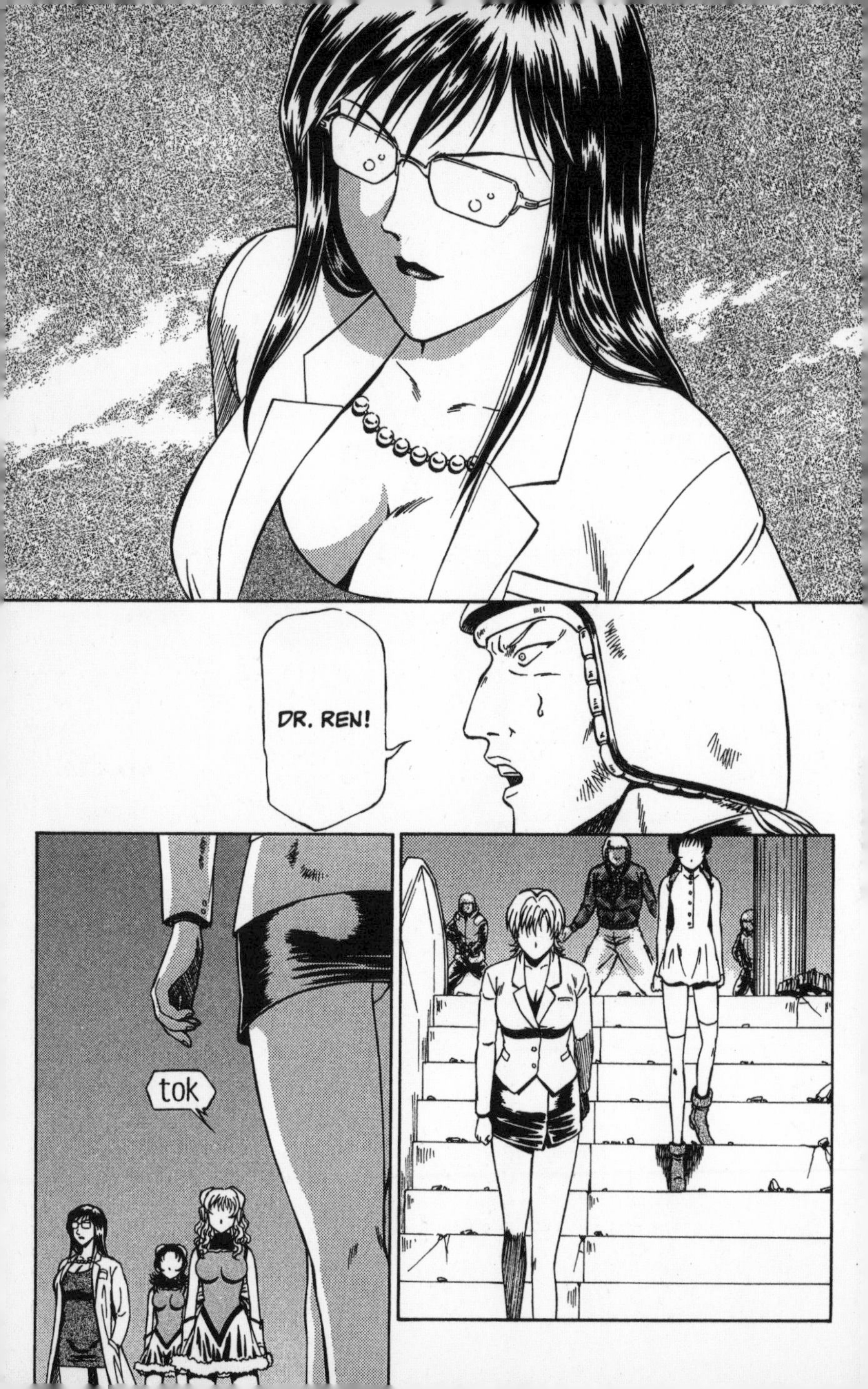
DR. REN!
tok

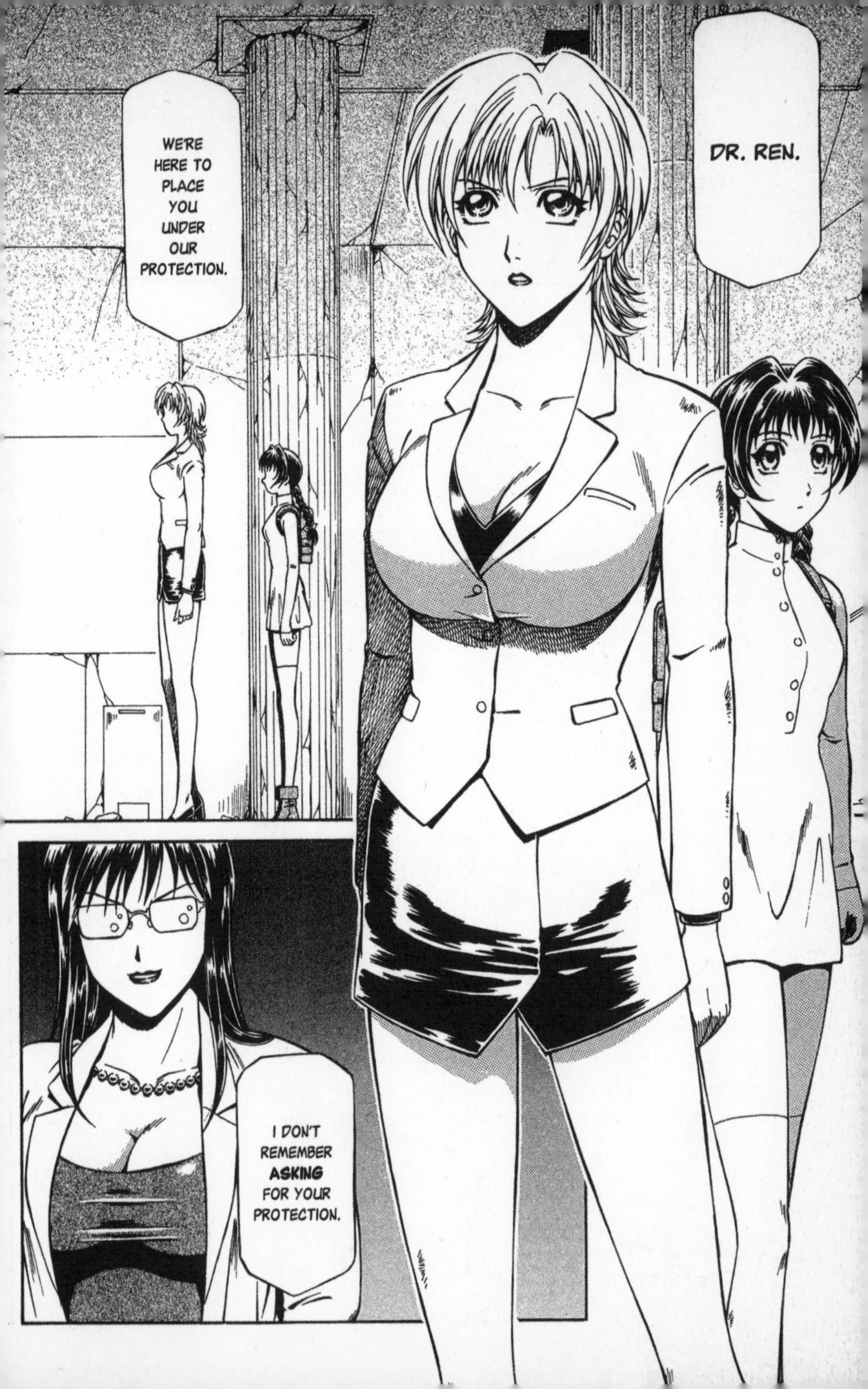
DR. REN.
WE'RE HERE TO PLACE YOU UNDER OUR PROTECTION.
I DON'T REMEMBER **ASKING** FOR YOUR PROTECTION.

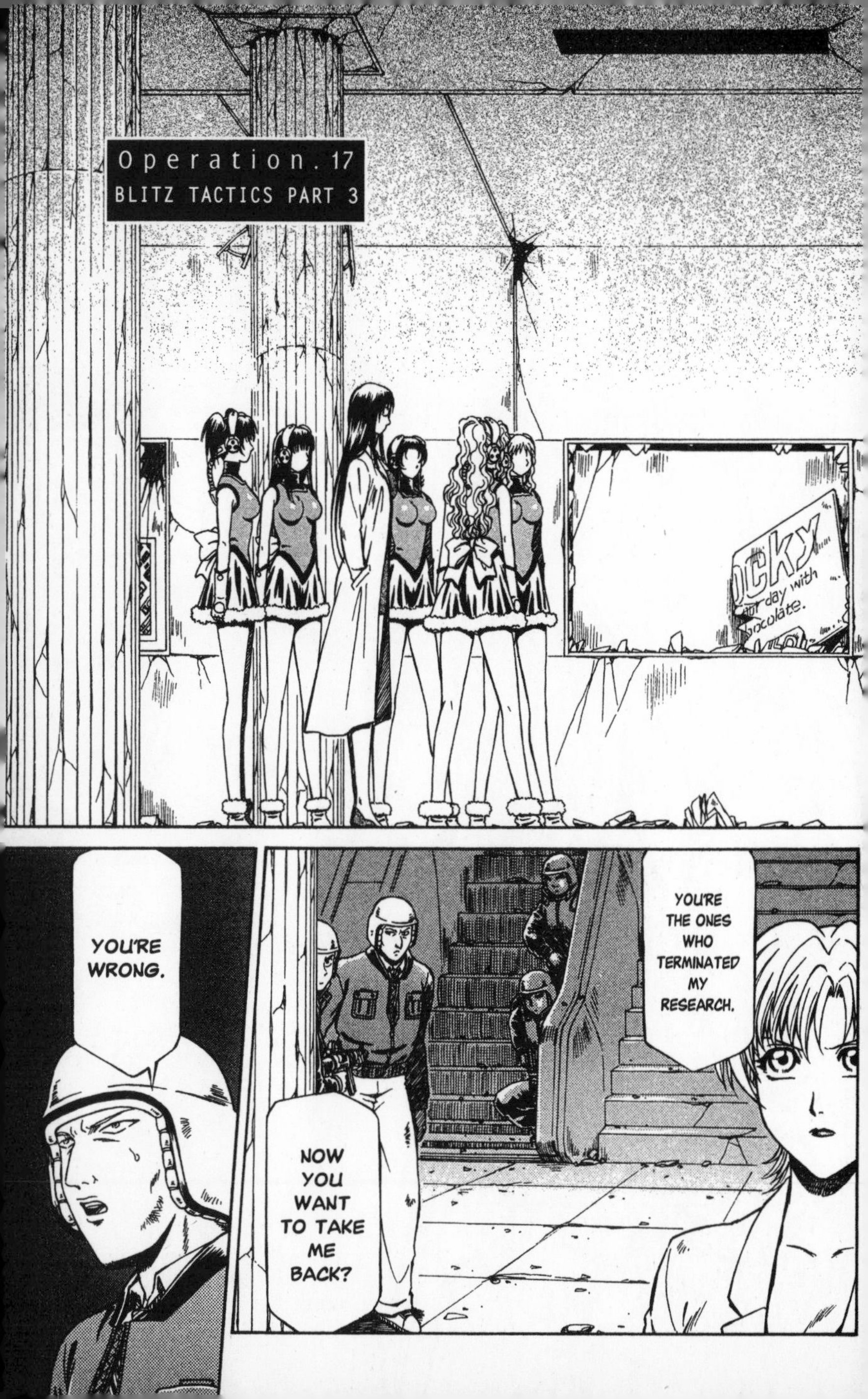
Operation. 17
BLITZ TACTICS PART 3
YOU'RE THE ONES WHO TERMINATED MY RESEARCH.
NOW YOU WANT TO TAKE ME BACK?
YOU'RE WRONG.

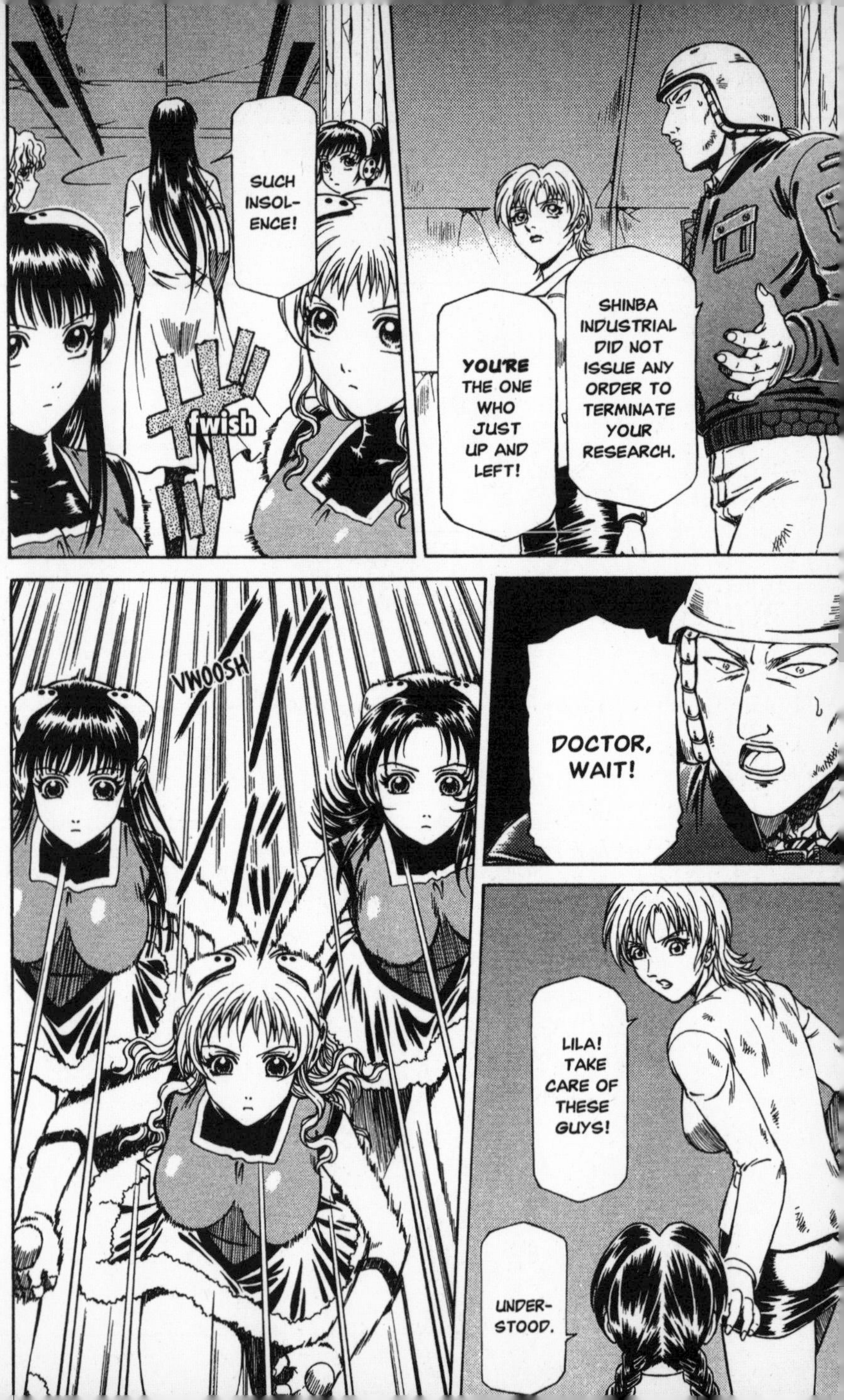
SHINBA INDUSTRIAL DID NOT ISSUE ANY ORDER TO TERMINATE YOUR RESEARCH.
YOU'RE THE ONE WHO JUST UP AND LEFT!
SUCH INSOL-ENCE!
fwish
DOCTOR, WAIT!
LILA! TAKE CARE OF THESE GUYS!
UNDER-STOOD.
VWOOSH

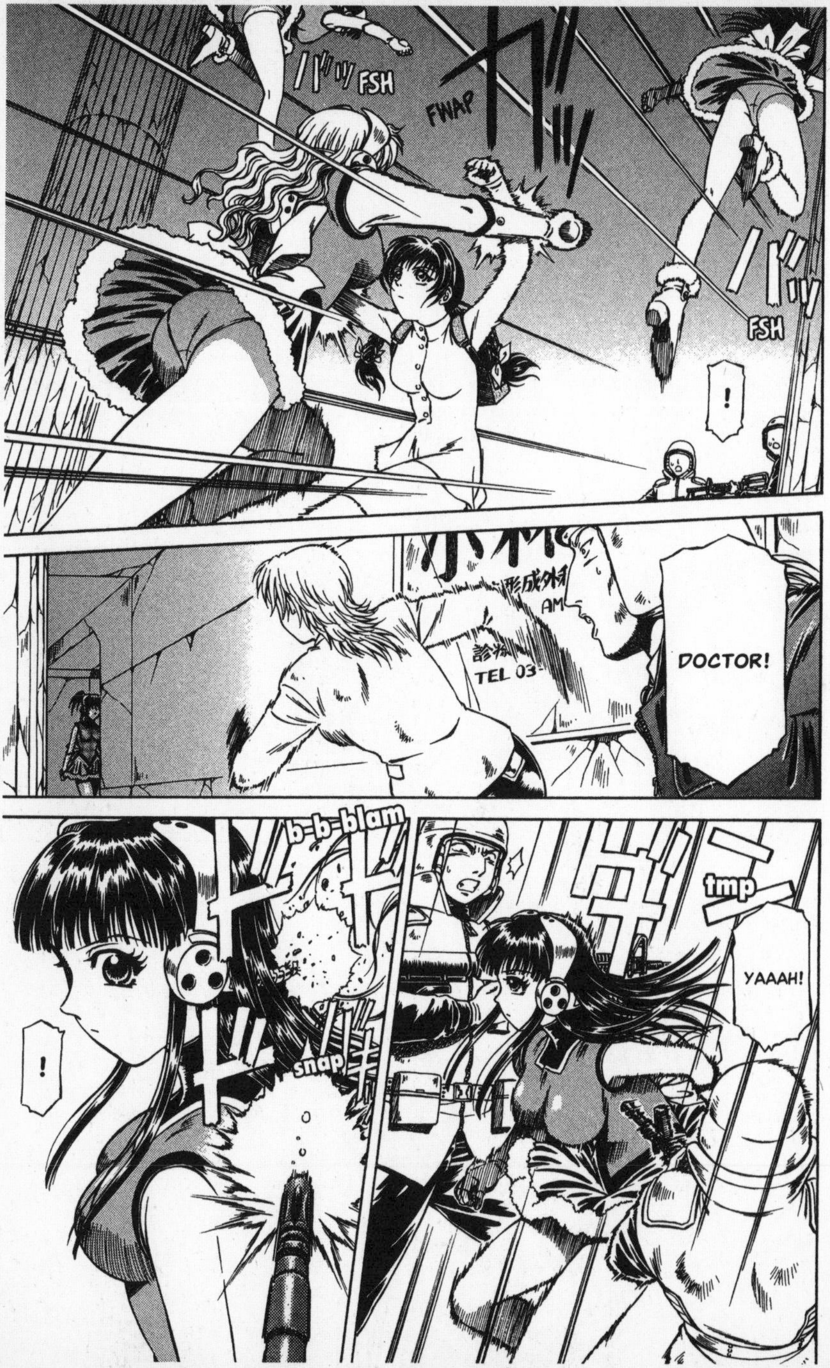
FSH
!
FWAP
FSH
DOCTOR!
TEL 03-
tmp
YAAAH!
b-b-blam
snap
!

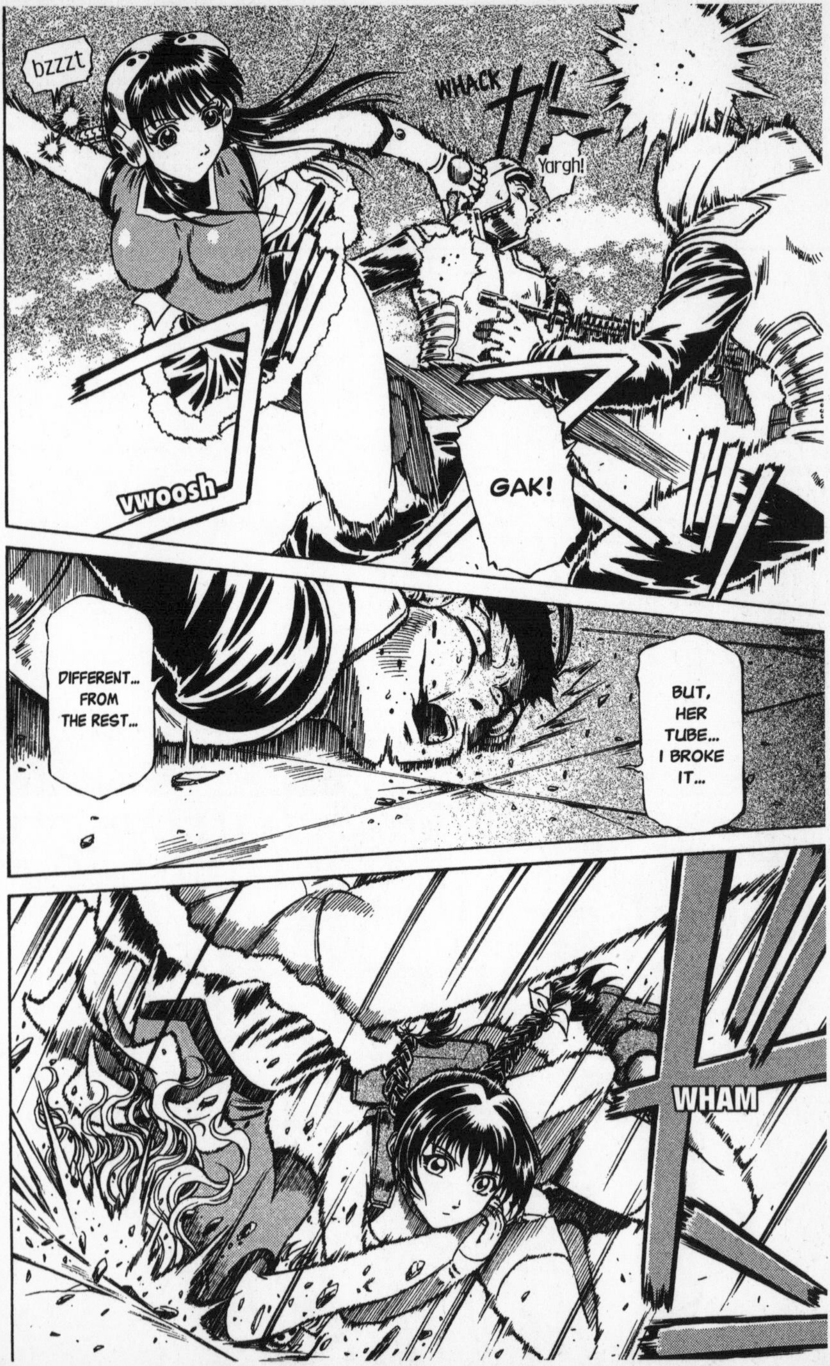
bzzzt
WHACK
Yargh!
vwoosh
GAK!
BUT, HER TUBE... I BROKE IT...
DIFFERENT... FROM THE REST...
WHAM

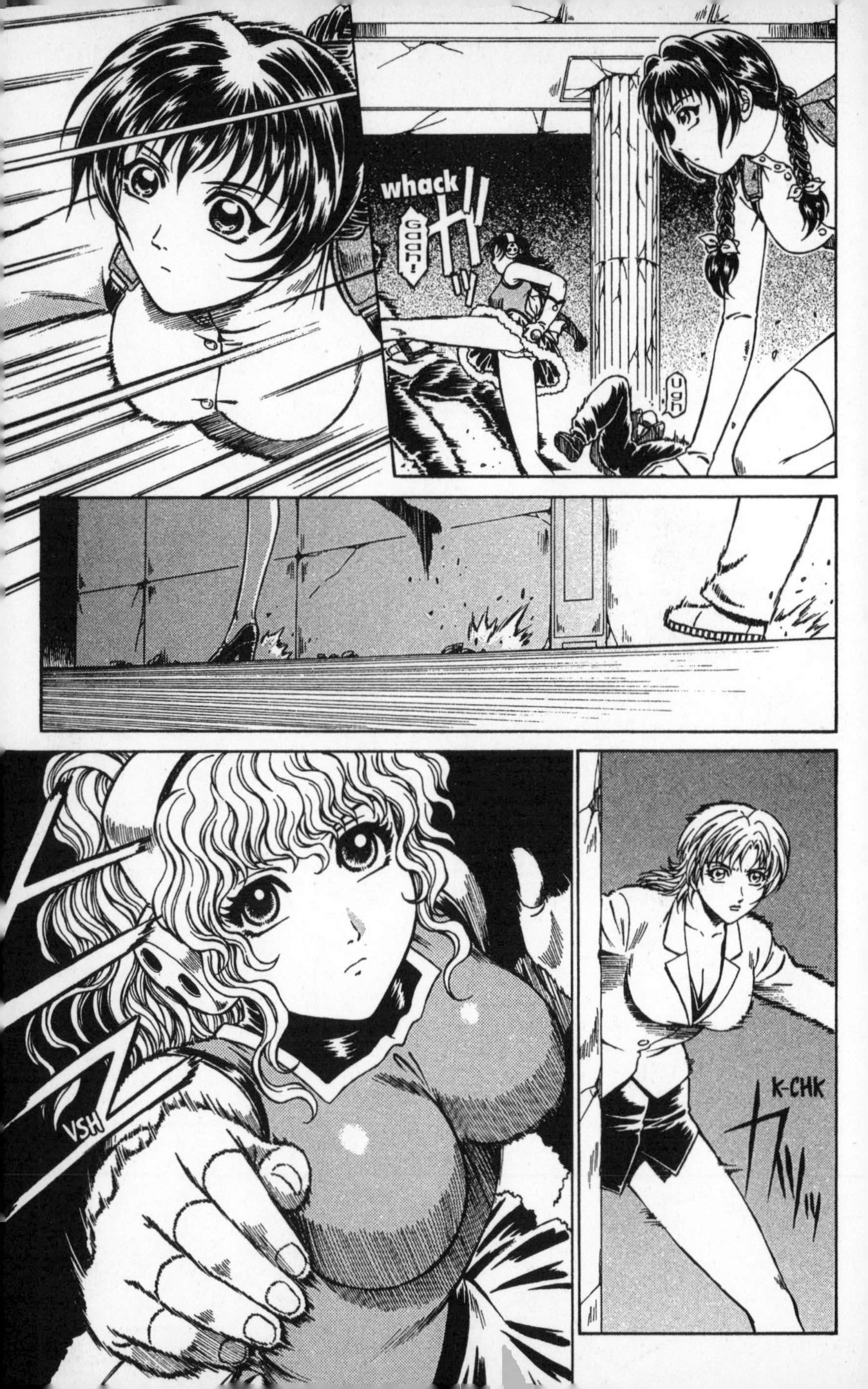
whack
Gaan!
Ugh
VSH
K-CHK

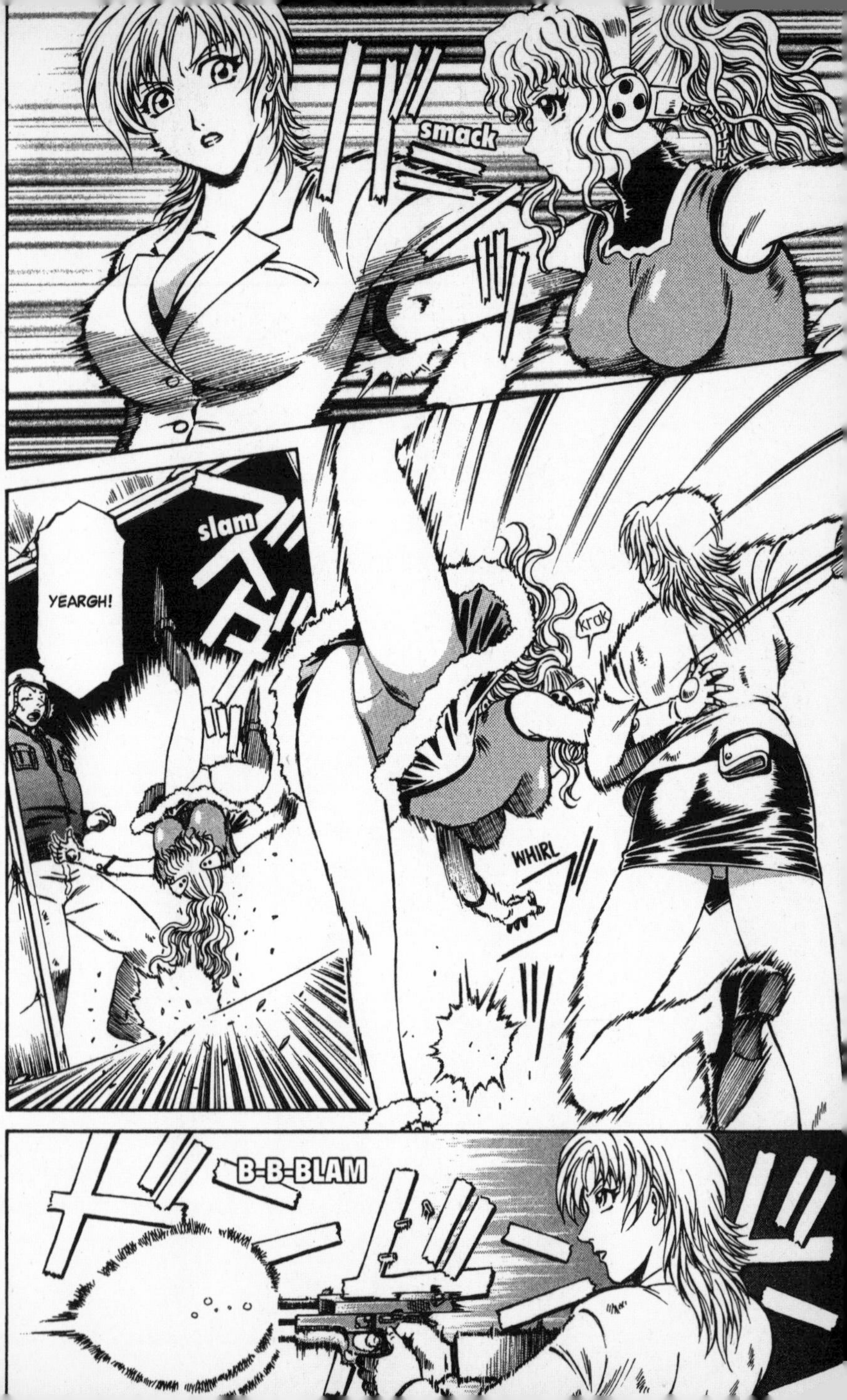

smack
slam
YEARGH!
krak
WHIRL
B-B-BLAM

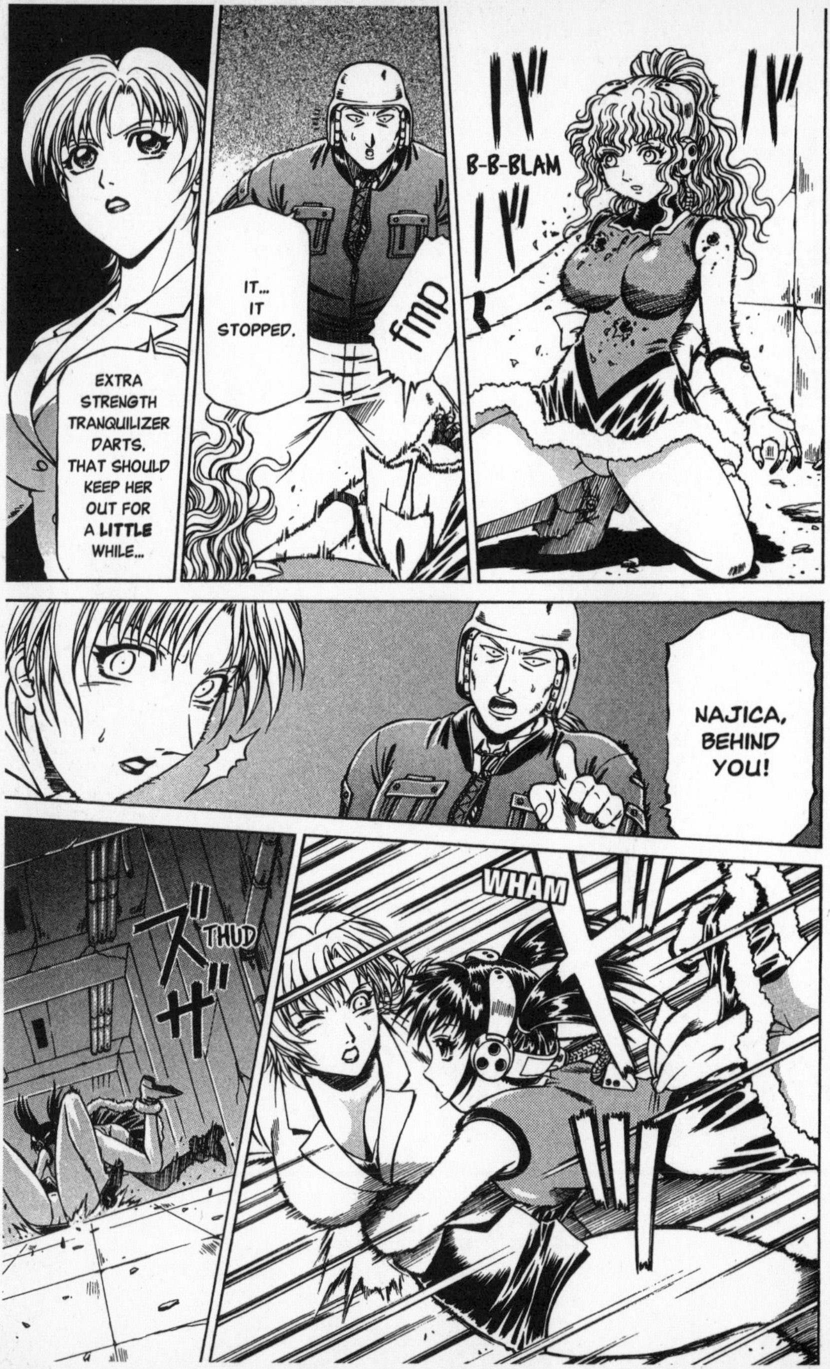
B-B-BLAM
fmp
IT... IT STOPPED.
EXTRA STRENGTH TRANQUILIZER DARTS. THAT SHOULD KEEP HER OUT FOR A **LITTLE** WHILE...
NAJICA, BEHIND YOU!
WHAM
THUD

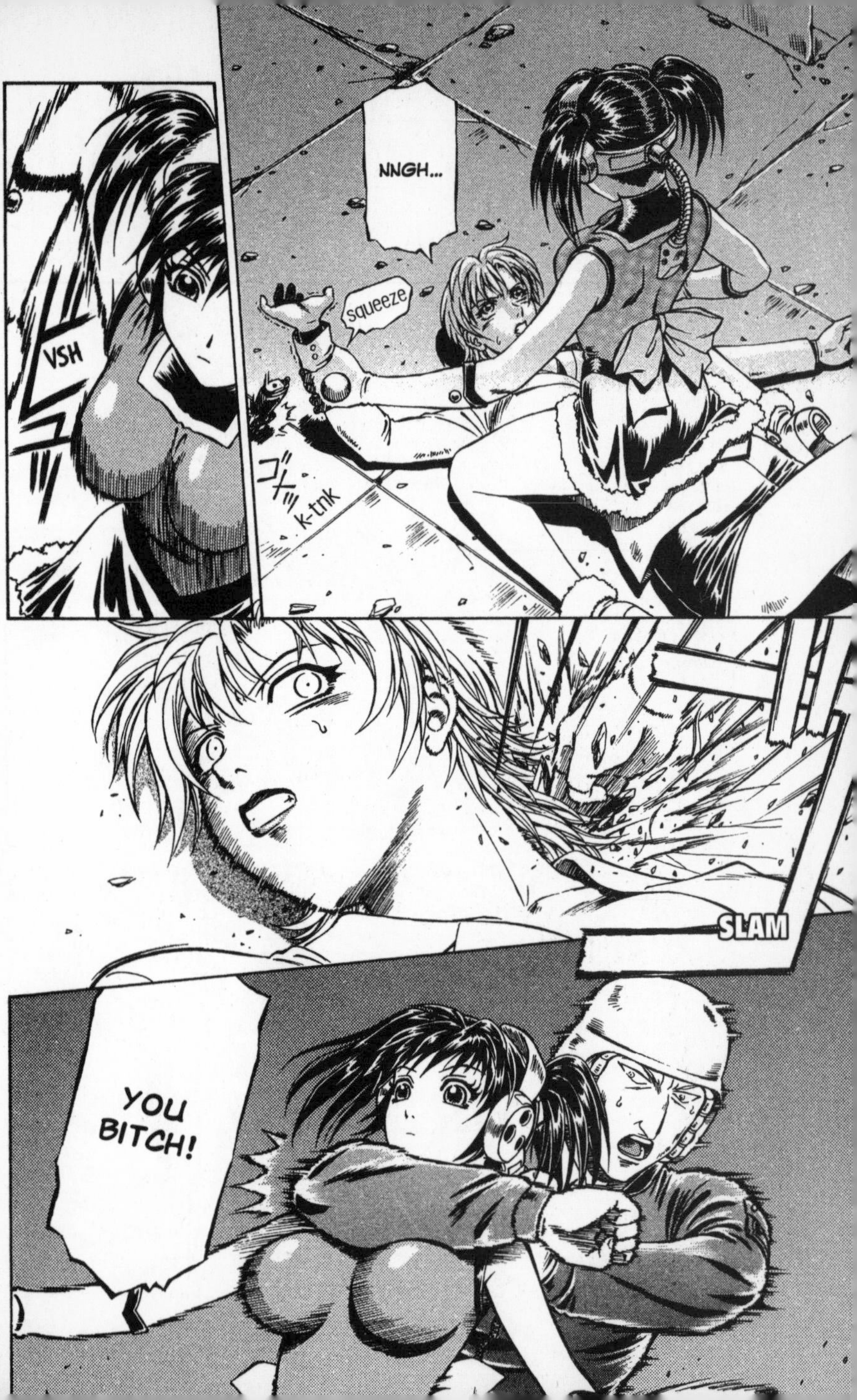
NNGH...
squeeze
VSH
ゴメッ
k-tnk
SLAM
YOU BITCH!

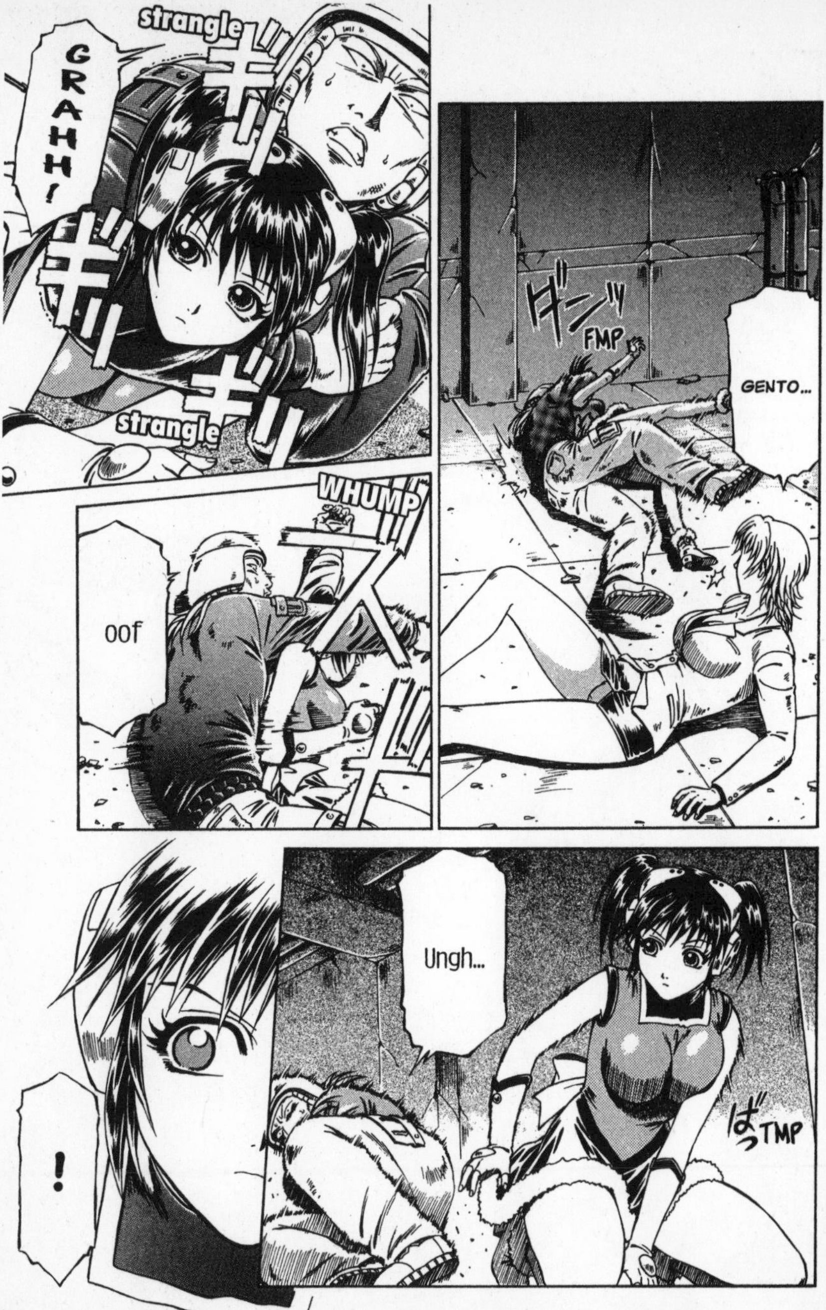

strangle
GRAHH!
strangle
WHUMP
oof
FMP
GENTO...
Ungh...
TMP
!

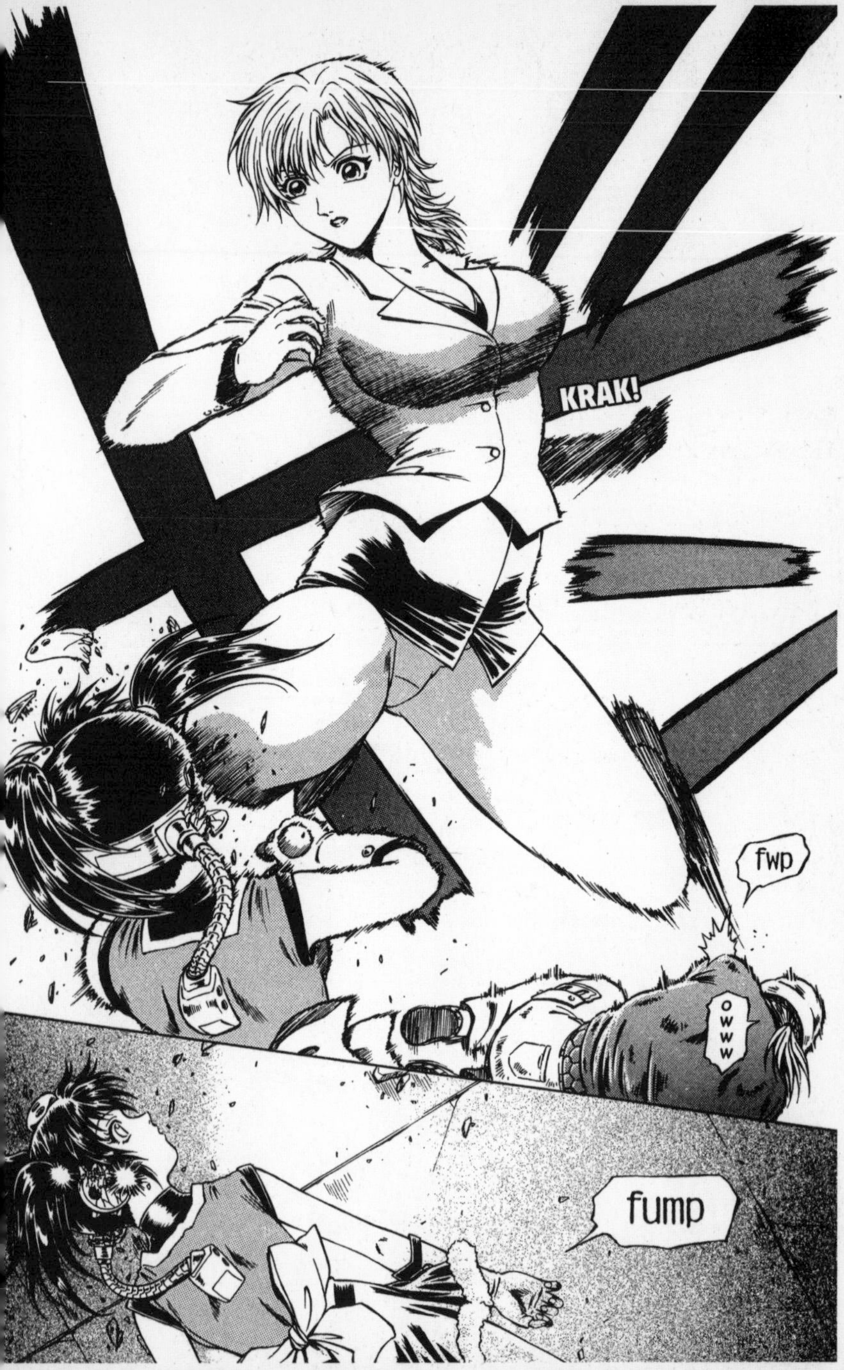
KRAK!
fwp
OWWW
fump

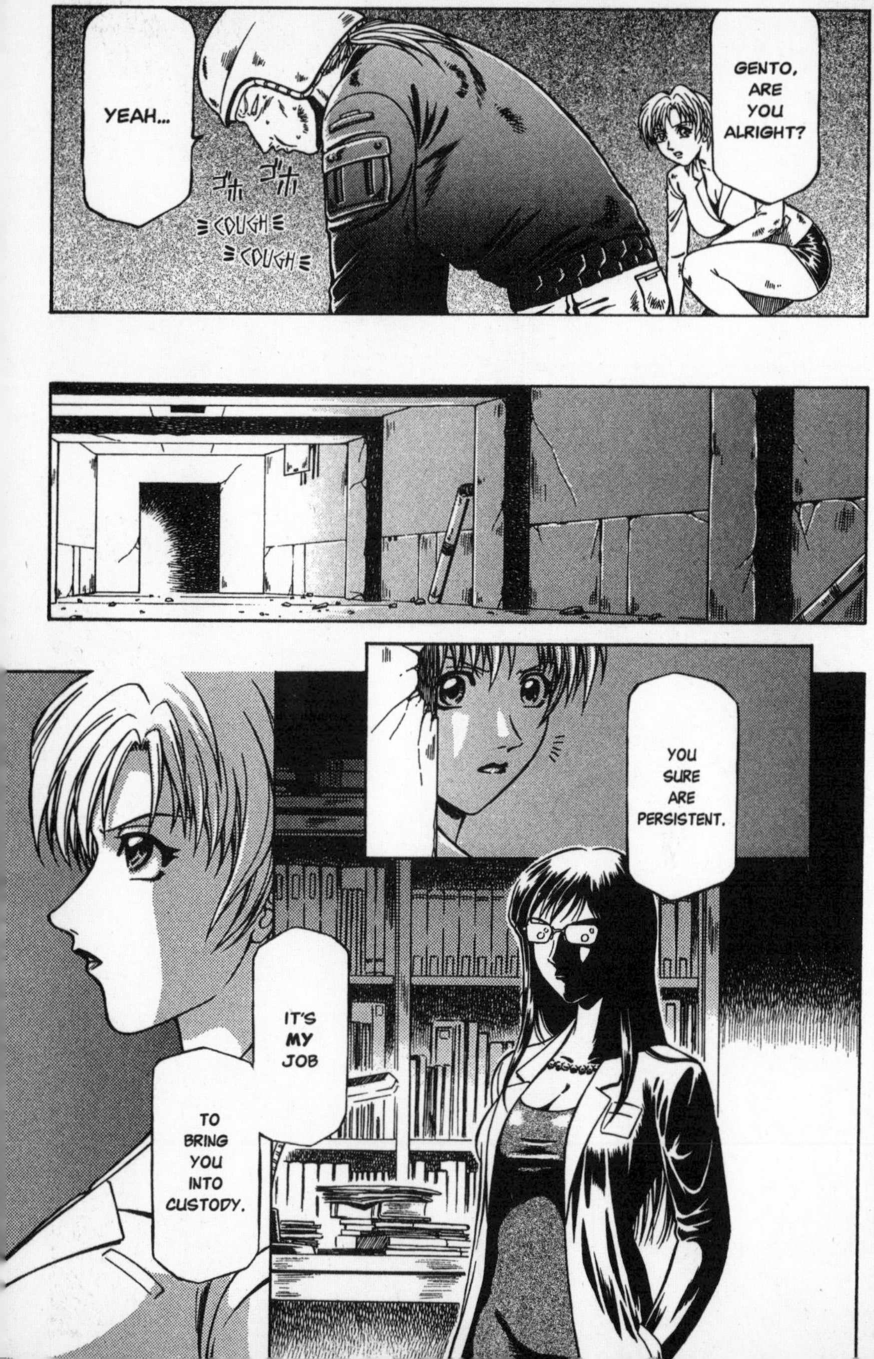
GENTO, ARE YOU ALRIGHT?
YEAH...
ゴホ ゴホ
COUGH COUGH
YOU SURE ARE PERSISTENT.
IT'S MY JOB
TO BRING YOU INTO CUSTODY.

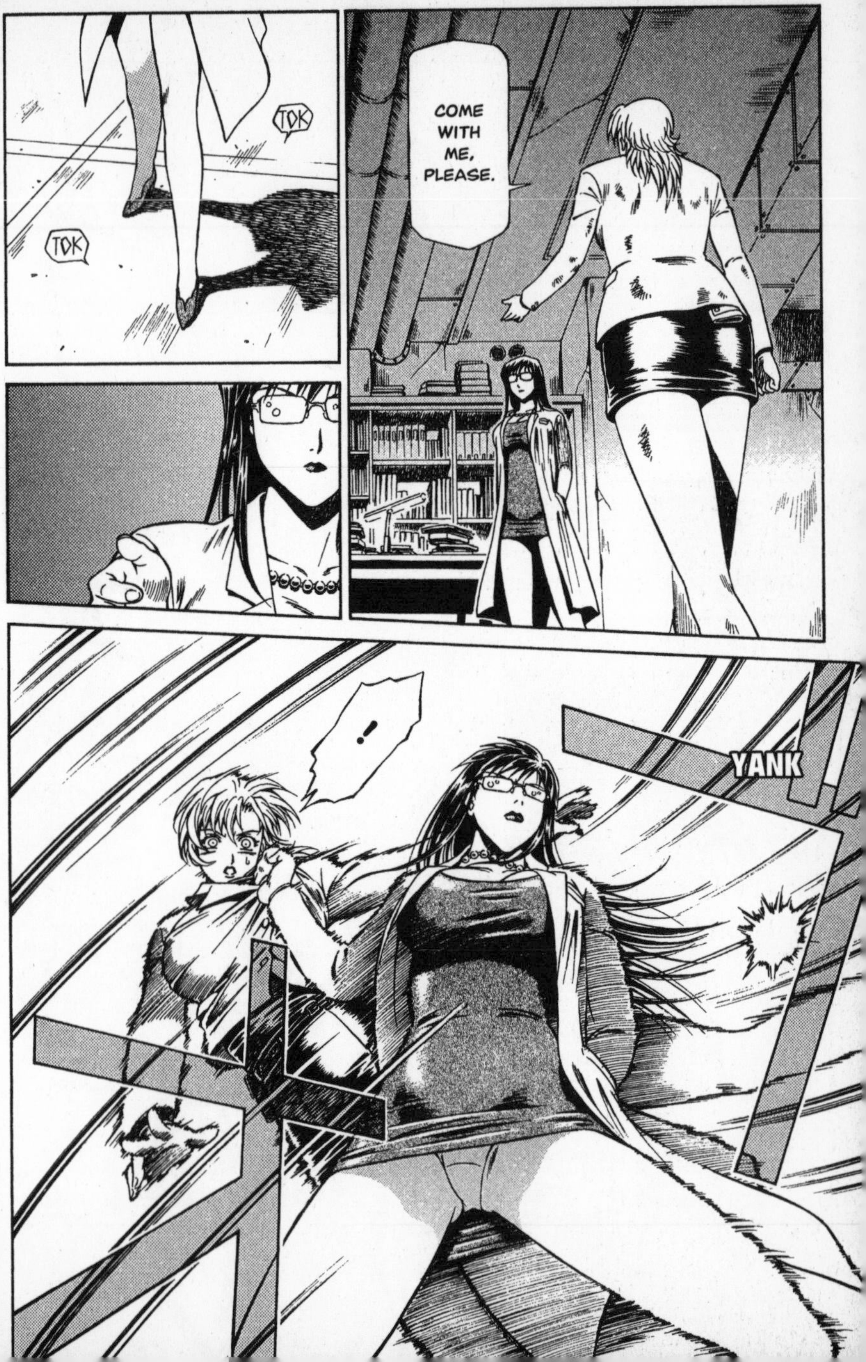
TOK
TOK
COME WITH ME, PLEASE.
!
YANK

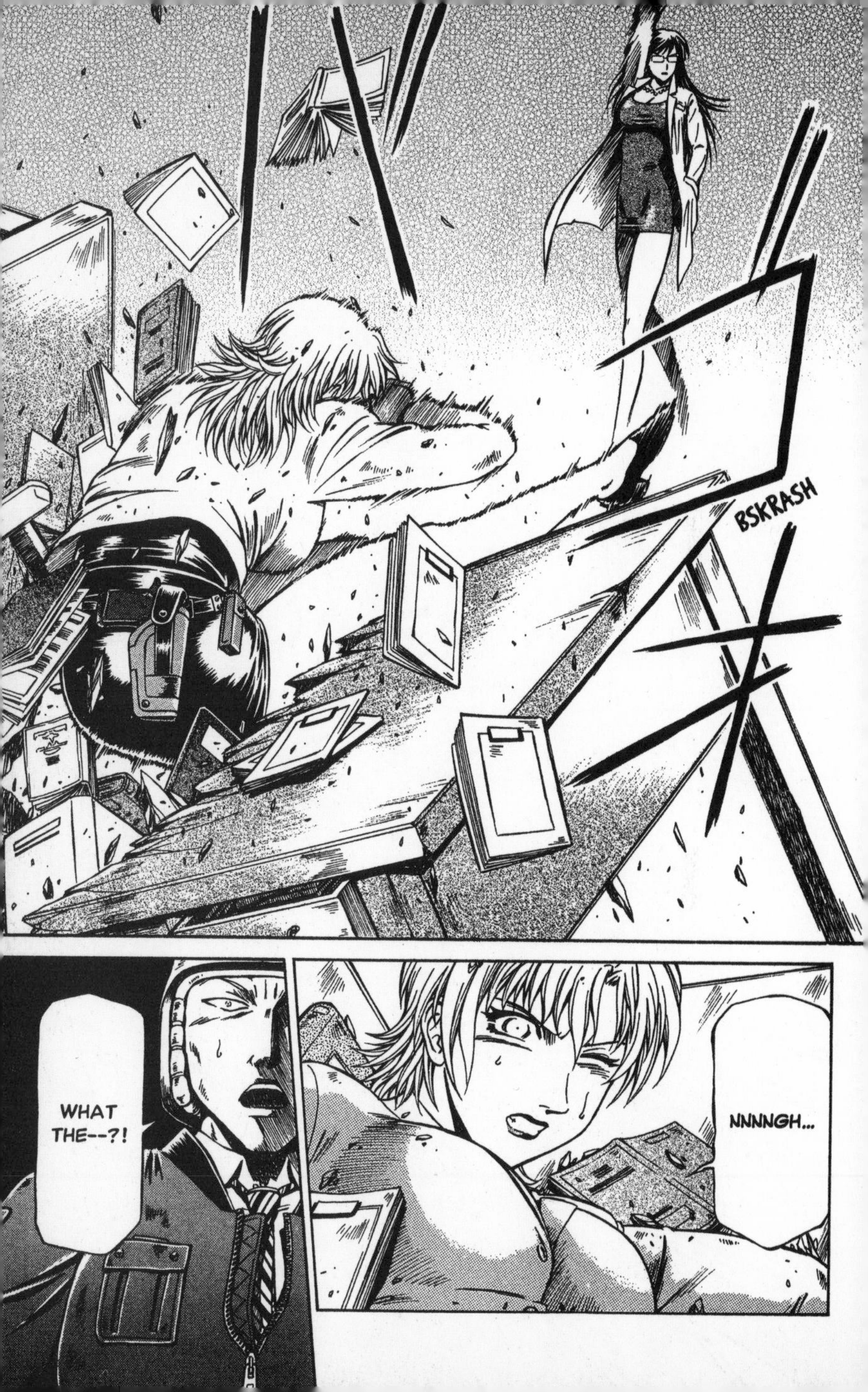
BSKRASH
WHAT THE--?!
NNNNGH...

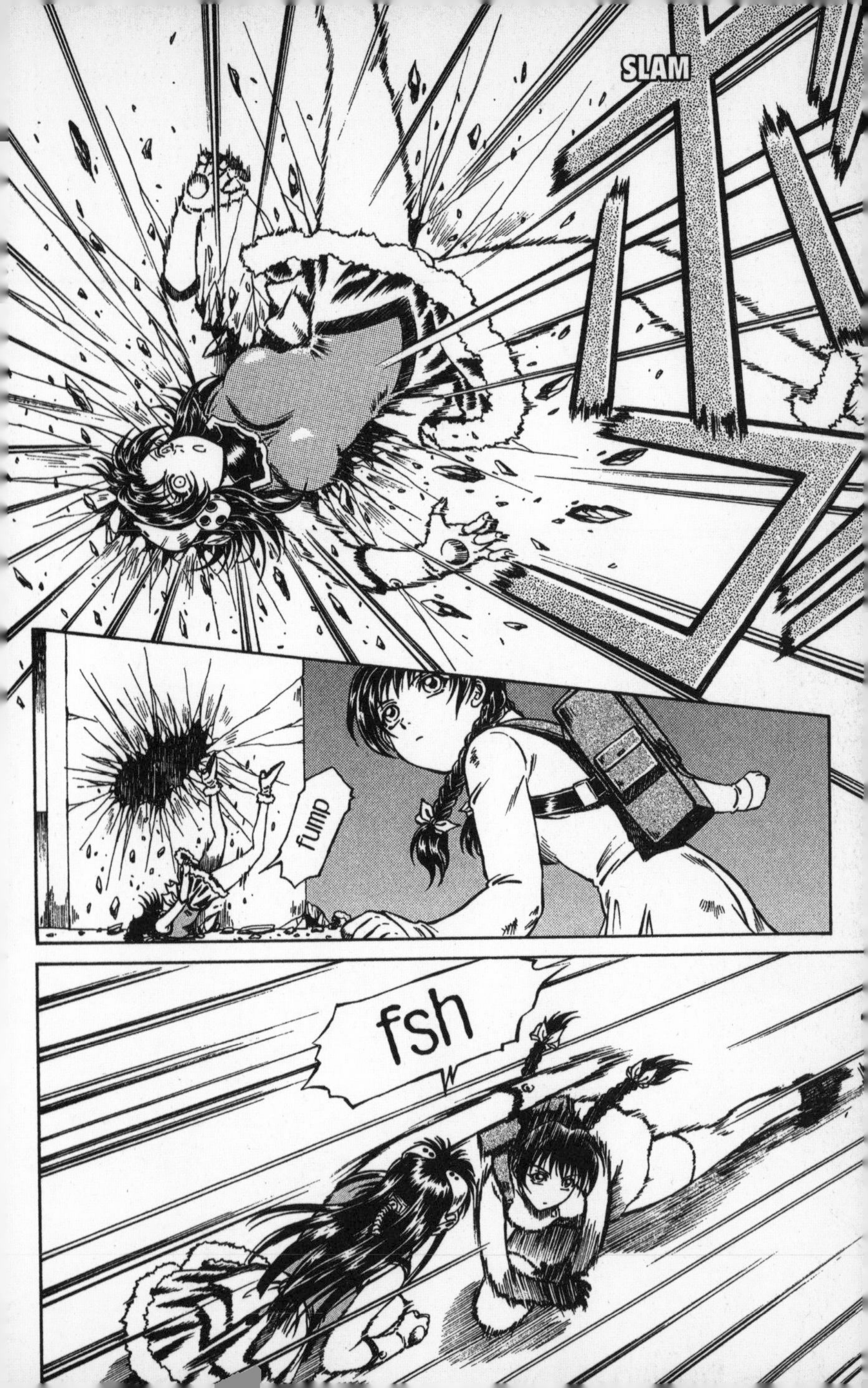
SLAM
fump
fsh

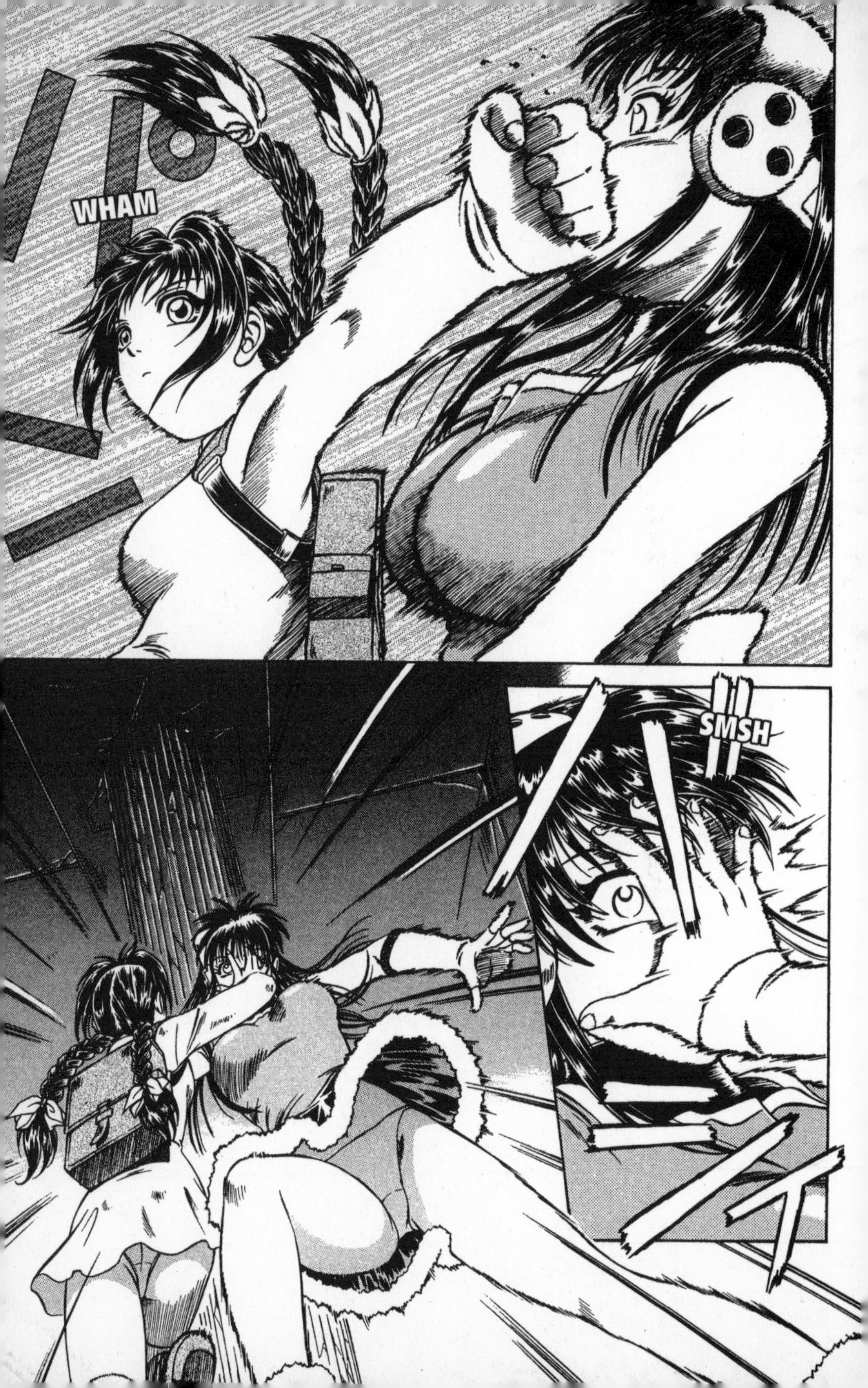
WHAM
SMSH

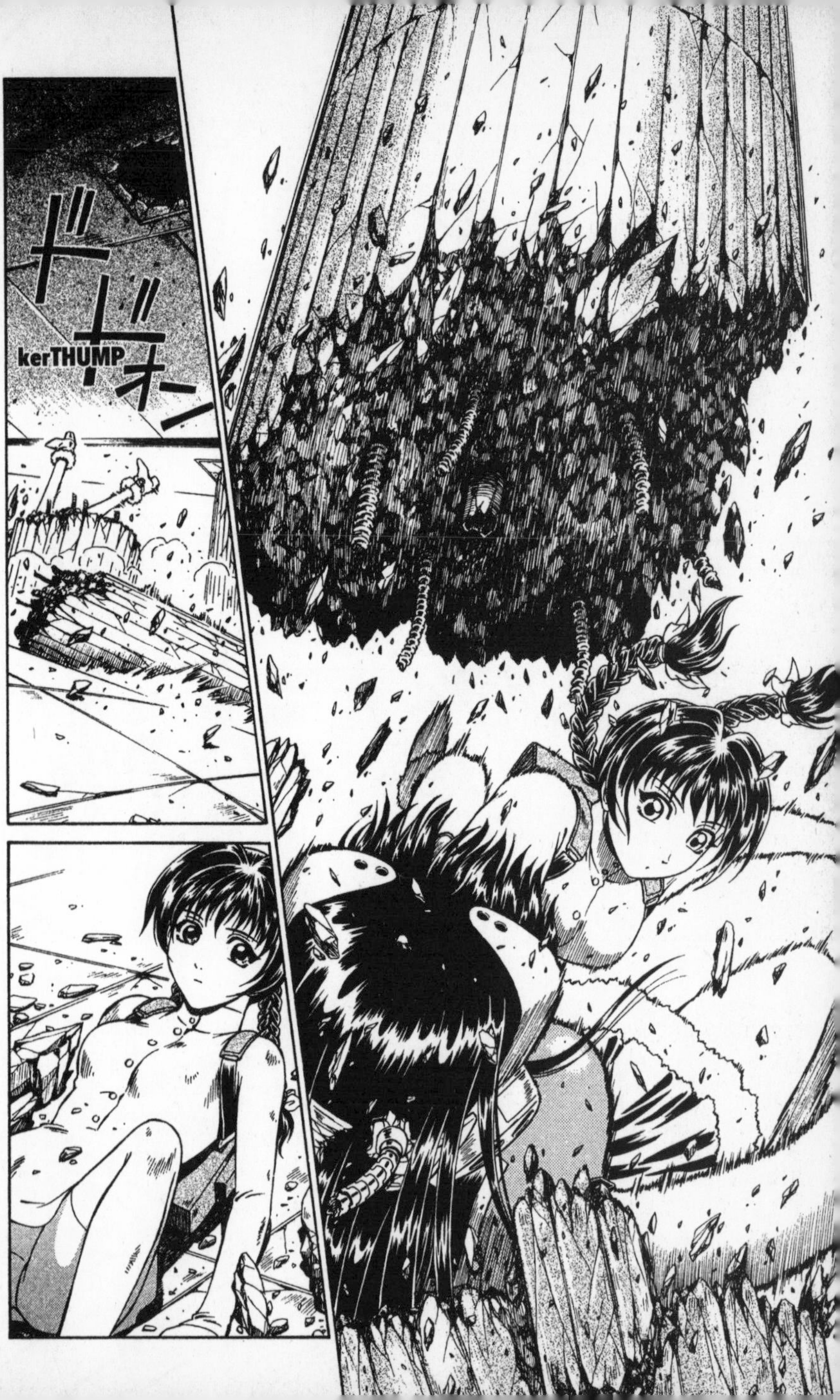
ドドォーン
kerTHUMP

!

SO,
WE
MEET
AGAIN.

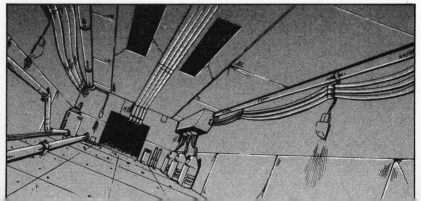

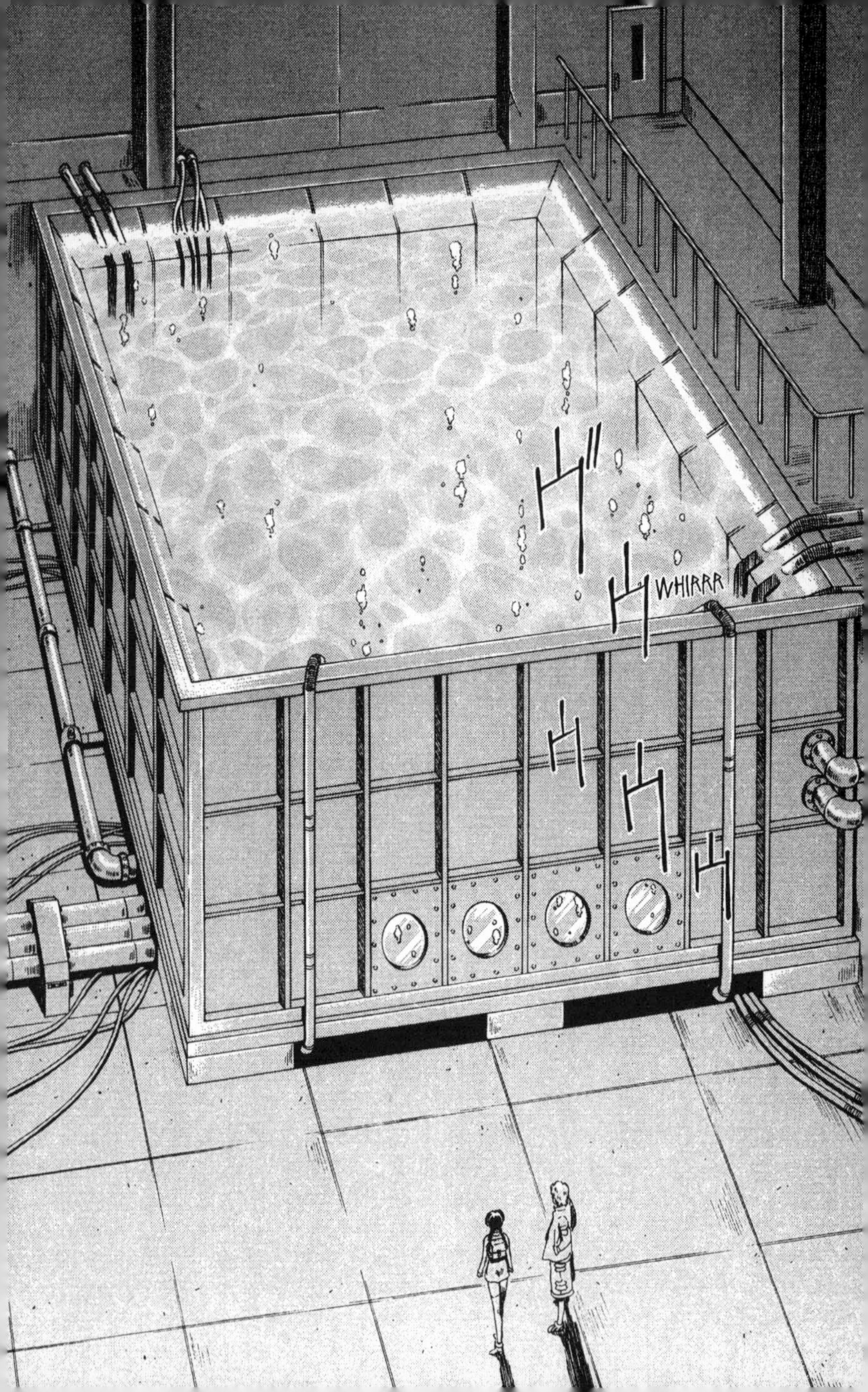
WHIRRR

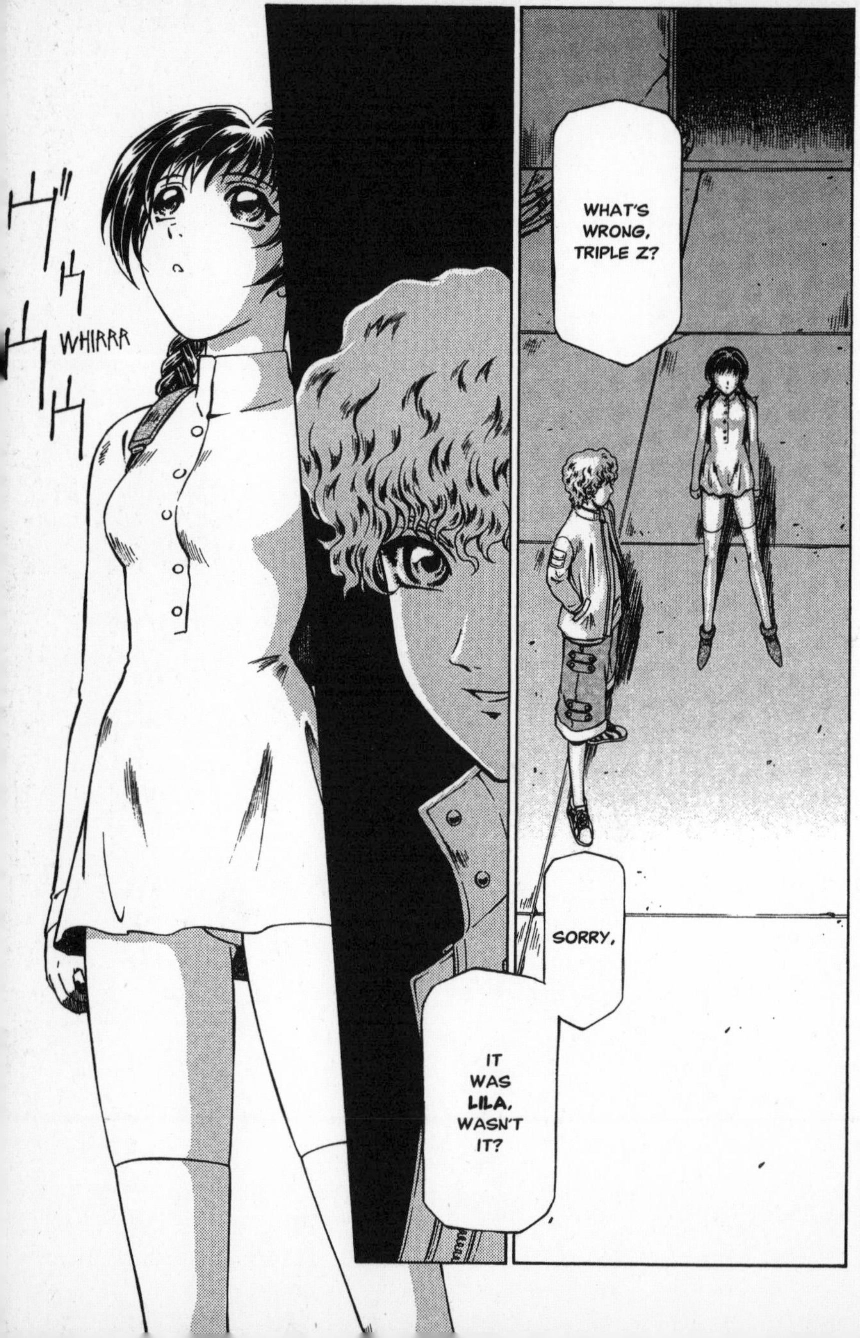

ヴゥゥゥ
WHIRRR
WHAT'S WRONG, TRIPLE Z?
SORRY,
IT WAS LILA, WASN'T IT?

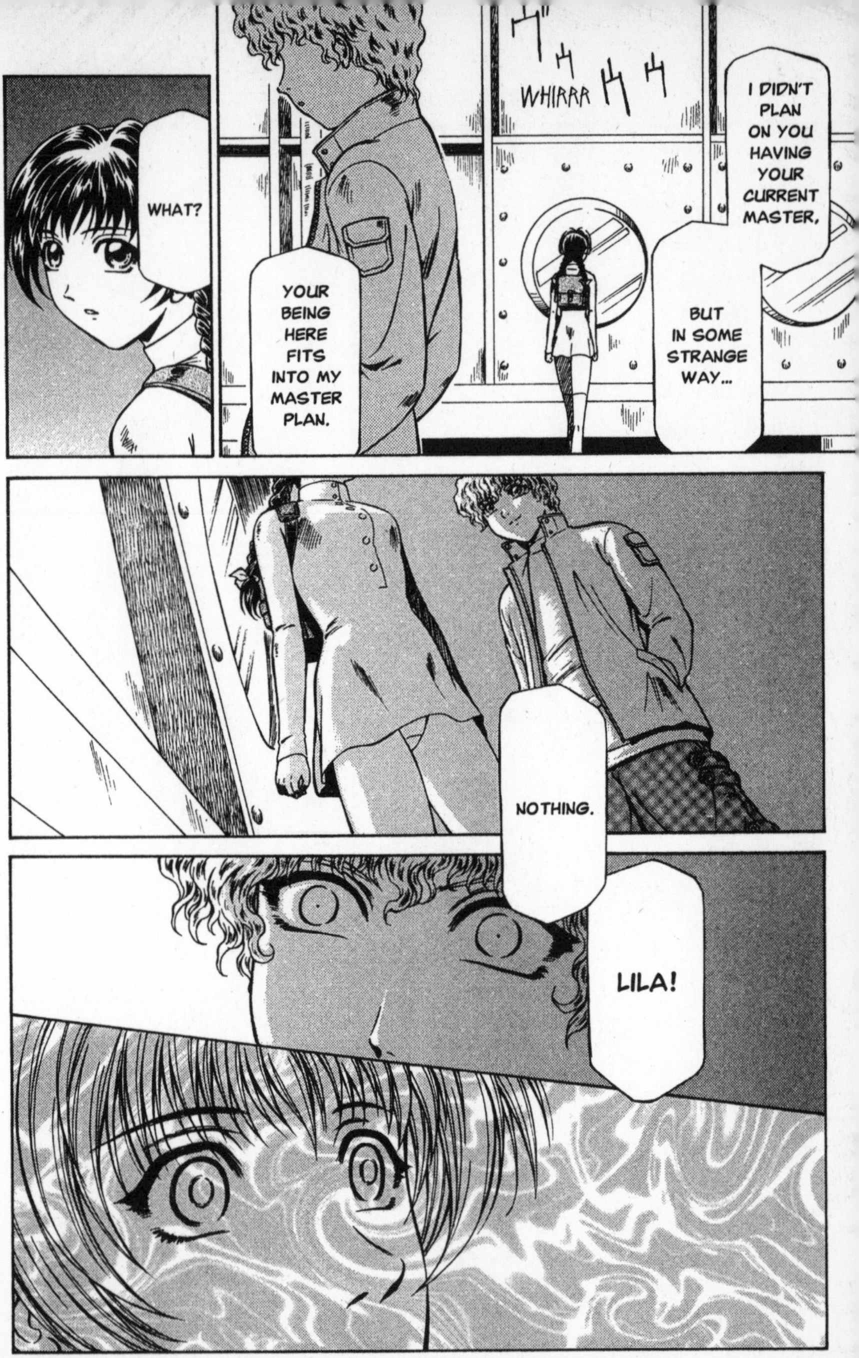
WHIRRR
I DIDN'T PLAN ON YOU HAVING YOUR CURRENT MASTER,
BUT IN SOME STRANGE WAY...
YOUR BEING HERE FITS INTO MY MASTER PLAN.
WHAT?
NOTHING.
LILA!

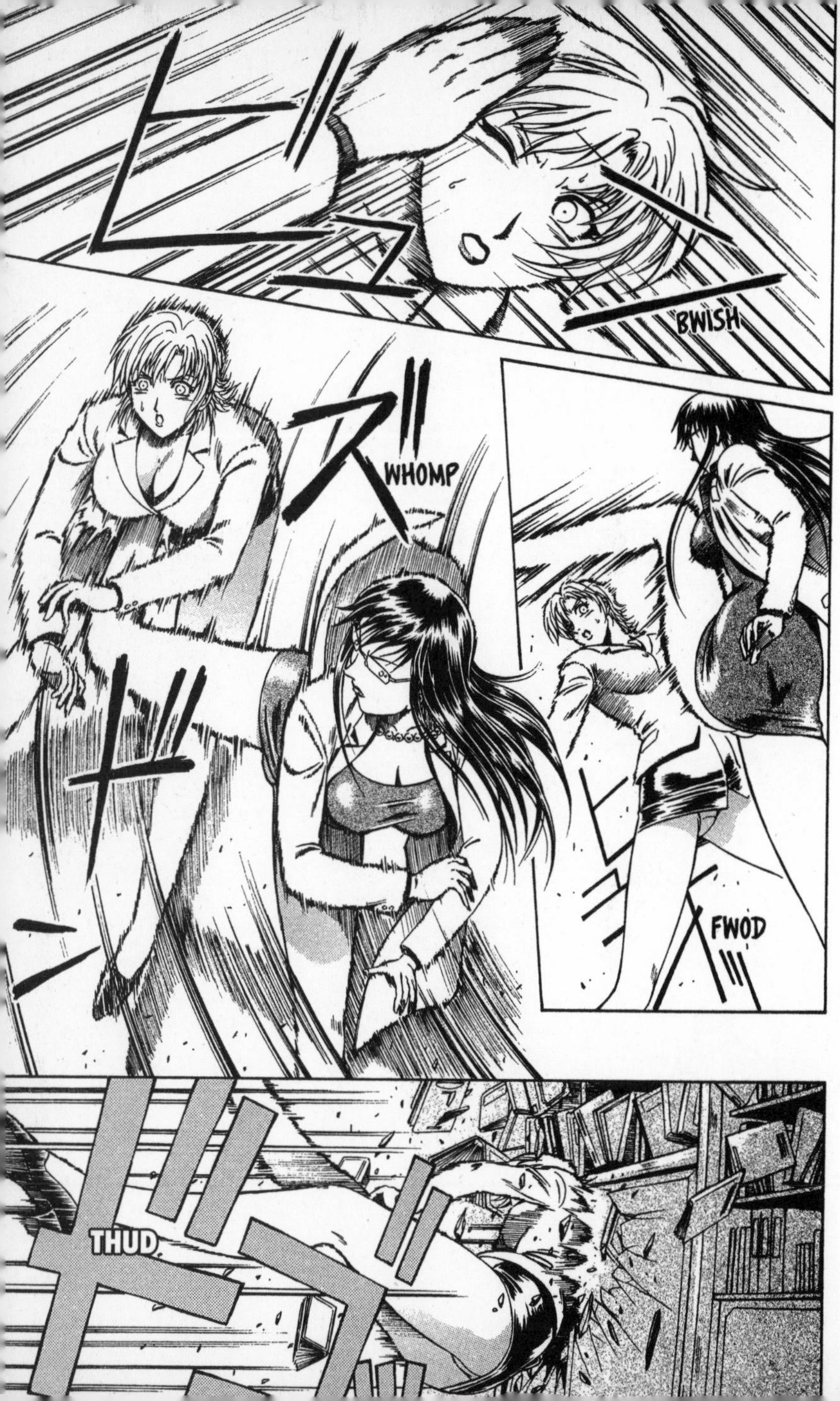
BWISH
FWOD
WHOMP
THUD

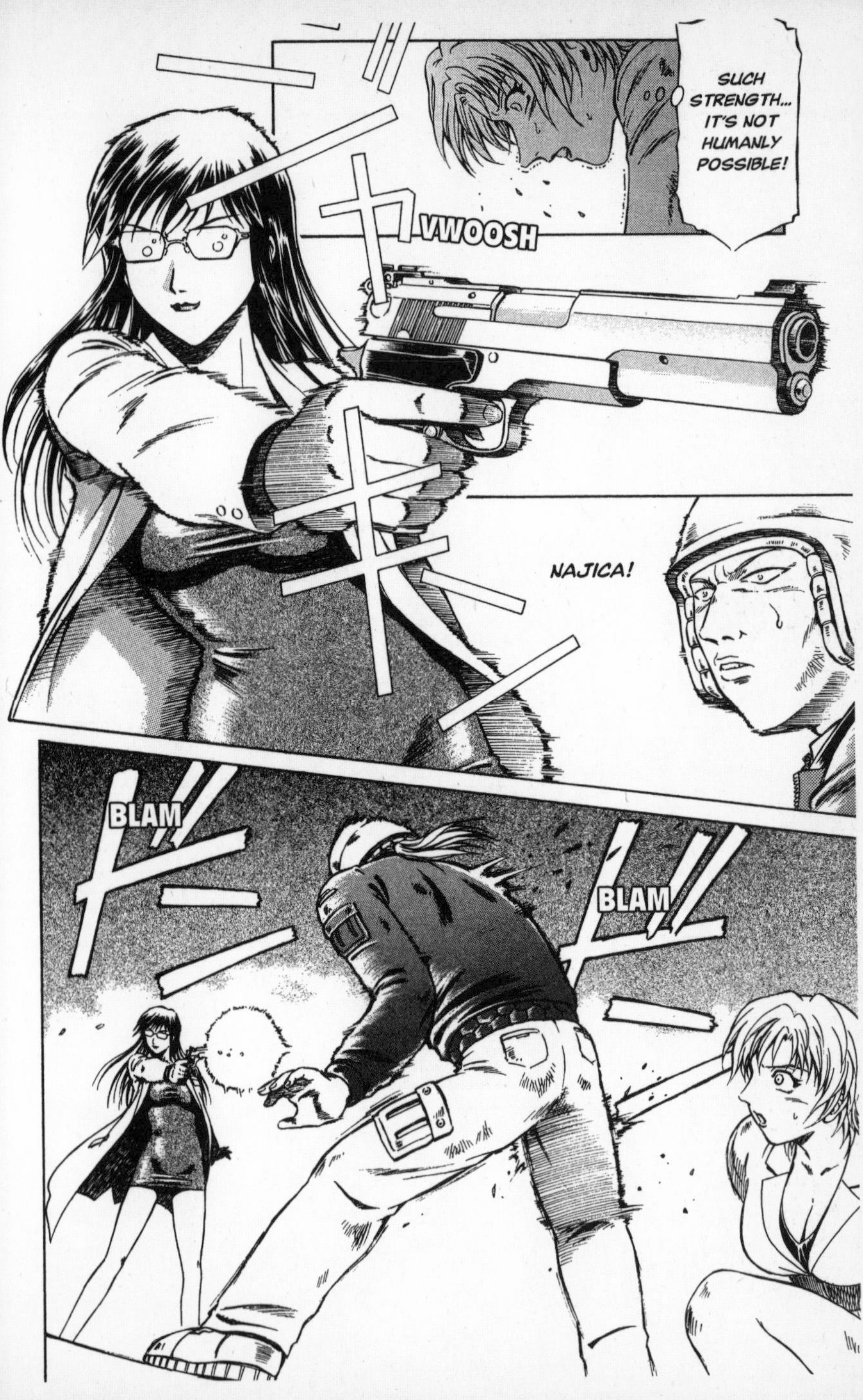
SUCH STRENGTH... IT'S NOT HUMANLY POSSIBLE!
VWOOSH
NAJICA!
BLAM
BLAM

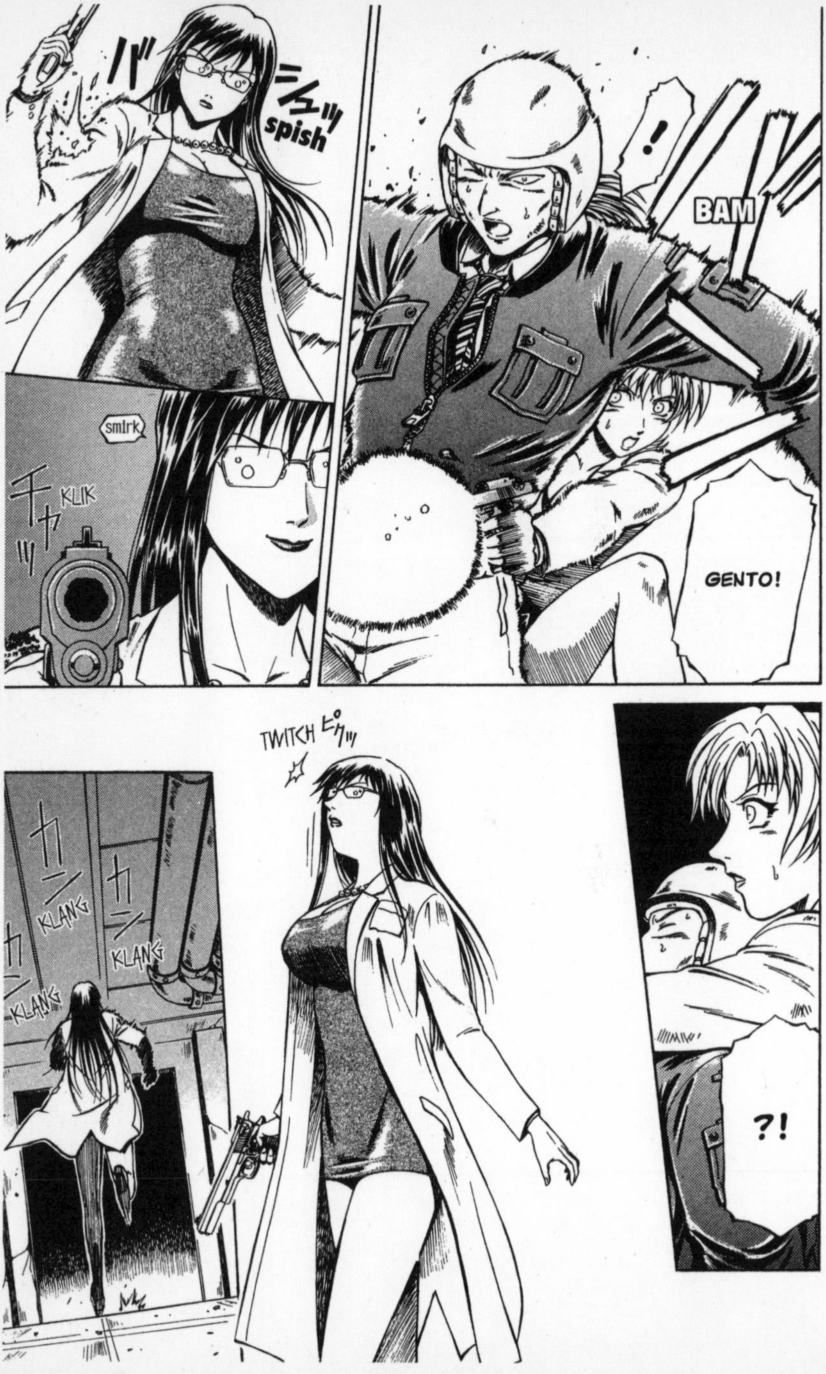
!
BAM
バシュッ
spish
GENTO!
smirk
チャッ
KLIK
?!
TWITCH ピクッ
カン
KLANG
カン
KLANG
カン
KLANG

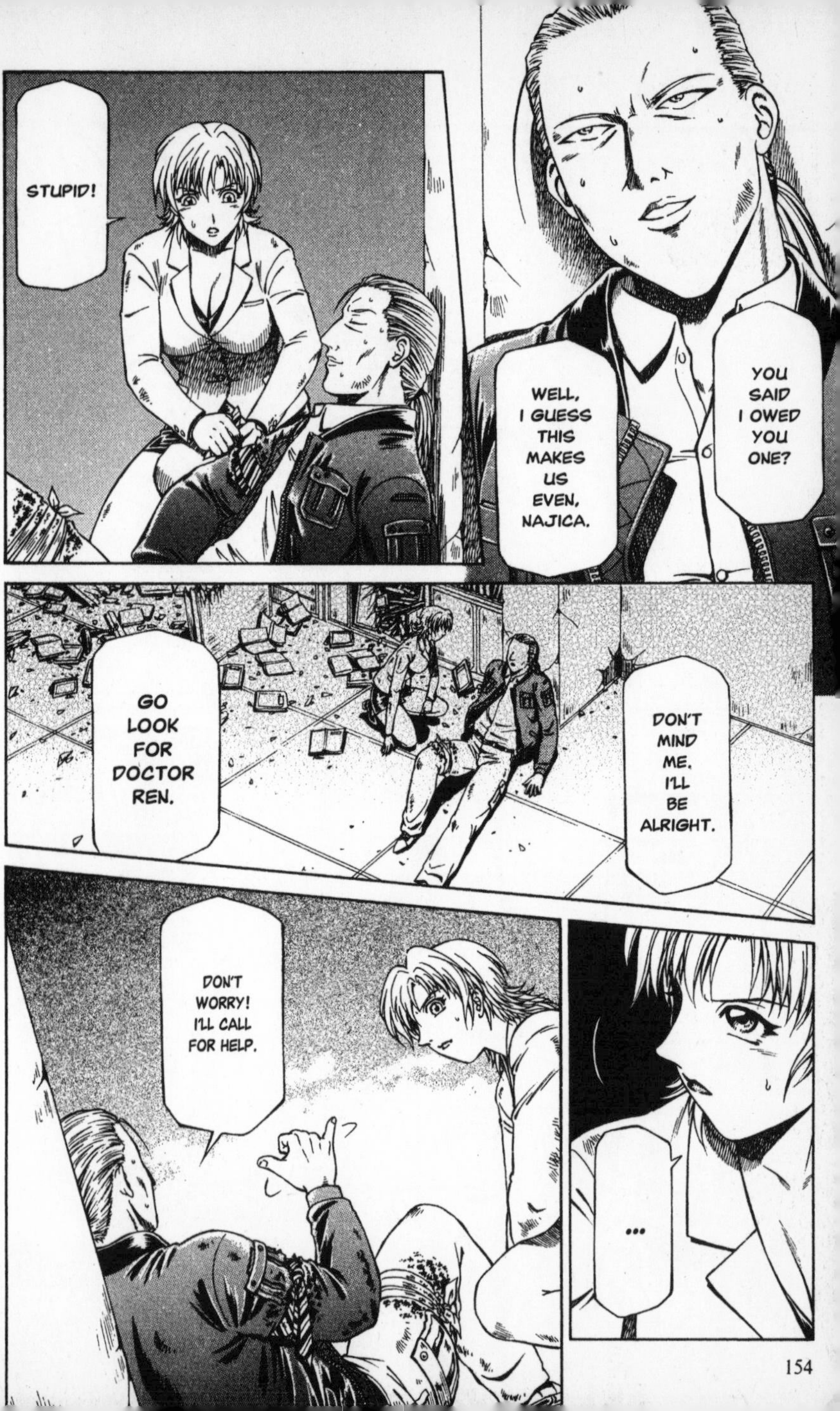
YOU SAID I OWED YOU ONE?
WELL, I GUESS THIS MAKES US EVEN, NAJICA.
STUPID!
DON'T MIND ME. I'LL BE ALRIGHT.
GO LOOK FOR DOCTOR REN.
...
DON'T WORRY! I'LL CALL FOR HELP.

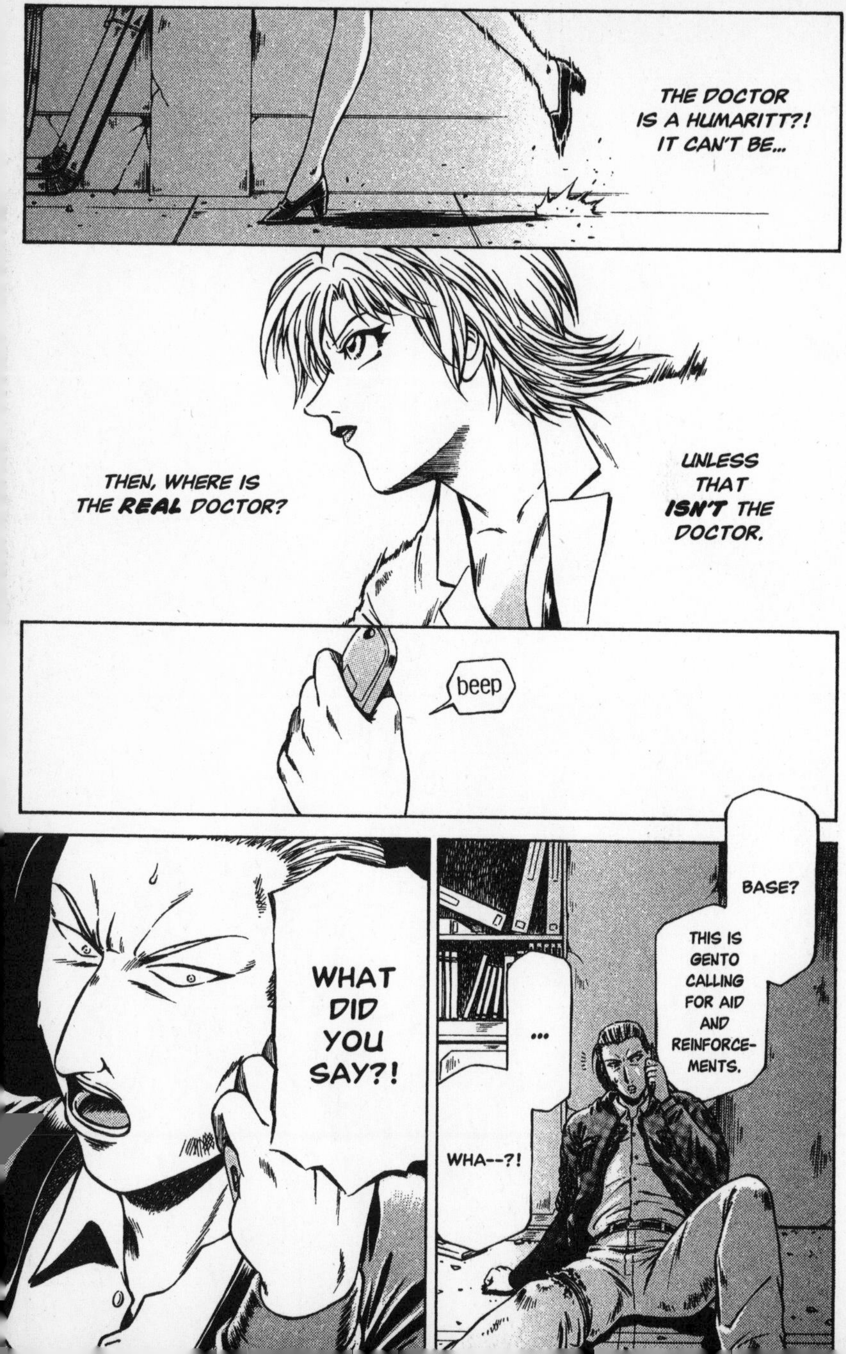
THE DOCTOR IS A HUMARITT?! IT CAN'T BE...
UNLESS THAT ISN'T THE DOCTOR.
THEN, WHERE IS THE REAL DOCTOR?
beep
BASE?
THIS IS GENTO CALLING FOR AID AND REINFORCE-MENTS.
...
WHA--?!
WHAT DID YOU SAY?!

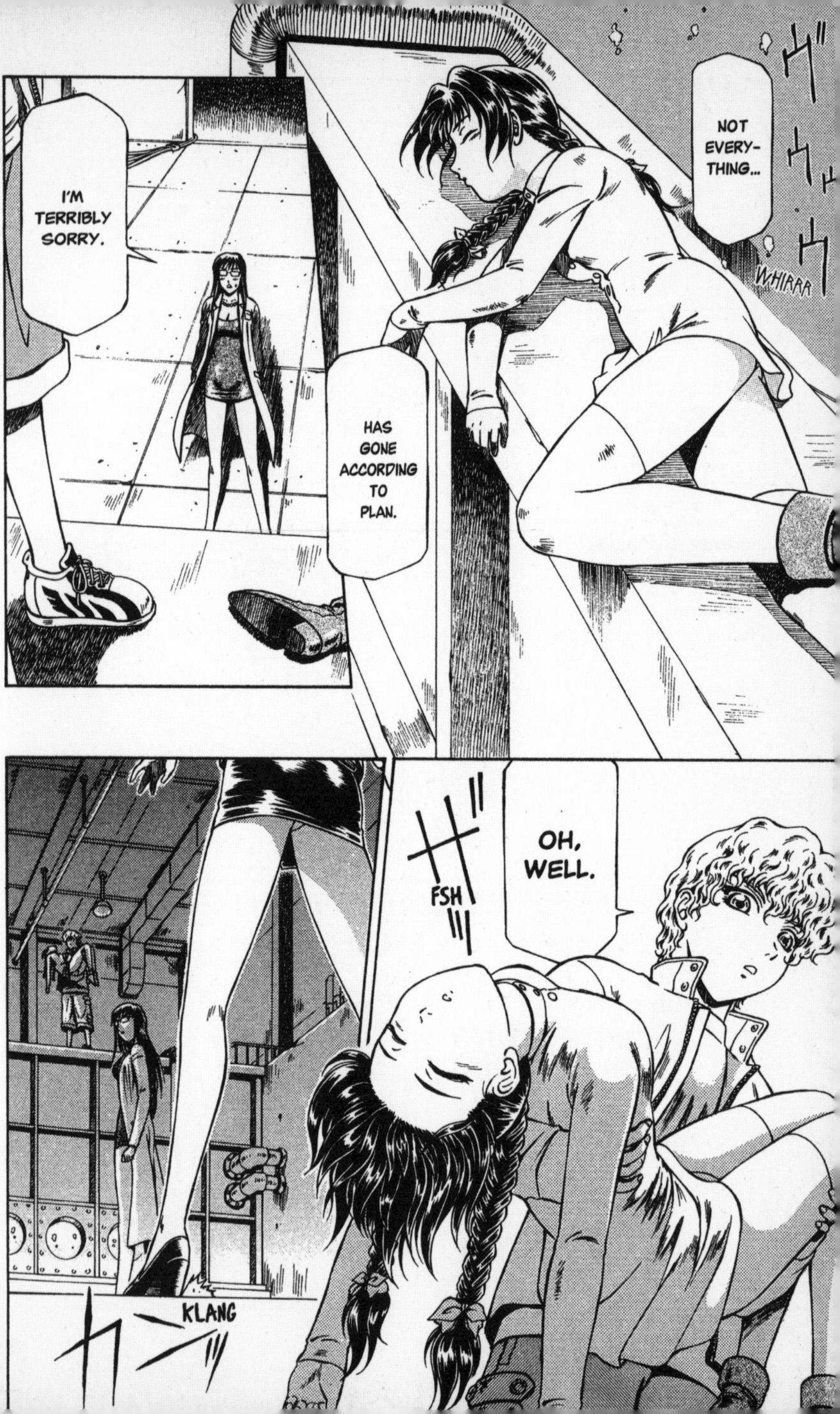
NOT EVERY-THING...
WHIRRR
HAS GONE ACCORDING TO PLAN.
I'M TERRIBLY SORRY.
OH, WELL.
FSH
KLANG

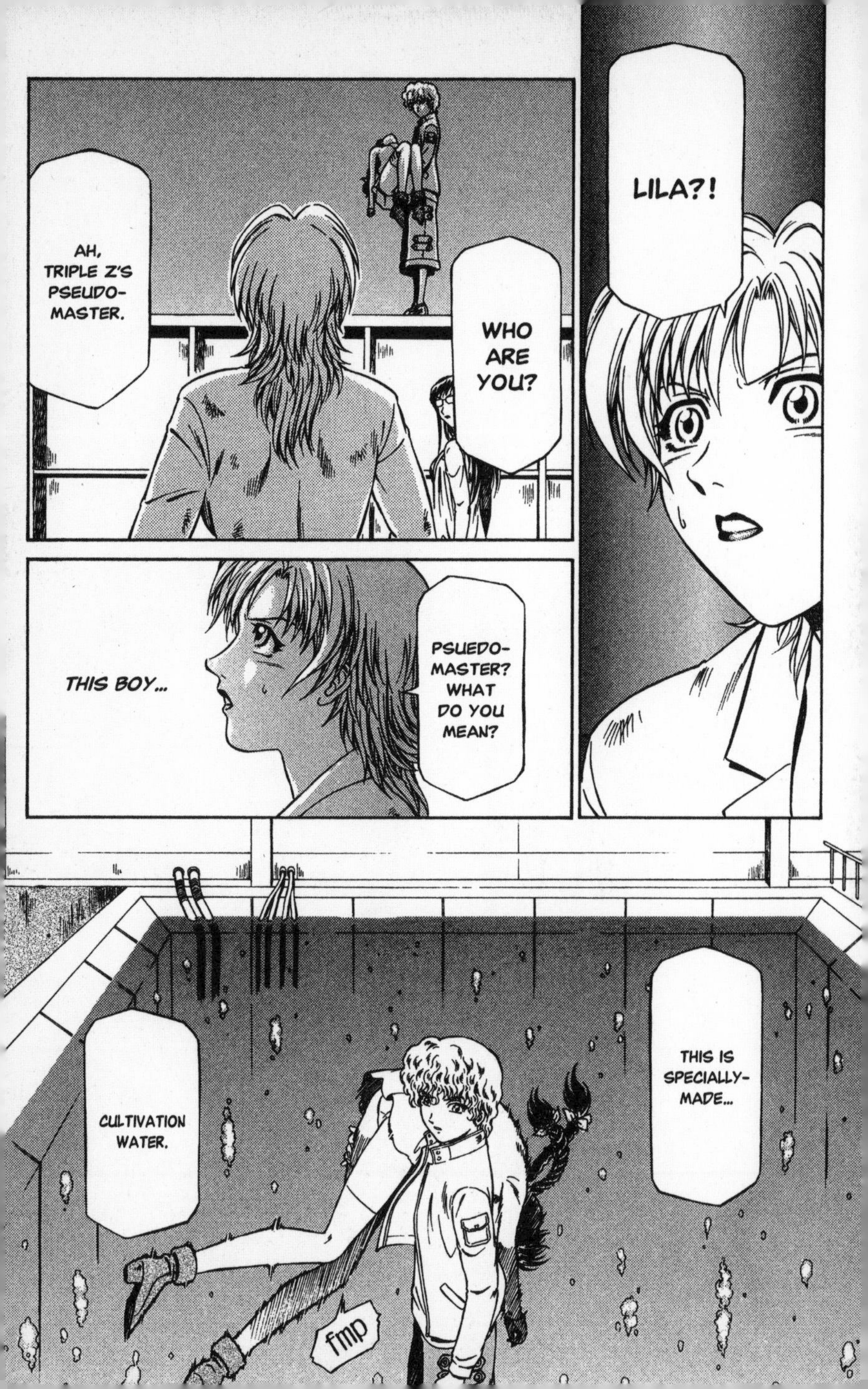

AH, TRIPLE Z'S PSEUDO-MASTER.
WHO ARE YOU?
LILA?!
THIS BOY...
PSUEDO-MASTER? WHAT DO YOU MEAN?
THIS IS SPECIALLY-MADE...
CULTIVATION WATER.
fmp

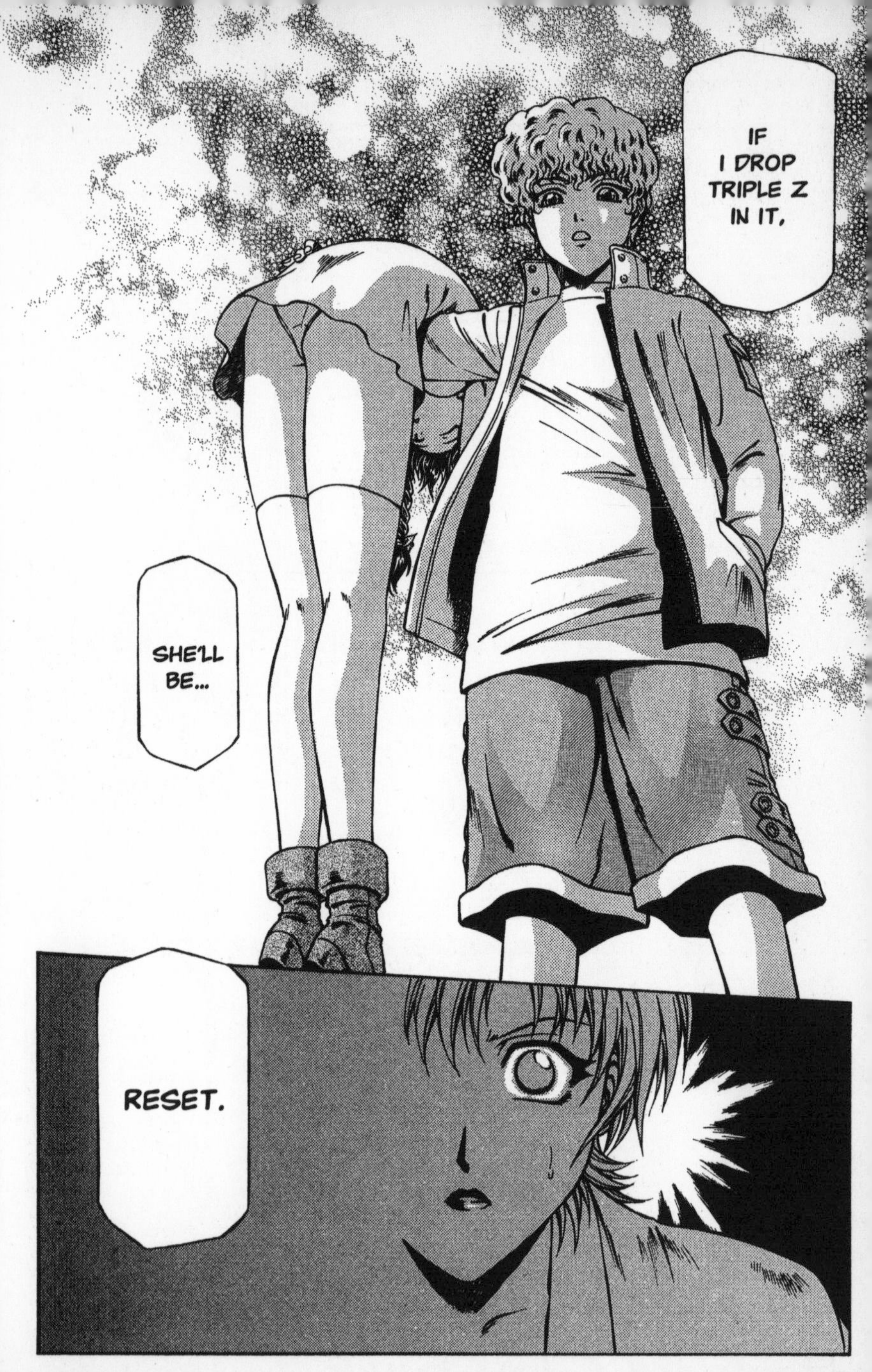
IF I DROP TRIPLE Z IN IT,
SHE'LL BE...
RESET.

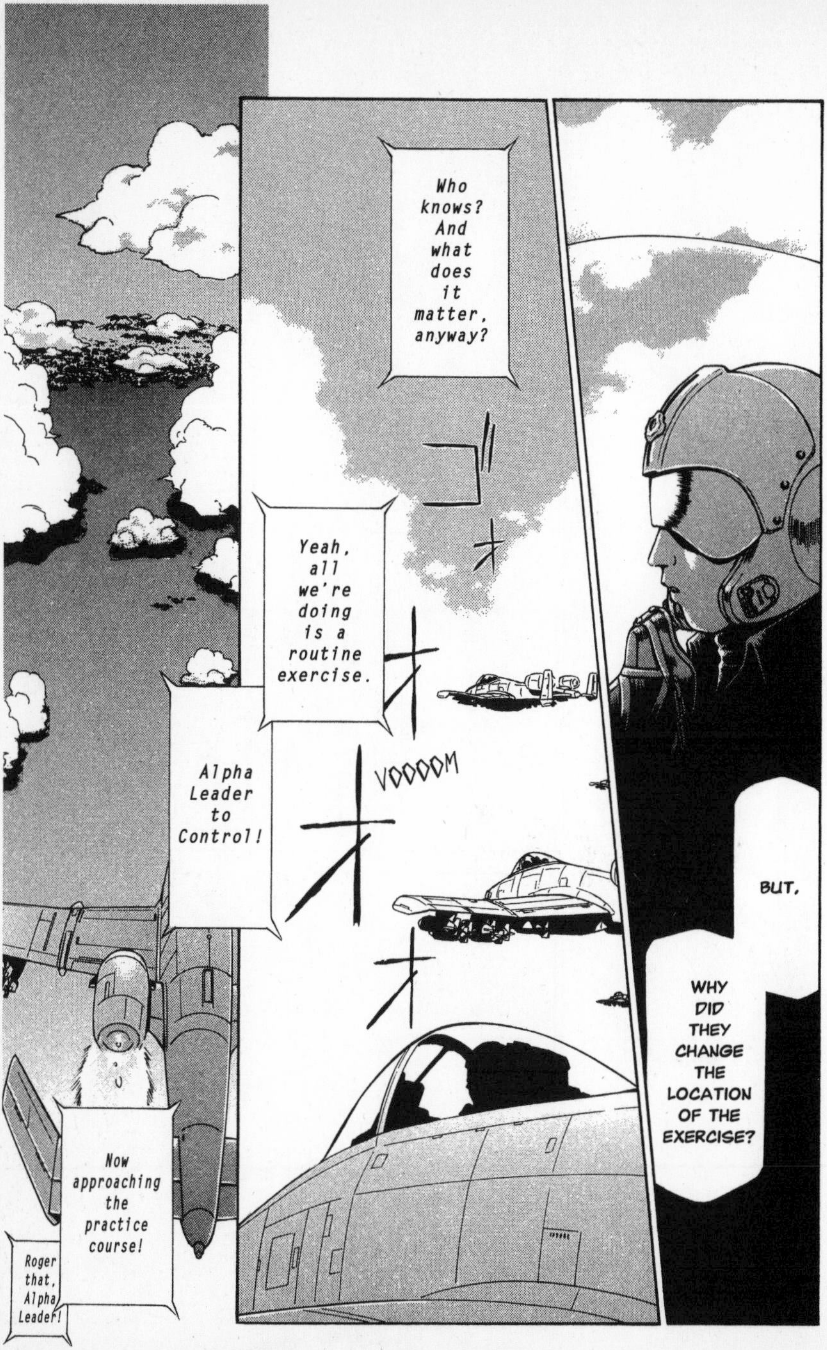
Alpha Leader to Control!
Now approaching the practice course!
Roger that, Alpha Leader!
Yeah, all we're doing is a routine exercise.
Who knows? And what does it matter, anyway?
VOOOOM
BUT,
WHY DID THEY CHANGE THE LOCATION OF THE EXERCISE?

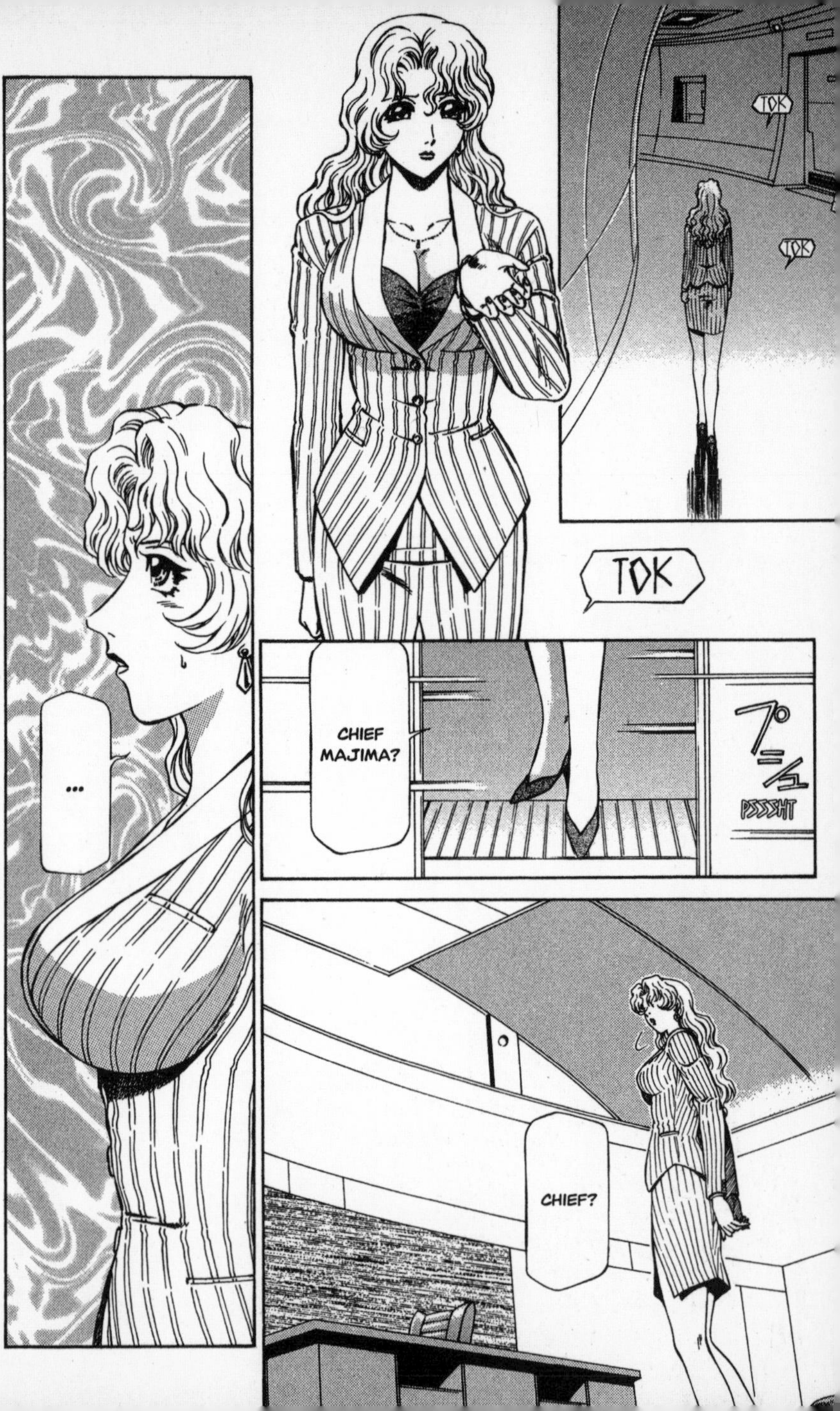
TOK
TOK
TOK
PSSSHT
CHIEF MAJIMA?
CHIEF?
...

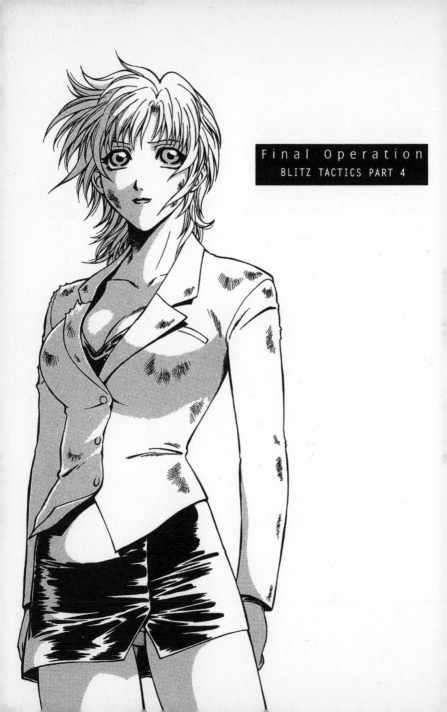

Final Operation
BLITZ TACTICS PART 4

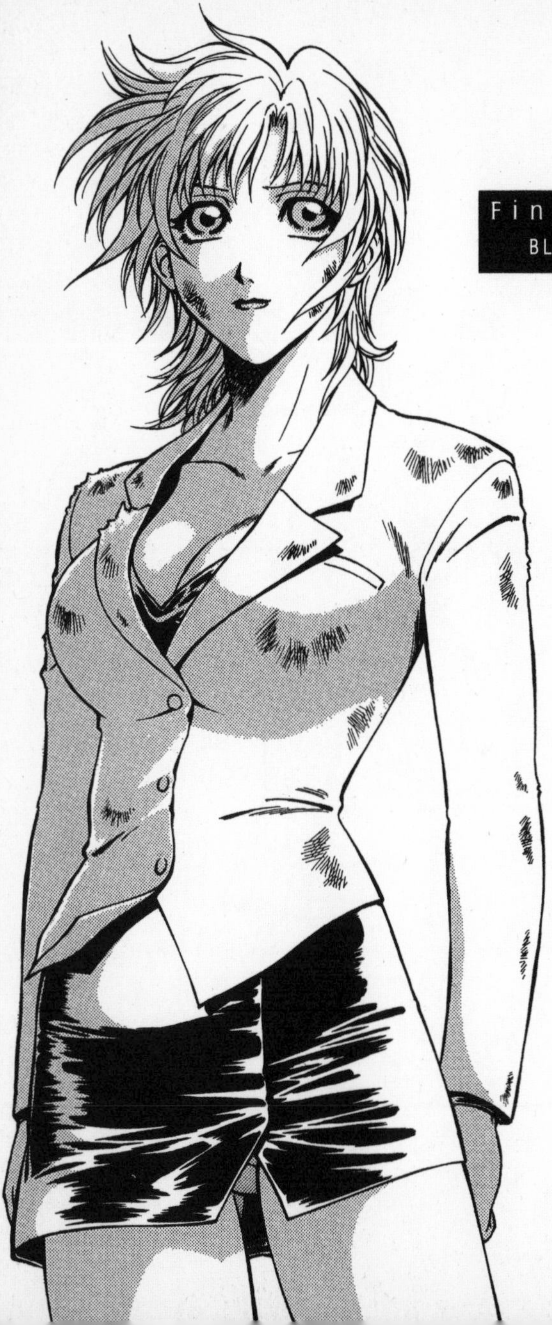

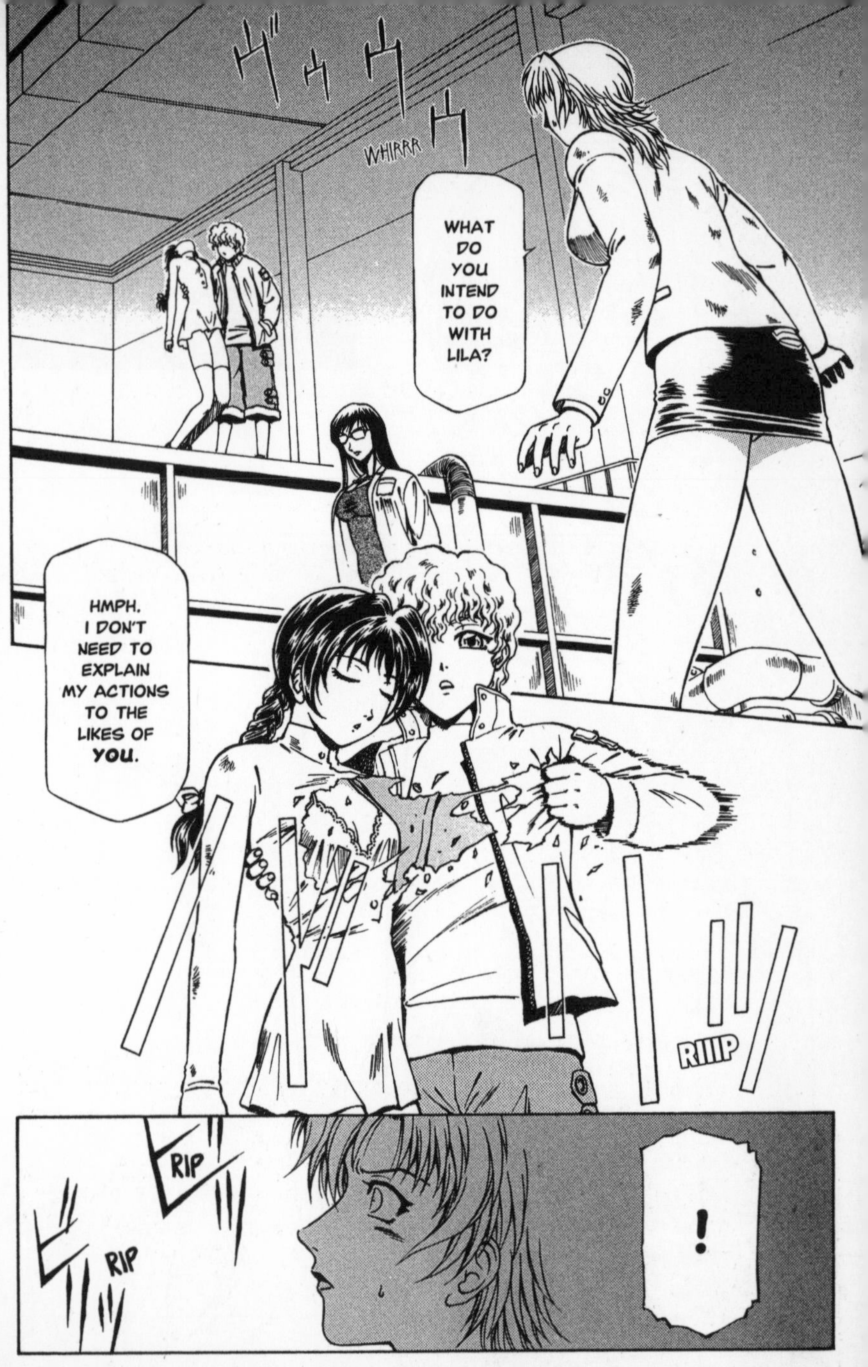
ヴゥウン
WHIRRR
WHAT DO YOU INTEND TO DO WITH LILA?
HMPH. I DON'T NEED TO EXPLAIN MY ACTIONS TO THE LIKES OF YOU.
RIIIP
RIP
RIP
!

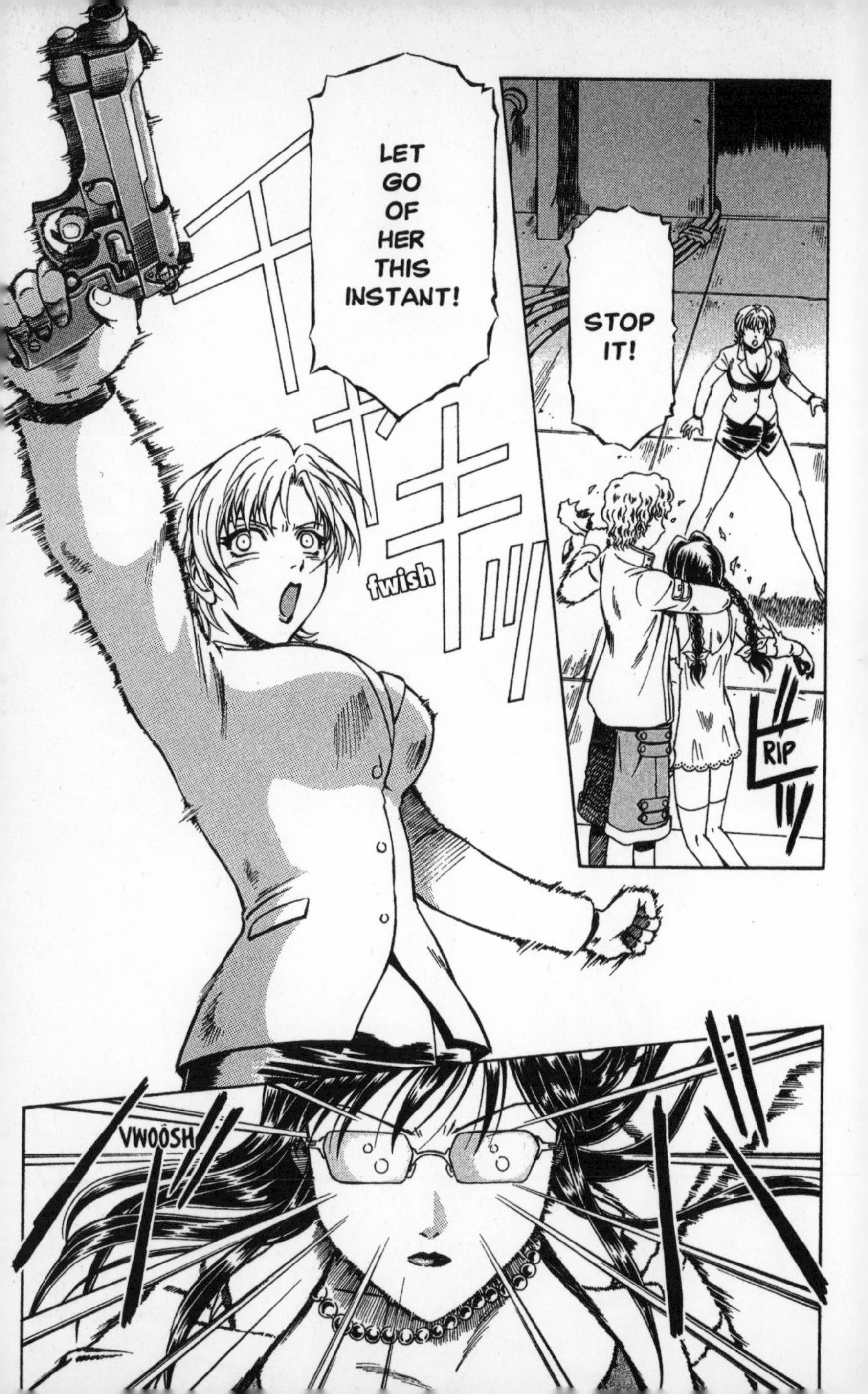
LET GO OF HER THIS INSTANT!
STOP IT!
RIP
fwish
VWOOSH

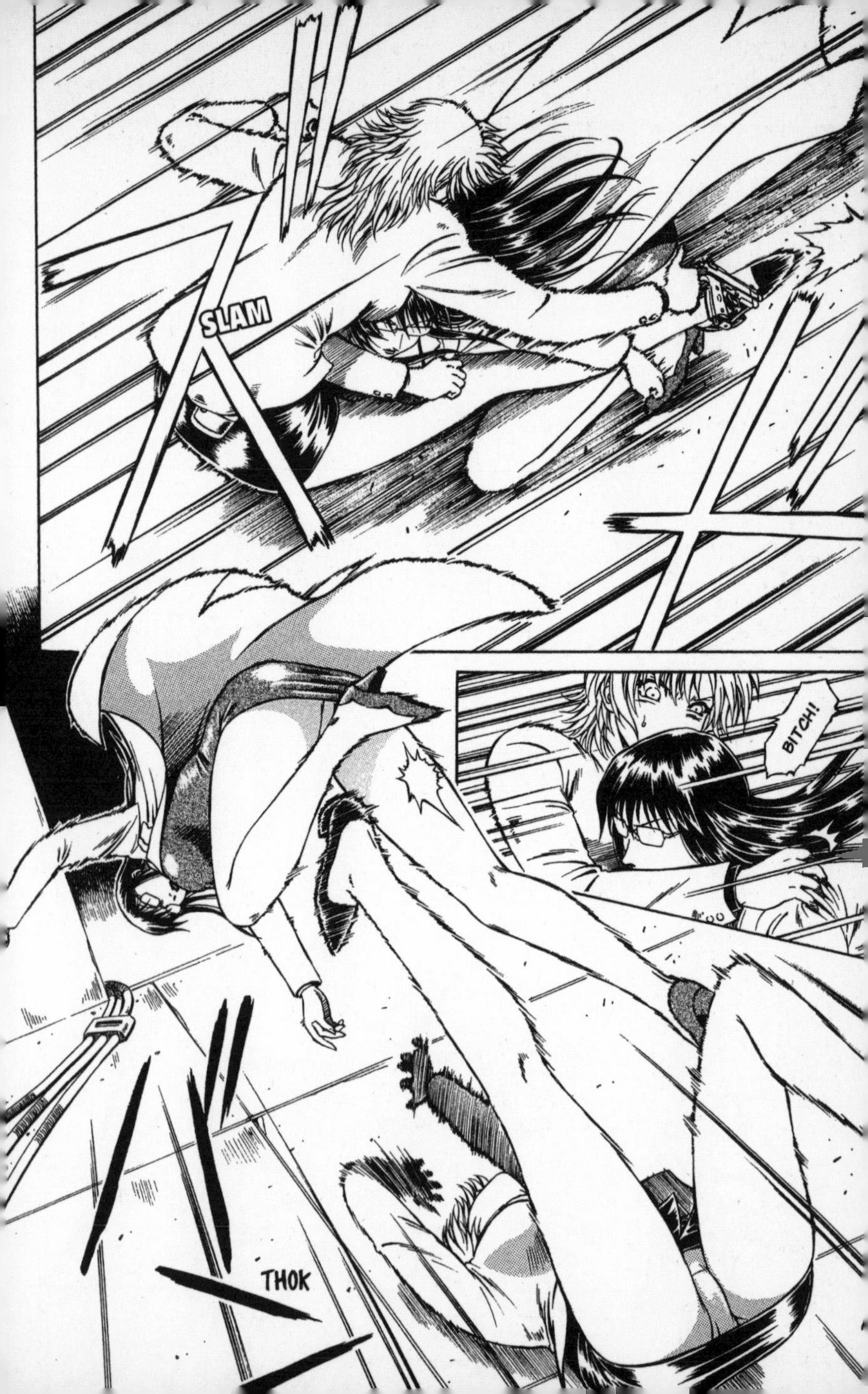
SLAM
BITCH!
THOK

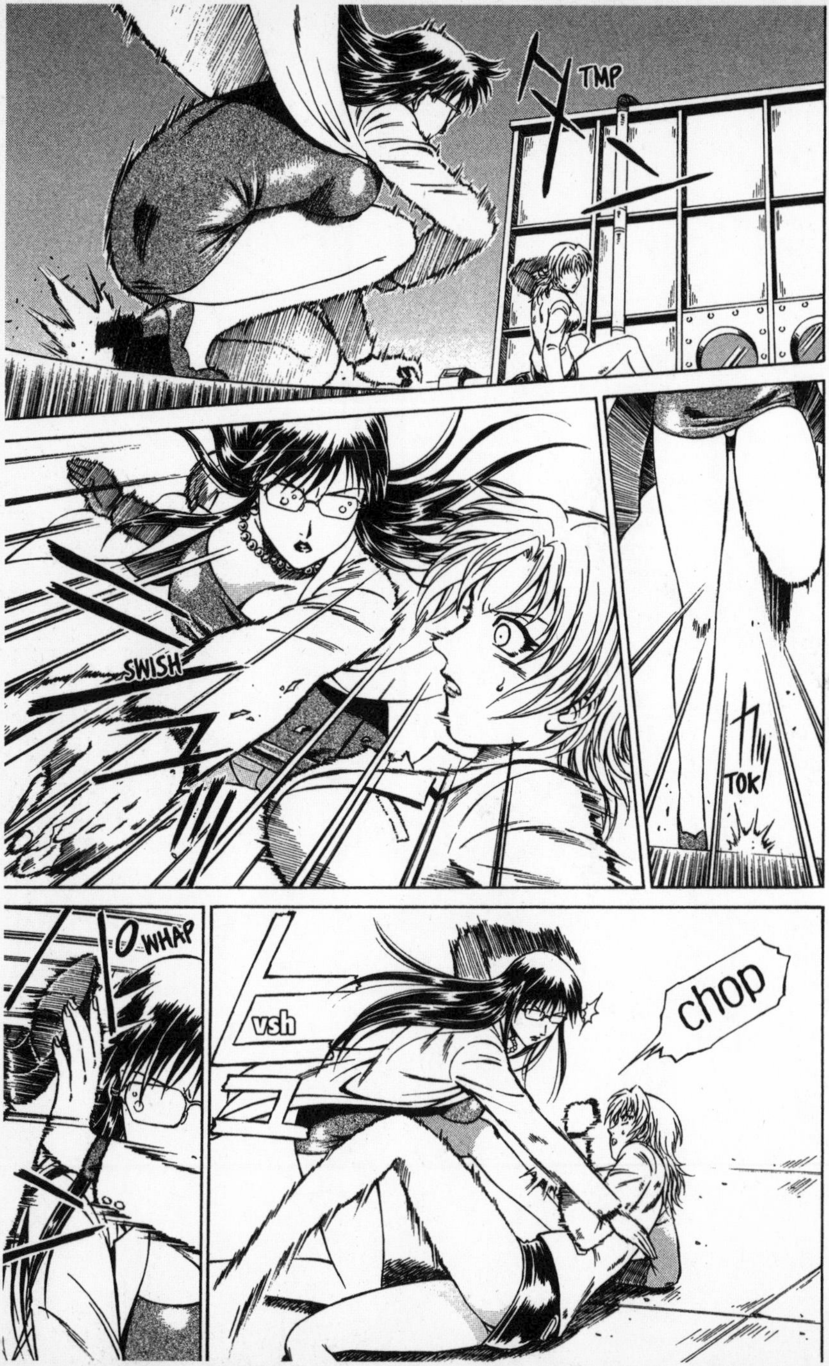
TMP
SWISH
TOK
WHAP
vsh
chop

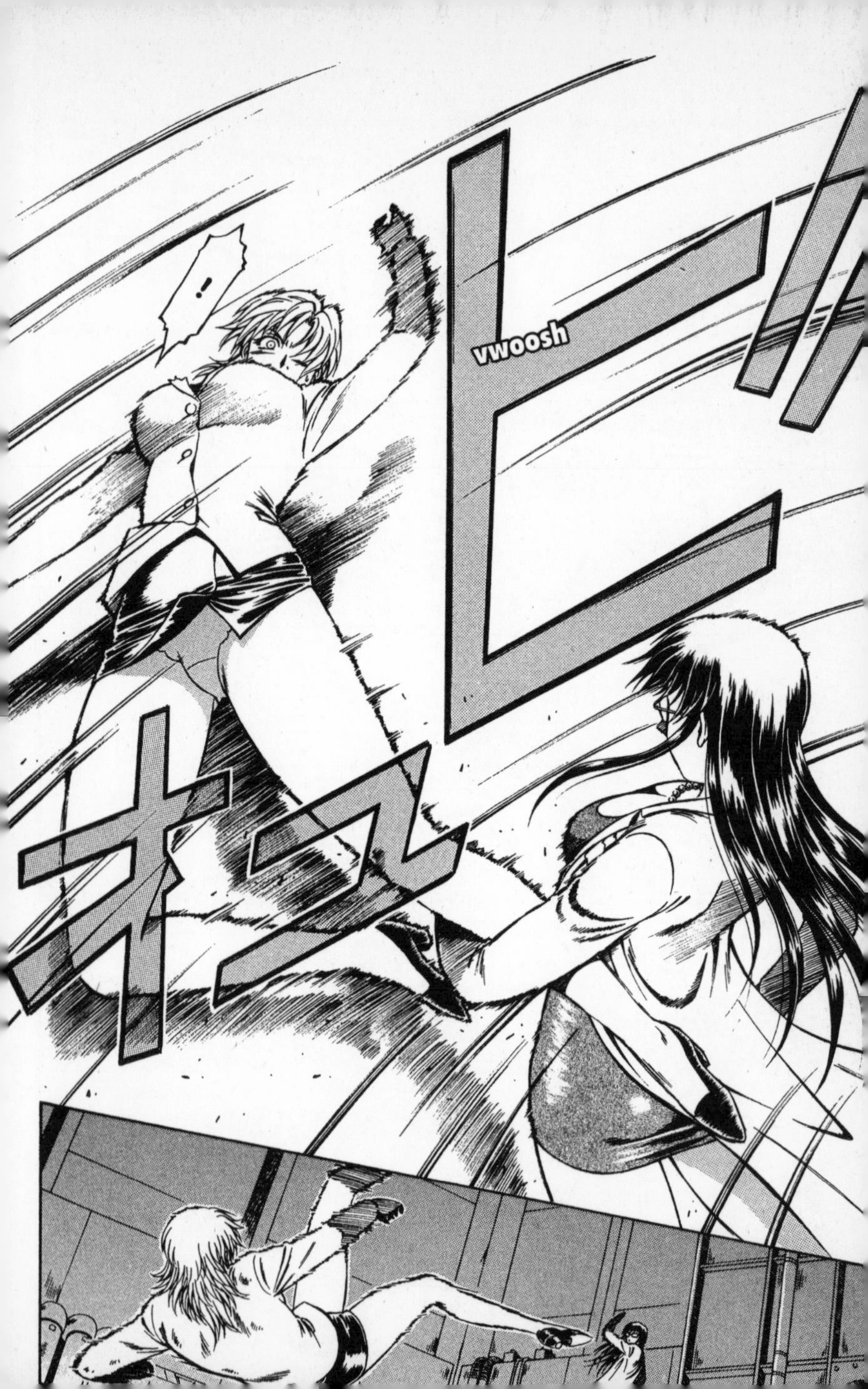
!
vwoosh

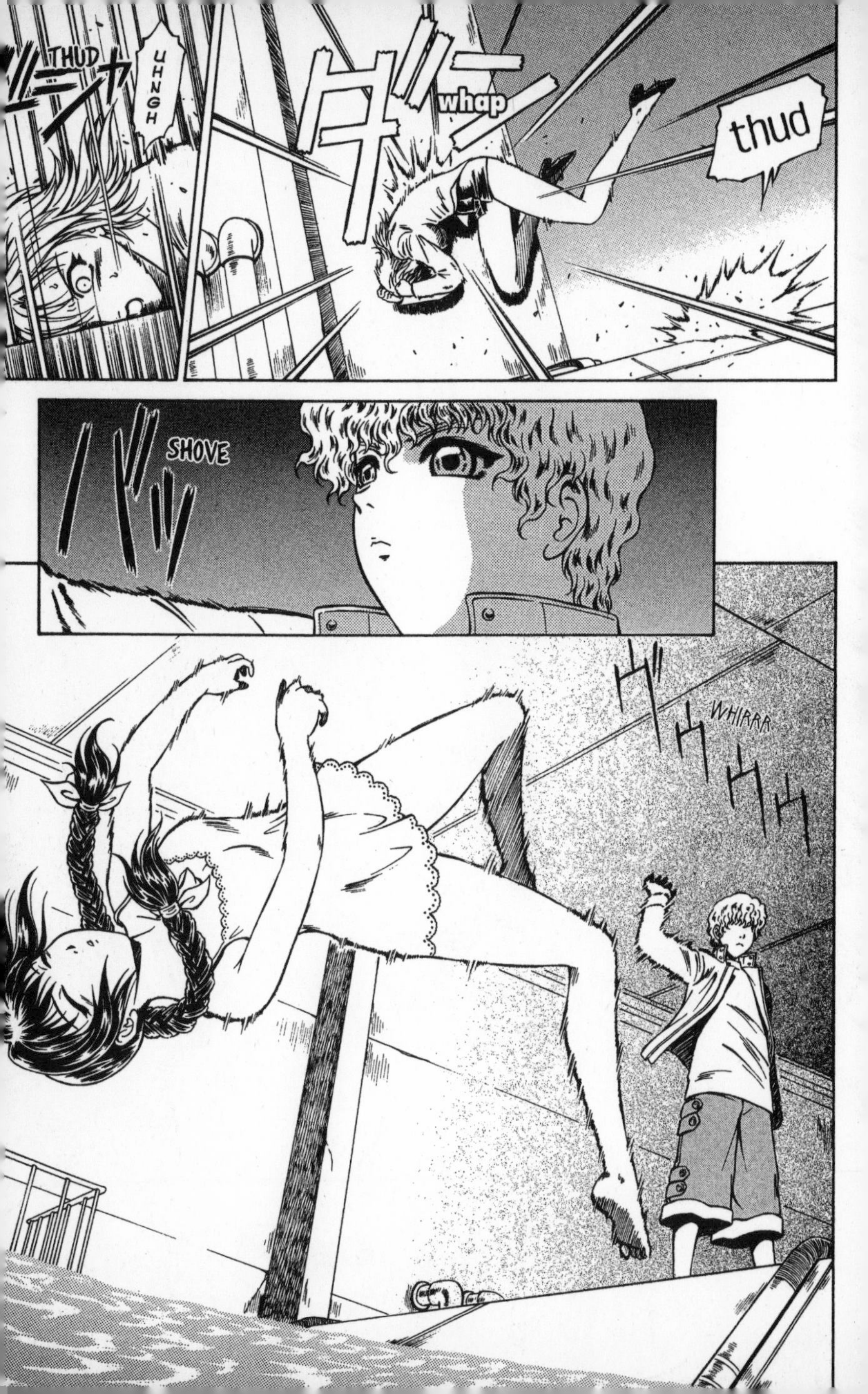
THUD
UHNGH
whap
thud
SHOVE
WHIRRR

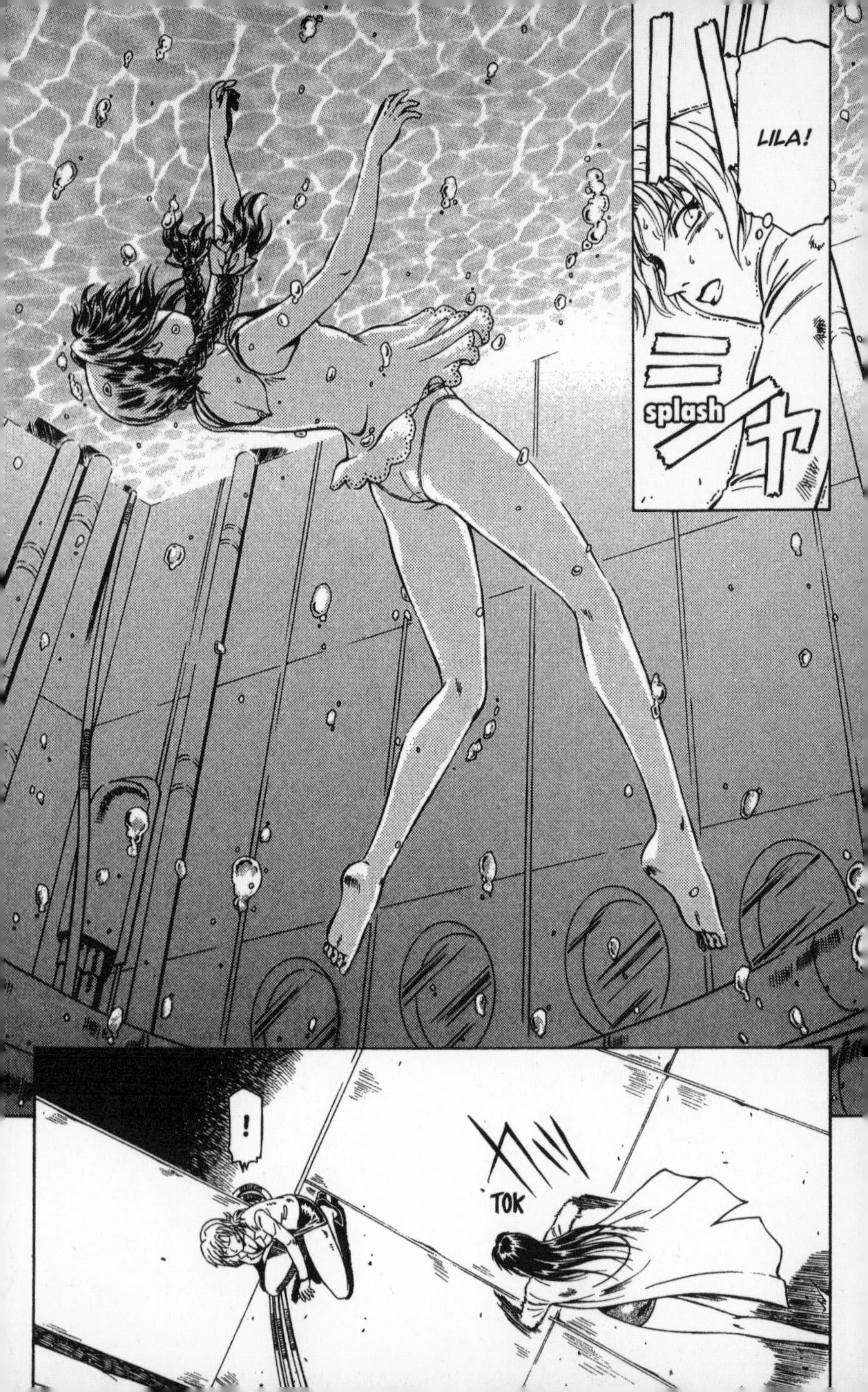
LILA!
splash
TOK
!

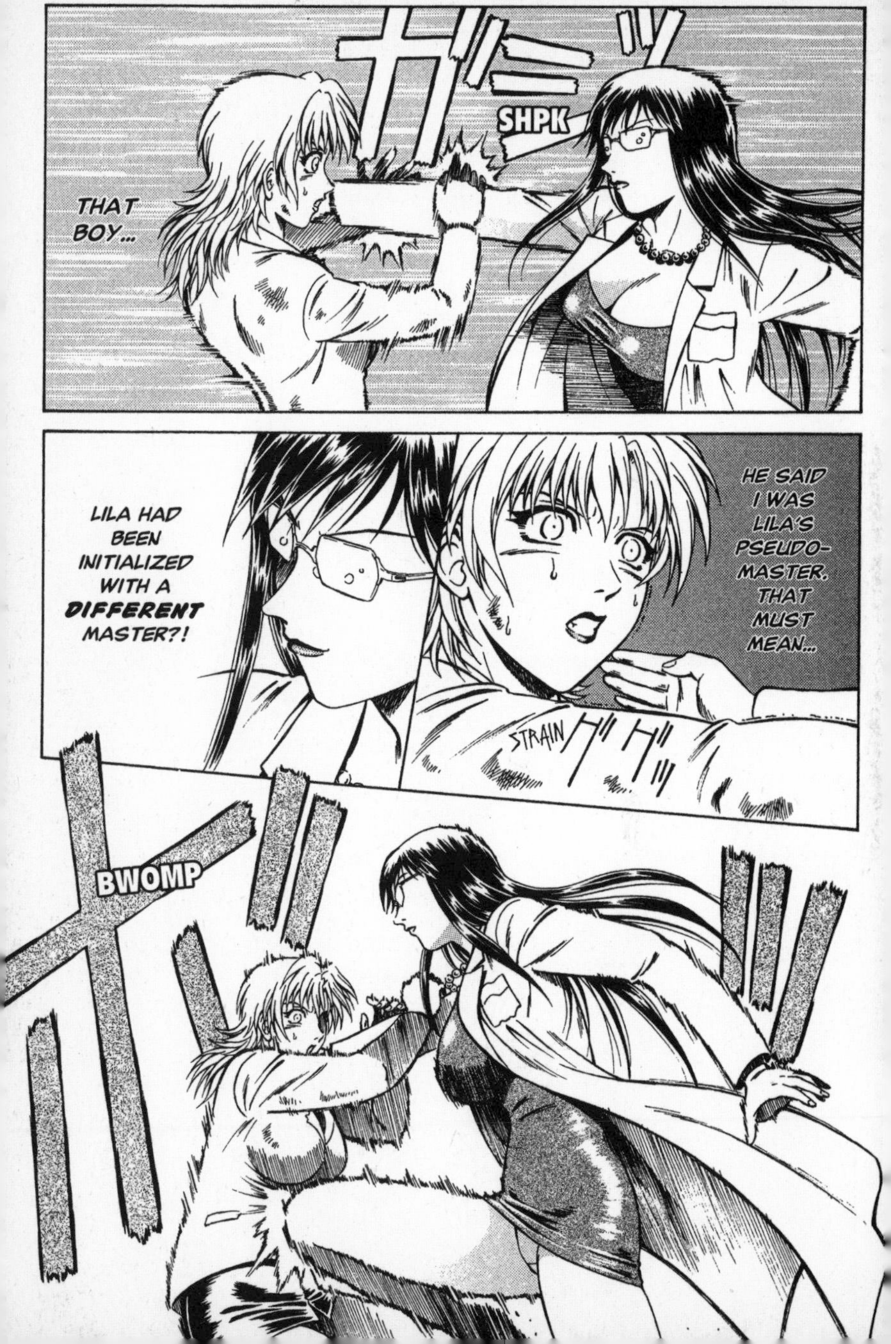
SHPK
THAT BOY...
HE SAID I WAS LILA'S PSEUDO-MASTER. THAT MUST MEAN...
LILA HAD BEEN INITIALIZED WITH A **DIFFERENT** MASTER?!
STRAIN
BWOMP

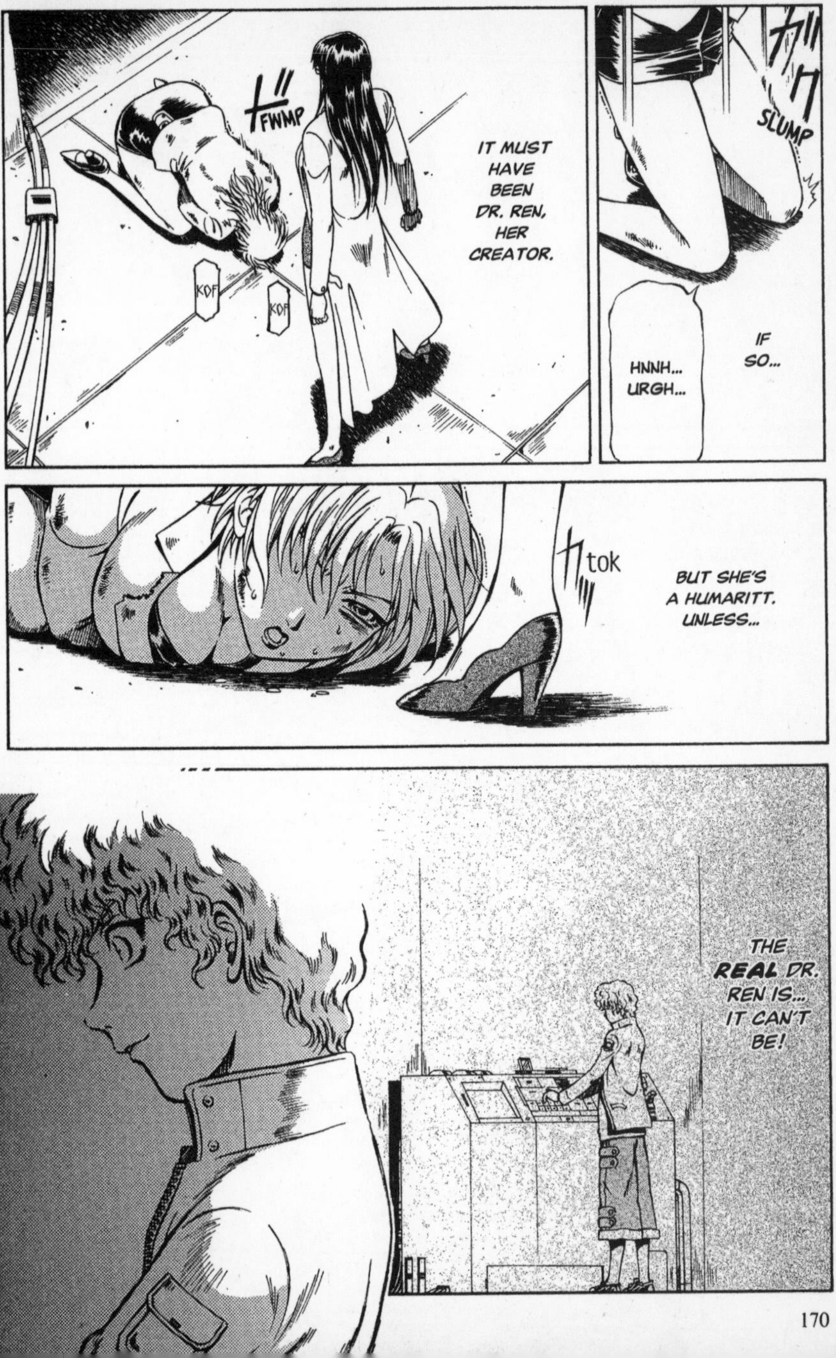
FWMP
KOF
KOF
IT MUST HAVE BEEN DR. REN, HER CREATOR.
SLUMP
HNNH... URGH...
IF SO...
tok
BUT SHE'S A HUMARITT. UNLESS...
THE REAL DR. REN IS... IT CAN'T BE!

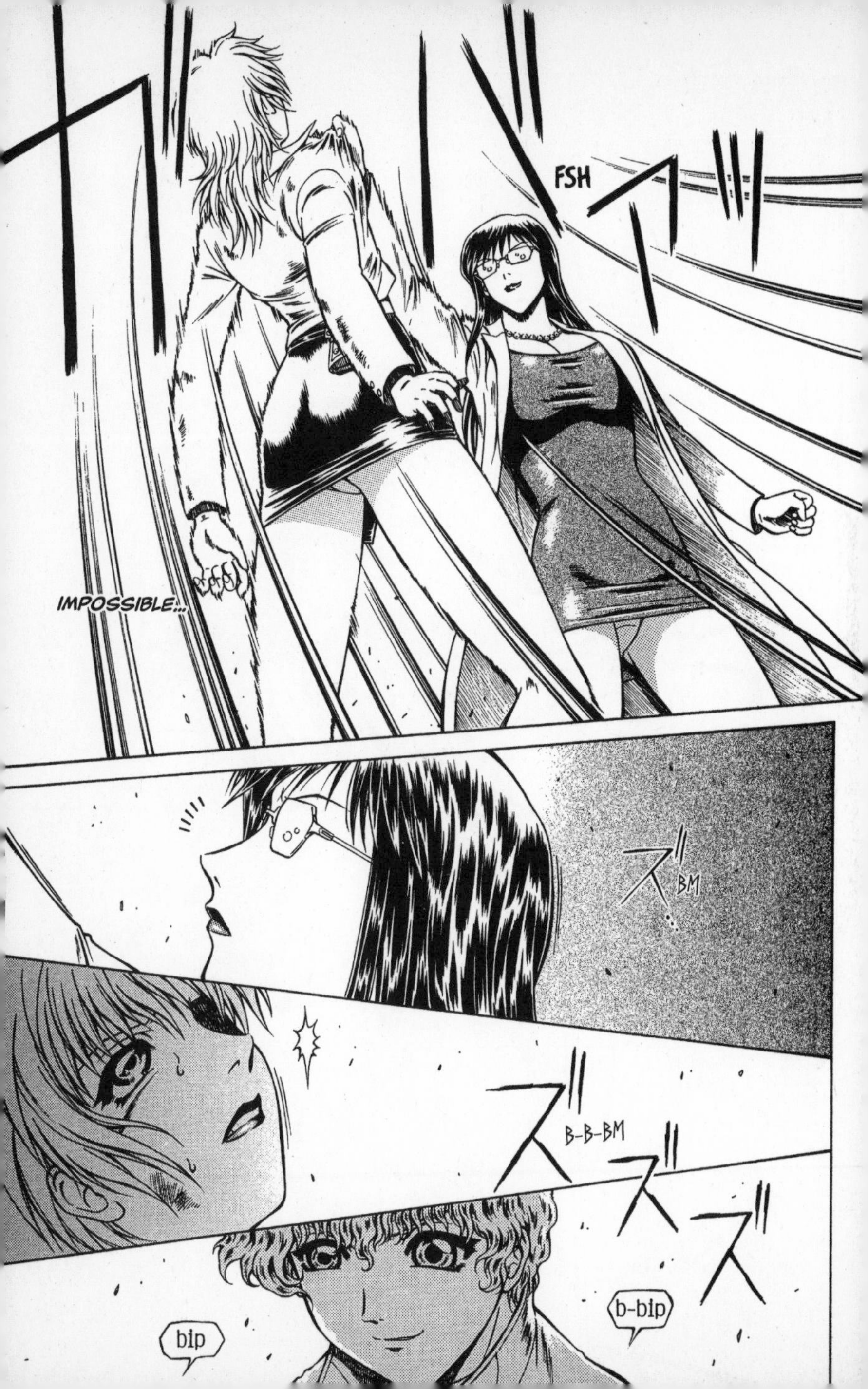
FSH
IMPOSSIBLE...
BM
B-B-BM
b-bip
bip

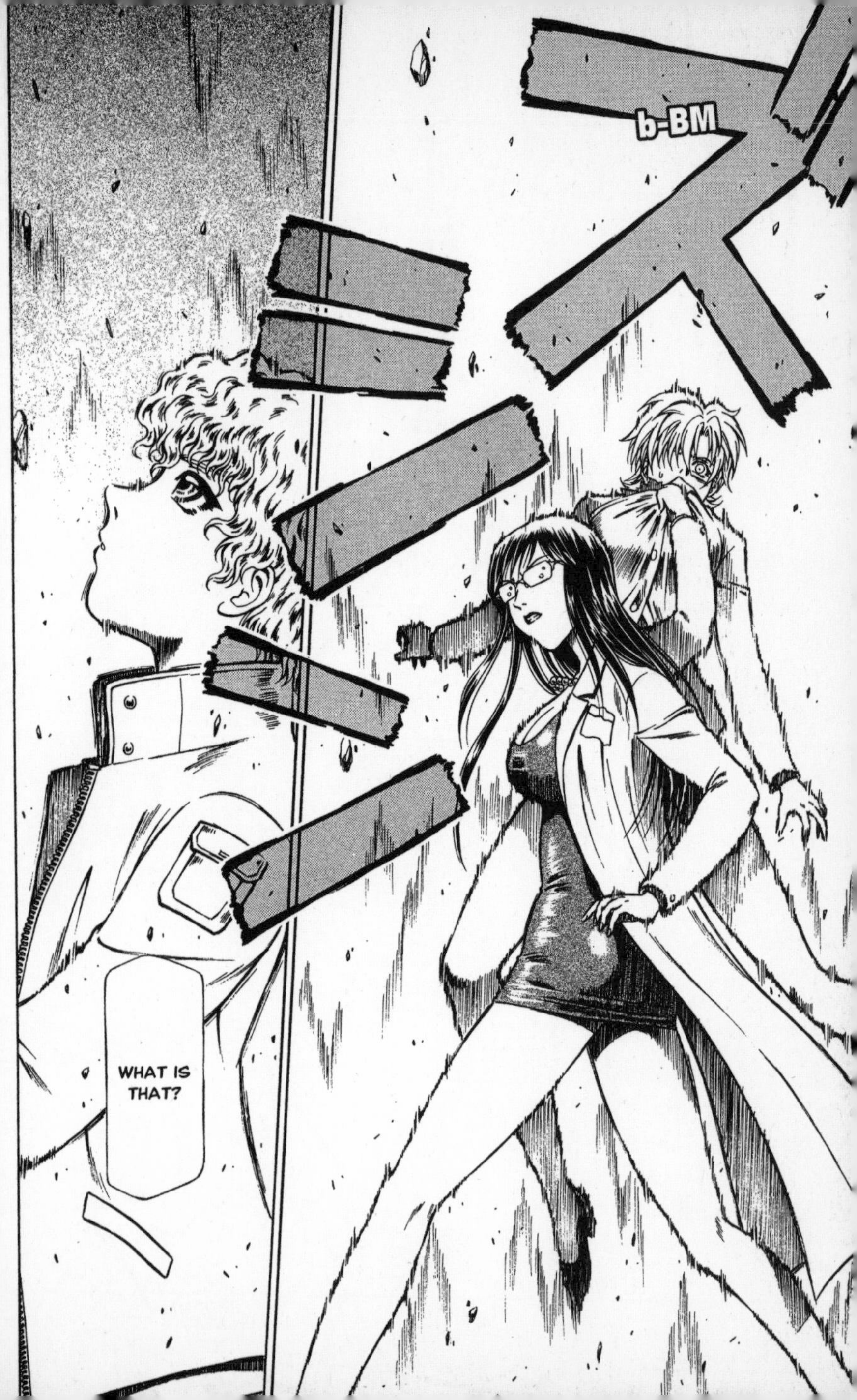
b-BM
WHAT IS THAT?

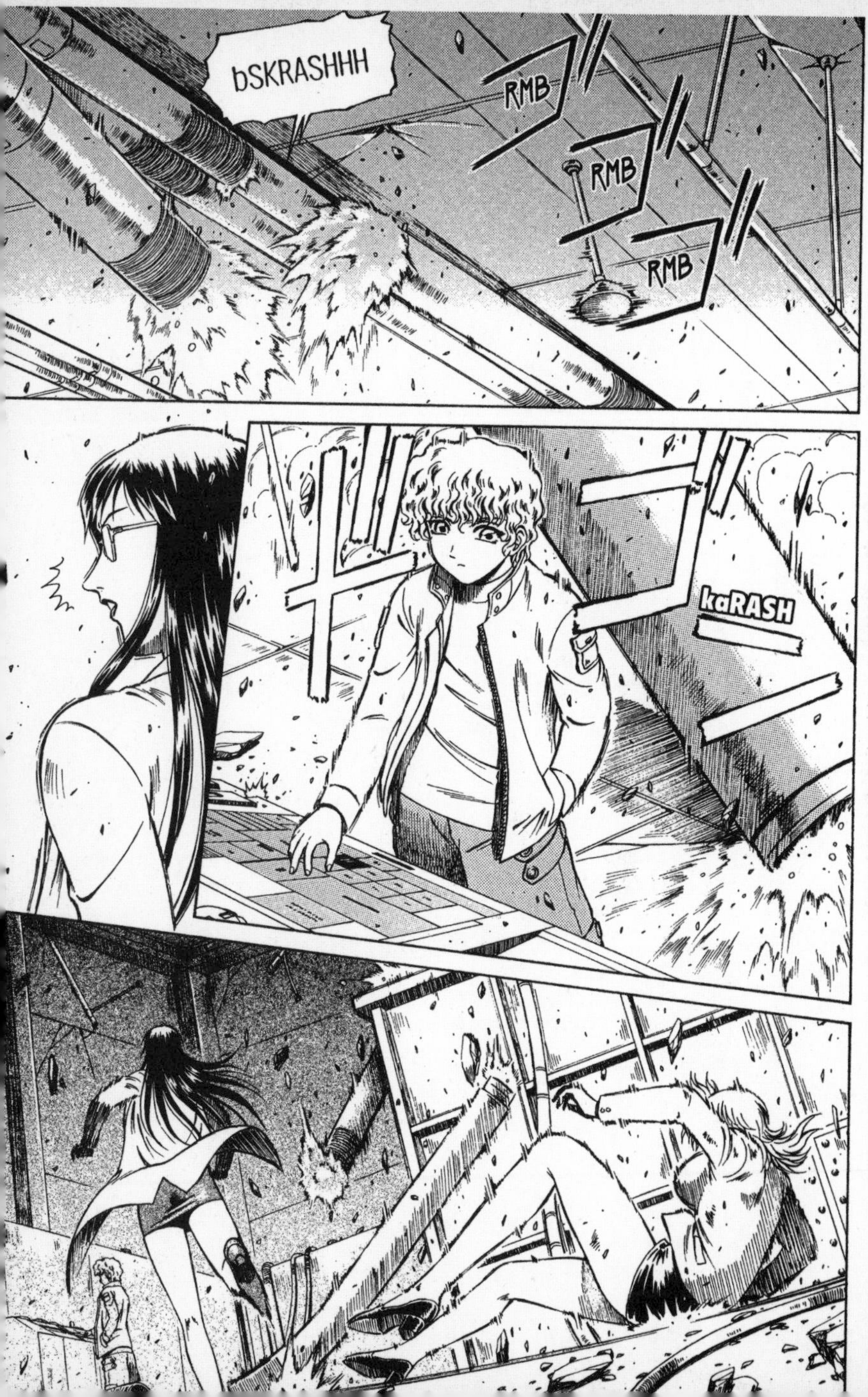

bSKRASHHH
RMB
RMB
RMB
kaRASH

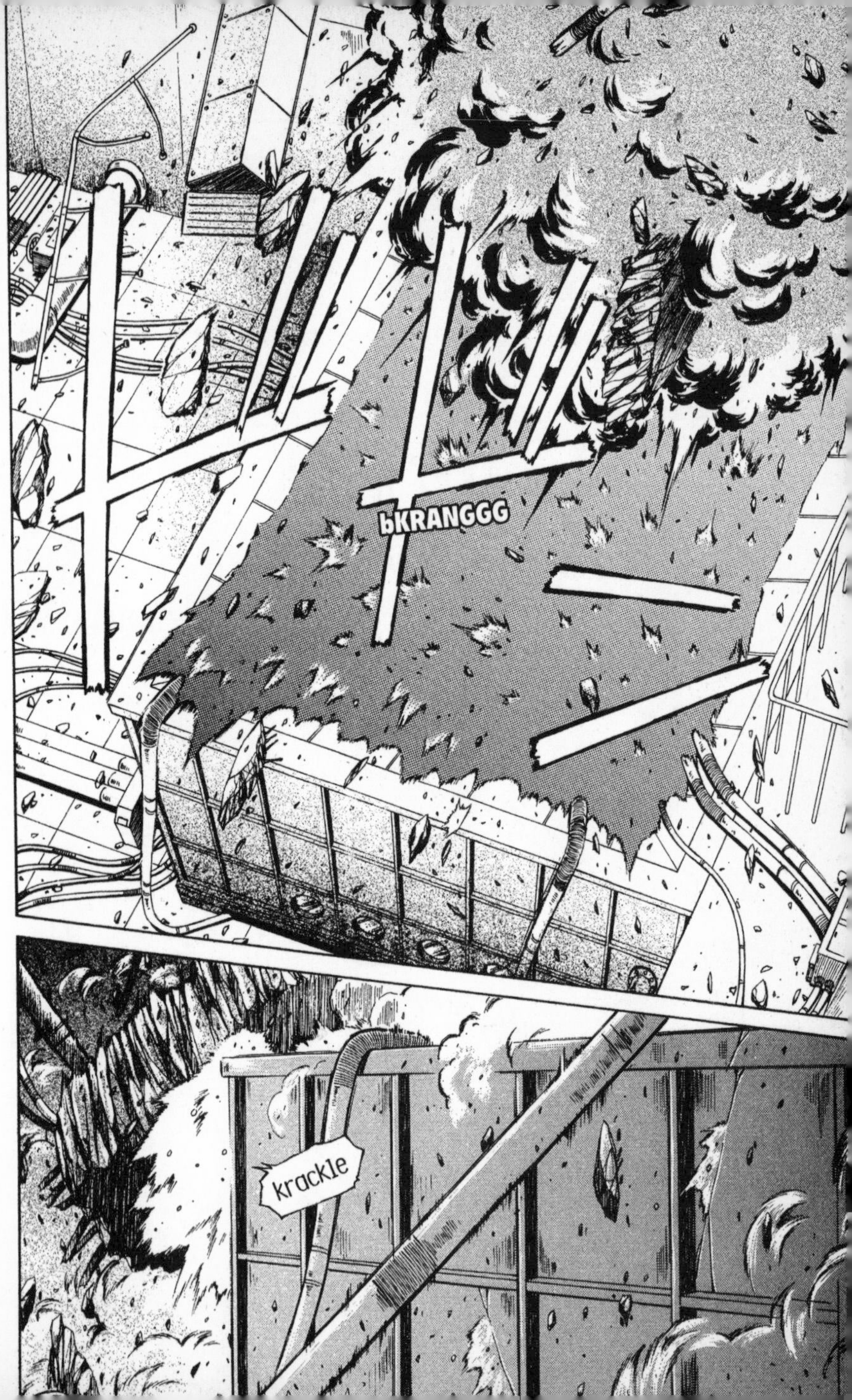
bKRANGGG
krackle

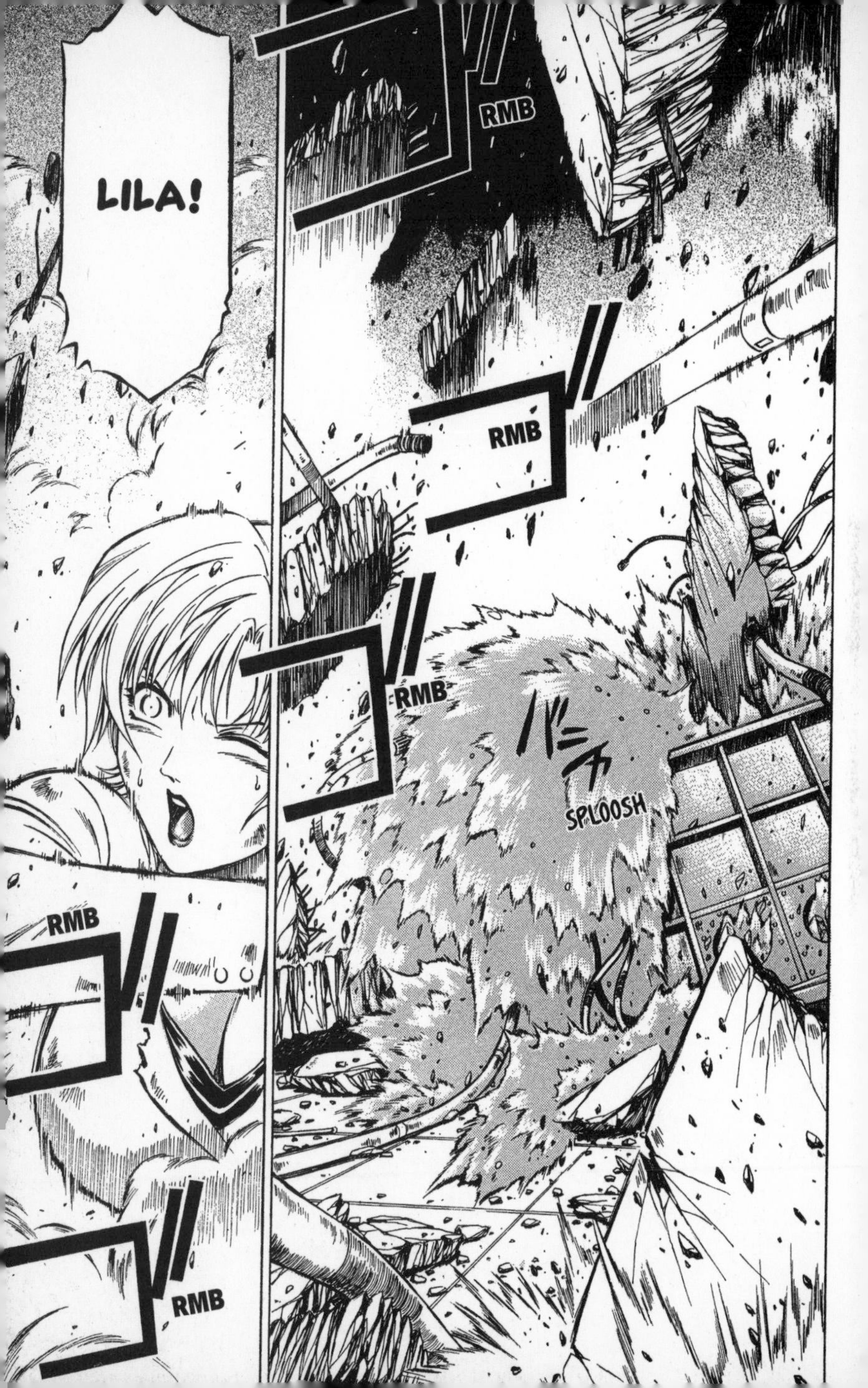
RMB
RMB
RMB
バシャ
SPLOOSH
LILA!
RMB
RMB

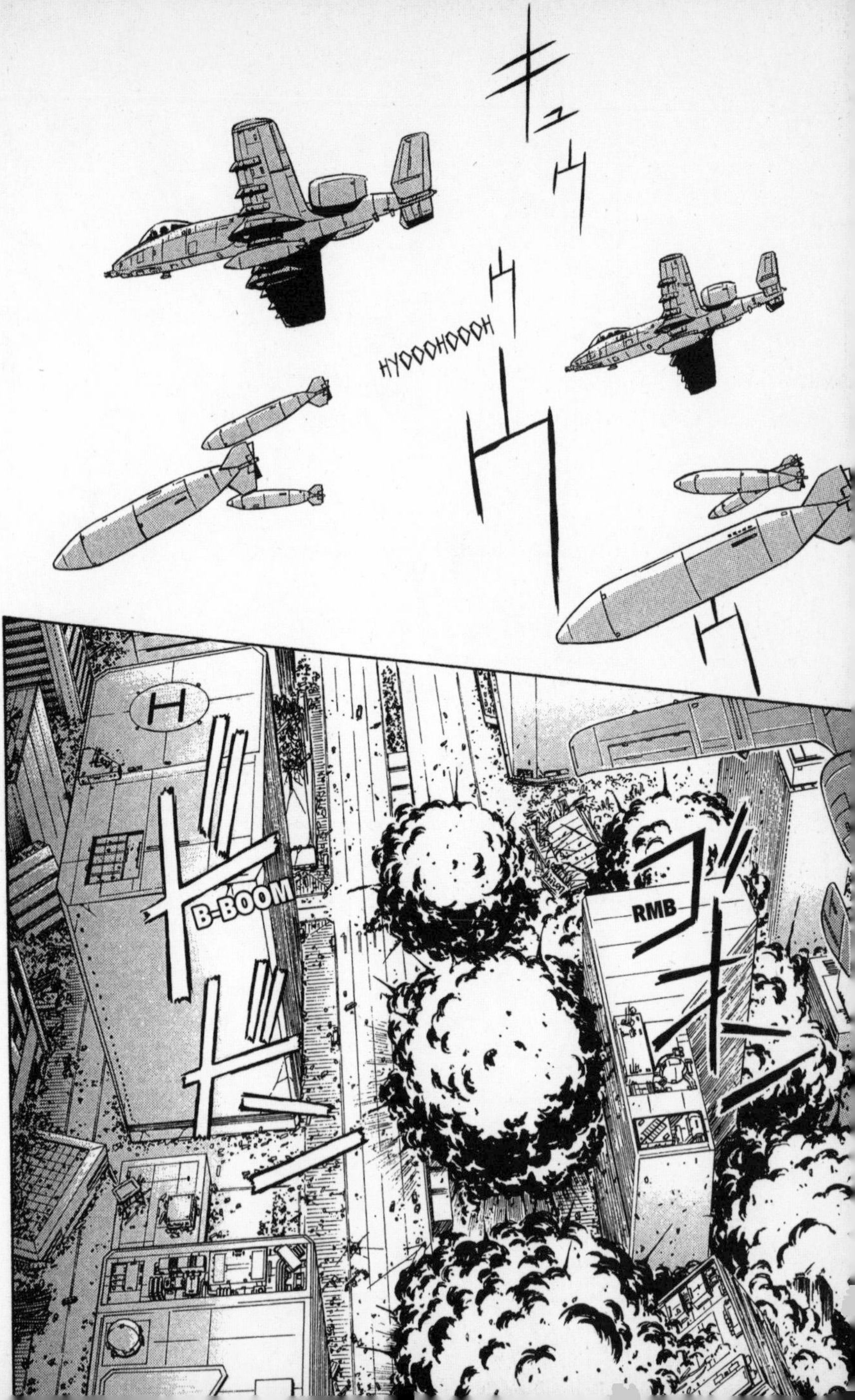
HYOOOHOOOH
B-BOOM
RMB

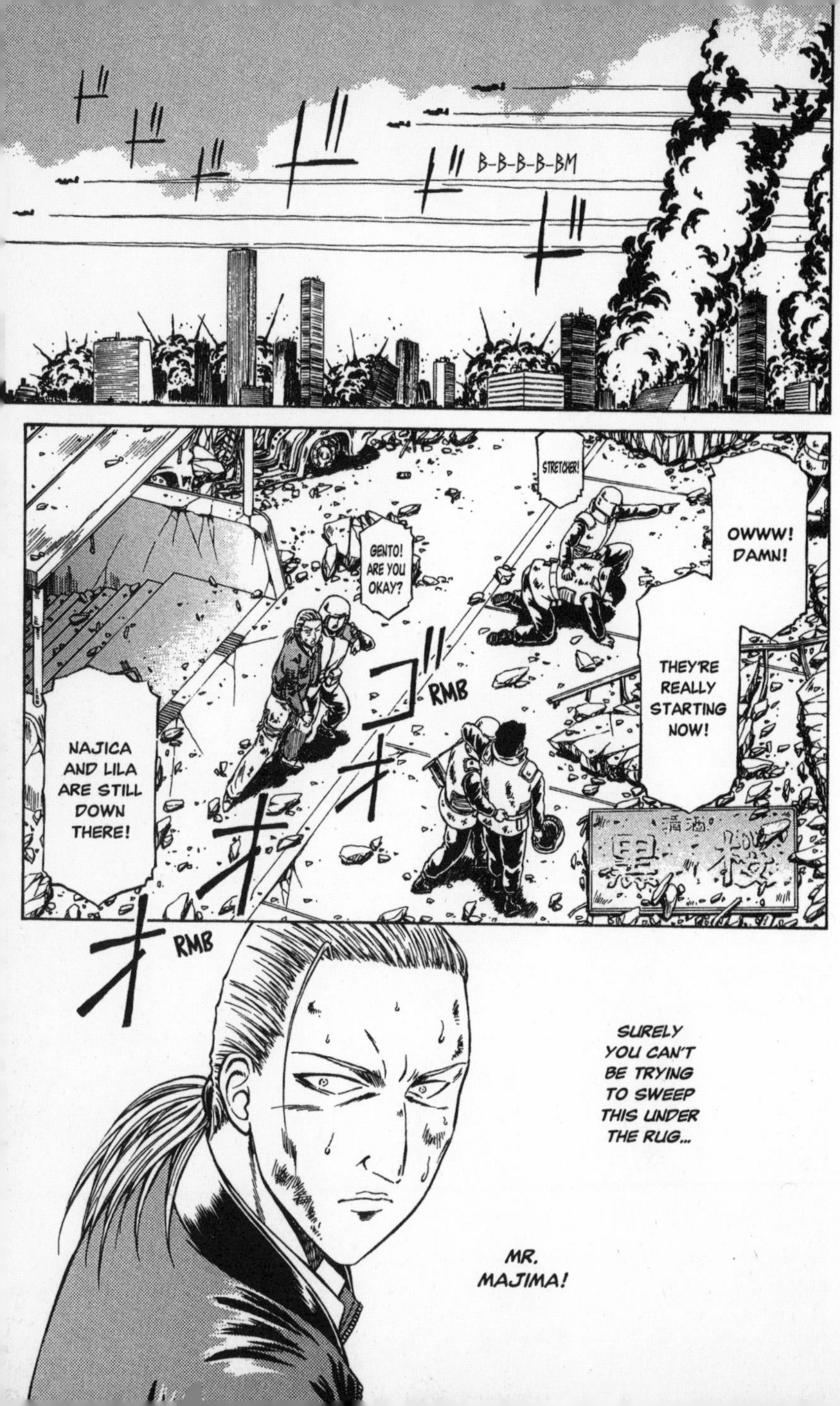
B-B-B-B-BM
STRETCHER!
OWWW! DAMN!
THEY'RE REALLY STARTING NOW!
GENTO! ARE YOU OKAY?
RMB
NAJICA AND LILA ARE STILL DOWN THERE!
RMB
SURELY YOU CAN'T BE TRYING TO SWEEP THIS UNDER THE RUG...
MR. MAJIMA!

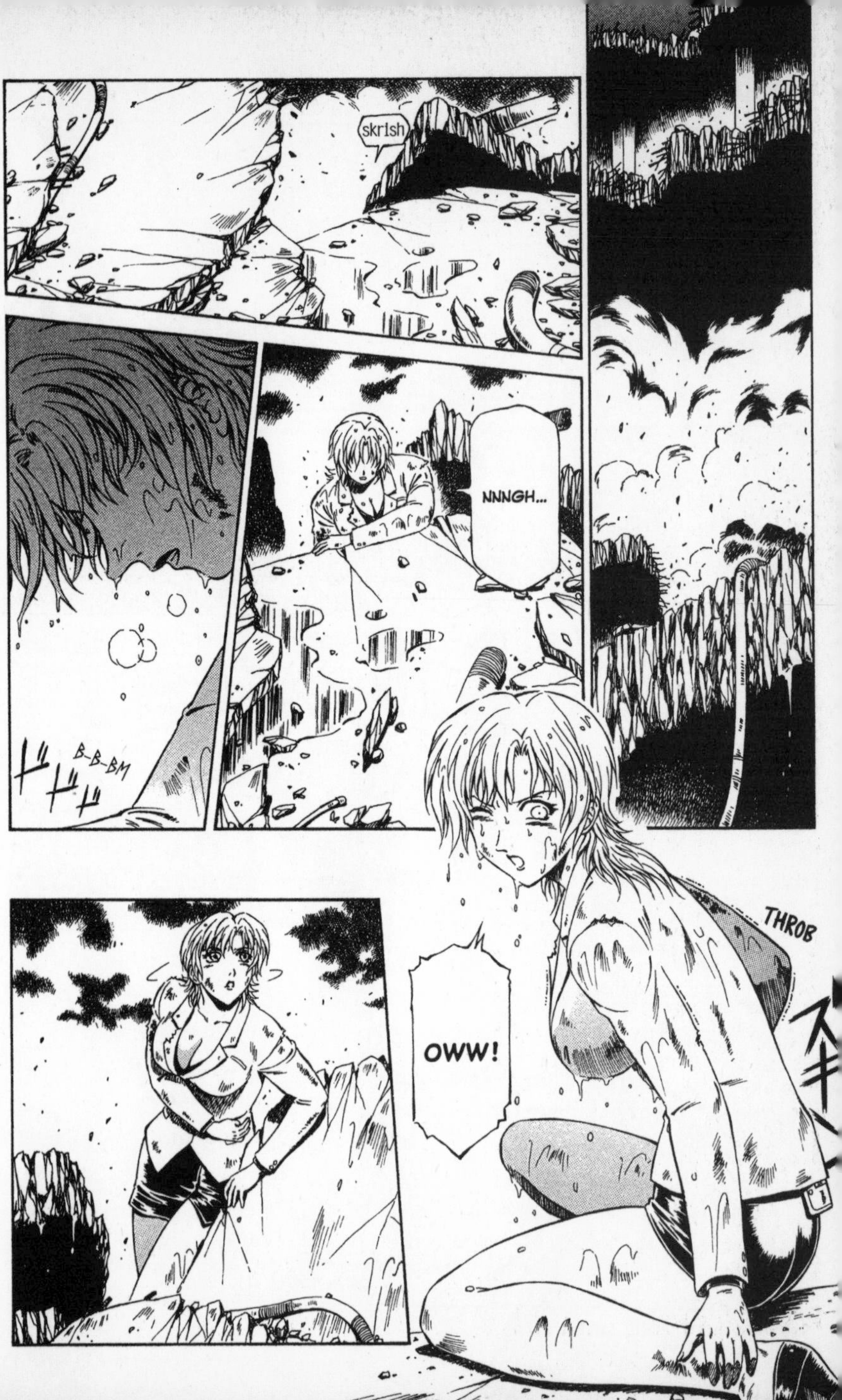
skrish
NNNGH...
B-B-BM
ドドド
THROB
OWW!

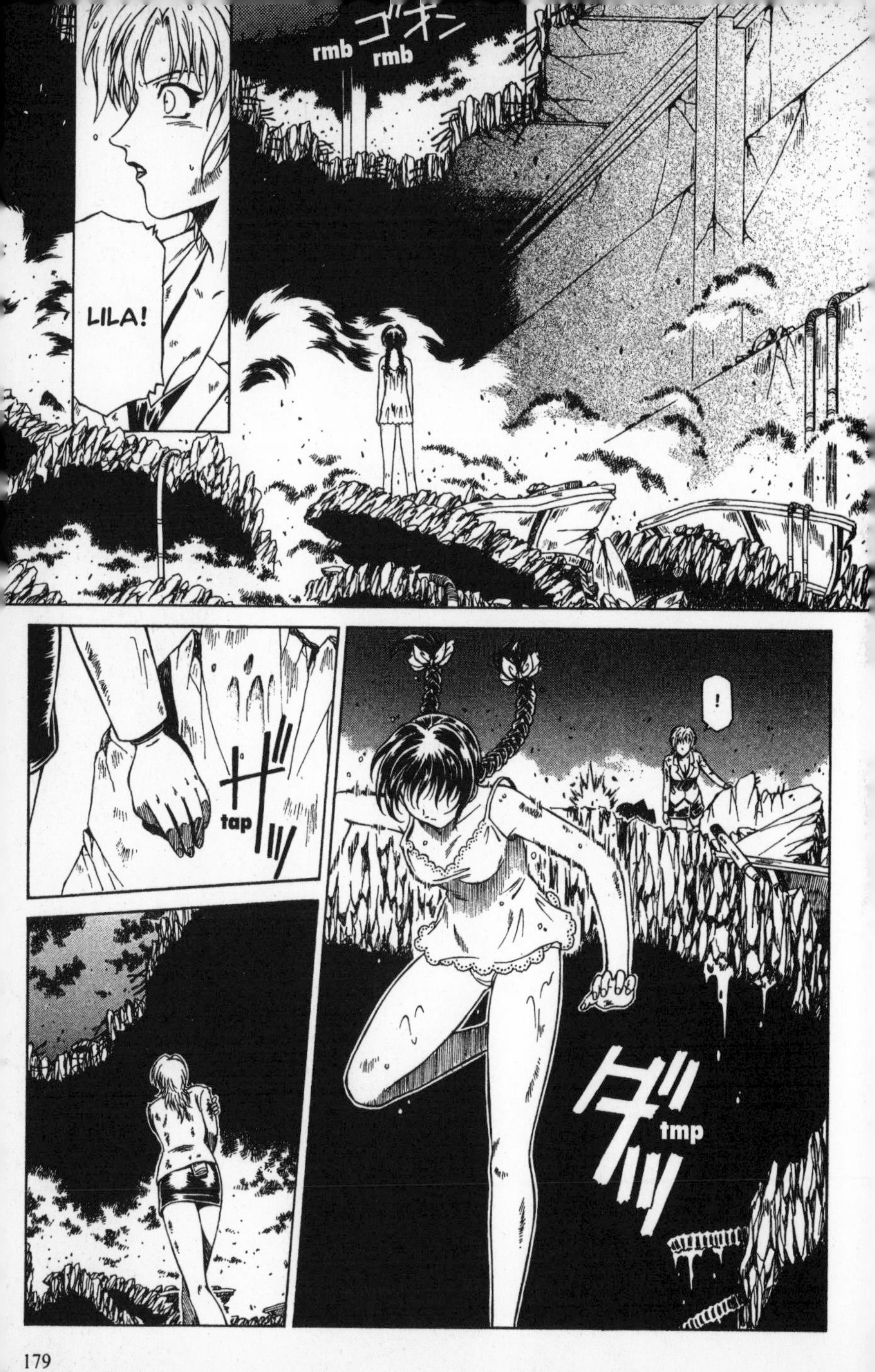
rmb ゴオン rmb
LILA!
ザッ tap
!
ダッ tmp

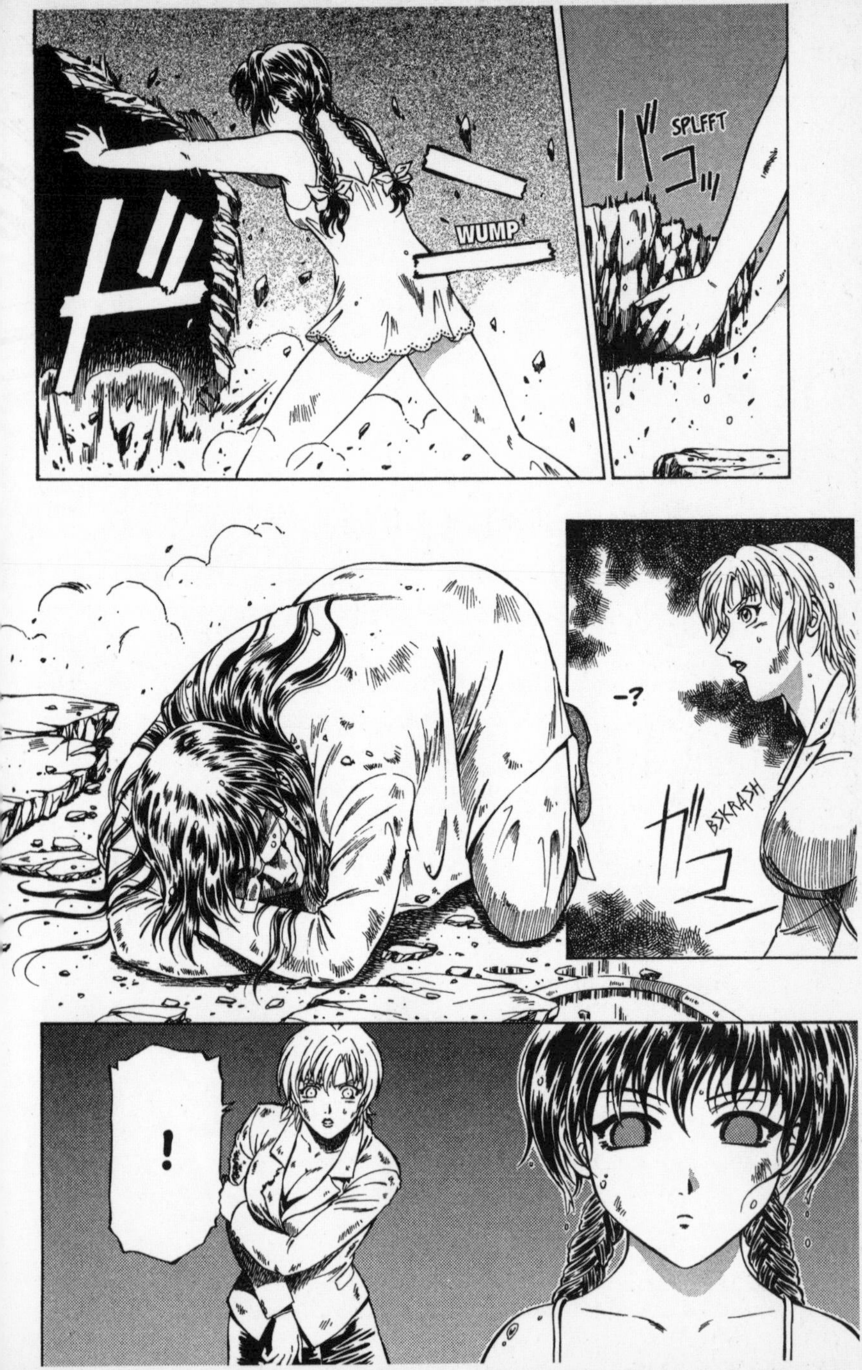

バコッ
SPLFFT
ドゴ
WUMP
-?
ガゴ
BSKRASH
!

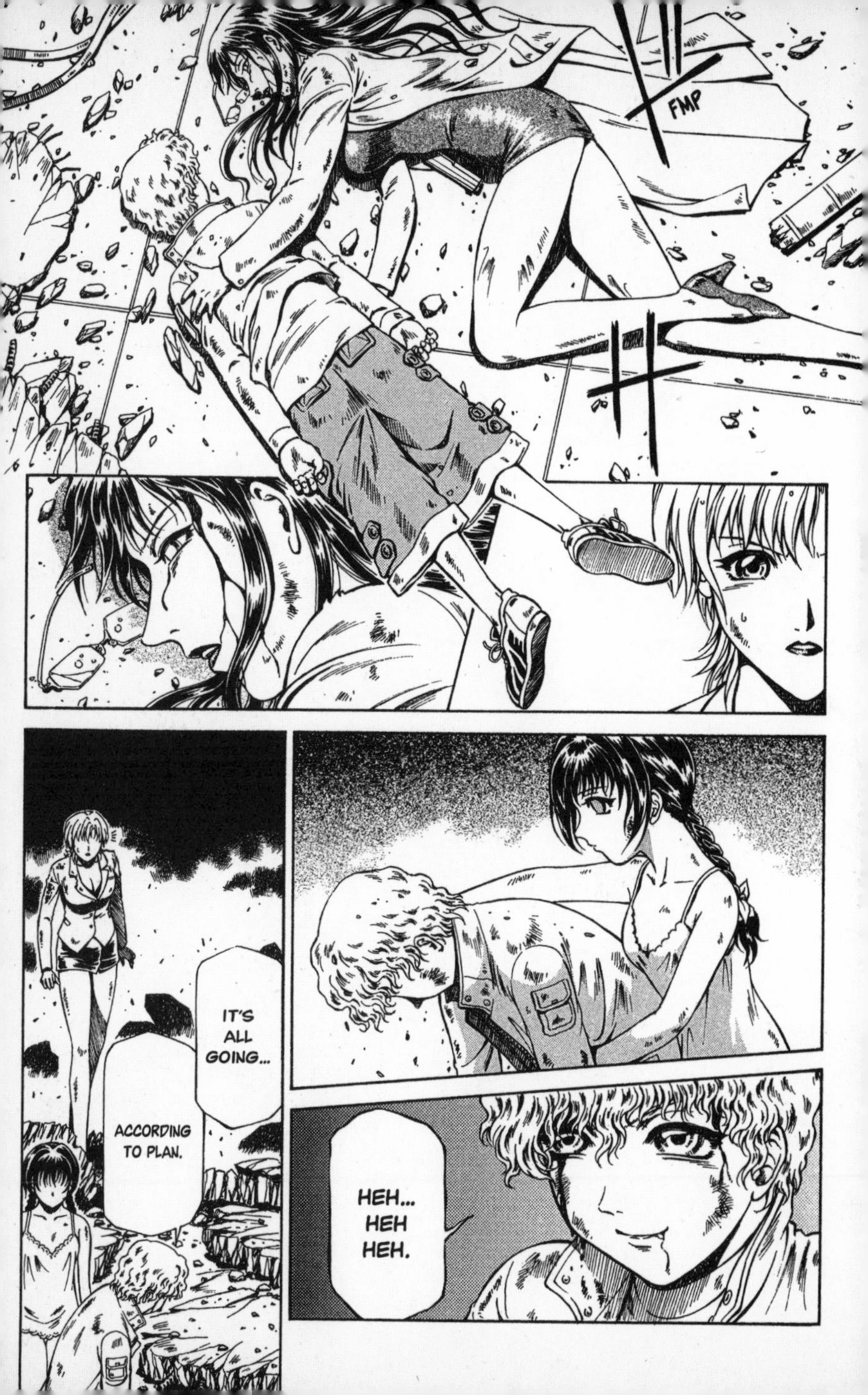
FMP
IT'S ALL GOING...
ACCORDING TO PLAN.
HEH... HEH HEH.

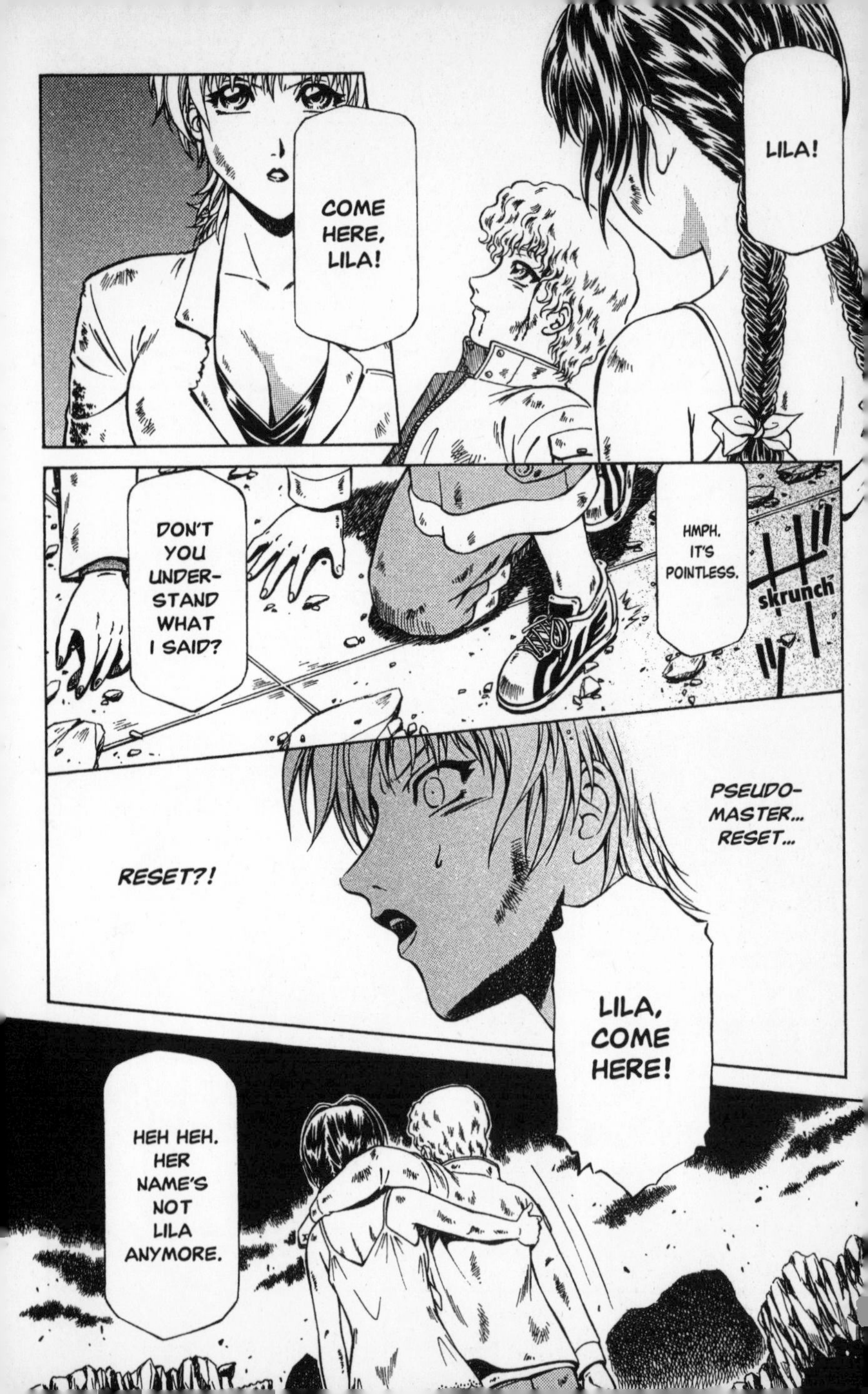
LILA!
COME HERE, LILA!
HMPH. IT'S POINTLESS.
skrunch
DON'T YOU UNDER-STAND WHAT I SAID?
PSEUDO-MASTER... RESET...
RESET?!
LILA, COME HERE!
HEH HEH. HER NAME'S NOT LILA ANYMORE.

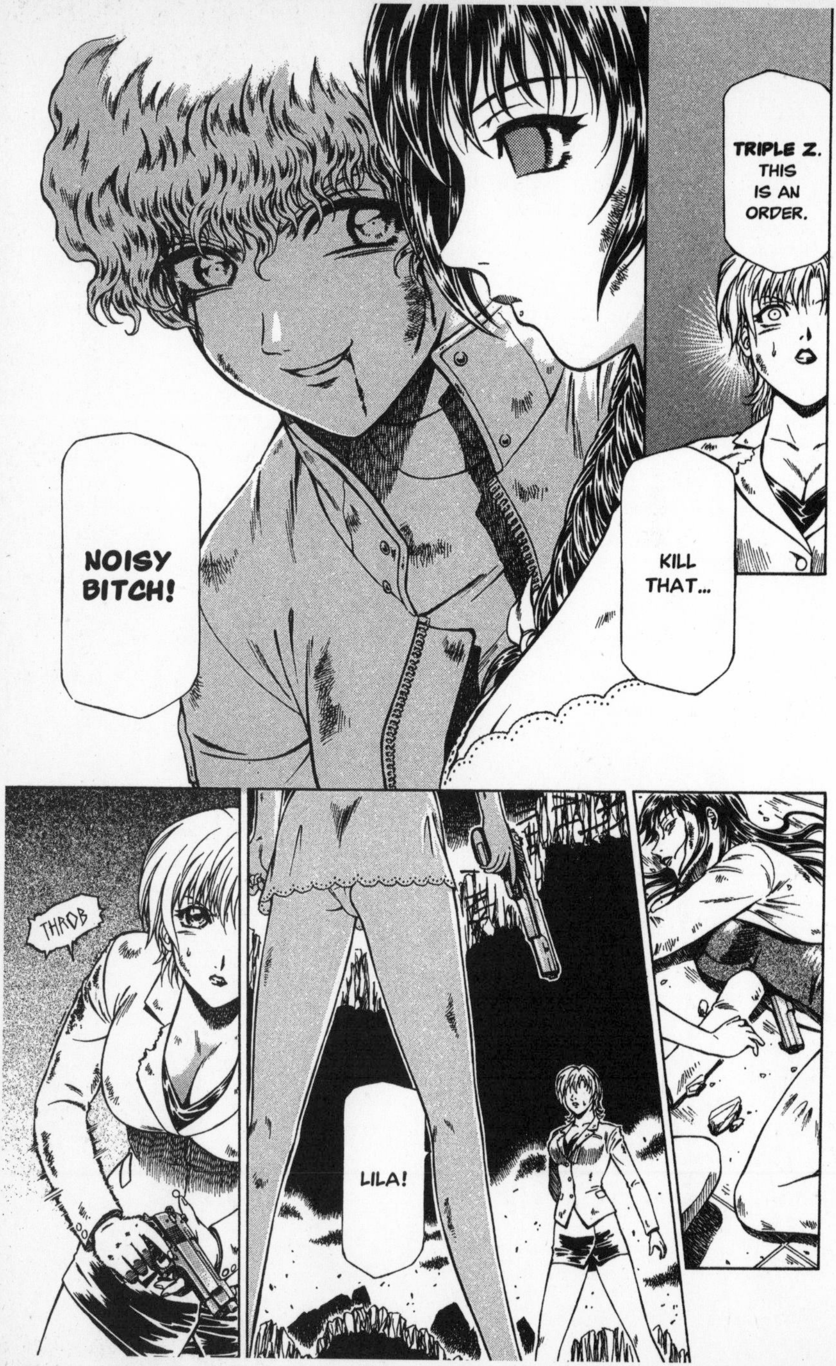
TRIPLE Z. THIS IS AN ORDER.
KILL THAT...
NOISY BITCH!
LILA!
THROB

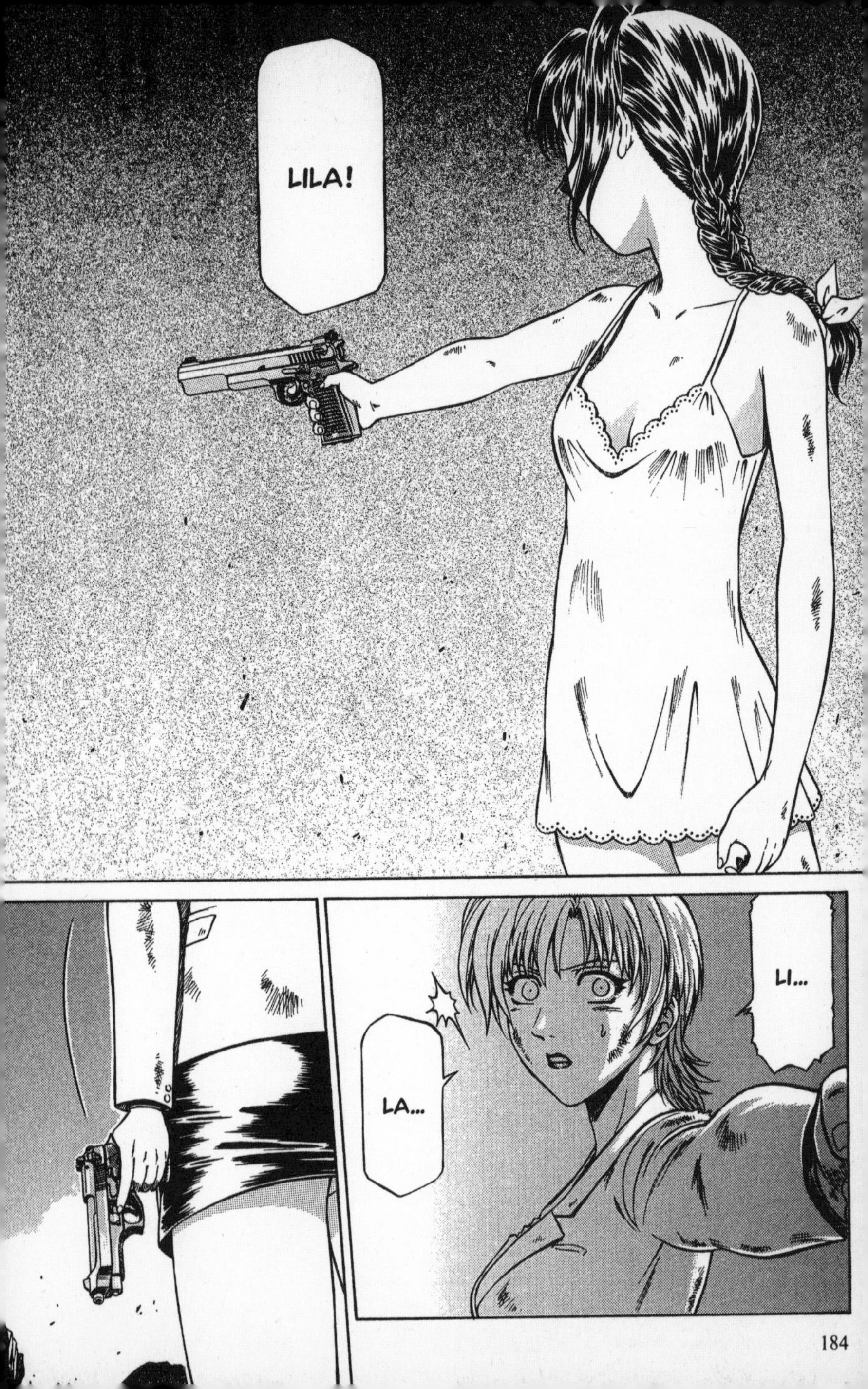
LILA!
LI...
LA...

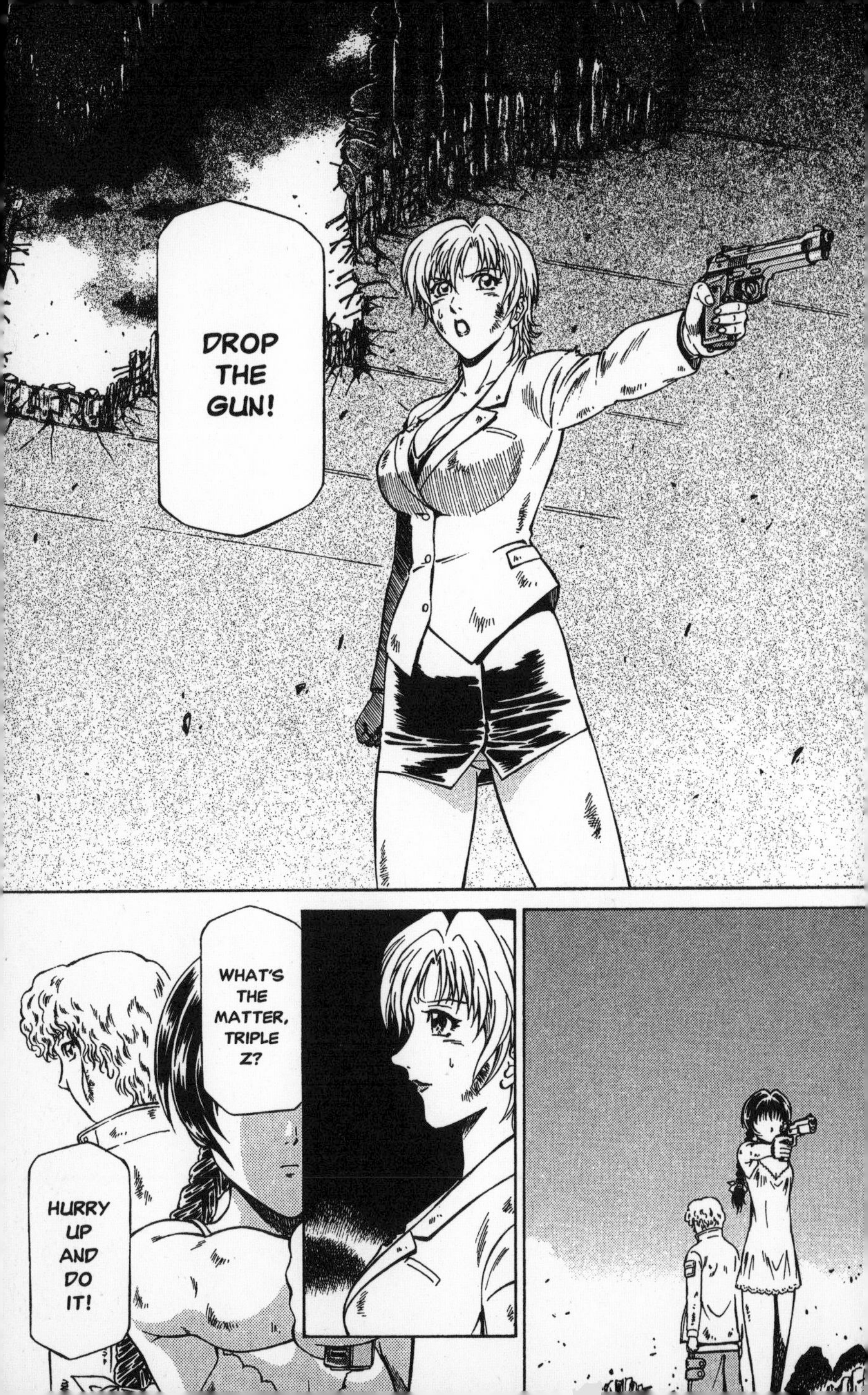
DROP THE GUN!
WHAT'S THE MATTER, TRIPLE Z?
HURRY UP AND DO IT!

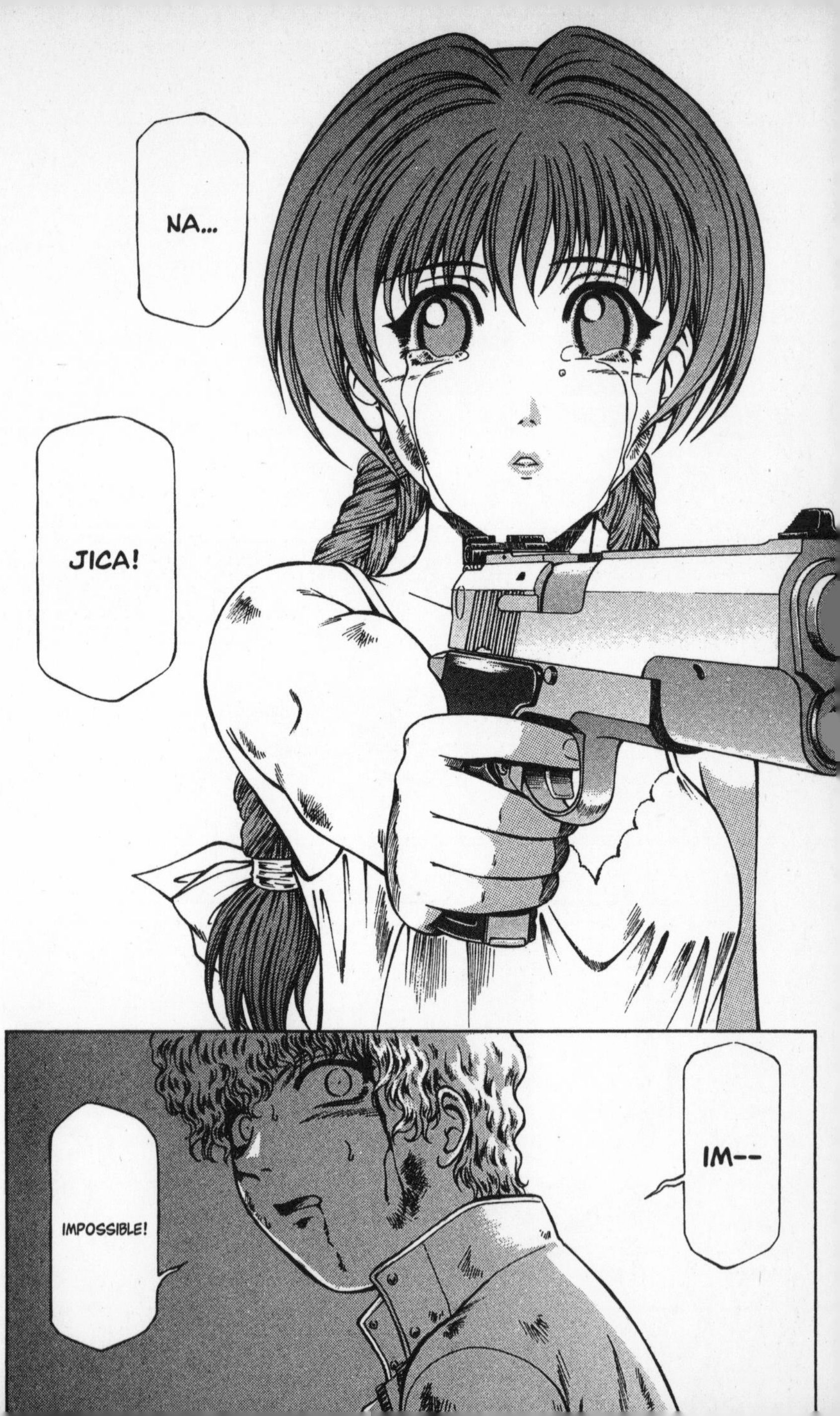
NA...
JICA!
IM--
IMPOSSIBLE!

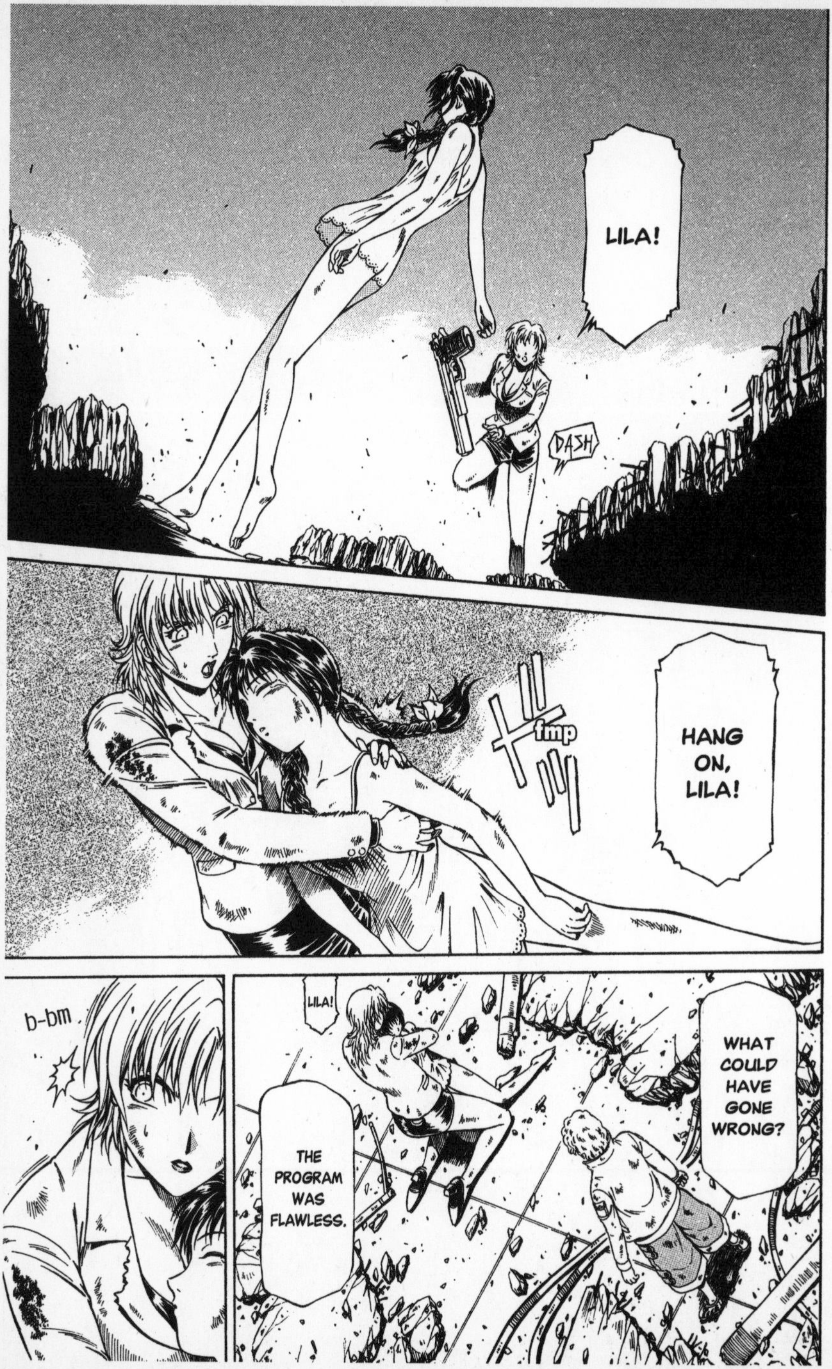

LILA!
DASH
HANG ON, LILA!
fmp
b-bm
LILA!
WHAT COULD HAVE GONE WRONG?
THE PROGRAM WAS FLAWLESS.

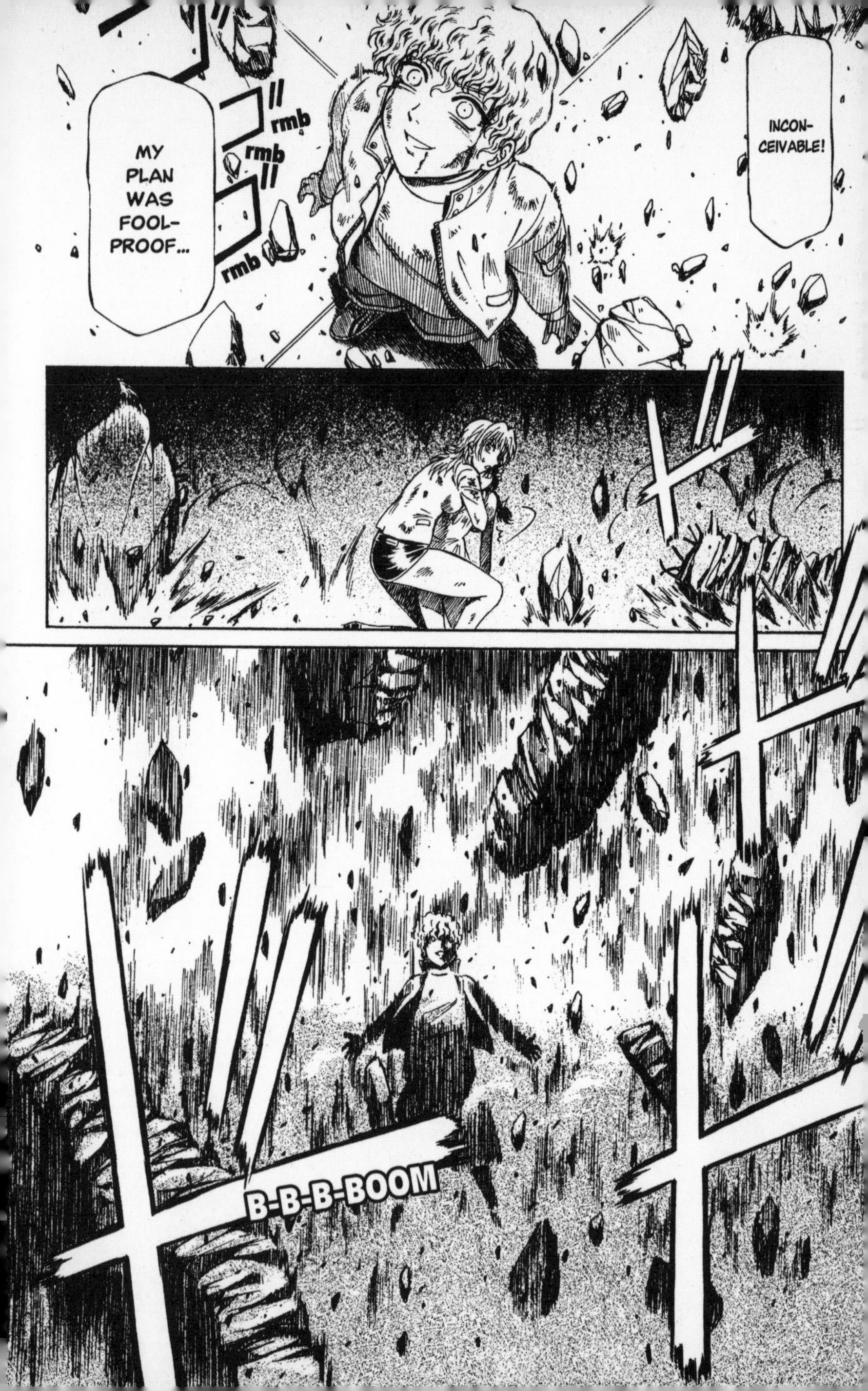
INCON-CEIVABLE!
rmb
rmb
rmb
MY PLAN WAS FOOL-PROOF...
B-B-B-BOOM

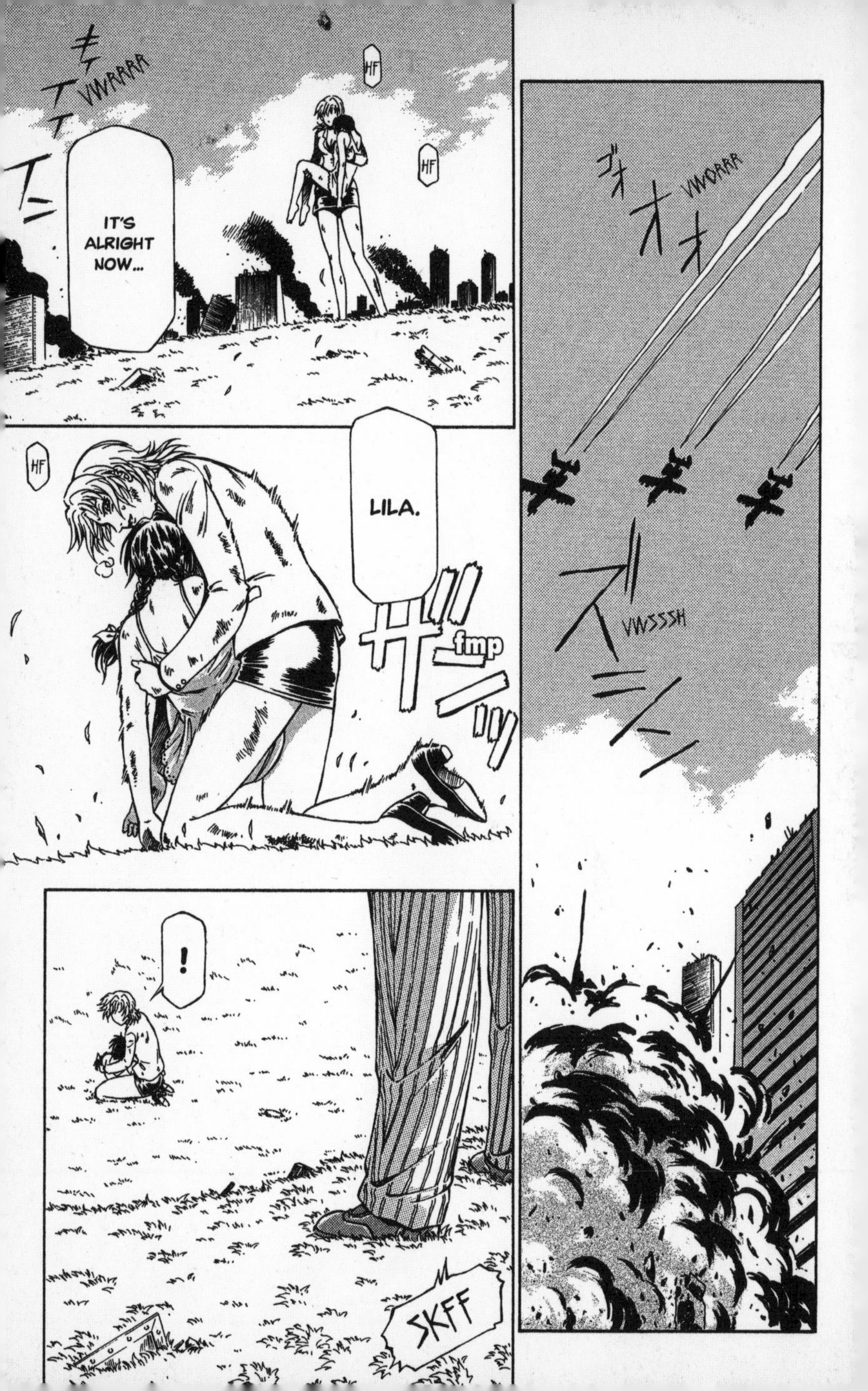
ゴオオオ
VWORRR
VWSSSH
VWRRRR
HF
HF
IT'S ALRIGHT NOW...
HF
LILA.
fmp
!
SKFF

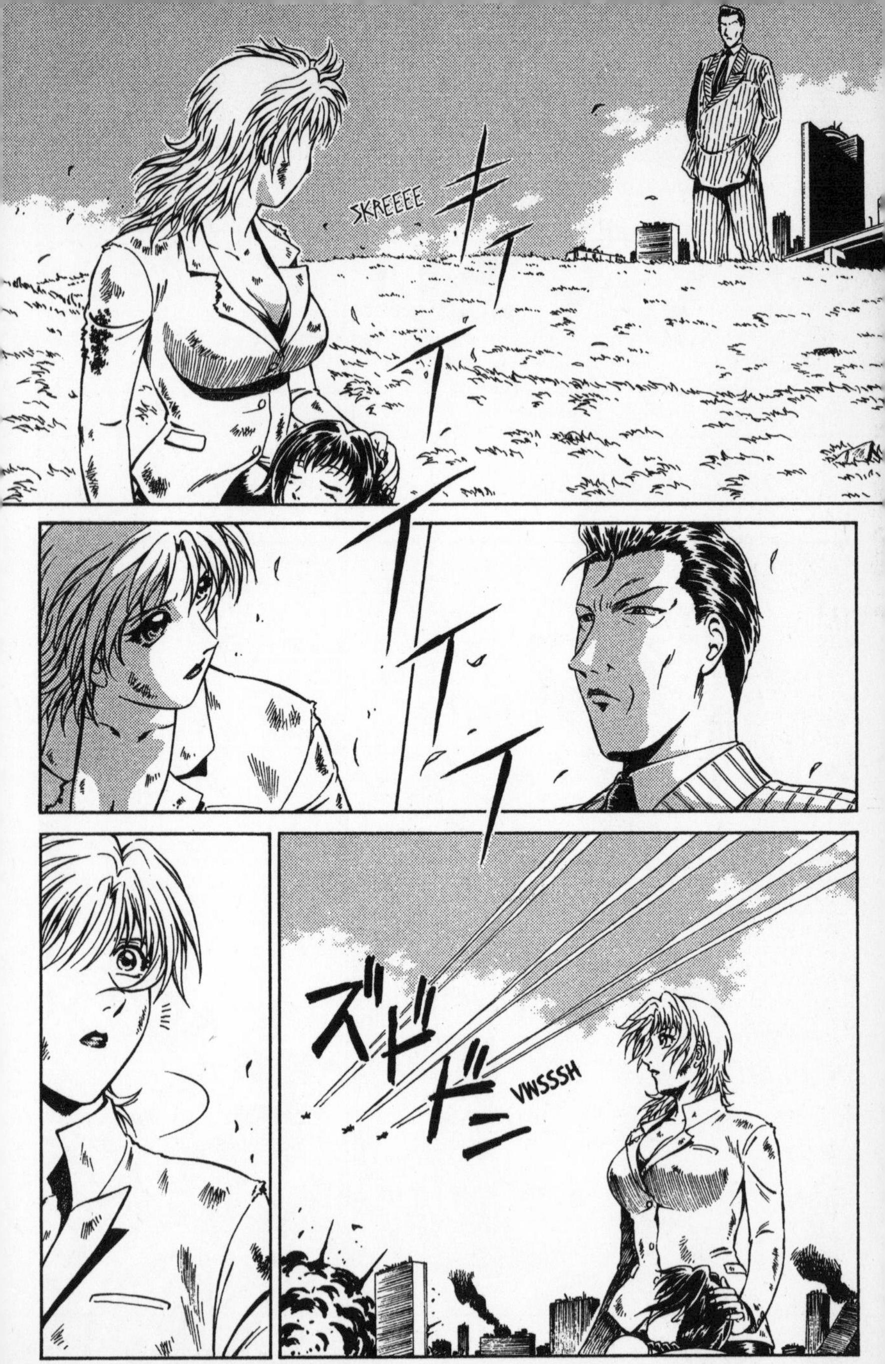
SKREEEE
VWSSSH

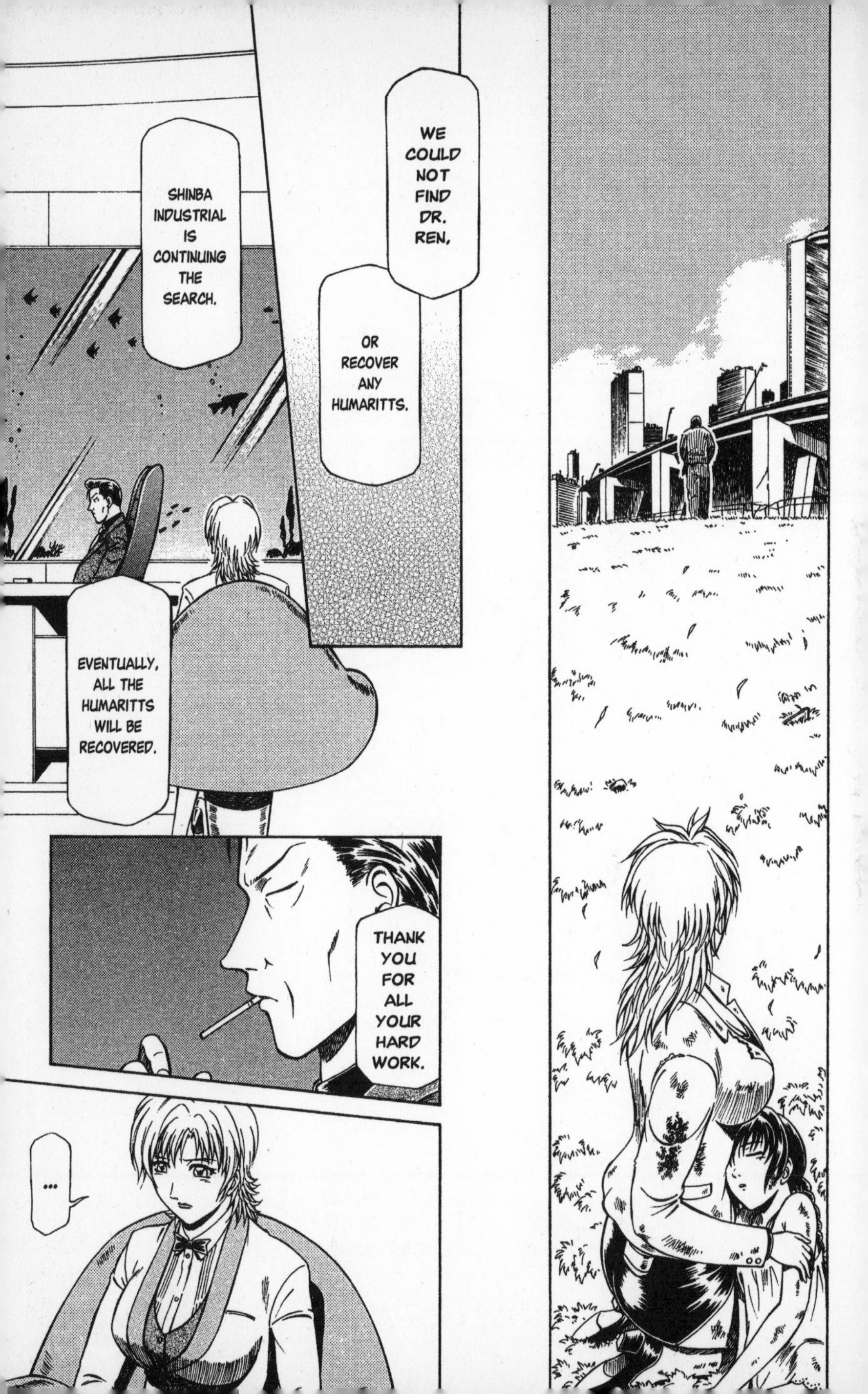
WE COULD NOT FIND DR. REN,
OR RECOVER ANY HUMARITTS.
SHINBA INDUSTRIAL IS CONTINUING THE SEARCH.
EVENTUALLY, ALL THE HUMARITTS WILL BE RECOVERED.
THANK YOU FOR ALL YOUR HARD WORK.
...

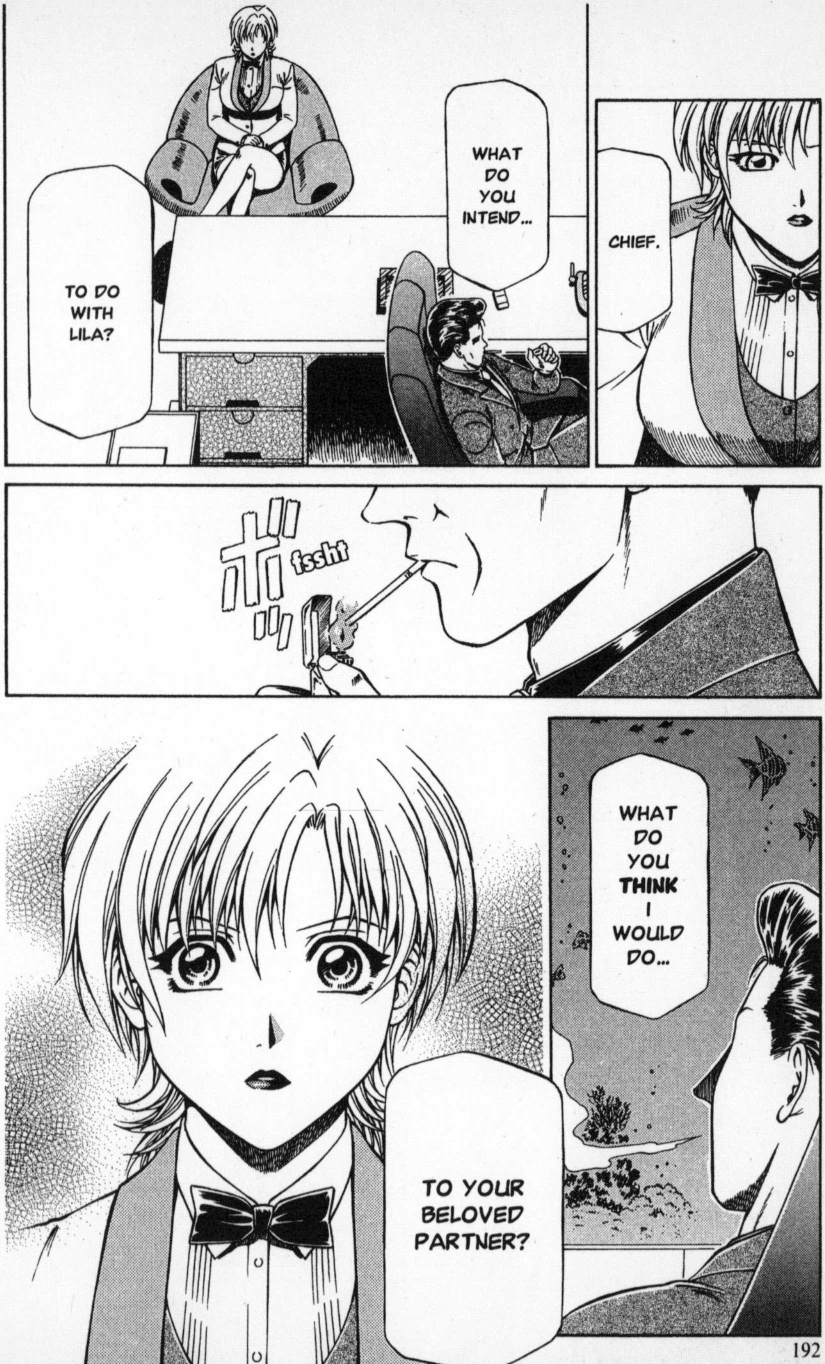
CHIEF.
WHAT DO YOU INTEND...
TO DO WITH LILA?
fssht
WHAT DO YOU THINK I WOULD DO...
TO YOUR BELOVED PARTNER?

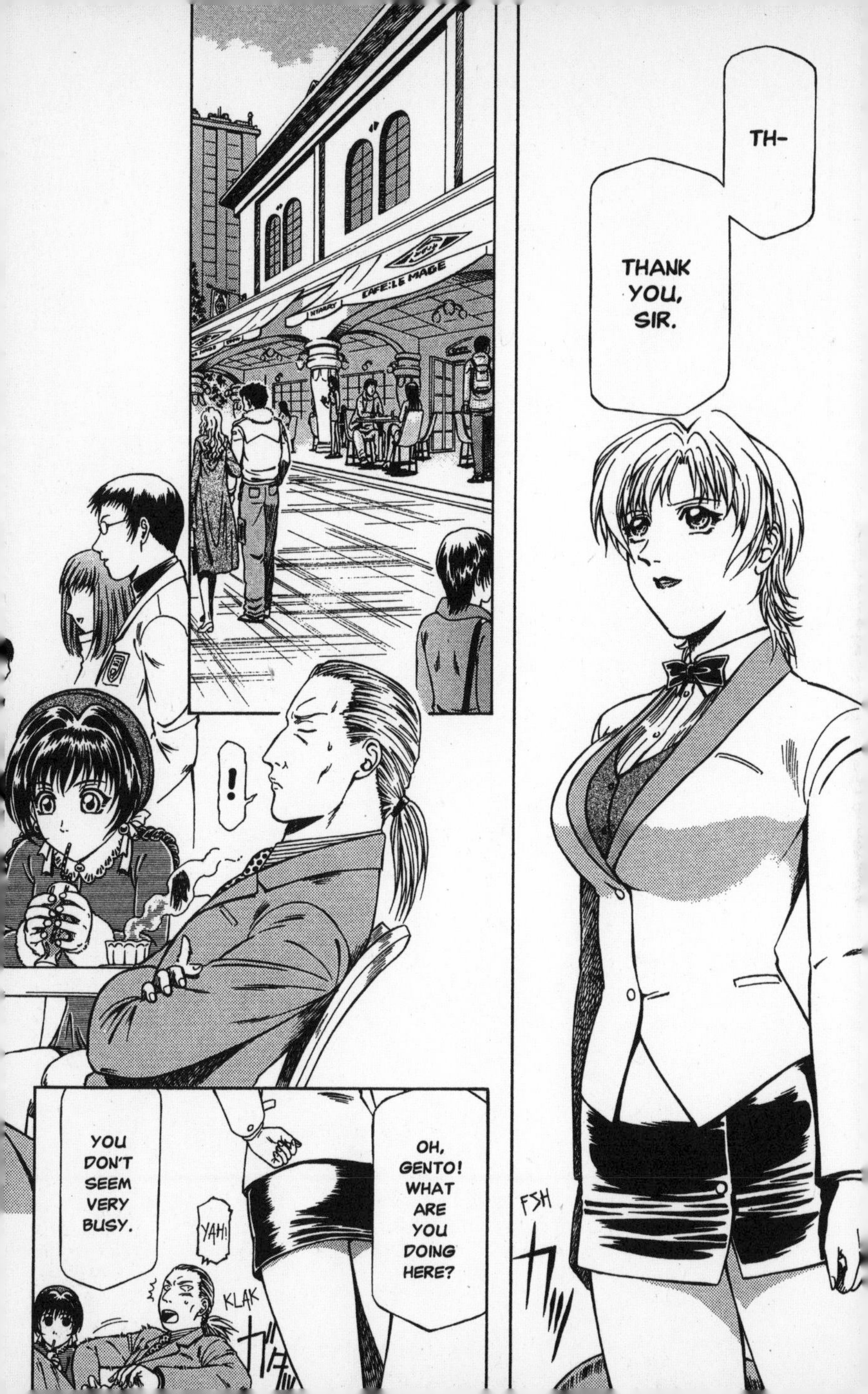
TH-
THANK YOU, SIR.
FSH
CAFE LE MAGE
!
OH, GENTO! WHAT ARE YOU DOING HERE?
YOU DON'T SEEM VERY BUSY.
YAH!
KLAK

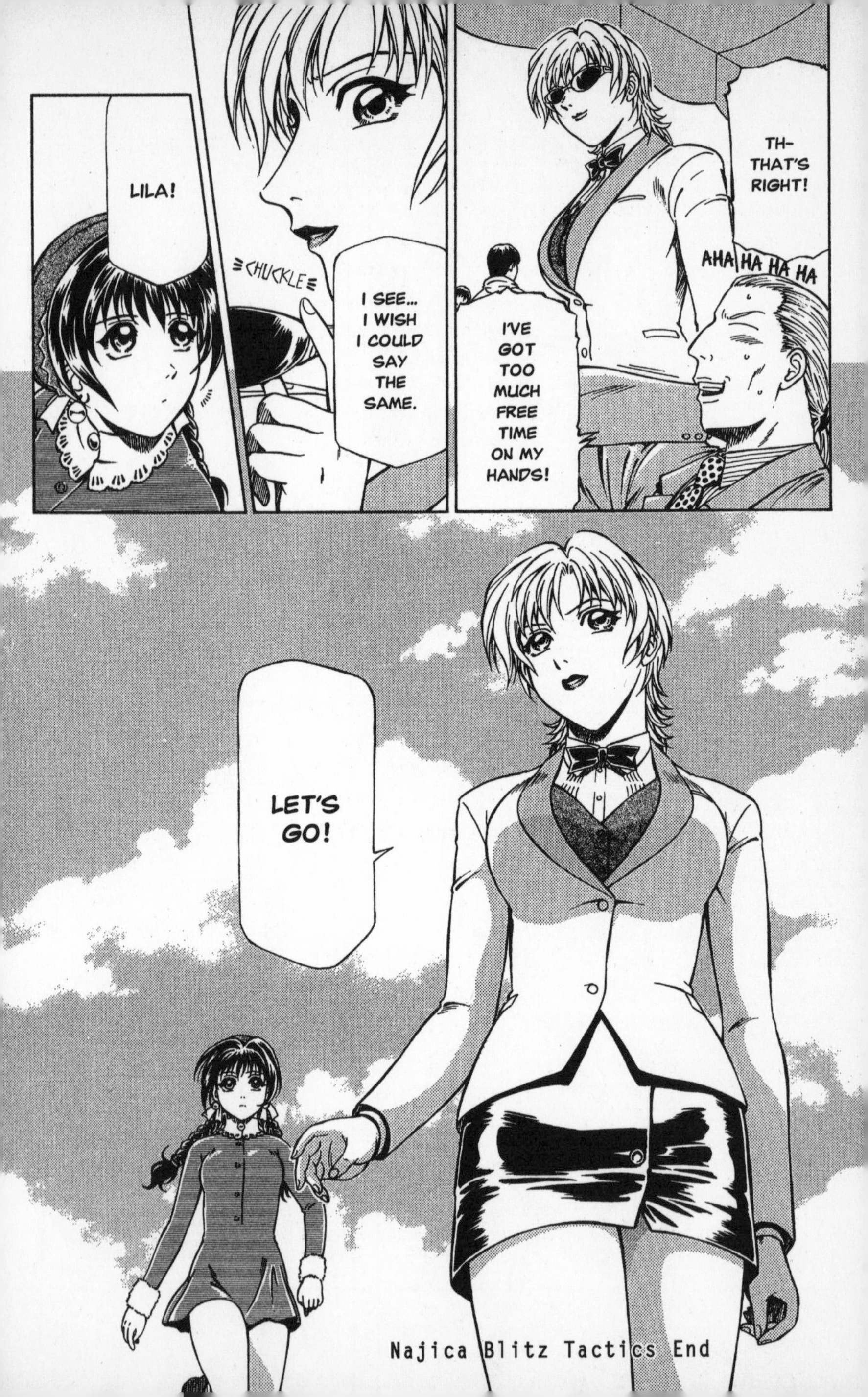
I'VE GOT TOO MUCH FREE TIME ON MY HANDS!
TH- THAT'S RIGHT!
AHA HA HA HA
I SEE... I WISH I COULD SAY THE SAME.
CHUCKLE
LILA!
LET'S GO!
Najica Blitz Tactics End

Najica Blitz Tactics
Volume 3

© 2003 by Takuya Tashiro/STUDIO FANTASIA • AFW/NAJICA Project/MEDIA FACTORY
First published in Japan in 2003 by MEDIA FACTORY, Inc.
English translation rights reserved by A.D.Vision, Inc.
Under the license from MEDIA FACTORY, Inc., Tokyo.

Translator	**JOSH COLE**
Lead Translator/Translation Supervisor	**JAVIER LOPEZ**
ADV Manga Translation Staff	**KAY BERTRAND, AMY FORSYTH, BRENDAN FRAYNE, HARUKA KANEKO-SMITH, EIKO McGREGOR AND MADOKA MOROE**
Print Production/Art Studio Manager	**LISA PUCKETT**
Pre-press Manager	**KLYS REEDYK**
Art Production Manager	**RYAN MASON**
Sr. Designer/Creative Manager	**JORGE ALVARADO**
Graphic Designer/Group Leader	**SHANNON RASBERRY**
Graphic Designers	**CHY LING AND KERRI KALINEC**
Graphic Artists	**HEATHER GARY, SHANNA JENSCHKE, AND GEORGE REYNOLDS**
Graphic Intern	**MARK MEZA**
International Coordinator	**TORU IWAKAMI**
International Coordinator	**ATSUSHI KANBAYASHI**
Publishing Editor	**SUSAN ITIN**
Assistant Editor	**MARGARET SCHAROLD**
Editorial Assistant	**VARSHA BHUCHAR**
Proofreaders	**SHERIDAN JACOBS AND STEVEN REED**
Editorial Intern	**JENNIFER VACCA**
Research/ Traffic Coordinator	**MARSHA ARNOLD**
Executive VP, CFO, COO	**KEVIN CORCORAN**
President, CEO & Publisher	**JOHN LEDFORD**

Email: editor@adv-manga.com
www.adv-manga.com
www.advfilms.com

For sales and distribution inquiries, please call 1.800.282.7202

is a division of A.D. Vision, Inc.
10114 W. Sam Houston Parkway, Suite 200, Houston, Texas 77099

ISBN: 1-4139-0140-9
First printing, December 2004
10 9 8 7 6 5 4 3 2 1
Printed in Canada

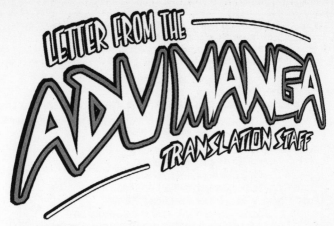

LETTER FROM THE ADV MANGA TRANSLATION STAFF

Dear Reader,

On behalf of the ADV Manga translation team, thank you for purchasing an ADV book. We are enthusiastic and committed to our work, and strive to carry our enthusiasm over into the book you hold in your hands.

Our goal is to retain the spirit of the original Japanese book. While great care has been taken to render a true and accurate translation, some cultural or readability issues may require a line to be adapted for greater accessibility to our readers. At times, manga titles that include culturally-specific concepts will feature a "Translator's Notes" section, which explains noteworthy references to the original text.

We hope our commitment to a faithful translation is evident in every ADV book you purchase.

Sincerely,

Javier Lopez
Lead Translator

Madoka Moroe

Haruka Kaneko-Smith

Eiko McGregor

Kay Bertrand

Joshua M. Cole

Brendan Frayne

Amy Forsyth

ADV MANGA™

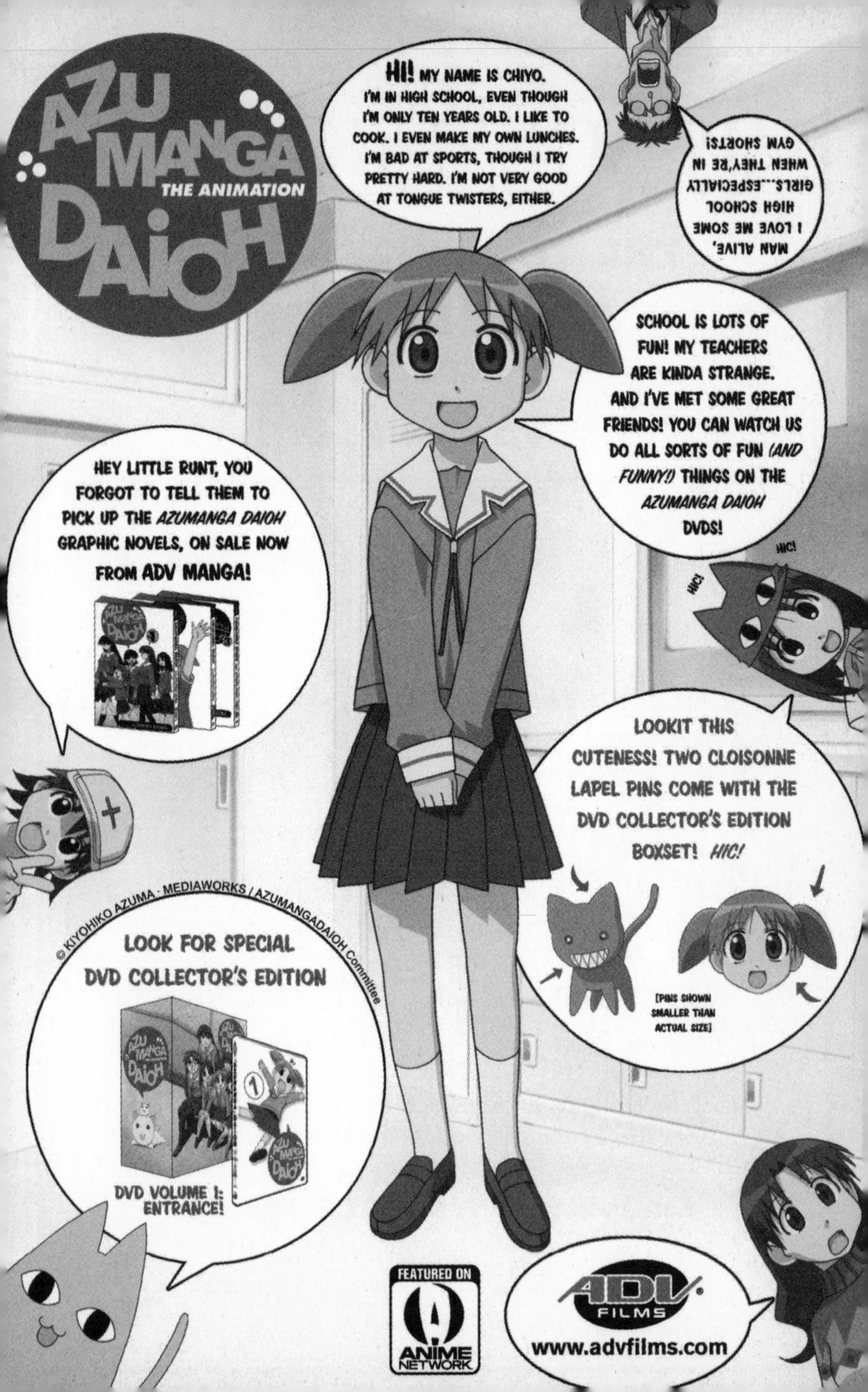
AZUMANGA DAIOH THE ANIMATION
HI! MY NAME IS CHIYO. I'M IN HIGH SCHOOL, EVEN THOUGH I'M ONLY TEN YEARS OLD. I LIKE TO COOK. I EVEN MAKE MY OWN LUNCHES. I'M BAD AT SPORTS, THOUGH I TRY PRETTY HARD. I'M NOT VERY GOOD AT TONGUE TWISTERS, EITHER.
MAN ALIVE, I LOVE ME SOME HIGH SCHOOL GIRLS...ESPECIALLY WHEN THEY'RE IN GYM SHORTS!
SCHOOL IS LOTS OF FUN! MY TEACHERS ARE KINDA STRANGE. AND I'VE MET SOME GREAT FRIENDS! YOU CAN WATCH US DO ALL SORTS OF FUN (AND FUNNY!) THINGS ON THE AZUMANGA DAIOH DVDS!
HEY LITTLE RUNT, YOU FORGOT TO TELL THEM TO PICK UP THE AZUMANGA DAIOH GRAPHIC NOVELS, ON SALE NOW FROM ADV MANGA!
HIC!
HIC!
LOOKIT THIS CUTENESS! TWO CLOISONNE LAPEL PINS COME WITH THE DVD COLLECTOR'S EDITION BOXSET! HIC!
[PINS SHOWN SMALLER THAN ACTUAL SIZE]
© KIYOHIKO AZUMA · MEDIAWORKS / AZUMANGADAIOH Committee
LOOK FOR SPECIAL DVD COLLECTOR'S EDITION
DVD VOLUME 1: ENTRANCE!
FEATURED ON ANIME NETWORK
ADV FILMS
www.advfilms.com

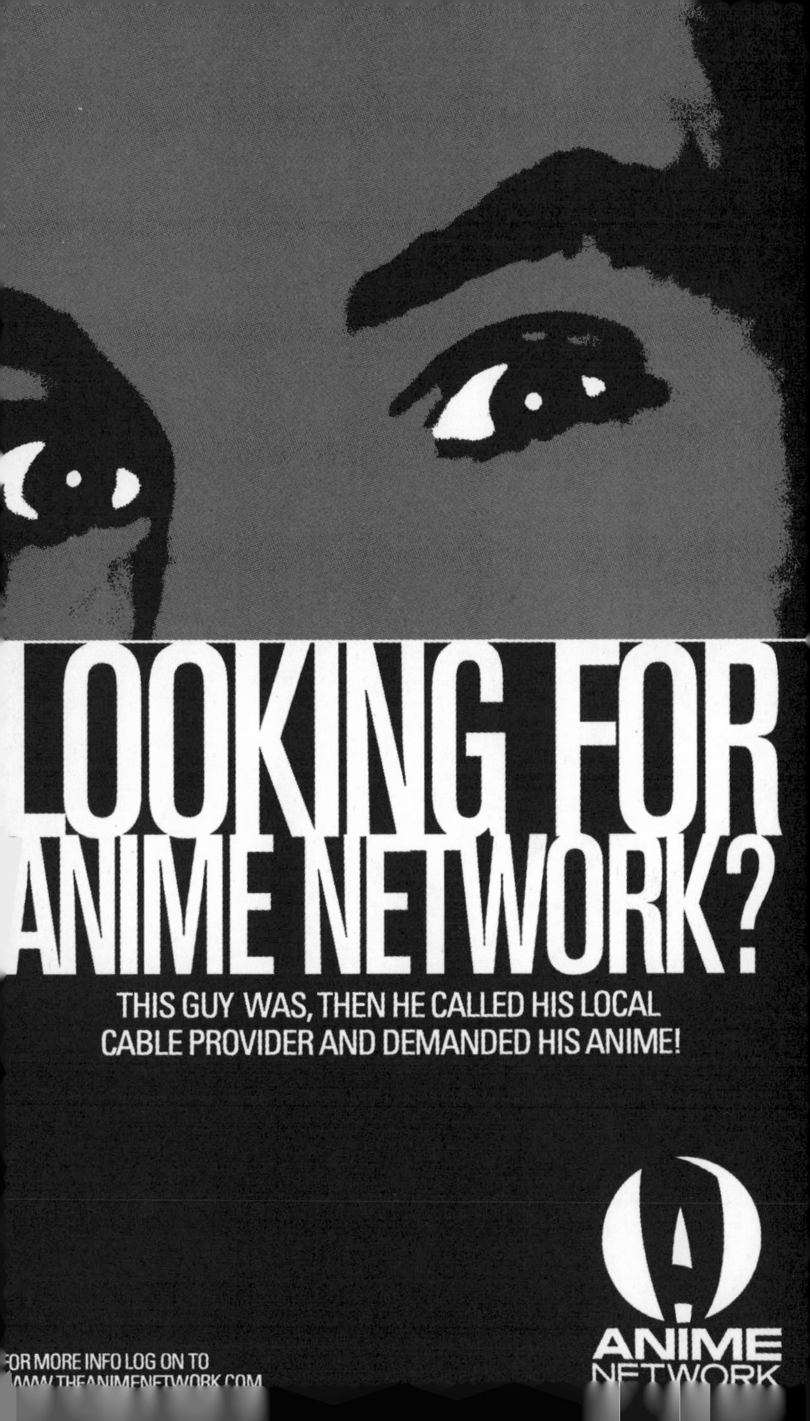
LOOKING FOR ANIME NETWORK?
THIS GUY WAS, THEN HE CALLED HIS LOCAL CABLE PROVIDER AND DEMANDED HIS ANIME!
ANIME NETWORK
FOR MORE INFO LOG ON TO
WWW.THEANIMENETWORK.COM

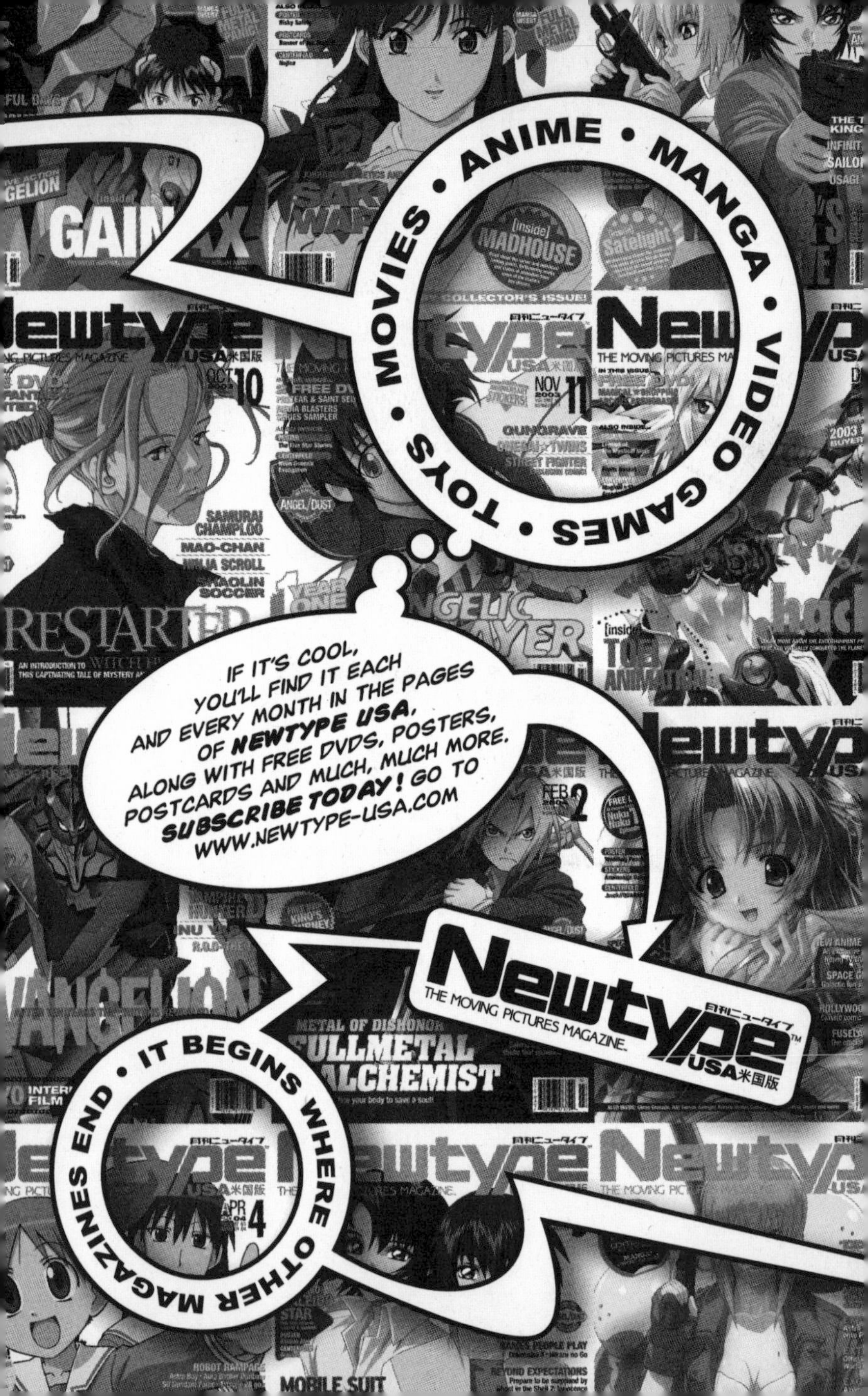
ANIME • MANGA • VIDEO GAMES • TOYS • MOVIES •
IF IT'S COOL, YOU'LL FIND IT EACH AND EVERY MONTH IN THE PAGES OF NEWTYPE USA, ALONG WITH FREE DVDS, POSTERS, POSTCARDS AND MUCH, MUCH MORE. SUBSCRIBE TODAY! GO TO WWW.NEWTYPE-USA.COM
Newtype USA 米国版 月刊ニュータイプ
THE MOVING PICTURES MAGAZINE.
IT BEGINS WHERE OTHER MAGAZINES END •